MULTINATIONAL CORPORATE EVOLUTION AND SUBSIDIARY DEVELOPMENT

Previous books involving Neil Hood

Hood, N. and S. Young (eds) (1979) *The Economics of Multinational Enterprise*

Hood, N. and S. Young (eds) (1984) *Industry, Policy and the Scottish Economy*

Young, S., N. Hood and J. Hamill (1988) *Foreign Multinationals and the British Economy*

Hood, N. and J. -E. Vahlne (eds) (1988) *Strategies in Global Competition*

Hood, N., R. Kilis and J. -E. Vahlne (eds) (1997) *Transition in the Baltic States*

Multinational Corporate Evolution and Subsidiary Development

Edited by

Julian Birkinshaw
and
Neil Hood

First published in Great Britain 1998 by
MACMILLAN PRESS LTD
Houndmills, Basingstoke, Hampshire RG21 6XS and London
Companies and representatives throughout the world

A catalogue record for this book is available from the British Library.

ISBN 0–333–72289–2

First published in the United States of America 1998 by
ST. MARTIN'S PRESS, INC.,
Scholarly and Reference Division,
175 Fifth Avenue, New York, N.Y. 10010

ISBN 0–312–21471–5

Library of Congress Cataloging-in-Publication Data
Multinational corporate evolution and subsidiary development / edited by Julian Birkinshaw and Neil Hood.
p. cm.
Includes bibliographical references and index.
ISBN 0–312–21471–5
1. International business enterprise. 2. Corporations, Foreign. 3. Subsidiary corporations. 4. International trade. 5. Competition, International. I. Birkinshaw, Julian M. II. Hood, Neil.
HD2755.5.M819 1998
658'.049—dc21 98–5593
CIP

This book is printed on paper suitable for recycling and made from fully managed and sustained forest sources.

10 9 8 7 6 5 4 3 2 1
07 06 05 04 03 02 01 00 99 98

Printed and bound in Great Britain by Antony Rowe Ltd, Chippenham, Wiltshire

To the memory of **Gunnar Hedlund**, one of the leading international business scholars of his generation

Contents

List of Appendices

List of Tables

List of Figures

Preface and Acknowledgements

This book emerged from the well-established interests of the editors in the processes which influence the development of subsidiaries. It was facilitated by the fact that the Annual Conference of the European International Business Academy was held at the Stockholm School of Economics in December 1996, and the editors were asked to help to shape that programme. Several of the sessions were focused on the topic of this volume and a number of the chapters are based on the papers presented on that occasion. In addition, the editors invited a range of other authors in different parts of the world who were known to be active researchers on subsidiary development.

The editors would like to acknowledge the superb work of the Institute of International Business staff in Stockholm, who made the EIBA conference so memorable. In addition they would like to record their sincere thanks to Irene Hood in Strathclyde International Business Unit, University of Strathclyde, Glasgow, for her sterling work in assisting in all aspects of the editorial process and her liaison with all the contributors.

JULIAN BIRKINSHAW
NEIL HOOD

List of Contributors

Allan Bird, Californian Polytechnic State University, USA

Julian Birkinshaw, Stockholm School of Economics, Sweden

Schon Beechler, Columbia University, USA

Sea-Jin Chang, Korea University, Korea

Ed Delany, E. Delany & Associates, Ireland

William Egelhoff, Fordham, USA

Mats Forsgren, Copenhagen Business School, Denmark

Luciano Fratocchi, University of Bologna, Italy

Liam Gorman, Irish Management Institute, Ireland

Ulf Holm, University of Uppsala, Sweden

Neil Hood, University of Strathclyde, UK

Jiatao Li, McKinsey, Hong Kong

Stephen McCormick, Irish Management Institute, Ireland

Marina Papanastassiou, Economic University of Athens, Greece

Robert Pearce, University of Reading, UK

Torben Pedersen, Copenhagen Business School, Denmark

Trond Randøy, Agder College, Norway

Philip Rosenzweig, IMD, Switzerland

Hellmut Schütte, Insead, France

Bernard Surlemont, University of Liège, Belgium

James H. Taggart, University of Strathclyde, UK

Sully Taylor, Portland State University, USA

1 Introduction and Overview

Julian Birkinshaw and Neil Hood

CONTEXT

Large multinational corporations (MNCs) have aroused the curiosity of researchers for many decades. While the MNC phenomenon can be defined remarkably simply – a firm that controls production assets in more than three countries, for example – its implications are far-reaching. A subfield of economics has grown up around the observation that the *raison d'être* of MNCs is their ability to internalise international transactions (Hymer, 1960/1976). In political economics, MNCs constitute a fundamental challenge to principles of national sovereignty (Servan-Schreiber, 1967). And in the field of management, MNCs represent the special case of organisations that span heterogeneous organisational environments (Westney, 1994).

Another distinctive, though certainly not unique, feature of MNCs is their large number of subsidiary companies. It is self-apparent that foreign subsidiaries have a critical role to play in the success of the MNC, whether in terms of their ability to sell the firm's products internationally or in terms of more high-value-added activities such as R&D or manufacturing. What is more surprising is that subsidiary-focused research has only become an important strand of MNC research in the last fifteen years. While there were occasional studies of foreign subsidiaries in the 1970s (for example, Brandt and Hulbert, 1976; Sim, 1977; Youssef, 1975), the field of 'MNC subsidiary management' research can probably be dated back to work done at the start of the 1980s by Garnier (1982). Hedlund (1980), Otterbeck (1981), and Picard (1980), which first examined questions of autonomy and formalisation in a systematic manner. Since that time there has been an explosion of research on MNC subsidiaries, concerned variously with parent–subsidiary relationships, subsidiary roles and strategies, subsidiary network relationships, subsidiary impact on the host country economy, and subsidiary resources and capabilities.

This collection of chapters by authors based in Europe, the USA and the Far East, represents another contribution to the growing body of literature on MNC subsidiaries. The theme that all the chapters address in some shape or form is that of subsidiary development. Subsidiary development refers broadly to the process through which MNC subsidiaries enhance their resources and capabilities, and in so doing add increasing levels of value to the MNC as a whole. This is, of course, a simplistic notion – subsidiaries can certainly become smaller or less focused, and they can destroy value if they are not effectively managed. But in the majority of cases, one does observe a process of development that begins with the subsidiary's founding as a market-access subsidiary or branch plant and leads to the accumulation of higher-order value-adding activities such as manufacturing, R&D and even divisional management (Birkinshaw and Hood, 1997; Forsgren, Holm and Johanson, 1995; Prahalad and Doz, 1981). To take just one example, 3M Canada was established in 1951 with sales and local manufacturing. In 1972 it began exporting certain product lines to the USA, and in the 1980s it attracted a series of world-scale manufacturing investments. In the 1990s 3M Canada also established several small development units, and took the initiative in launching a couple of new products (Birkinshaw, 1995).

Subsidiary development is an important phenomenon for several reasons. The first is that multinational corporate evolution is driven in large part by the changes that are exhibited in its foreign subsidiaries. The process of subsidiary development is itself indicative of the much discussed trend towards greater international dispersal of value-adding activities in MNCs. As more and more strategic resources accumulate away from the traditional centre, it becomes impossible to fully understand the phenomenon of the MNC by just talking to or surveying head office managers. The opinions, attitudes and activities of subsidiary managers are equally critical.

The second reason is that the subsidiary draws from and contributes to the development of the economy of its host country. Much has been written about the importance of technological spillovers from foreign direct investment (FDI) and the emergence of leading-edge clusters that foreign firms tap into in various ways (for example, Kokko, 1992; Porter, 1990). Perhaps more importantly, there are examples of countries like Ireland, Scotland, Singapore and Canada in which foreign-owned subsidiaries make up 50 per cent or more of the industrial sector. Clearly in such countries the phenomenon of subsidiary development is not an academic exercise – it lies at the heart of fundamental economic questions such as national competitiveness, investment attraction and job creation.

Finally, and more esoterically, the phenomenon of subsidiary development represents an interesting or 'special' case of firm growth. Building on Penrose's (1959) *The Theory of the Growth of the Firm*, it is evident that the growth or development of the subsidiary is driven by certain factors (the motivation of the general manager, the opportunities in the local environment, and so on) and constrained by others (access to financial resources, credibility with HQ, and so on). Several of the chapters in this volume address these issues in more detail, and provide the foundations for theorising about the nature of the development process in subsidiary companies versus independent companies. The point, in simple terms, is that subsidiary development *per se* is an interesting academic phenomenon, which deserves further scrutiny.

Subsidiary development, in summary, represents an emerging field of inquiry that has important implications for multinational corporate evolution. This volume presents the first collection of chapters – to our knowledge – that deals explicitly with the phenomenon of subsidiary development, and it is a testament to the importance of the topic that we were able to put together twelve empirical chapters that were all written in the last couple of years and have not been published elsewhere.

This introductory chapter is in two sections. First, it contains a brief review of the MNC subsidiary management literature, picking up on three streams of research that are identified as the 'HQ–subsidiary relationship', 'subsidiary role', and 'subsidiary development' schools respectively. In this section, there is also some speculation on the reasons for the emergence of the subsidiary development school of thinking. Second, the twelve chapters in this volume are introduced, in terms of their key ideas, their empirical base, and their positioning in the literature.

MNC SUBSIDIARY MANAGEMENT RESEARCH

The focus on this review is on research with an explicit subsidiary focus. Since 1980 there has been a steady stream of research on MNC subsidiaries, its emphasis gradually changing over time in keeping with changes in the underlying research phenomenon and the trends in management thought. Any attempt to categorise such a body of research is difficult and prone to over-simplification, but nevertheless worthwhile as a way of tracking the evolution in thinking that has occurred over the past twenty years. Three broad schools of thought can be identified, as indicated in Table 1.1, and elaborated below.

Headquarters–Subsidiary Relationships

Perhaps the obvious starting point for research into foreign subsidiaries is to try to understand how they are connected to the corporate headquarters. Accordingly, most of the early research in the late 1970s and 1980s was concerned with various facets of the HQ–subsidiary relationship: centralisation (Garnier, 1982; Hedlund, 1981; Gates and Egelhoff, 1986), formalisation (Hedlund, 1981; Negandhi and Baliga, 1981), and control and co-ordination (Brandt and Hulbert, 1976; Cray, 1984; Welge, 1981). The results from this stream of research were not very conclusive, however, and in retrospect it seems likely that Ghoshal and Nohria's (1989) concept of a differentiated network – in which each subsidiary is controlled through different mechanisms according to its role – provides an explanation for the lack of consistency in early findings.

It should be remembered that this focus on headquarters–subsidiary relationships was entirely consistent with the prevailing view of MNCs at that time – that is, as hierarchical, centre-dominated corporations, whose foreign subsidiaries were typically limited to local sales and manufacturing. Implicitly, this research stream assumed that the subsidiary was engaged

Table 1.1 Three streams of research on subsidiary management

Stream	*HQ–subsidiary relationship*	*Subsidiary role*	*Subsidiary development*
Focus on research	Aspects of dyadic relationship between subsidiary and HQ	Internal, corporate and environmental factors explaining different subsidiary roles	Changes in role and activities of subsidiary over time
Assumptions about nature of MNC	Hierarchy: subsidiaries are controlled by HQ	Heterarchy/network: subsidiaries have different roles, and have relationships with multiple units inside/outside the firm	
Research approach	Cross-sectional/static		Longitudinal/dynamic
Theoretical foundations	Transaction cost theory, contingency theory	Social network theory	Evolutionary theory, resource-based theory
Key contributions	Brandt and Hulbert (1976) Hedlund (1981) Otterbeck (1981)	Bartlett and Ghoshal (1986) Etemad and Dulude (1986) White and Poynter (1984)	Prahalad and Doz (1981) Birkinshaw and Hood (1997) Jarillo and Martinez (1990)
Related research focusing on the corporate level	Egelhoff (1980) Stopford and Wells (1972) Vernon (1966)	Bartlett and Ghoshal (1989) Hedlund (1986)	Kogut and Zander (1995) Malnight (1996)

principally in a dyadic relationship with its headquarters (rather than as part of a network), and that it was acting as an instrument of the parent company (rather than as a semi-autonomous unit with a mind of its own). Much of this work also appeared to assume that headquarters could manage all subsidiaries in the same way, rather than as a differentiated network (Bartlett and Ghoshal, 1986).

The emergence of alternative conceptions of the MNC in the mid-1980s – heterarchies, transnationals, networks and the like – essentially brought the headquarters–subsidiary relationship stream of research to an end. This is probably appropriate, given the increasingly complex web of relationships that subsidiary managers have to manage. But at the same time we should not throw the baby out with the bathwater – network models are indeed attractive, but it should not be overlooked that the subsidiary's most critical relationship was, and still is, with its corporate headquarters.

Subsidiary Roles

Beginning with White and Poynter's (1984) research on Canadian subsidiaries, the 1980s saw an explosion of studies focused on the various roles played by subsidiary companies. White and Poynter, for example, identified miniature replica, product specialist, rationalised manufacturer, strategic independent, and marketing satellites. Other studies took rather different approaches but typically ended up with three or four types of subsidiary (Bartlett and Ghoshal, 1986; Birkinshaw and Morrison, 1995; D'Cruz, 1986; Ghoshal and Nohria, 1989; Gupta and Govindarajan, 1991; Jarillo and Martinez, 1990; Taggart, 1997; and so on).

The recognition that subsidiaries have different roles was indeed an important step forward. Rather than focusing just on the headquarters–subsidiary relationship, researchers realised that that relationship was one of many factors that were responsible for defining the set of activities undertaken by the subsidiary (namely, its role). The other important determinants of the subsidiary's role included its industry sector (Jarillo and Martinez, 1990), the local business environment (Ghoshal and Nohria, 1989), relationships with sister subsidiaries (Gupta and

Govindarajan, 1991) and the entrepreneurial drive of subsidiary management (Birkinshaw, 1995; Crookell, 1986). This body of research both contributed to, and drew from, the emerging network conceptualisations of the MNC in that it saw the subsidiary unit as one node in a network of internal and external relationships (Ghoshal and Bartlett, 1991; Hedlund, 1986). It also recognised for the first time that the subsidiary, rather than its relationship with HQ, was an important unit of analysis.

Space restrictions prevent a thorough analysis of the subsidiary role stream of research, but it should be made clear that there were several distinct lines of thinking within this broader stream. The most common approach was probably to model the subsidiary's role as 'assigned' by corporate management. Bartlett and Ghoshal (1986), for example, clearly saw subsidiaries being give specific roles according to their existing capabilities and the strategic importance of their local market. The second approach was to see the subsidiary as a more autonomous entity that was capable of defining its own 'strategy'. Such an approach was evident in early Canadian studies (Etemad and Dulude, 1986; White and Poynter, 1984), and it continues to gain a lot of support in such countries as Canada, Ireland and Scotland (Birkinshaw, 1995; Delany, this volume, Chapter 6). Finally, there have been some studies in which the local environment is seen as having a deterministic impact on the role of the subsidiary (for example, Ghoshal and Nohria, 1989). Obviously the reality for most subsidiaries is that different factors – corporate, subsidiary and local-environmental – all have some impact on the set of activities they undertake, but most research has tended to focus on one set of factors (Birkinshaw *et al.*, 1998).

Subsidiary Development

The third stream of research differs from the first two in that it is focused on a dynamic question, not a static one, namely: How and why do the activities of the subsidiary change over time? This stream of research builds on the network perspective of MNCs but it also adds in an explicit resources and/or capabilities component. The basic idea is that over time the subsidiary accumulates valuable capabilities through its network relationships, which leads to an enhanced status (*vis-à-vis* headquarters) and thus an extension of the scope of its activities (Birkinshaw and Hood, 1997).

Some of the reasons why subsidiary development is an important phenomenon have already been discussed, but it is also interesting to speculate on the reasons for its current popularity. One of these is the emergence of a parallel 'evolutionary perspective' on the MNC as a whole (Kogut and Zander, 1993; Madhok, 1997; Malnight, 1996), which in turn draws on the dynamic-capabilities view of the firm currently in vogue (Nelson and Winter, 1982; Penrose, 1959; Teece *et al.*, 1997). Clearly, subsidiary-level research can draw from these bodies of thought, in terms of the mechanisms for capability development and the factors that facilitate and impede the process. Less obviously, subsidiary-level research has great potential to contribute to the current debate on resource and capability-based theories of the firm, because it shows that 'the firm' is not necessarily the appropriate unit of analysis. If capabilities are actually heterogeneously distributed between subsidiaries, as a network perspective would suggest, then research needs to consider more seriously questions of internal resource transfer and utilisation, in addition to the well-developed arguments about the scarcity, non-tradability and inimitability of resources as the foundation of competitive advantage.

The other reason for the emergence of subsidiary development research is that it is consistent with several business trends. Inward investment, for example, is becoming increasingly competitive, with the result that existing subsidiaries are being actively encouraged to expand their presence in the host country. Internal benchmarking is pushing firms to think about which subsidiary units are most effective, and encouraging a process of internal competition and specialisation in subsidiaries. And the empowerment movement encourages subsidiary managers to take initiative in the development and selling of their own distinctive capabilities.

While the current thrust of research in this area is relatively recent, elements of it can be discerned at least as far back as the early 1980s, when Prahalad and Doz (1981) argued that MNCs should increasingly use subtle or informal mechanisms to retain control over those subsidiaries that had developed unique or valuable resources of their own. A number of the well-known studies of subsidiary roles, such as Jarillo and Martinez (1990) and Gupta and Govindarajan (1994) also gave some consideration to a development process, in terms of roles changing over time as subsidiaries developed new capabilities or as their environments changed. Moreover, in the case of the Canadian research in this area (for example, Etemad and Dulude, 1986), such changes in roles were actually prescribed – White and Poynter (1984: 69), for example, noted that 'through the careful development of local capabilities the subsidiary manager can contribute to the evolution of the Canadian subsidiary's strategy.'

However, it is only in the last few years that research on the subsidiary development process *per se* has emerged. In putting this volume together, the editors sought to capture as much of the leading-edge thinking in this area as was possible. Many of the chapters are still grounded in what has been identified as the subsidiary-roles stream, but with some explicit consideration of the ways these roles change over time. Others represent attempts to model specific elements of the development process. The end product that has emerged gives some important insights into the theoretical and empirical concerns hinted at above, as well as providing an exciting new research agenda for researchers of MNC subsidiaries.

OUTLINE OF THE BOOK

The book is divided into three parts. Part I, 'Corporate Strategy and Subsidiary Development', consists of chapters on the roles of foreign subsidiaries, how they are developing over time, and how they impact the strategy and structure of the corporation. The chapters in this group sit on the boundary between the subsidiary role and subsidiary development streams of research. They all look at the role of the subsidiary, but they go further by considering how the changes in such roles are influencing the evolution of the corporation as a whole. Part II, 'Centres of Excellence in Multinational Networks', looks at the emergence of highly evolved subsidiaries with leading-edge capabilities. While the chapters in it do not address the dynamic question of role change, they are particularly relevant here because they help to develop an understanding of some of the internal drivers for subsidiary development. Finally, Part III, 'Corporate Process and Subsidiary Development', consists of five chapters that look explicitly at various aspects of the subsidiary development process.

Part I: Corporate Strategy and Subsidiary Development

The first chapter (Chapter 2), by James Taggart of the University of Strathclyde, is entitled 'Identification and Development of Strategy at Subsidiary Level' Taggart looks at the changes in subsidiary strategy over time using a sample of UK subsidiaries. The research is rooted in the subsidiary role stream referred to earlier, in that it categorises subsidiary strategy using Porter's (1986) configuration-coordination framework. However, it also goes further, by plotting the anticipated changes in subsidiary strategy over time. In doing this, Taggart reveals several interesting insights. First, the overall trend is towards greater co-ordination with other units; second, the 'detached' subsidiary with weak coordination and geographic concentration is a transitional phase that all subsidiary managers would like to move out of; and third, the 'strategic auxiliary' with high coordination and geographical concentration is the desired end point for most subsidiary managers. Overall, Taggart's work provides some important insight into the objectives of the managers running these subsidiaries. The next question, of course, is whether these objectives end up being realised, or whether headquarters managers have different outcomes in mind.

Marina Papanasstasiou (Economic University of Athens) and Robert Pearce (University of Reading) wrote Chapter 3, 'Individualism and Interdependence in the Technological Development of MNEs: The Strategic Positioning of R&D in Overseas Subsidiaries'. Papanastassiou and Pearce's focus is on the R&D activities of foreign-owned subsidiaries. Specifically, they examine the roles of a sample of UK subsidiaries according to the nature of the R&D they undertake, and they also look at the anticipated growth or decline of their R&D. This analysis leads them towards one very important conclusion: that many subsidiaries are undergoing a process of 'creative transition', which shifts them away from locally focused product development and in the direction of more creative research activities that are valuable to the corporation as a whole. Papanastassiou and Pearce build on this insight to speculate on the corporate-level challenge of managing a network of creative and interdependent subsidiaries.

Chapter 4 is by Trond Randøy and Jiatao Li of Agder College and McKinsey Inc., respectively. Entitled, 'Global Resource Flows and MNE Network Integration', it looks at the patterns of integration and resource flow in multinational corporations. They build a typology of subsidiaries according to the inflow and outflow of resources (product, knowledge, capital), and then examine the characteristics of foreign-owned US subsidiaries according to this typology. Unlike most of the other chapters in this volume, Randøy and Li use secondary data, which allows them to cover a large number of subsidiaries in twenty-five different industries. The key finding from this research is that distinctive subsidiary types can be discerned on an industry-by-industry basis. The 'resource networker', for example, with high resource inflows and outflows, is predominantly found only in the office machines and electronic components industries.

Chapter 5, by Hellmut Schütte of INSEAD, is entitled 'Between Headquarters and Subsidiaries: The RHQ Solution'. While at first glance a study of regional headquarters has little to do with foreign subsidiaries, it becomes clear in Schütte's study that the RHQ is a sort of 'super-subsidiary' that faces many of the same issues (development, decline, role change, and so on) that more run-of-the-mill subsidiaries do. The chapter reports on an exploratory study of Japanese RHQs in Europe and European or American RHQs in South-East Asia. Two key findings should be highlighted here. First, RHQs are clearly gaining in power (namely, taking on greater responsibilities for their regions), especially in corporations with area-based or matrix structures. Second, the RHQ managers typically felt greater allegiance to their region than to the parent, and indeed saw their role more as one of regional integration than of hierarchical control. RHQs, it seems, are complex organisational creations that raise some important questions for researchers of MNC subsidiaries.

Part II: Centres of Excellence in Multinational Networks

Mats Forsgren and Torben Pedersen of Copenhagen Business School wrote Chapter 6, 'Centres of Excellence in Multinational Companies: The Case of Denmark'. They review the MNC subsidiary literature in some detail, and suggest that a true centre of excellence has to meet some strict criteria. It has to have R&D and strong exports, rather like a world product mandate subsidiary, but in addition it has also to have strong interdependencies with the rest of the multinational network (unlike a world product mandate). Furthermore, the centre should also have strong links into the local economy (namely, high embeddedness). Forsgren and Pedersen undertake an empirical analysis of foreign-owned subsidiaries in Denmark, and conclude that there are very few subsidiaries that meet all these criteria. This finding is important, because it suggests that subsidiaries probably have to choose – to some degree – between their local embeddedness, their integration into the corporate system, and the extent of their product autonomy.

In Chapter 7, Bernard Surlemont of the University of Liège looks at another aspect of centres of excellence in his chapter, 'A Typology of Centres Within Multinational Corporations: An Empirical Investigation'. Surlemont characterises centres according to their scope (namely, how broad a set of activities they are involved with) and their domain (namely, how many units around the world they control). Using data on Belgian co-ordination centres, the chapter shows that most are either 'administrative' centres (high scope, low domain) or 'strategic' centres (low, high), and that the characteristics of each are substantially different. The chapter also speculates on the paths of development, and the ways subsidiary and HQ managers can influence them. A key line of thought running throughout it is that the interplay between the actions of subsidiary and HQ management is what determines the centre's role.

Chapter 8 by Luciano Fratochii (University of Bologna) and Ulf Holm (University of Uppsala) takes a look at centres of excellence from a headquarters perspective. Their chapter, 'Centres of Excellence in the International Firm', uses data on the twenty largest Swedish MNCs to try to understand the emergence of marketing and production centres in foreign subsidiaries. The chapter has two key findings. First, the emergence of marketing and manufacturing centres is partially a function of the level of internationalisation: marketing centres are established first, with manufacturing centres later. Second, the psychic distance between the foreign subsidiary and HQ is an important predictor of marketing centres. This chapter is unusual in the extent to which it provides relatively objective data about the existence of foreign centres of excellence, and it is the only one in this collection that draws comparisons across multiple countries.

Part III: Corporate Process and Subsidiary Development

In Chapter 9, Bill Egelhoff (Fordham University), Liam Gorman and Stephen McCormick (Irish Management Institute) put forward a very detailed account of the subsidiary development process, under the title 'Using technology as a Path to Subsidiary Development'. This builds on the technology transfer literature and the recent thinking on subsidiary initiative to examine the ways subsidiaries use their technological capabilities to extend their business domain. Based on a sample of sixteen Irish subsidiaries, the chapter describes three development paths: aggressive, incremental, and *status quo*. Aggressive development, the authors conclude, is driven most effectively by strong general management, leading-edge technology, and through a process of backward integration. This study highlights the importance of internal subsidiary factors as the engine of development. It also points to the implications for HQ managers of subsidiaries that are attempting to enhance their value added.

Chapter 10, by Ed Delany, an independent consultant, also reports on a study of foreign-owned subsidiaries in Ireland. Entitled 'Strategic Development of Multinational Subsidiaries in Ireland', this chapter builds on the same theme as Chapter 9 but takes it one step further. Delany makes the distinction between 'subversive' and 'boy scout' subsidiaries, arguing that the former is the only way to achieve development. He then elaborates on three types of initiatives undertaken in his sample companies: domain consolidation, domain defending, and domain extending. In the final part of the chapter an eight-stage process model is put forward for subsidiary initiatives. It is interesting to observe that both chapters on Irish subsidiaries (9 and 10) provide very rich stories about subsidiary initiative. Certainly Ireland is not a unique case – similar stories have been told from Canada and Scotland, for example – but at the same time there would appear to be some characteristic of Ireland, or Irish investment, that make 'subversive' subsidiary activity so pervasive.

Chapter 11, by Julian Birkinshaw of the Stockholm School of Economics, takes up the question of subsidiary development from a host-country perspective. Entitled 'Foreign-Owned Subsidiaries and Regional Development: The Case of Sweden', it focuses on the impact that different groups of subsidiaries have had on the Swedish economy. Sweden, the author suggests, is in a rather unusual position given its relatively recent interest in attracting foreign direct investment. The result is a curious mixture of subsidiaries: a group of very large, acquired firms such as ABB and Saab with a major impact on the Swedish economy; a large group of sales and marketing subsidiaries with very limited job creation or investment; and a smaller middle group of organically grown subsidiaries with R&D and/or manufacturing. Birkinshaw documents four short case-studies of subsidiaries in the latter group, concluding that the development process as observed in Ireland (above) is not replicated in Sweden. Instead, there appears to be an emerging 'centre of excellence' model with rather limited prospects for additional Swedish investment. The implications for the Swedish economy are discussed.

Sea-Jin Chang (Korea University) and Philip Rosenzweig (IMD) take a very detailed look at one case of subsidiary development in Chapter 12, 'Functional and Line of Business Evolution Processes in MNC Subsidiaries: Sony in the USA, 1972–1995'. This chapter complements the preceding three by providing solid evidence of the evolution of the activities undertaken by Sony in the USA in the last 25 years. As they show, development is observed on two dimensions: functional extension (sales, manufacturing, development, business management), and line-of-business extension (colour TVs, audio equipment, magnetic tape, and so on). At each stage they identify the key factors promoting development and those inhibiting it. A generic process model is also put forward. Interestingly, one insight that emerges from this study is the importance of headquarters managers as the drivers of the development process. Unlike the Irish studies in Chapters 9 and 10, subsidiary management in Sony appeared to work closely with their HQ bosses, rather than as subversive elements. Whether this is an artefact of contrasting researchers perspectives or more objective differences in company culture is of course impossible to discern, but it is certainly an issue worthy of further study.

Finally, in Chapter 13 Schon Beechler (Columbia University), Allan Bird (California Polytechnic) and Sully Taylor (Portland State University) look at one specific aspect of subsidiary development in their chapter, 'Organisational Learning in Japanese MNCs: Four Affiliate Archetypes'. This chapter is an inductive study of the development process that takes place between subsidiary and parent company. The authors build on the well-established point that the subsidiary's management systems face competing pressures from the HQ and from the host country, but they take the argument much further, by detailing the learning processes (or lack of learning) that lead to a resolution of the competing pressures. The most attractive model, they argue is the open hybrid in which there is active subsidiary-level learning about the strengths and weaknesses of the existing model, which feed back not only into the subsidiary's management system but also into the management systems of the MNC as a whole.

CONCLUDING REMARKS

The chapters in this volume cover a wide variety of issues and a large number of countries, but at the same time there are a number of noticeable gaps that we were unable to fill. South-East Asia, for example, represents an extremely important area for business but is represented in this volume only through the work of Schütte. Latin America, the Middle East, Eastern Europe and Russia are not represented at all. This may just be a 'sampling error' on the part of the book's authors, but it could also be indicative of a more widespread tendency to research subsidiaries in established markets. Of course, there is a lot of research done on questions of market entry and joint venture management in developing countries, but as such new entrants become significant subsidiaries in their own right there is need for them to be researched using the sorts of tools and lenses discussed in this volume.

Equally evident in this collection of chapters is the preference to sample subsidiaries by host country not by parent country. Fratochii and Holm's study of Swedish MNCs is the one exception. Again, there are sound reasons for focusing on a readily accessible sample that is close to home, but it results in a lot of unanswered questions – about the differences between subsidiaries of the same parent, and about the opinions of HQ managers (which are rarely solicited).

But these gaps aside, chapters in current collection represent some of the leading-edge thinking about MNC subsidiaries, and indeed about the way the MNC as a whole works. The phenomenon of subsidiary development will continue to grow in importance, and it raises a plethora of new research issues. It is hoped that the ideas raised in this volume will provide a suitable foundation on which others can move forward and take the research of MNC subsidiaries to higher levels.

References

Bartlett, C.A. and S. Ghoshal (1986) 'Tap Your Subsidiaries for Global Reach', *Harvard Business Review*, 64 (6), 87–94.

Bartlett, C.A. and S. Ghoshal (1989) *Managing Across Borders: The Transnational Solution*, Boston, Mass.: Harvard Business School Press.

Birkinshaw, J.M. (1995) *Entrepreneurship in Multinational Corporations: The Initiative Process in Canadian Subsidiaries*, unpublished doctoral dissertation, Western Business School, London, Ontario, Canada.

Birkinshaw, J.M. and N. Hood (1997) 'An Empirical Study of Development Processes in Foreign Owned subsidiaries in Canada and Scotland', *Management International Review*, 37 (4), 339–64.

Birkinshaw, J.M., N. Hood and S. Jonsson (1998) 'Building Firm Specific Advantage in MNCs: The Role of Subsidiary Initiative', *Strategic Management Journal* (forthcoming).

Birkinshaw, J.M. and A.J. Morrison (1995) 'Configurations of Strategy and Structure in Multinational Subsidiaries', *Journal of International Business Studies*, 26 (4), 729–54.

Brandt, K. and J. Hulbert (1976) 'Patterns of Communications in the Multinational Corporation: An Empirical Study', *Journal of International Business Studies*, 7 (spring), 57–64.

Cray, D. (1984) 'Control and Coordination in Multinational Corporations', *Journal of International Business Studies*, 15 (3), 85–98.

Crookell, H.H. (1986) 'Specialization and International Competitiveness', in H. Etemad and L.S. Dulude (eds), *Managing the Multinational Subsidiary*, London: Croom Helm.

D'Cruz, J. (1986) 'Strategic Management of Subsidiaries', in H. Etemad and L.S. Dulude (eds), *Managing the Multinational Subsidiary* Response to Environmental Changes and to Host Nation R&D Policies, London: Croom Helm.

Etemad, H. and L.S. Dulude (eds) (1986) *Managing the Multinational Subsidiary* Response to Environmental Changes and to Host Nation R&D Policies, London: Croom Helm.

Forsgren, M., U. Holm and J. Johanson (1995) 'Division Headquarters Go Abroad – A Step in the Internationalization of the Multinational Corporation', *Journal of Management Studies*, 32 (4), 475–91.

Garnier, G.H. (1982) 'Context and Decision Making Autonomy in the Foreign Affiliates of U.S. Multinational Corporations', *Academy of Management Journal*, 25, 893–908.

Gates, S. and W.G. Egelhoff (1986) 'Centralization in Headquarters-Subsidiary Relationships', *Journal of International Business Studies*, 17 (2), 71–92.

Ghoshal, S. and C.A. Bartlett (1991) 'The Multinational Corporation as an Interorganizational Network', *Academy of Management Review*, 15 (4), 603–25.

Ghoshal, S. and N. Nohria (1989) 'Internal Differentiations Within Multinational Corporations', *Strategic Management Journal*, 10, 323–37.

Gupta, A.K. and V. Govindarajan (1991) 'Knowledge Flows and the Structure of Control within Multinational Corporations', *Academy of Management Review*, 16 (4), 768–92.

Gupta, A.K. and V. Govindarajan (1994) 'Organizing for Knowledge Within MNCs', *International Business Review*, 3 (4), 443–57.

Hedlund, G. (1980) 'The Role of Foreign Subsidiaries in Strategic Decision-making in Swedish Multinational Corporations', *Strategic Management Journal*, 1, 23–36.

Hedlund, G. (1981) 'Autonomy of Subsidiaries and Formalization of Headquarters-Subsidiary Relationships in Swedish MNCs', in L. Otterbeck (ed.), The Management of headquarters–subsidiary relations in Multinational Corporations, Aldershot, UK: Gower.

Hedlund, G. (1986) 'The Hypermodern MNC: A Heterarchy?', *Human Resource Management*, 25, 9–36.

Hymer, S. (1960/1976) *The International Operations of National firms: A Study of Direct Investment*, Cambridge, Mass.: MIT Press.

Jarillo, J.C. and J. Martinez (1990) 'Different Roles for Subsidiaries: The Case of Multinational Corporations', *Strategic Management Journal*, 11, 501–12.

Kogut, B. and U. Zander (1993) 'Knowledge of the Firm and the Evolutionary Theory of the Multinational Corporation', *Journal of International Business Studies*, 24 (4), 625–45.

Kokko, A. (1992) *Foreign Direct Investment, Host Country Characteristics, and Spillovers*, Economic Research Institute, Stockholm School of Economics.

Madhok, A. (1997) 'Cost, Value and Foreign Market Entry Mode: The Transaction and the Firm', *Strategic Management Journal*, 18, 39–61.

Malnight, T. (1996) 'The Transition from Decentralized to Network-based MNC Structures: An Evolutionary Perspective', *Journal of International Business Studies*, 27 (1), 43–66.

Negandhi, A.R. and B.R. Baliga (1981) 'Internal Functioning of American, German and Japanese Multinational Corporations', in L. Otterbeck (ed.), *The Management of Headquarters–Subsidiary Relations in Multinational Corporations*, Aldershot, UK: Gower.

Nelson, R. and S. Winter (1982) *An Evolutionary Theory of Economic Change*, Cambridge, Mass.: Harvard University Press.

Otterbeck, L. (ed.) (1981) *The Management of Headquarters–Subsidiary Relations in Multinational Corporations*, Aldershot: Gower.

Penrose, E.T. (1959) *The Theory of the Growth of the Firm*, Oxford: Blackwell.

Picard, J. (1980) 'Organization Structures and Integrative Devices in European Multinational Corporations', *Columbia Journal of World Business*, 4, 9–18.

Porter, M.E. (1986) *Competition in Global Industries*, Boston, Mass.: Harvard Business School Press.

Porter, M.E. (1990) *The Competitive Advantage of Nations*, New York: Free Press.

Prahalad, C.K. and Y.L. Doz (1981) 'An Approach to Strategic Control in MNCs', *Sloan Management Review*, Summer, 5–13.

Servan-Schreiber, J-J (1967) *Le Dèfi Américan (the American Challenge)*, London: Hamish Hamilton.

Sim, A.B. (1977) Decentralized Management of Subsidiaries and Their Performance', *Management International Review*, 2, 45–52.

Stopford, J. and L.T. Wells (1972) *Managing the Multinational Enterprise: Organizations of the Firm and Ownership of Subsidiaries*, New York: Basic Books.

Taggart, J. (1997) 'Autonomy and Procedural Justice: A Framework for Evaluating Subsidiary Strategy', *Journal of International Business Studies*, 28 (1), 51–77.

Teece, D., G. Pisano and A. Shuen (1997) 'Firm Capabilities, Resources, and the Concept of Strategy', Strategic Management Journal, 18 (7), 509–534.

Vernon, R. (1966) 'International Investments and International Trade in the Product Cycle', *Quarterly Journal of Economics*, 80, 190–207.

Welge, M. (1981) 'The Effective Design of Headquarter–Subsidiary Relationships in German MNCs', in L. Otterbeck (ed.) *The Management of Headquarters–subsidiary Relations in Multinational Corporations*, Aldershot: Gower.

Westney, D.E. (1993) 'Institutionalization Theory and the Multinational corporation', in S. Ghoshal and D.E. Westney (eds), *Organization Theory and the Multinational Corporation*, New York: St Martin's Press.

White, R.E. and T.A. Poynter (1984) 'Strategies for Foreign-owned Subsidiaries in Canada', *Business Quarterly*, 48 (4) Summer, 59–69.

Youssef, S.M. (1975) 'Contextual Factors Influencing Control Strategy of Multinational Corporations', *Academy of Management Journal*, 18 (19), 136–143.

Part I
Corporate Strategy and Subsidiary Development

2 Identification and Development of Strategy at Subsidiary Level

James H. Taggart

INTRODUCTION

The general strategic management literature is far from unanimous on whether the strategy-making process is (or should be) rational, partly rational, or unable to be anything but non-rational (Hofer and Schendel, 1978; Porter, 1980; Quinn, 1980; Johnson, 1988). Conceptual and practical considerations suggest that the middle course is not only that of least resistance, but also the one that gives practitioners the best chance of evolving a practical strategy using some form of incrementalism coupled with a rational analysis that identifies major sources of internal and environmental risk. This is particularly important when a firm moves from one strategy to another, whether to move away from poor positioning within its industry or to avoid the lifecycle risk by moving on from a successful strategy before it hits the decline stage. Evidence suggests that there is a dynamic involved in the strategy process that gravitates towards the evolutionary rather than the incremental, whether it be at functional (Ronstadt, 1978), subsidiary (White and Poynter, 1984; Taggart, 1996c) or corporate level (Morrison, 1990). Thus, whether the study is based on organisational design (Mintzberg, 1980), control mechanisms (Doz and Prahalad, 1981), contingency theory (Ginsberg and Venkatraman, 1985), the strategy–structure interface (Amburgey and Dacin, 1994), or biology modelling (Taggart, 1995), sensitivity to the firm's operating environment is the central issue in strategy change.

The purpose of this chapter is threefold. First, it will explore the question of strategy evolution in multinational subsidiaries using the coordination–configuration (C–C) framework first developed by Porter (1986) to prescribe broad strategy directions for multinational corporations (MNCs), and more recently extended by Roth (1992) to cover the activities of medium-size firms operating in global industries. Second, when the pattern of strategy evolution has been established and described, evidence will be sought of simultaneous movement along other strategy dimensions or variables in order to increase the interpretability of strategy change, and perhaps to suggest some causative process. Third, following the configurations aspect of organisational strategy (Meyer *et al.*, 1993) linkages will be evaluated between the C–C basis of strategy evolution developed here and the integration–responsiveness dimensions of Prahalad and Doz (1987). Throughout, the concept of strategy evolution as an emergent property of MNC subsidiaries will be reflected upon.

CONCEPTUAL BACKGROUND

Porter's (1986) C–C paradigm is one of two dominant models of international strategy developed in the 1980s. While limited to only two dimensions, it has substantial analytical and descriptive power in terms of the strategy choices faced by an MNC. On the coordination dimension, the firm has to decide how to link into various value-adding activities across its international network in such a way that its competitive position is strengthened and its performance optimised. The typical MNC faces a wide range of choices here; it can decide to minimise the level of coordination among its plants and subsidiaries world-wide, and allow each operating unit a great deal of responsibility and autonomy. In terms of White and Poynter's (1984) model of subsidiary strategy, this suggests the 'miniature replica' type of subsidiary that carries out a full range of functional and operational tasks at local level. While admirably suited to countries with hostile trading conditions, low coordination makes it difficult for the MNC to garner many of the potential economies of global operations. With high coordination, the MNC will have improved flexibility in dealing with international suppliers, customers and competitors; while successful coordination may take a number of years and a substantial investment to develop, Porter maintains that it allows great sustainability of competitive advantage.

Configuration of value-chain activities is closely linked to matters of international location, which has been a long-running focus of study by economists with interests in international business (Dunning, 1958 and 1995; Vernon, 1966; Wells, 1972; Rugman, 1980; Dunning and Archer, 1987). In evaluating the optimum locational strategy for its world-wide activities, the MNC has many choices; it can dispense activities across many or all countries where it operates (low configuration) or it may concentrate particular activities and/or functions in a small number of countries, especially in its home base. As suggested above, this choice may be applied to each value-chain activity individually, so that an MNC may have dispersed manufacturing and concentrated marketing, or vice versa, or any particular combination between the extremes. Again, low configuration may be related with the miniature replica subsidiary, though the devolution of activities to country level also gives the subsidiary much flexibility to respond to the local situation. Takeuchi and Porter (1986) conclude that of all functional activities, marketing may yield most configurational benefits to an MNC because of its inherent flexibility. In general, an MNC may enhance competitive advantage by dispersion where communication and transportation costs are high, or by concentration where economies of scale are significant.

Putting these dimensions together, Porter evolved four basic strategy prescriptions (see Figure 2.1). High coordination and high configuration yield a 'purest global strategy', typified by companies like Microsoft and Toyota; high coordination coupled with dispersed activities leads to a 'high foreign investment strategy' that requires the extensive coordination among the network of subsidiaries that is often found in the electronics industry (Motorola, NEC). The 'country-centred strategy' is the result of combining low coordination with dispersed activities, and subsidiaries in this situation often operate as the quasi-independent firms found in the international food industry (Unilever, United Biscuits). The fourth quadrant is the 'export-based strategy', often practised by newly internationalising firms and those whose marketing activity (but very little else) is widely dispersed internationally (Boeing, Rolls-Royce).

Figure 2.1 Coordination-configuration framework

Co-ordination of activities	Geographically dispersed	Geographically concentrated
High	**Corporate strategy** High foreign investment with extensive coordination among subsidiaries ***Subsidiary strategy*** *Confederate subsidiary*	**Corporate strategy** Purest global strategy ***Subsidiary strategy*** *Strategic auxiliary*
Low	**Corporate strategy** Country-centred ***Subsidiary strategy*** *Autarchic subsidiary*	**Corporate strategy** Export-based ***Subsidiary strategy*** *Detached subsidiary*

Configuration of activities

Source: Derived from Porter (1986) and extended by author.

Empirical evaluation of coordination as a strategic dimension has been carried out by Ghoshal and Bartlett (1988), Roth and Morrison (1990), Nohria and Garcia-Pont (1991), and Agarwal and Ramaswami (1992). Martinez and Jarillo (1991) found a powerful relationship between subsidiary role and the level of coordination applied to it. Configuration has been empirically evaluated by Roth and Morrison (1992), and Yip (1994), who found that an important ingredient of successful global strategy is concentration of activities; Birkinshaw and Morrison (1995) conclude that this is also a key determinant of subsidiary roles. Roth (1992) has provided strong empirical evaluation of the C–C framework, and Moon (1994) has carried out some interesting adaptations of the model. Taggart (1996a) has brought together the findings of Martinez and Jarillo (1991) and Birkinshaw and Morrison (1995) above to develop a C–C paradigm focused on MNC subsidiary strategy. It depends on the degree of coordination and configuration experienced by the subsidiary, and its strategy prescriptions, which correspond to the corporate roles defined by Porter, are shown in Figure 2.1.

Porter's purest global strategy requires a small number of value-chain activities carried out by a highly focused subsidiary involved in the role of *strategic auxiliary* with fairly limited autonomy. The *confederate subsidiary* also makes few decisions locally, but its behaviour is participative and responsive; it is well suited to working with the extensive and integrated network characteristic of the 'high foreign investment' corporate strategy. In the third quadrant we find subsidiaries with more autonomy (due to lower levels of coordination) and a significant number of value-chain activities performed locally; this *autarchic subsidiary* corresponds to the country-centred strategy. In the export-based quadrant we would not normally expect to find many manufacturing subsidiaries except where they were fairly young, or in a transition phase, or where they were part of a highly diversified parent that exerted little day-to-day control over the non-core parts of its international network; this type is referred to as the *detached subsidiary*.

The second dominant MNC strategy paradigm of the 1980s was the integration–responsiveness (I–R) framework developed by Prahalad and Doz (1987), later evaluated empirically by Roth and Morrison (1990) and Johnson (1995). It has also been partially developed as a model of subsidiary strategy by Jarillo and Martinez (1990), and more fully by Taggart (1997a). The need for local responsiveness is due to market and regulatory imperatives that vary substantially between countries, and the pressure for integration arises from the MNC's needs to exploit international market imperfections while maximising scale economies. Prahalad and Doz propose a spectrum of strategies running from high–integration–low–responsiveness (integrated product strategy) to low–integration–high–responsiveness (locally responsive strategy), with a midway multifocal strategy for firms that have to take account of both sets of pressures. Prahalad and Doz recognised that coordination of activities had a role to play in both integration and responsiveness, and this suggested link with the Porter paradigm will be explored below because it affects our interpretation of subsidiary strategy.

RESEARCH PROBLEM

In developing their model of subsidiary strategy, White and Poynter (1984) implied the possibility of development from one strategy to another over time. Thus, a miniature replica (adopter type) could develop into an innovator type through the addition of value-adding activities at the plant either at the behest of headquarters or through the affiliate's initiative. Similarly, it could develop into a product specialist or rationalised manufacturer by increasing its market scope. Finally, it could become a strategic independent by adding to both value-added scope and market scope. This conceptual pattern of strategic development was confirmed by an empirical study of MNC manufacturing subsidiaries in Scotland carried out by Young *et al.* (1988). Prahalad and Doz's own work (1987) on the I–R framework proposes that researchers should collect strategy data from 'three years ago', as well as current information in order that strategy change over time may be detected and evaluated. This proposal was taken a step further by Jarillo and Martinez (1990), who carried out an evaluation of the I–R framework as it applies at subsidiary level. In their study of 50 selected manufacturing affiliates in Spain, they asked respondents to answer the questionnaire for 'three years time' as well as giving past and current data. This allowed them to chart the progress of three groups of firms (autonomous, receptive and active subsidiaries) over three points in time. A similar technique was applied by Taggart (1996b) in a study of 128 MNC manufacturing subsidiaries in Scotland, and by Taggart and Hood (1995) with a sample of 103 German subsidiaries in the British sales; in both studies, the time period was lengthened from three to five years, forward and back. Thus, in considering the suitability of C–C as a framework for evaluating subsidiary strategy, we arrive at the first and central research problem addressed here, namely:

> RP1: Is there a well-defined taxonomy of manufacturing subsidiaries that develops over time in a consistent manner?

Miller and Friesen (1984: 35) make a general criticism that it is often difficult to evaluate the robustness of a taxonomy, because researchers use all their data in generating the groups of companies and leave none to establish the stability and internal consistency of the taxonomy. This criticism may well be levelled at, for example, Jarillo and Martinez (1990) and Taggart (1996b). In their empirical evaluation of the White and Poynter model, Young *et al.* (1988) included a number of other variables that were used to develop the interpretation of subsidiary strategy types evolved from the data; these included aspects of decision-making autonomy and material flows within the MNC network. Roth and Morrison's (1990) evaluation of the I–R framework followed the Miller and Friesen guideline fairly rigorously, and their taxonomy was tested along a number of alternative dimensions including performance characteristics, nature of innovation, extent of marketing differentiation, customer scope, and degree of cost control. Although their study of procedural justice was unidimensional, Kim and Mauborgne (1993) adopted a similar approach, using a number of additional variables to test the robustness and improve the interpretability of their findings; the additional parameters included organisational commitment, trust in headquarters, concerns about decision outcomes, and perspectives on the reward system. Finally, Johnson's (1995) evaluation of the I–R framework within a single industry used the variables proposed by Roth and Morrison (1990), together with aspects of quality and positioning. All of this suggests that the second research problem addressed here should be:

> RP2: Does the taxonomy evolved from the C–C framework differentiate across other key strategy dimensions in some systematic way that illuminates the process of strategy evolution?

A principal thrust of Miller and Friesen's work (1977, 1978, 1980, 1982, 1984) is that firms exhibit a natural tendency to come together in a fairly small number (compared with that theoretically possible) of 'quantum states' or 'configurations'.

Crucial to this view of the organisational world is that such configurations will be discernible only if interdependencies can be demonstrated to exist among various types of strategy dimension. Further, such an approach adds to the precision and power of empirical analysis and increases its explanatory capability (Meyer *et al.*, 1993). While this research project has not been conceived on such a configurational approach, the general approach can be used to evaluate the links between the C–C paradigm and the I–R dimensions described above. Also, following the 'quantum' notion adapted from the physical sciences, comparisons along the integration and responsiveness dimensions may help explain strategy evolution within the C–C context. The third research problem addressed here, then, is:

> RP3: To what extent do measures of integration and local responsiveness help to evaluate the consistency of a C–C-based taxonomy of subsidiary strategy and its evolution over time?

RESEARCH METHOD

Sample

Two random samples of 25 and 500 companies were drawn from Jordan's listing of US and other foreign-owned manufacturing firms located in the UK; the first sample was used to test the research instrument, and 22 (88 per cent) responded to a request for a meeting to do so. The pre-tested postal questionnaire was sent to the chief executive of each subsidiary in the large sample, from whom 171 (34.2 per cent) valid responses were received. Just over half were from chief executives with 23 per cent each from other directors and other managers. A postal questionnaire was deemed to be the appropriate data collection method for reasons of generalisability of results and cost efficiency. Eighty-five (50 per cent) of the responding subsidiaries were broadly involved in some aspect of engineering, 31 (18 per cent) were operating in the chemicals industry, and 58 (32 per cent) were spread over other manufacturing classifications. The representative responding subsidiary employed around 990, had been established for just over 22 years in the UK, and had annual sales of some £197 million of which £74 million (37.5 per cent) were exported.

Measures

Both coordination and configuration dimensions were measured by four variables each; for coordination, these were level of technical transfer between subsidiaries, linked marketing activity between subsidiaries, linked production requirements between subsidiaries, and linked purchasing requirements between subsidiaries; for configuration, location of strategic skills within the MNC, location of other resources, location of R&D within the MNC, and location of purchasing activity. All were measured on a five-point, Likert-type scale. The variables were drawn from Porter (1986), Martinez and Jarillo (1991) and Roth (1992), and were pre-tested with the subsample of 22 MNC subsidiaries and adjusted marginally to make the wording more precise for the final research instrument. Both sets of measures were accepted as valid and reliable. (Correlations in both sets of measurements were high (all at $p \leq 0.001$) for 'five years ago' and 'current' (see 'Data Analysis' below). The Cronbach alphas for the coordination measures were 0.72 (five years ago) and 0.69 (current); for configuration, the alphas were 0.78 and 0.76 respectively.)

Integration was measured with six variables: manufacturing decisions linked to local or world-wide market areas, product and quality specifications developed by HQ or subsidiary, extent to which the subsidiary serves MNC customers worldwide, centralising and sharing of technology development within the internal network, dependence of the subsidiary on linkages within the internal network, and centralisation of production planning. Local responsiveness comprised five variables: homogeneity of customers and their needs, extent to which competitors and their strategies are easily identified, stability of technology, lifecycle of product line, and the homogeneity of the executive group All of these variables were drawn from the original work of Prahalad and Doz (1987), and the wording of some was changed marginally after the pre-test; they were measured on a five-point, Likert-type scale. Both sets of measures were taken as valid and reliable. (Correlations within both sets of variables were high for both time periods (with all but a few at $p \leq 0.05$). Alphas for integration were 0.72 (five years ago) and 0.68 (current), and for responsiveness 0.59 and 0.60, respectively. Both these values are well above the minimum suggested by Nunally (1967) and accepted by Roth and Morrison (1992).)

Additional strategy variables to test the C–C framework were drawn from various sources, where they had been found valid in other research: market scope (White and Poynter, 1984) was measured on a six-classification choice ('mainly UK' to 'world-wide'); nature of R&D (Young *et al.*, 1988; Taggart, 1997b) also used a six-classification scale ('none' to 'generation of new technology for corporate parent'); proportion of output sent to other group plants for further processing (Kobrin, 1991) was measured by a six-band scale of percentages, as was the proportion of inputs from other group plants (Egelhoff, 1988); finally, the nature of production operations (Roth and Morrison, 1992) was measured by a five-point Likert-type scale ('assembly only' to 'fully fledged manufacturing'). All five variables were subjected to the pre-test before inclusion in the final research instrument.

Data Analysis

A four-stage data analysis procedure was carried out. First, factor analysis was used to ensure that the multi-variable dimensions could be reduced to one factor in each case; loadings varied from 0.52 to 0.83, but were mainly in the range 0.65 to 0.75. The second phase involved the use of cluster analysis to identify groups of companies along the two principal strategic dimensions, coordination and configuration. Since both correlations and alphas were high for both dimensions, the respective sets of variables were aggregated and averaged, thus allowing each subsidiary to be identified by a single value along each dimension (Ghoshal and Bartlett, 1988). These values were used as inputs for the cluster analysis, both hierarchical and non-hierarchical methods being used in combination (Sharma, 1996: 217). Following Prahalad and Doz (1987), respondents were asked on the research instrument to indicate for each variable the position 'five years ago' and the current position. Some researchers have also asked respondents for a forecast of the position in five years time (Jarillo and Martinez, 1990; Taggart, 1996b). This is a perfectly respectable extension of the technique, but is not used here in order to focus attention on known aspects of strategy evolution. Thus, clustering was carried out for 'five years ago' and the current position. Individual members of each cluster were identified and tracked to identify strategy trajectories over the five years in question.

In stage three, analysis of variance was carried out to detect significant differences among the clusters along the five additional strategic variables, namely market and value-added scope, outputs and inputs, and nature of production technology. As RP2 concerns systematic variation rather than some hypothesised relationship, the appropriate *post hoc* technique is Duncan's multi-range test. For the final stage, aggregated values of integration and responsiveness were used for further analysis of variance. As an additional step, firms were coded according to whether they had or had not moved into a different strategic group over the time period, and the integration and responsiveness variables used to evaluate causative relationships. Since the dependent variable is dichotomous in this case, the appropriate technique is logit regression.

RESULTS

Factor analysis on each of the four multi-variable dimensions indicated that the appropriate variables loaded heavily on single factors as follows: coordination, 0.65 to 0.77; configuration, 0.58 to 0.95; integration, 0.45 to 0.77; responsiveness, 0.53 to 0.66. The variables thus load uniquely and significantly on their respective dimensions, indicating that a robust model has been derived. In addition, this analysis determined that the four strategic dimensions are mutually orthogonal, thus functionally independent of one another.

The aggregated data for coordination and configuration were subject to both hierarchical and non-hierarchical clustering. The 'five years ago' dendrogram suggested that four clusters of firm were present; the 'current' analysis indicated four or five clusters, with five being the better solution. Non-hierarchical analysis showed that the four-cluster solution for 'five years ago' explained 70.8 per cent of total variance; for 'current' data the four-cluster solution explained 69.7 per cent of total variance, and the five-cluster solution 76.2 per cent. Because Figure 2.1 is a four-quadrant model, the four-cluster solution was selected as being most amenable to theoretical interpretation (Roth and Morrison, 1990; Johnson, 1995). Variable means are shown in Table 2.1; the *F*-statistic should be interpreted with care; it does not denote significance in the usual way, because the four groups have been constructed on the basis of substantial differences in the aggregates of these variables. However, Table 2.1 does support the view noted above that a robust model has been derived here.

The evolution of strategy types is shown in Figure 2.2; the initial group of 51 *detached subsidiaries* increases very substantially in coordination levels to become the basis of a group of 46 *strategic auxiliaries*, while the initial group of 42 *strategic auxiliaries* becomes the basis of a new group of 36 affiliates with the same strategy, and again movement is due to an increase in coordination levels. The initial group of 44 *autarchic subsidiaries* is the basis for a new group of 53 located within the same quadrant, but with higher levels of both coordination and configuration; similarly, the original group of 34 *confederate subsidiaries* increases coordination, but drops back on configuration to form the basis of a new group of 36 *confederates.* The overall picture is one of substantially larger increases in coordination than in configuration, and substantially more movement among subsidiaries that were originally *autarchic* or *detached.*

The detailed dynamic of strategic evolution is much more complex than is portrayed in the schematic Figure 2.2. Of the 51 subsidiaries originating in cluster 1 (*detached subsidiary*), 23 join the 'current' cluster 1 (lower-level *strategic auxiliaries*), 6 more increase along both dimensions to move into current cluster 3 (higher-level *strategic auxiliaries*), 6 increase in coordination but drop back in configuration to join the current group of *confederate subsidiaries*, and 16 increase coordination but reduce configuration to become part of the new cluster of *autarchic subsidiaries.* The original group of 44 *autarchic subsidiaries* contributes 34 firms to the current cluster, 3 become *detached*

Table 2.1 Four-cluster solution: cluster analysis
High scores denote high levels of coordination and configuration (min = 1, max = 5).

		Cluster 1 Detached	*Cluster 2 Confederate*	*Cluster 3 Strategic auxiliary*	*Cluster 4 Autarchic*	*F-statistic*
Five years ago		$n = 51$	$n = 34$	$n = 42$	$n = 44$	
Coordination	Technological transfer between subsidiaries	1.92	3.74	2.71	1.93	23.94[a]
	Linked marketing activity between subsidiaries	1.69	3.38	2.31	1.27	36.59[a]
	Linked product requirements between subsidiaries	1.63	3.56	1.60	1.43	42.91[a]
	Linked purchasing between subsidiaries	1.82	2.79	2.14	1.43	13.51[a]
Configuration	Location of strategic skills and resources within MNC	2.12	2.03	3.64	1.20	116.60[a]
	Location of R&D within MNC	2.86	2.62	4.38	1.32	48.79[a]
	Location of other skills and resources	2.24	2.18	3.98	1.20	69.59[a]
	Location of purchasing activity within MNC	1.65	1.53	2.81	1.00	29.76[a]
Current		$n = 46$	$n = 36$	$n = 36$	$n = 53$	
Coordination	Technological transfer between subsidiaries	3.37	4.19	3.42	2.62	17.86[a]
	Linked marketing activity between subsidiaries	3.09	4.19	3.28	1.75	55.61[a]
	Linked product requirements between subsidiaries	2.50	4.22	2.25	1.74	42.82[a]
	Linked purchasing between subsidiaries	2.93	3.67	3.11	1.91	24.31[a]
Configuration	Location of strategic skills and resources within MNC	2.41	1.92	3.58	1.64	69.23[a]
	Location of R&D within MNC	3.28	2.53	4.19	1.83	32.72[a]
	Location of other skills and resources	2.46	2.06	3.81	1.70	42.16[a]
	Location of purchasing activity within MNC	1.82	1.50	3.03	1.17	41.25[a]

[a] Significant at $p < 0.000$.

subsidiaries (increase in configuration), 3 become *confederate* (increased in coordination), and 4 become *strategic auxiliaries* (very large increase along both dimensions).

Figure 2.2 Strategy evolution

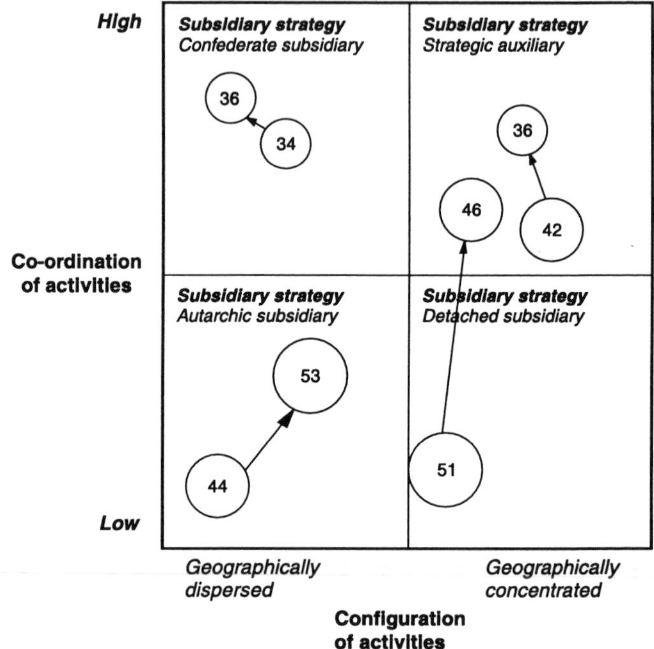

The number of subsidiaries is shown within each circle

The initial cluster of 34 *confederates* give 21 members to the new cluster, 9 become *detached* (decrease along both dimensions), only one moves into the *strategic auxiliary* quadrant (increase in configuration), and 3 drop substantially in coordination and increase somewhat in configuration to join the current *autarchic* cluster. Of the original 42 members of the *strategic auxiliary* cluster, none moves to the *autarchic* quadrant, 11 move to the lower-level *strategic auxiliary* group. (drop in configuration), and 6 increase coordination levels but reduce configuration to join the current *confederate* group. This series of evolutions is shown in Figure 2.3. Overall, the significant move-

Table 2.2 Comparison of operation variables means among four-cluster solutions

	Cluster 1 Detached	*Cluster 2 Confederate*	*Cluster 3 Strategic auxiliary*	*Cluster 4 Autarchic*	*F-statistic*	*p-value*	*Difference*[a] *between clusters*
Five years ago	$n = 51$	$n = 34$	$n = 44$	$n = 44$			
Market scope	2.51	3.55	2.17	2.88	4.07	0.008	2 > 1, 3
Nature of R&D	3.27	4.03	2.33	4.16	16.65	0.000	3 < 1, 2
Outputs to other group plants	1.67	2.30	1.69	1.51	3.20	0.024	2 > 1, 3, 4
Inputs from other group plants	3.04	3.30	3.31	1.86	7.60	0.000	4 < 1, 2, 3
Level of production technology	4.33	4.55	3.93	4.53	2.68	0.048	3 < 2, 4
Integration	2.07	2.44	2.18	1.56	9.07	0.000	4 < 1, 2, 3; 1 < 2
Responsiveness	2.25	2.14	2.04	2.17	0.77	0.514	nil
Current data	$n = 46$	$n = 36$	$n = 36$	$n = 53$			
Market scope	3.36	4.02	2.45	3.14	5.17	0.032	1 > 3; 2 > 3, 4
Nature of R&D	3.70	4.41	2.70	3.86	9.33	0.000	3 < 1, 2
Outputs to other group plants	2.30	2.47	1.73	1.80	3.00	0.032	2 > 3, 4
Inputs from other group plants	3.43	3.38	3.45	2.20	7.14	0.000	4 < 1, 2, 3
Level of production technology	3.93	4.62	4.24	4.53	3.93	0.010	1 < 2, 4
Integration	2.47	2.69	2.40	1.70	19.09	0.000	4 < 1, 2, 3
Responsiveness	2.16	2.13	2.06	2.14	0.19	0.901	nil

[a]Based on Duncan's multiple-range test, $p \leq 0.05$.

ments in coordination noted above are confirmed by the more detailed evolutions of Figure 2.3, but the previously more static role of configuration is shown to be somewhat misleading; at this disaggregated level, changes in configuration among the sample firms are shown to be much more substantial than previously recognised. Naturally, each movement in the strategy space is accompanied by more than changes in coordination and/or configuration, and this is explored further in the next stage.

Figure 2.3 Dynamics of evolution

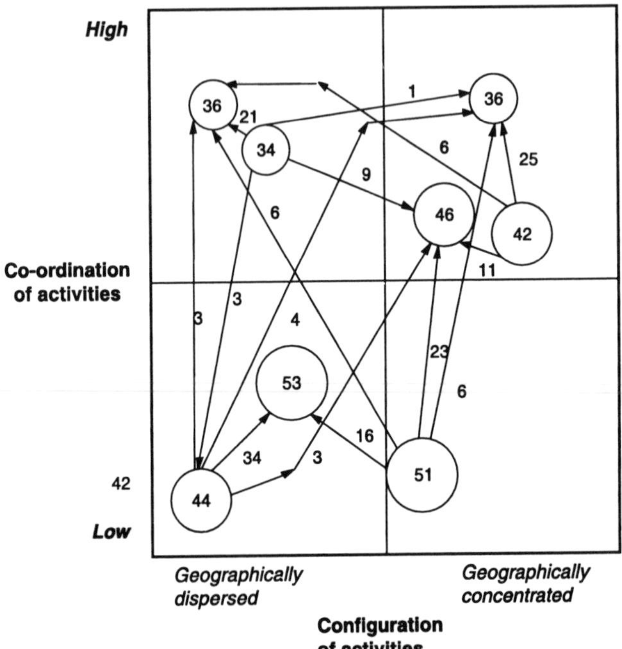

The third stage evaluates the power of the C–C framework to differentiate across a range of strategy variables, namely market scope, nature of R&D, material outputs and inputs to and from other group plants, and the level of production technology used by the subsidiary. The ANOVA results are reported in Table 2.2 and the significant differences in these variables across the clusters indicate an acceptable degree of internal consistency in the cluster solutions. The final column of this table underlines this consistency, as the relationships between the clusters in the two solutions (five years ago, current) is very similar. In other words, we have additional and powerful confirmation that the model derived here is both meaningful and robust, linked directly to a number of key strategic variables, and not merely a function of opportune variation in coordination and configuration.

The differences in the variable means across the two solutions linked to the dynamic in Figure 2.3, suggest some interesting comparisons that were tested for significance (*t*-test for correlated samples, $p \leq 0.05$). Thus, firms that were in cluster 1 (*detached subsidiaries*) five years ago and are also in cluster 1 (lower-level *strategic auxiliary*) currently are characterised by expanded market scope increased levels of R&D, an increased proportion of material outputs sent to other group plants for further processing, and an increased proportion of material inputs from other group plants. Companies moving out of cluster 1 over the five-year period are also characterised by expanded market scope and increased levels of R&D. Stable membership of cluster 2 (*confederate subsidiary*) is associated with higher outputs to other group plants, while movements out of this cluster are not characterised by significance movement along any of the five variables. Subsidiaries that begin in cluster 3 (*strategic auxiliary*) and remain in this group (higher-level *strategic auxiliary*) are marked by increasing complexity of R&D and increasing levels of production technology. Movement out of this group is also associated with increasing levels of R&D complexity (through a lesser extent), increased market scope, and increased levels of outputs to other group subsidiaries. Affiliates that remain within the *autarchic* classification are characterised by increasing levels of inputs from other group subsidiaries and increased market scope, while firms moving out of this group show no particular change in the selected variables. Two specific subgroups are perhaps worthy of note involving firms that were *strategic auxiliaries* five years ago; those that become lower-level *strategic auxiliaries* are characterised by increased levels of outputs to other group subsidiaries, while these becoming *confederates* are marked by increased complexity of R&D.

In the final stage, integration and responsiveness were used as evaluative variables to test the C–C framework. ANOVA results are shown in Table 2.2, and it is clear that in both time periods integration is a powerful differentiator of cluster 4 (*autarchic subsidiaries*), but responsiveness has no role to play.

To examine how these dimensions are linked to strategy evolution, a comparison was made between firms that remained groups over the five-year period and those that did not. Logistic regression was carried out using this measure of strategy stability as the dependent variable, and changes in integration and responsiveness as the predictor variable. The following equations emerged:

Cluster 1: $\text{logit (strategy stability)} = -0.29 + 0.11(\text{integration}) - \underline{1.28\ (\text{responsiveness})}$

Cluster 2: $\text{logit (strategy stability)} = 0.46 - 0.46(\text{integration}) - 1.69\ (\text{responsiveness})$

Cluster 3: $\text{logit (strategy stability)} = 0.16 + \underline{1.41(\text{integration})} + 0.20\ (\text{responsiveness})$

Cluster 4: $\text{logit (strategy stability)} = 2.26 - \underline{2.63\ (\text{integration})} - 0.17\ (\text{responsiveness})$

Thus, a stable strategy configuration is associated with reducing levels of both integration and responsiveness among *confederate* and *autarchic* subsidiaries, with increasing levels of both integration and responsiveness among *strategic auxiliaries*, and with increases in integration and reductions in responsiveness among detached affiliates. However, only the underlined coefficients (above) are significant ($p \leq 0.10$), and so these equations are indicative only, suggesting weak associations between strategy stability and increments in levels of integration and responsiveness.

DISCUSSION

The application of coordination and configuration at affiliate level produces a well-defined and internally consistent taxonomy of subsidiary strategy, consisting of four groups that broadly match a conceptual typology. The *detached subsidiary* is perhaps the most interesting group because, theoretically speaking, it probably should not exist at all except as a transitional form as the corresponding corporate strategy (export-centred) calls for marketing affiliates with little or no manufacturing. A group of 51 such subsidiaries is found in the 'five years ago' data, but the quadrant is empty when the current data is applied; this seems to confirm the transitory nature of *detached subsidiaries.* This group evolves into a current cluster of 46 lower-level strategic auxiliaries, which, of course, also has some members that originate in other clusters.

The original *detached subsidiaries* are characterised, naturally, by low coordination and relatively high concentration of activities, though it is also marked by fairly low intra-MNC linkages as indicated by the low proportion of outputs (< 5 per cent) going to other group plants for further processing. Market scope is limited to the UK with a few selected countries in Continental Europe, and a number of the firms are involved in the development of new and improved products for these markets. The strategy evolution to the current position is marked by a large increase in coordination, with configuration being fairly static. The 23 firms that were members of this cluster in both time periods showed substantial increases in market scope and in the proportion of outputs going to other group plants, with the proportion of inputs from group plants also growing somewhat. The remaining 28 firms that moved into other clusters showed an increase in R&D complexity, with a significant number of firms moving into product development and improvement.

It may well be that the *detached subsidiary* represents an initial move by foreign MNCs to set up in the UK with the objective at that stage being to serve previously existing customers in that market. As its skills and resources develop, it may well be allocated additional countries in continental Europe to service, as well as increasing its penetration of the UK market. Thus, the earlier suggestion of a transition role for this subsidiary type may indicate that it shares some characteristics with the host market penetrator (Taggart and Hood, 1995). In particular, Hood and Taggart (1997) have pointed out the frequency with which German affiliates in the UK adopt this type of early stage market entry strategy.

Confederate subsidiaries were the smallest of the four groups five years ago and were, of course, characterised by high coordination and fairly low configuration; the level of integration among these firms was the highest for all groups. *Confederates* were also marked by very high levels of market scope (Europe with selected other parts of the world) and more complex R&D, with many of the affiliates involved in new product development. This group had the highest level of production technology, the highest proportion of outputs going to other group subsidiaries for further processing (7 per cent) and a high level of inputs (15 per cent) coming from other group subsidiaries. The 'current' group of *confederate subsidiaries* shows a rise in coordination and a fall in configuration, with levels of integration also increasing somewhat. The 21 firms that were members of the group at both time periods showed some increase in the proportion of outputs transferred to other group plants for further processing, while the 13 firms that moved into other clusters showed fairly large increases in market scope but a sharp drop in the level of production technology in use.

In many ways, the *confederate* resembles White and Poynter's (1984) rationalised manufacturer, though it also perhaps characteristic of fragmented international industries. The UK market is unlikely to be its first priority, and it puts more emphasis on serving its parent's customers world-wide, as well as producing parts and subassemblies to shipment to other group subsidiaries. Typically, this type of affiliate will be found within a globalising MNC rather than one that puts high weighting on a pan-Europe strategy. Policy-makers may be attracted to this type as its longevity is not significantly related to the success of the UK (or any other regional) economy; the downside risk is that the *confederate* identified here is likely to be replicated many times throughout its international network, and may be a candidate for closure for reasons of plant efficiency and/or technological obsolescence.

The *strategic auxiliary* group is perhaps the most interesting; it represents the highest level of complexity in terms of international network strategy; the original group of 44 firms evolves into an even more complex group of 36, while a second group of somewhat lower-level *strategic auxiliaries* moves into this quadrant, based on erstwhile *detached subsidiaries.* The original high coordination high configuration group was also marked by high levels of integration, though noticeably less so in the latter than *confederates.* The increase in coordination over the five years was paralleled by an increase in integration, while configuration decreased slightly. The 25 firms that remained members of this classification throughout increased R&D levels somewhat from a very low level, but not nearly as much as the 17 firms that evolved into other groups. The same pattern showed with market scope and the proportion of outputs going to other group plants for further processing. Conversely, the constant members of the group increased the level of production technology slightly more than the others.

The *strategic auxiliary* is a similar type to the strategic leader of Bartlett and Ghoshal (1986) and also shares characteristics with the recently identified collaborator subsidiary (Taggart 1997c). It is likely to operate under fairly close supervision from headquarters but, if the relationship at the interface is good, then the relative lack of autonomy may be more than made up for by its high technological capability and wide access to world markets. Indeed, many of these subsidiaries may be involved in second-stage internationalisation (Taggart and Berry, 1997), though if affiliate-generated moves into wider market areas are to be substantial, many of the firms in this group will have to negotiate or massage more operating autonomy away from headquarters.

The *autarchic subsidiaries* start out in a position of very low coordination and configuration, but the combined movement of this group along both dimensions is the largest for any cluster. Indeed, by the end of the of the five year period, this group has evolved strongly in the direction of the *strategic auxiliary* quadrant; this is accompanied by only a small increase in integration. For the 34 companies that remained within this classification and the 10 companies that moved, similar changes were noted in the levels of the operational strategic variables with the exception of R&D, where the movers showed no difference at all while the constant *autarchic subsidiaries* increased marginally.

Perhaps the key aspect of *autarchics* is the vigour of their diagonal movement shown in Figure 2.2. Taggart and Taggart (1996) have recently indicated that such powerful strategy evolution is a function of the nature of leadership within the subsidiary and of the management team's ability to coax increased autonomy and flexibility from an often reluctant headquarters. This, in turn, requires excellent relationships at the HQ–subsidiary interface.

It will be understood from Table 2.2 and the preceding discussion that levels of integration appear to vary in some systematic way with levels of coordination, but not with configuration; in contrast, levels of local responsiveness do not seem to be associated with any particular levels of or changes in either coordination or configuration. Taking the sample as a whole, there is somewhat less variability in responsiveness than in integration, but the key point is that varying levels of the former are not expressed in the 4-cluster taxonomy, while integration seems to vary systematically. It is also clear from Figure 2.2 that the taxonomy expresses the intrinsic variation in coordination substantially more than that in configuration; again, the descriptive statistics for the sample show that levels of configuration vary at least as much as those of coordination, so the taxonomy is emphasising coordination variability at the expense of configuration. This may be due to the fact that the central thrust of this research – that the C–C framework may be usefully applied at subsidiary level – is not wholly tenable. More likely is that this research, while obliquely recognising the 'configurations' concept of Miller and Friesen (1984), has not taken full account of it. It is, of course, inherently unlikely that the real strategy space of a group of MNC subsidiaries could be realistically described by only two strategic dimensions. The results of this research suggests that such a framework can be the basis for a robust taxonomy that describes strategic posture and strategy evolution in a consistent manner, but they also suggest that the addition of integration, responsiveness, market scope, R&D complexity, level of production technology in use, and material outputs and inputs to and from other group plants may well be the basis for a series of 'configurations' that add substantially to our understanding of the nature of subsidiary strategy. In particular, such configurations would be rich in explanatory power if they fully expressed the variability in local responsiveness and configuration.

CONCLUSIONS

This research set out to apply the C–C framework at MNC affiliate level and to determine whether a taxonomy corresponding to a four-way conceptual typology of subsidiary strategy (*detached, confederate* and *autarchic subsidiaries*, and *strategic auxiliaries*) could consistently explain strategy evolution as well as variation along a number of other strategic dimensions. A group of *detached subsidiaries* for 'five years ago' was found to evolve away from this quadrant, which was then found to be devoid of companies in the 'current' period. More than half of the original *detached subsidiaries* become *strategic auxiliaries*, with a significant number also moving into the *autarchic* quadrant. The bulk of the *confederate subsidiaries* remained in this quadrant, though some became *strategic auxiliaries.* Most of the original *strategic auxiliaries* remained within the same classification, as did more than three-quarters of the *autarchic subsidiaries*, though these evolved strongly in the direction of the *strategic auxiliary* quadrant. Overall, then, the *detached subsidiary* was seen to be a temporary phase, while *strategic auxiliary* was either the preferred end point or eventual target of a large proportion of the sample. Increases in coordination were generally substantial over the five year period, and thus was defined as the main characteristic of strategy evolution. Changes in configuration were less marked, comprising both increases and decreases.

Evaluating the movement of these strategic groups along a number of alternative strategy dimensions underlined the validity of Miller and Friesen's (1984: 4–8) contention that richness and robustness of strategy configurations may be achieved only by the inclusion of larger numbers of significant strategy dimensions. The development of such strategy configuration was not the aim of this research, but the importance of this incremental step is strongly suggested by the taxonomy's relative insensitivity to overall variations in configuration, and by its failure to encompass variations in local responsiveness.

These findings appear to have three principal implications for corporate management teams. First, while the C–C paradigm has been a well-used managerial tool over the last decade, it has been viewed (by HQ managers and others) as a tool to be used primarily at corporate level. It is clear from the results presented here that it is equally applicable at subsidiary level, and it produces a robust and flexible model of subsidiary strategy that links its dimensions tightly to other strategic variables including integration, responsiveness, market and value scope. It therefore presents corporate managers with a precise methodology for allocating appropriate strategic roles to subsidiaries throughout the international network in such a way that overall resource utility is maximised. Second, the model provides an explanatory tool in the often sensitive task of persuading host governments that a particular local subsidiary is on a positive development trajectory and that its continued existence – at least in the medium term – is assured by the role it plays within its international network. This will be true so long as the subsidiary in question is moving away from the *detached* quadrant. On the distaff side, the model also gives policy-makers an independent measure of the same development trajectory. Third, it is clear that subsidiary managers can make as much use of this tool as their counterparts at headquarters. For a liberal and confident corporate management team, this will be seen as a positive evolution; in this case, cooperation across the HQ–subsidiary interface will improve the MNC's overall competitive advantage. Where a more hierarchical attitude exists in the home country, subsidiary management awareness and use of this model to negotiate with HQ is more likely to exacerbate existing interface problems.

References

Agarwal, S. and S.N. Ramaswami (1992) 'Choice of Foreign Market Entry Mode: Impact of Ownership, Location and Internationalization Factors', *Journal of International Business Studies*, 23 (1), 1–27.

Amburgey, T.L. and T. Dacin (1994) 'As the Left Foot Follows the Right: The Dynamics of Strategic and Structural Change', *Academy of Management Journal*, 37 (6), 1427–452.

Bartlett, C. and S. Ghoshal (1986) 'Tap Your Subsidiaries for Global Reach', *Harvard Business Review*, November–December, 87–94.

Birkinshaw, J.M. and A.J. Morrison (1995) 'Configurations of Strategy and Structure in Subsidiaries of Multinational Corporations', *Journal of International Business Studies*, 26 (4), 729–54.

Doz, Y.L. and C.K. Prahalad (1981) 'Headquarters' Influence and Strategic Control in MNCs', *Sloan Management Review*, Fall, 15–29.

Dunning, J.H. (1958) *American Investment in British Manufacturing Industry*, London: Allen & Unwin.

Dunning, J.H. (1995) 'Reappraising the Eclectic Paradigm in an Age of Alliance Capitalism', *Journal of International Business Studies*, 26 (3), 461–92.

Dunning, J.H. and H. Archer (1987) 'The Eclectic Paradigm and the Growth of UK Multinational Enterprises, 1870–1983', University of Reading Discussion Chapters in International Investment and Business Studies, no. 109.

Egelhoff, W.G. (1988) 'Strategy and Structure in Multinational Corporations: a Revision of the Stopford and Wells Model', *Strategic Management Journal*, 9, 1–14.

Ghoshal, S. and C.A. Bartlett (1988) 'Creation, Adoption and Diffusion of Innovations by Subsidiaries of Multinational Corporations', *Journal of International Business Studies*, 19 (3), 365–88.

Ginsberg, A. and N. Venkatraman (1985) 'Contingency Perspectives of Organizational Strategy: a Critical Review of the Empirical Research', *Academy of Management Review*, 10, 421–34.

Hofer, C. and D. Schendel (1978) *Strategy Formulation: Analytical Concepts*, St Paul, Minn.: West.

Hood, N. and J.H. Taggart (1997) 'German Foreign Direct Investment in UK and Ireland: Survey Evidence', *Regional Studies*, 31 (2), 137–48.

Jarillo, J.C. and J.I. Martinez (1990) 'Different Roles for Subsidiaries: The case of multinational corporations in Spain', *Strategic Management Journal*, 11, 501–12.

Johnson, G. (1988) 'Re-thinking Incrementalism', *Strategic Management Journal*, 9, 75–91.

Johnson, J.H. Jr (1995) 'An Empirical Analysis of the I–R Framework: US Construction Equipment Industry Firms in Global Competition', *Journal of International Business Studies*, 26 (3), 621–35.

Kim, W.C. and R.A. Mauborgne (1993) 'Procedural Justice, Attitudes and Subsidiary Top Management Compliance with Multinationals' Corporate Strategic Decisions', *Academy of Management Journal*, 36 (3), 502–26.

Kobrin, S.J. (1991) 'An Empirical Analysis of the Determinants of Global Integration', *Strategic Management Journal*, 12, 17–31.

Martinez, J.I. and J.C. Jarillo (1991) 'Co-ordination Demands of International Strategies', *Journal of International Business Studies*, 22 (3), 429–44.

Meyer, A.D., A.S. Tsui and C.R. Hinings (1993) 'Configurational Approaches to Organisational Analysis', *Academy of Management Journal*, 36 (6), 1175–195.

Miller, D. and P. Friesen (1977) 'Strategy Making in Concept: Ten Empirical Archetypes', *Journal of Management Studies*, 19, 131–51.

Miller, D. and P. Friesen (1978) 'Archetypes of Strategy Formulation', *Management Science*, 24, 921–33.

Miller, D. and P. Friesen (1980) 'Archetypes of Organisational Transition', *Administrative Science Quarterly*, 25, 268–99.

Miller, D. and P. Friesen (1982) 'Structural Change and Performance: Quantum vs. Piecemeal–Incremental Approaches', *Academy of Management Journal*, 25, 867–92.

Miller, D. and P. Friesen (1984) *Organizations: A Quantum View*, Englewood Cliffs, NJ: Prentice-Hall.

Mintzberg, H. (1980) 'Structure in 5's: A Synthesis of the Research on Organization Design', *Management Science*, 26, 322–41.

Moon, W.C. (1994) 'A Revised Framework of Global Strategy: Extending the C–C Framework', *International Executive*, 36 (5), 557–74.

Morrison, A.J. (1990) *Strategies in Global Industries: How US Businesses Compete*, Quorum Books: New York.

Nohria, N. and C. Garcia-Pont (1991) 'Global Strategic Linkages and Industry Structure', *Strategic Management Journal*, 12, 105–24.

Nunnally, J. (1967) *Psychometric theory*, New York: McGraw-Hill.

Porter, M.E. (1986) 'Changing Patterns of International Competition', *California Management Review*, 28, 9–40.

Porter, M. (1980) *Competitive Strategy: Techniques for Analysing Industries and Competitors*, New York, Free Press.

Prahalad, C.K. and Y.L. Doz (1987) *The Multinational Mission: Balancing Local Demands and Global Vision*, New York: The Free Press.

Quinn, J.B. (1980) *Strategies for Change: Logical Incrementalism*, Homewood, Ill.: Irwin.

Ronstadt, R.C. (1978) 'International R&D: the Establishment and Evolution of Research and Development Abroad by Seven US Multinationals', *Journal of International Business Studies* 9 (1), 7–24.

Roth, K. and A.J. Morrison (1990) 'An Empirical Analysis of the I–R Framework in Global Industries', *Journal of International Business Studies*, 21 (4), 541–64.

Roth, K. (1992) 'International Configuration and Coordination Archetypes for Medium-sized Firms in Global Industries', *Journal of International Business Studies*, 23 (3), 533–50.

Roth, K. and A.J. Morrison (1992) 'Implementing Global Strategy: Characteristics of Global Subsidiary Mandates', *Journal of International Business Studies*, 23 (4), 715–35.

Rugman, A.M. (1980) 'Internationalisation as a General Theory of Foreign Direct Investment: a Reappraisal of the Literature', *Weltwirtschaftliches*, 116 (2), 365–79.

Sharma, S. (1996) *Applied Multivariate Analysis*, New York: Wiley.

Taggart, J.H. (1995) 'Strategy Formulation in Declining Industries: A Biology Paradigm', *Journal of Marketing Management*, 11 (4), 295–314.

Taggart, J.H. (1996a) 'An Empirical Evaluation of the C–C Paradigm', SIBU Working Paper 96/6, University of Strathclyde.

Taggart, J.H. (1996b) 'Multinational Manufacturing Subsidiaries in Scotland: Strategic Role and Economic Impact', *International Business Review*, 5 (5), 447–68.

Taggart, J.H. (1996c) 'Evolution of Multinational Strategy: Evidence from Scottish Manufacturing Subsidiaries', *Journal of Marketing Management*, 12 (6), 533–49.

Taggart, J.H. (1997a) 'An Evaluation of the I–R Grid: MNC Manufacturing Subsidiaries in the UK', *Management International Review*, 37 (4), 295–318.

Taggart, J.H. (1997b) 'R&D Intensity in UK Subsidiaries of Manufacturing Multinational Corporations', *Technovation*, 17 (2), 73–82.

Taggart, J.H. (1997c) 'Autonomy and Procedural Justice: A Framework for Evaluating Subsidiary Strategy', *Journal of International Business Studies*, 28 (1), 51–76.

Taggart, J.H. and N. Hood (1995) 'Perspectives on Subsidiary Strategy in German Companies Manufacturing in the British Isles', Conference Proceedings, Academy of International Business, Bradford.

Taggart, J.H and J.M. Taggart (1996) 'Subsidiary Strategy in Peripheral Economies', in B. Fynes and S. Ennis (eds), *Competing from the Periphery*, London: Dryden.

Taggart, J.H. and M.M.J. Berry (1997) 'Second Stage Internationalisation: Evidence from MNC Manufacturing Subsidiaries in the UK', *Journal of Marketing Management*, 13 (1) 179–92.

Takeuchi, H. and M.E. Porter (1986) 'Three Roles of Marketing in Global strategy', in Michael E. Porter (ed.), *Competition in Global Industries.*, Boston, Mass.: Harvard Business School Press.

Vernon, R. (1966) 'International Investment and International Trade in the Product Cycle', *Quarterly Journal of Economics*, 80 (May), 190–207.

Wells, L.T. (1972) *The Product Life Cycle and International Trade*, Boston, Mass.: Harvard University Press.

White, R.E. and T.A. Poynter (1984) 'Strategies for Foreign-Owned Subsidiaries in Canada', *Business Quarterly*, 48(4), Summer, 59–69.

Yip, G.S. (1994) 'Industry Drivers of Global Strategy and Organisation', *International Executive*, 36 (5), 529–56.

Young, S., N. Hood and S. Dunlop (1988) 'Global Strategies, Multinational Subsidiary Roles and Economic Impact in Scotland', *Regional Studies*, 22 (6), 487–97.

3 Individualism and Interdependence in the Technological Development of MNEs: The Strategic Positioning of R&D in Overseas Subsidiaries

Marina Papanastassiou and Robert Pearce

INTRODUCTION

The growth of decentralised R&D in MNEs is central to the ways these companies approach the new competitive pressures of the global economy of the late twentieth century.(For recent evidence and analysis of R&D in MNEs see Dunning (1994), Dunning and Narula (1995), Fors (1996), Håkanson and Nobel (1993a, 1993b), Howells and Wood (1993), Papanastassiou (1995), Pearce (1989), Pearce and Singh (1992a, 1992b), Taggart (1993).) As these companies seek to define positions for technology in the generation of sustained competitiveness, roles for overseas R&D laboratories can emerge at three distinct levels. In the short term, the pressures of global competition mean that MNEs need to produce their well-established products as effectively as possible. Laboratories operating within the subsidiaries that produce such products may support their operations by assisting in the adaptation of the manufacturing process to host-country conditions and of the products to local tastes. However, to carry competitiveness into the medium term, MNEs need to substantially upgrade their product range, introducing new generations that embody new concepts that extend the industry's scope. As a weapon in global competition, such product innovation needs to embody clear international dimensions. (For analysis of approaches to innovation in a global context see Ghoshal and Bartlett (1988), Bartlett and Ghoshal (1989, 1990), Papanastassiou and Pearce (1996), Pearce and Papanastassiou (1996a).) Though such radical evolution of product scope is still likely to embody substantial elements of the company's existing stock of knowledge (that is, remain within an established technological trajectory), these major operations in product development will also require the crucial addition of new technology inputs in order to operationalise this knowledge in the emerging commercial context. Since this context is now a global one, a vital role emerges for overseas R&D in taking these major steps in product development. On the supply side, overseas laboratories can provide new elements of technology that complement the group's initial stock in crucial ways, while on the demand side overseas laboratories work with other functions in local subsidiaries to make the process of product development responsive to specific market conditions.

Finally, in the long term, companies need to regenerate the core of their knowledge assets through substantial amounts of speculative research that is intended to provide eventually a basis for more fundamentally original new products that may perhaps ultimately even reflect an alteration in the direction of the technological trajectory of the firm or industry. In implementing programmes of basic and applied research to cover such speculative possibilities, a wide range of scientific disciplines may need to be accessed, and in cases where the science bases of other countries provide the best traditions in relevant technological areas overseas laboratories in these countries will be a crucial facet of MNEs' pursuit of such knowledge expansion. Labs that play mainly this role often operate on a stand-alone basis, independent of any other (for example, manufacturing) activity of the parent MNE in the country in question (Pearce and Singh, 1992a).

In this chapter the predominant concern is with the first two of these levels of overseas R&D, and in particular with the way an extension of the R&D function within subsidiaries represents a key element in the transition from the dependent role of supplying established products to the individualistic (though still substantially interdependent) one of product development.(Other studies that include discussion of the position of R&D in the operations of MNE subsidiaries include Hood *et al.*, (1994), Molero and Buesa (1993), Molero *et al.* (1995), Roth and Morrison (1992).) We investigate various aspects of the positioning of R&D in the activity of the subsidiaries of foreign MNEs operating in the UK through the results of a survey carried out in 1993–94. The questionnaire was sent to 812 such manufacturing subsidiaries, with satisfactory replies received from 190 of them.(The survey was carried out as part of a project financed by the ESRC. It was intended to survey all relevant manufacturing subsidiaries that could be found in the National Register Publishing Company's *International Directory of Corporate Affiliations.*)

R&D AND INTERDEPENDENT INDIVIDUALISM

This chapter seeks to encompass two closely interrelated levels of investigation. The first of these assesses in general terms the positioning of R&D in MNE subsidiaries in the UK, looking at its prevalence, its roles and its motivation. The second focuses on the more detailed theme of the extent to which R&D contributes to the distinction between types of subsidiaries, and most explicitly its contribution to the emergence of those (world or regional mandate) subsidiaries that take responsibility for the development (as well as production and marketing) of parts of their MNE group's product range.

While the quantitative intensity of international competition in most major industries places pressure on MNEs to produce their established products as cost-effectively as possible, qualitative elements of global heterogeneity also open up dynamic competitive perspectives that need to be accessed if these companies are to address the potentials of sustained progress and growth. Globally competing enterprises need to articulate their medium-term development through globalised programmes of market responsiveness and knowledge acquisition and application. Overseas subsidiaries with an individualised creativity (product development mandates) can play crucial roles in the ways MNEs use global heterogeneity in a positive fashion. We may discern two ways this can occur. First, such subsidiaries may apply a new group-level technology to their own regional market (regional product mandate) by developing from it a distinctive product variant that fully responds to the relevant local tastes and characteristics. Though operating within a programme that is defined by a new group-level technology, the subsidiaries that undertake this role need a high level of individualised R&D competence that can work with its marketing personnel to develop the distinctive product variant.

In the second alternative the subsidiary-level development may be more unique and self-contained, and therefore perhaps open up wider markets (a world product mandate). Here the new product concept, and the core elements of new technology, may emerge in an individualised subsidiary that then stakes its claim to responsibility for its full commercial development and world-wide supply. A key word here, however, may be responsibility (Pearce, 1989, 1992). Even where the crucial elements of the core technology emerge at the subsidiary level the capacity for its full elaboration is likely to be beyond the scope of most such national units. Access to supporting R&D inputs from elsewhere in the group may ensure the most effective completion of all facets of the new technology from the point of view of the subsidiary, and also encourage an optimal use of group-wide technological scope. Another factor in the use of such R&D interdependencies is that it helps to ensure that new technological possibilities can emerge, and be enthusiastically supported and nurtured at the subsidiary level, but with a clear group-level understanding of how these new dimensions relate to the MNE's overall technological trajectory.

An optimal use of these supportive elements in decentralised R&D in MNEs would allow the positive emergence and application of individualised creative scope to occur within mandated subsidiaries in ways that also augment the coherent progress of group-level technology. Valuable two-way interdependencies can be discerned. As already observed, the full elaboration of the new technological possibilities that emerge within one subsidiary may need complementary inputs from elsewhere in the group. At the same time, elements of new subsidiary-level knowledge may not only support its own product development ambitions but also have the potential to enrich the technological scope of other subsidiaries that are working on other parts of the group's product range. Approaching globalised R&D through subsidiaries requires MNEs to be aware of the benefits of both individualism and interdependency. This also underlines that there is no longer likely to be a viable dichotomy between MNEs that adopt centralised or decentralised approaches to R&D. The logical aim now appears to be for extensive decentralised originality that remains open to centralised monitoring and evaluation in order to ensure that it supports the enrichment and coherent evolution of a clearly articulated group-level technological trajectory.

Our investigation of MNE subsidiaries in the UK discerned four possible roles that these might play.(For more detailed discussion of these roles see Pearce (1996), Pearce and Papanastassiou (1996b), Papanastassiou and Pearce (1997a).) Here these roles, and their relative importance in responding subsidiaries, are briefly introduced along with speculations as to their likely requirements for R&D support. The first subsidiary role was defined as 'to produce for the UK market products that are already established in our MNE group's product range' (ESTPROD/UK). Though we have suggested elsewhere (Pearce, 1996) that, as would be expected in the context of globalised competition, this role is in relative decline, it still takes a prominent residual position among responding subsidiaries. Thus 8.1 per cent of respondents felt this was their only role, 37.3 per cent felt it took a predominant position, 27.0 per cent believed it retained a secondary position and only 27.6 per cent considered it played no part in their operations. In terms of the globalised technology perspectives of MNEs, these subsidiaries are likely to be highly dependent, concerned only to apply standardised (centrally created) technology to their own markets. Where in-house R&D plays a role then this is likely to be the very localised one of adapting technology that is already embodied in established products to host country conditions.

The second role was defined as 'to play a role in the MNE's European supply network by specialising in the production and export of part of the established product range' (ESTPROD/EUR). Overall this role was of similar relevance to the first with 3.2 per cent of responding subsidiaries rating it their only one, 46.5 per cent feeling it took a predominant position, 21.6 per cent a secondary one and 28.6 per cent considering it played no part in their activities. Since these ESTPROD/EUR subsidiaries operate in an externally determined position as constituents of centrally coordinated networks, in order to specialise in the production of limited parts of a well-established product range for supply to a wider geographical market area, there would seem less reason for them to have in-house R&D than ESTPROD/UK. In the latter, a reaction to a distinct local market with which they can generate close affinity is viable and beneficial. However, if individual ESTPROD/EUR subsidiaries are unlikely to need (or to be allowed – where they are expected to conform to a predetermined role in a cohesive network) R&D that is uniquely supportive of their own operations, the whole integrated European system of such facilities is likely to require such backing for adaptation of its received technology. It may then be decided to locate such network-supporting R&D units within one or more of the producing subsidiaries.(An alternative might be to set up a laboratory independent from any production unit. This would establish its neutrality and mitigate tensions that could arise from co-location with one production subsidiary.) Overall this might suggest that ESTPROD/EUR subsidiaries are less likely to possess R&D units than ESTPROD/UK, but that where they do they may then be more substantial and powerful. Also, such R&D in ESTPROD/EUR subsidiaries would still be essentially dependent within the globalised technological perspectives of the MNE, but apply its work to regionalised aims (rather than the localised ones of ESTPROD/UK laboratories).

The third subsidiary role was defined as 'to play a role in the MNE group's European supply network by producing and exporting component parts for assembly elsewhere' (COMPART). Only 1.1 per cent of respondents considered this their only role, and only 6.1 per cent more felt it a predominant one, while 22.7 per cent believed it was limited to a secondary role, and 70.2 per cent did not play it at all. If this COMPART role is played within a network that is seeking cost-effective supply of well-established products it is unlikely to need in-house R&D support. However, such COMPART operations could be associated with subsidiaries that have mandates to develop new products for the European (or world) markets, and may be closely involved in this creative process. In this case their own R&D unit could then be a strong asset in asserting an individualised position in supporting the operations of the mandated subsidiary.

The final subsidiary role defined for respondents was 'to develop, produce and market for the UK and/or European (or wider) markets new products additional to the MNE group's existing range' (DEVELPROD). The relative prevalence of this role is compatible with its emergence as a strong element in the heterogeneity of the contemporary MNE's approach to the global strategic environment. Thus 8.7 per cent of respondents rated this their only role, 27.2 per cent felt it a predominant one, 34.2 per cent believed it took a secondary status, while 29.9 per cent did not yet include it in their activity. We would clearly expect that the performance of the DEVELPROD role would be more likely to require in-house R&D support than any of the others. Also, in line with previous discussion, this R&D is expected to be central to the proactive positioning of these subsidiaries. Thus the ideal status of such subsidiaries may be one of interdependent individualism, fully exploiting distinctive creative attributes in (or accessible to) their operations but doing so in ways that also enhance (rather than disrupt) beneficial synergies with the logical evolution of group-wide scope. Labs in DEVELPROD subsidiaries thus enter the globalised technology perspectives of their MNEs in a much more positive way than those in the ESTPROD types of subsidiary, moving from dependency to the exercise of an individualism that will, to varying degrees and in various ways, be modulated by interdependencies with wider group creativity. From strong positions within the evolution of the group-level technological trajectory DEVELPROD laboratories may support either regionalised or globalised commercial objectives (Regional Product Mandate or World Product Mandate subsidiaries).

R&D IN UK SUBSIDIARIES OF MNEs

A question in the survey of UK-based MNE subsidiaries asked respondents to evaluate the importance to their operations of seven potential sources of technology. (See Papanastassiou and Pearce (1997a, 1997b), Pearce (1996) for detailed discussion of the full scope of this question.) One of these was defined as 'R&D carried out by our own laboratory'. As Table 3.1 shows, only 40.8 per cent of respondents did not use the output of an in-house R&D unit as part of their technology scope, while 3.4 per cent considered it the only source of their technology, 35.8 per cent a major source and 20.1 per cent a secondary source.

Support from an in-house R&D unit emerges as least prevalent in ESTPROD/UK subsidiaries, which have the largest proportion not using such laboratories at all and the smallest proportion considering their contribution to technological scope as being a major source. The results in Table 3.1 validate only part of our hypothesis of a dichotomous status for R&D in ESTPROD/EUR subsidiaries. Thus rather more of these, as predicted, found a strong (major or only source) position for in-house R&D than was the case for ESTPROD/UK subsidiaries but less (contrary to our expectation) operated without such support. The unexpected persistence of R&D units in ESTPROD/EUR subsidiaries may reflect the selection process through which subsidiaries acquire this role. Thus it may be that in assembling a network of facilities to play this role MNE group planners view the presence of R&D and other creative attributes as reflecting favourably on the quality and potential of a subsidiary, even though there is no obvious use for these functions in the position that the unit is expected to take. If this is so then the process of rationalising these subsidiaries into their networked role may eventually see the decline of those R&D units that may (perhaps for reasons of morale or relations with host-country governments, and so on) have been allowed to persist into the early phases of accession to this position.

As hypothesised, the use of their own R&D laboratory is decisively strongest in the DEVELPROD subsidiaries, where by far the smallest proportion of them operate without such a facility and notably the largest proportion rate the input of one to be a major (or only) source of technology. Though a third of COMPART subsidiaries operate without in- house R&D support, half of them rated such laboratories as a major source of their technology. This suggests that there exists a clear tendency for COMPART facilities to operate interdependently with the creative activity of DEVELPROD subsidiaries, rather than dependently in support of ESTPROD/EUR networks.

Table 3.1 In-house R&D as a source of technology in MNE subsidiaries in the UK

	Importance of in-house R&D (percentage of subsidiaries) [a]				
	Only source of technology	*Major source of technology*	*Secondary source of technology*	*Not a source of technology*	*TOTAL*
By industry					
Food		75.0		25.0	100.0
Automobiles		38.9	5.6	55.6	100.0
Aerospace		16.7	16.7	66.7	100.0
Electronics and electrical appliances	2.2	30.4	30.4	37.0	100.0
Mechanical engineering	3.8	26.9	19.2	50.0	100.0
Instruments	9.1	45.5	9.1	36.4	100.0
Industrial and agricultural chemicals	6.9	44.8	20.7	27.6	100.0
Pharmaceuticals and consumer chemicals		50.0	30.0	20.0	100.0
Metal manufacture and products	9.1	27.3	9.1	54.5	100.0
Other manufacturing		21.4	28.6	50.0	100.0
TOTAL	3.4	35.8	20.1	40.8	100.0
By home country					
USA	1.5	46.2	18.5	33.8	100.0
Japan	4.7	21.9	20.3	53.1	100.0

Europe	4.7	37.2	23.3	34.9	100.0
TOTAL[b]	3.4	35.8	20.1	40.8	100.0
By subsidiary type[c]					
ESTPROD/UK		32.9	19.0	48.1	100.0
ESTPROD/EUR	3.4	36.8	24.1	35.6	100.0
COMPART		50.0	16.7	33.3	100.0
DEVELPROD	7.9	58.7	11.1	22.2	100.0

Subsidiary types:

ESKPROD/UK: *to produce for the UK market products that are already established in our MNE group's product range.*
ESTPROD/EUR: *to play a role in the MNE group's European supply network by specialising in the production and export of part of the established product range.*
COMPART: *to play a role in the MNE group's European supply network by producing and exporting component parts for assembly elsewhere.*
DEVELPROD: *to develop, produce and market for the UK and/or European (or wider) markets, new products additional to the MNE group's existing range.*

[a] The percentage of respondents that graded 'R&D carried out by our own laboratory' at each level as a source of their technology.
[b] Includes subsidiaries of MNEs from Australia and Canada.
[c] Subsidiaries that said a particular role was either their only one or their predominant one.
Source: Authors' survey 1993–4.

In Table 3.2 the analysis of 'R&D carried out by our own laboratory' (OWNLAB) as a source of subsidiary technology is extended by placing it alongside two other types of R&D that could be accessed (as technology sources) by these operations. The first of these additional sources of R&D is 'R&D carried out for us by another R&D laboratory of our MNE group' (GROUPLAB). When these two sources of R&D are summarised into average responses in Table 3.2, it is clear that overall GROUPLAB is somewhat the more prevalent. (To some extent this reflects the fact that more subsidiaries use GROUPLAB inputs than greater intensity of use when it is accessed. Thus only 27 per cent of subsidiaries had no use for GROUPLAB compared with 41 per cent that did not use OWNLAB. By contrast, 66 per cent of subsidiaries that used OWNLAB at all felt it took a major (or only) position as a source of technology, while only 57 per cent of those using GROUPLAB felt it took this position.) However, as hypothesised, the relative positioning of OWNLAB and GROUPLAB varies considerably between types of subsidiary. For both ESTPROD/UK and ESTPROD/EUR it is GROUPLAB that is clearly the more important source of R&D as a technological input. This reflects the fact that where in-house R&D (OWNLAB) occurs in subsidiaries producing established products, its role is merely to mediate in the effective application of technology whose use is already pervasive in the group, rather than to seek any degree of individualisation of the subsidiaries' own knowledge scope. In DEVELPROD subsidiaries (and to a less clear-cut degree in COMPART facilities) the position is reversed, with OWNLAB moving into the predominant position as a source of R&D. Similarly, while (as Table 3.1 also showed) OWNLAB is more important in DEVELPROD/COMPART subsidiaries than in the ESTPROD ones, GROUPLAB is stronger in the ESTPROD units than in the former pair of roles. Thus the move to the more creative roles places a priority on an increased availability of R&D scope within the subsidiary. However, while OWNLAB provides the individualistic technology momentum in such operations a quite substantial (if somewhat reduced) continued access to other R&D capacity in the group also reflects the benefits from the exercise of such distinctive scope in an interdependent fashion.

These results can provide a stylised view of R&D repositioning as subsidiaries move into more creative roles.(Of course, causation is indeterminate here. Thus subsidiaries may acquire R&D that is unnecessary for their current role in order to generate the scope to claim a move to a higher-value-added role.) In the most technologically dependent phases of an ESTPROD role, subsidiaries may not incorporate an in-house R&D unit, instead securing any necessary work on the adaptation of the relevant group technology from other MNE laboratories that perhaps already have experience of it. Here GROUPLAB substitutes for work that OWNLAB would have carried out. If subsidiary-level individualisation increases the amount of technological work needed then eventually an in-house laboratory may emerge. At first this may mainly do the types of work that would earlier have been secured from other group laboratories. However, if the subsidiary makes the full creative transition (Papanastassiou, 1995; Papanastassiou and Pearce, 1994) to a DEVELPROD role then the proactive position of OWNLAB also finds a new status for GROUPLAB inputs. Now the in-house laboratory articulates a programme of R&D to support its subsidiary's product development objectives, but may not feel it necessary (or viable) to perform all of this itself. Instead, it may commission such additional R&D from other group laboratories, so that GROUPLAB now complements (rather than, as earlier, substitutes) OWNLAB activity. We have already indicated that the individualisation of a subsidiary's scope through its own R&D may benefit the MNE group most when still exercised through such types of creative interdependence.

Table 3.2 Sources of R&D used by MNE subsidiaries in the UK

	Source of R&D (average response)[a]		
	OWNLAB	*GROUPLAB*	*LOCALINST*
By industry			
Food	2.50	1.78	1.67
Automobiles	1.83	2.65	1.39
Aerospace	1.50	1.83	1.33
Electronics and electrical appliances	1.98	2.33	1.32

Table 3.2 (*contd.*)

	Source of R&D (average response)[a]		
	OWNLAB	*GROUPLAB*	*LOCALINST*
Mechanical engineering	1.85	2.00	1.62
Instruments	2.27	2.18	1.73
Industrial and agricultural chemicals	2.31	2.31	1.52
Metal manufacture and products	1.91	1.82	1.36
Pharmaceuticals and consumer chemicals	2.30	2.40	1.60
Other manufacturing	1.71	2.14	1.50
TOTAL	2.02	2.22	1.48
By home country			
USA	2.15	2.18	1.62
Japan	1.78	2.23	1.27
Europe	2.12	2.25	1.55
TOTAL[b]	2.02	2.22	1.48
By subsidiary type[c]			
ESTPROD/UK	1.85	2.29	1.39
ESTPROD/EUR	2.08	2.27	1.41
COMPART	2.17	2.08	1.58
DEVELPROD	2.52	2.05	1.62

Sources of R&D: OWNLAB = R&D carried out by own laboratory.
GROUPLAB = R&D carried out for us by another R&D laboratory of our MNE group.
LOCALINST = R&D carried out for us by local scientific institutions (e.g., universities, independent laboratories, industry laboratories).

[a] Responding subsidiaries were asked to grade each source of R&D as (1) our only source, (2) a major source, (3) a secondary source, (4) not a source. The average response is calculated by allocating a value of 4 to 'our only source', 3 to a 'major source', 2 to a 'secondary source', 1 to 'not a source'.

[b] Includes subsidiaries of MNEs from Australia and Canada.

[c] Subsidiaries that said a particular role was either their only one or their predominant one. For definitions of subsidiary types see Table 4.1.

Source: Authors' survey 1993–4.

The second of the additional R&D sources covered in Table 3.2 was defined as 'R&D carried out for us by local scientific institutions (for example, universities; independent laboratories; industry laboratories)' (LOCALINST). If the scope of the local science base is a factor in attracting the more creative types of MNE subsidiary to a particular country, then there are two ways this indigenous technology scope can be accessed. First, it may be internalised in the type of OWNLAB units already evaluated. Second, it can be secured through externalised contractual routes in the form of collaborative R&D arrangements with local institutions. As Table 3.2 shows, the LOCALINST means of securing R&D inputs initially appears relatively underdeveloped in the MNE subsidiaries' operations in the UK, with only 44 per cent of respondents making any use of such collaborations and only 3 per cent considering that this was more than a secondary source of technology. However, it is likely that such collaborative R&D with independent local laboratories would be most effectively implemented through an in-house MNE laboratory and would then be logically interpreted as a secondary technology source mediated through the OWNLAB (as a lead source). Then, if we now assume that LOCALINST R&D can only be accessed through an in-house lab, we can suggest that up to 75 per cent of subsidiaries with OWNLAB R&D allowed their laboratories to supplement their work through such collaborations. Table 3.2 confirms, to a moderate degree, that LOCALINST is more prevalent as a technology source in the more creatively ambitious (DEVELPROD/COMPART) subsidiaries.

Responding subsidiaries that possessed R&D laboratories were asked to report if they expected growth or decline in these facilities in the near future. The results reported in Table 3.3 generally underwrite a continued momentum in decentralised R&D in these companies, with 39.8 per cent of respondents anticipating laboratory growth and only 11.9 per cent expecting laboratory decline. Both Japanese and US subsidiaries recorded a decisive net expectation of growth in their R&D laboratories, but subsidiaries of European MNEs did provide a net expectation of decline. For the Japanese and US subsidiaries the reported expectation is compatible with growing intra-subsidiary creativity as they aim to claim leading positions in their group's strategic approach to the European market (that is, regionalised dimensions replace localised ones and require more R&D support to do so). In the European subsidiaries' case there may also be a growing consciousness of specific need for a regional technology strategy, with a decision to focus the key creative elements of this on home-country (that is, Continental parent) operations. This then results in a decline in decentralised (for example, UK-based) R&D within Europe. (A global technology strategy for these companies (within which the European element operates) may then simultaneously apply outside Europe (for example, in North America and Asia).)

Table 3.3 Anticipated changes in size of R&D laboratories of MNE subsidiaries in the UK, by industry and home country [a]

	Anticipated change (percentage of respondents)	
	Growth	*Decline*
By industry		
Food	42.9	14.3
Automobiles	42.9	0
Electronics and electrical appliances	55.6	0
Mechanical engineering	46.7	0
Instruments	0	50.0
Industrial and agricultural chemicals	19.0	30.0
Pharmaceuticals and consumer chemicals	37.5	25.0
Other manufacturing	50.0	0
TOTAL	39.8	11.9
By home country		
USA	42.8	4.7
Japan	59.3	7.4
Europe	21.4	29.6
TOTAL[b]	39.8	11.9

[a] Responding MNE subsidiaries that possessed an R&D laboratory were asked if they anticipated its growth or decline in the near future.

[b] Indicates laboratories of MNEs from Australia and Canada.

Source: Authors' survey 1993–4.

Regressions were run using replies to these questions as dependent variables (Table 3.4(b)). These tests included dummy variables for industry and home-country and the roles of subsidiaries as independent variables. (The miscellaneous other manufacturing group served as omitted industry dummy and European MNE subsidiaries as omitted home-country dummy.) Apart from confirming anticipated growth in Japanese and US subsidiaries, the tests also provided significant results for the DEVELPROD role. This further substantiates the view that increasing commitment to product development in a subsidiary is positively related to the incorporation of R&D capacity within its scope. Though in neither case reaching significance, the signs on ESTPROD/EUR do suggest that the more prevalent is this role in a subsidiary the more likely is a decline in its R&D capacity. This would be compatible with our suggestion earlier that many ESTPROD/EUR subsidiaries may be carrying R&D capacity in excess of their needs. While this scenario is necessarily speculative, it may have some worrying implications for host countries (for example, the UK in this case). Thus subsidiaries with a certain degree of creative (high-value-added) scope may gain the essentially cost-based ESTPROD/EUR role and then later shed those characteristics that could individualise their situation in the MNE. Once this R&D has gone, the subsidiary can only sustain its networked position by low-cost supply of standardised inputs. The need to avoid 'unnecessary' overheads in retaining the ESTPROD/EUR position then makes it increasingly difficult to set up the potential to accede to the DEVELPROD role.

ROLES OF MNE SUBSIDIARIES' R&D LABORATORIES

A question in the survey asked those manufacturing subsidiaries that possessed R&D units to evaluate the relative importance of four roles in their activity. Somewhat the most pervasive of these roles (Table 3.5) was the one aimed at providing an individualised product scope and creative competence to the subsidiary, that is, 'to play a role in the development of new products for our distinctive markets'. This was rated their lab's only role by 5.9 per cent of responding subsidiaries, a

Table 3.4 Regressions with anticipated changes in size of R&D laboratories as dependent variables

	Dependent variable	
	Anticipated growth	*Anticipated decline*
Intercept	–01869	0.1648
	(–0.60)	(0.87)
Food	0.0713	0.0390
	(1.23)	(1.12)
Automobiles	0.0900	0.0592
	(0.31)	(0.33)
Electronics and electrical appliances	0.1037[a]	–0.0096
	(1.77)	(–0.27)
Mechanical engineering	0.0553	–0.0014
	(1.52)	(–0.06)
Instruments	–0.0511	0.1501[c]
	(0.97)	(4.72)
Industrial and agricultural chemicals	0.0434	0.1028[b]
	(0.54)	(2.11)
Pharmaceuticals and consumer chemicals	0.0452	0.0212
	(1.45)	(1.13)
USA	0.0266[b]	–0.0210[c]
	(2.37)	(–2.98)
Japan	0.0404[c]	–0.0083
	(3.35)	(–1.13)
ESTPROD/UK	0.0077	–0.0332
	(0.12)	(–0.84)
ESTPROD/EUR	–0.0713	0.0575
	(–1.09)	(1.44)
COMPART	–0.0327	0.0397
	(–0.41)	(0.82)
DEVELPROD	0.1098[a]	–0.0744[a]
	(1.78)	(–1.93)
R^2	0.2820	0.4323
F	2.17[b]	4.11[c]
n	99	97

[a] = significant at 10%.
[b] = significant at 5%.
[c] = significant at 1%.
n = number of observations.

major role by 75.2 per cent, a secondary one by 15.8 per cent and not part of its role by only 3.0 per cent. The other prevalent role also involved the laboratories providing direct support to the production unit with which they were associated, though here perhaps more to help them to perform effectively an externally determined role in group supply programmes (either to local or regional markets) than to create original scope within the subsidiary itself. Thus 'adaptation of existing products and/or processes to make them suitable to our market and conditions' was reported as the only role of 2.0 per cent of subsidiaries' laboratories, a major one for 65.3 per cent, a secondary one in 25.7 per cent of cases and not part of the role in 6.9 per cent.

It is interesting to note (Table 3.5) that where subsidiaries that played predominantly one or other of the ESTPROD roles had an R&D unit its activity seems likely to be rather more oriented to product development than to adaptation of established technology. This suggests that in such cases the subsidiaries feel that in order to defend their possession of R&D, and to generate a positive perspective on the future evolution of the overall operation, their laboratories should particularly support emerging product development scope. By contrast, where subsidiaries predominantly encompass the DEVELPROD role their laboratories still retain a substantial secondary commitment to adaptation of established technology.

The third laboratory role evaluated by subsidiaries was defined as 'to provide advice on adaptation and/or development to other producing subsidiaries of our MNE group'. Table 3.4 indicates that while clearly less important than direct support of their own subsidiaries, this manifestation of MNEs' technological interdependency was quite pervasive. (It was never rated as a lab's only role and a major one in only 27.7 per cent of cases, but 44.6 per cent of subsidiaries did consider it a secondary role of their labs.) This laboratory role was decisively most important within the operations of the COMPART subsidiaries. Taking this with the strong commitment of these COMPART subsidiaries' laboratories to product development, we find a further indication that a significant element in this component supply role is to work creatively with DEVELPROD operations. Thus here the strong involvement of COMPART subsidiaries in providing advice to other subsidiaries seems

Table 3.5 Roles of R&D laboratories of MNE subsidiaries in the UK

	Importance of laboratory roles[a] *(average response*[b]*)*			
	A	*B*	*C*	*D*
By industry				
Food	2.71	3.00	2.57	1.57
Automobiles	2.86	3.00	1.86	1.43
Electronics and electrical appliances	2.59	2.73	1.89	1.54
Mechanical engineering	2.60	3.00	1.87	1.40
Instruments	2.20	3.17	1.80	1.60
Industrial and agricultural chemicals	2.81	2.81	2.38	1.86
Pharmaceuticals and consumer chemicals	2.38	2.50	1.75	2.38
Other manufacturing	2.54	2.82	1.73	1.45
TOTAL	2.62	2.84	2.00	1.64
By home country				
USA	2.52	2.90	2.19	1.76
Japan	2.78	2.93	1.74	1.54
Europe	2.59	2.63	1.96	1.56
TOTAL[c]	2.62	2.84	2.00	1.64
By subsidiary type[d]				
ESTPROD/UK	2.53	2.81	2.08	1.81
ESTPROD/EUR	2.68	2.83	2.11	1.73

COMPART	2.57	3.00	2.86	2.29
DEVELPROD	2.67	2.94	1.98	1.60

Roles of laboratories:
A = Adaptation of existing products and/or processes to make them suitable to our market and conditions.
B = To play a role in the development of new products for our distinctive markets.
C = To provide advice on adaptation and/or development to other producing subsidaries of our MNE group.
D = To carry out basic research (not directly related to our current products) as part of a wider MNE-group-level research programme.

---

[a] Respondents were asked to evaluate each laboratory role as (i) its only role, (ii) a major role, (iii) a secondary role, (iv) not a part of its role.
[b] The average response is calculated by allocating a value of 4 to 'its only role', 3 to 'a major role', 2 to 'a secondary role', and 1 to 'not a part of its role'.
[c] Includes laboratories of MNEs from Australia and Canada.
[d] Subsidiaries that said a particular role was either only one or their prdominant one. For definitions of subsidiary types see Table 4.1.
Source: Authors' survey 1993–4.

likely to be part of a mutually supportive product development operation to which, ultimately, they will provide custom-created component parts. This third role is most strongly incorporated in US subsidiaries' laboratories, perhaps indicating a more ingrained tradition of networked integration and interdependence in these MNE's European operations. By contrast, it is very weak in Japanese subsidiaries compared with their strong commitment to the two in-house roles, suggesting that in the absence so far of fully-fledged European networks these companies' UK-based operations act as bridgeheads for the regional application of existing products (adaptation) and technology (development). (Defence of this high-value-added position as Japanese companies widen their European-networked dimensions will be a significant challenge for UK government inward-investment policy.) The weak position of this role in European-MNE laboratories in the UK, alongside the also limited position of product development, is compatible with the suggestion that growing regionalised dimensions in these companies involve increased centralisation of core technology operations in their Continental parent facilities.

The final laboratory role was defined as 'to carry out basic research (not directly related our current products) as part of a wider MNE-group-level research programme'. This relates to the third (long-term) aim of globalised technology programmes of MNEs that we distinguish in the introduction, seeking to tap into distinctive research scope and scientific traditions of host countries. The separation of the pre-competitive aims of this role from current commercial technology make it likely that where a host country's potential inputs to this type of work are powerful they can be most effectively applied in laboratories that operate independently from producing subsidiaries. Nevertheless, cases could plausibly emerge where the skills and resources put into place to support the wider objectives of subsidiaries' laboratories might also usefully provide supplementary inputs into their groups' pure research programmes. This type of work emerged as completely absent from the activity of 57.0 per cent of the laboratories of responding subsidiaries. On the other hand where, it did occur it often asserted a more than spin-off or residual position, being reported as a major (or only) role in 20.0 per cent of cases.

CONCLUSIONS

Technology has always had a strong influence on analytical thinking on the MNE. The early perception (Hymer, 1960) that national firms seeking to compete internationally would need a very distinctive source of competitive advantage in order to do so quickly targeted knowledge as an obvious example of such an asset. Again, the understanding (Buckley and Casson, 1976) that firms entering into overseas production were taking a decision to internalise (rather than externalise through a market) the internationalised use of a key source of their competitive advantage found the characteristics of technology to provide a clear illustrative case. Thus knowledge could be transferred relatively cheaply and effectively between parts (albeit in different countries) of the same firm, (though Teece's work (1976, 1977) did demonstrate that internal technology transfer was far from costless and that therefore it should not be construed as a public good within MNEs), while external markets for knowledge were subject to very significant elements of inherent failure.(For a review of the empirical investigation of technology as a determinant of overseas production see Pearce (1993: 32–34).)

However, complementing this understanding of the role of technology as a crucial motivating factor in the emergence of MNEs was the perception (Vernon, 1966; Hirsch, 1967) that within these companies the creation of knowledge, and its innovation into successful commercial products, was likely to be a highly centralised activity. An obvious implication of this was then that all the really creative R&D activity in MNEs would also be centralised. Only rather routine adaptation of products (and manufacturing processes) to local conditions was believed to provide any role for overseas R&D units.

The arguments of this chapter suggest that the contemporary MNE (reacting to the intensified nature of global competition) is still motivated by the same attributes and characteristics of technology, but now needs to operationalise its response in a much more decentralised and differentiated fashion. The persistent evolution of their core stock of technology remains central to the sustained long-term competitiveness of leading companies. At the same time the ability to apply the current commercial manifestation of this knowledge as effectively as possible throughout the global marketplace is also a crucial element in MNEs' technology programmes. However, the globalised dimensions now increasingly interjected not only intensify and deepen the challenges to technology creation and application in MNEs but also provide new potentials for the enrichment of the programmes through which they pursue these objectives. The expanding scope of decentralised R&D in these companies is central to meeting these challenges and embracing these potentials.

It is, therefore, a key managerial challenge in the contemporary MNE to achieve decentralised access to, and creative use of, technology in ways that can thus enrich both the knowledge available to the group and the effectiveness with which it is applied commercially. In a global environment that increasingly demands decisive response to both market and technological heterogeneity, the use of creative (product development) subsidiaries seems the best way of monitoring such aspects of competitive knowledge on behalf of the MNE group. Allowing them to develop their own individualised scope around their perceptions is then the best way to motivate such subsidiaries to do this job well. From this positioning they should benefit the group in two ways: first, through their own innovative operations (that is, product development), which then directly increase the current scope of the group, and second, by making their original perceptions on market trends and technological progress available to the group so that, more indirectly, they can also influence decisions on the group's overall evolution.

By looking at the technological dimension of their creative subsidiaries in this light, MNE central management should understand that they need to be encouraged to individualise their knowledge scope and creative skills in ways that still retain valuable interdependencies with the group's overall technological progress. Usually this will mean enriching the group's technological scope in evolutionary ways. Occasionally, however, it could challenge the scope and limits of core technology in more radical or revolutionary ways. When this happens it becomes a key responsibility of central technological planning to decide if it should be attempted to decisively assimilate these challenging new perspectives into group progress, to suppress them, or to allow them a certain degree of further investigation as a tentative and provisional independent strand. Such radical possibilities should usually not be allowed to proceed in more or less unsupervised ways that may disrupt other parts of creative programmes, reduce the degree of cohesion and coherence of technological progress and, at an extreme, lead to technological anarchy.

A useful viewpoint from which MNE central planners can evaluate these dimensions of the ways in which creative subsidiaries individualise their technology is to understand that they do so (particularly through in-house R&D units) by deriving distinctive perspectives from positions in two technological communities. The first of these is that of the MNE group itself, while the second is the scientific heritage and research base of the host country. Where the first of these prevails the local element may strengthen the subsidiary's scope in valuable ways that nevertheless remain securely anchored in the mainstream technology of the group. Usefully enhanced application of core technology emerges, but with limited contributions to longer-term progress (but also with less danger of reducing coherence and balance in group operations). Where it is the second community that prevails, the subsidiary's distinctive technology may be much more radical and much less firmly grounded in current group technology. There is a bigger potential here (substantial reinforcing of the longer-term technological development of the group), but also a greater danger in terms of loss of control over key areas of knowledge evolution. The most successful MNEs, in terms of central management of technology, may ultimately be those that can harness even the more radical of decentralised creative perceptions to group-level evolutionary processes without thereby lessening the incentives to overseas subsidiaries and laboratories to pursue the more idiosyncratic possibilities of their local environments.

References

Bartlett, C.A. and S. Ghoshal (1989) *Managing Across Borders: The Transnational Solution*, Boston, Mass.: Harvard Business School Press.

Bartlett, C.A. and S. Ghoshal (1990) 'Managing Innovation in the Transnational Corporation', in C.A. Bartlett, Y. Doz and G. Hedlund (eds), *Managing the Global Firm*, London: Routledge, 215–55.

Buckley, P.J. and M.C. Casson (1976) *The Future of the Multinational Enterprise*, London: Macmillan.

Dunning, J.H. (1994) *Multinational Enterprises and the Globalisation of Innovatory Capacity, Research Policy*, 23, 67–88.

Dunning, J.H. and R. Narula (1995) 'The R&D Activities of Foreign Firms in the United State', *International Studies of Management and Organisation*, 25 (1–2), 39–73.

Fors, G. (1996) *R&D and Technology Transfer by Multinational Enterprises*, Stockholm: Industrial Institute for Economic and Social Research.

Ghoshal, S. and C.A. Bartlett (1988) 'Creation, Adoption and Diffusion of Innovations by Subsidiaries of Multinational Corporations', *Journal of International Business Studies*, 19 (3), 365–88.

Håkanson, L. and R. Nobel (1993a) 'Foreign Research and Development in Swedish Multinationals', *Research Policy*, 22, 373–96.

Håkanson, L. and R. Nobel (1993b) 'Determinants of Foreign R&D in Swedish Multinationals, *Research Policy*, 22, 397–411.

Hirsch, S. (1967) *The Location of Industry and International Competitiveness*, Oxford University Press.

Hood, N., S. Young and D. Lal (1994) 'Strategic Evolution within Japanese Manufacturing Plants in Europe: UK Evidence', *International Business Review*, 3 (2), 97–122.

Howells, J. and M. Wood (1993) *The Globalisation of Production and Technology*, London: Belhaven.

Hymer, S.H. (1960) 'The International Operations of National Firms: A Study of Direct Investment', PhD thesis, MIT.

Molero, J. and M. Buesa (1993) 'Multinational Companies and Technological Change: Basic Traits and Taxonomy of the Behaviour of German Industrial Companies in Spain', *Research Policy*, 22, 265–278.

Molero, J., M. Buesa and M. Casado (1995) 'Technological Strategies of MNCs in Intermediate Countries: The Case of Spain', in J. Molero (ed), *Technological Innovation, Multinational Corporations and New International Competitiveness*, Luxembourg: Harwood, 265–91.

Papanastassiou, M. (1995) 'Creation and Development of Technology by MNEs' Subsidiaries in Europe: The Cases of UK, Greece, Belgium and Portugal', PhD thesis, University of Reading.

Papanastassiou, M. and R.D. Pearce (1994) 'Host-Country Determinants of the Market Strategies of US Companies' Overseas Subsidiaries', *Journal of the Economics of Business*, 1 (2), 199–217.

Papanastassiou, M. and R.D. Pearce (1996) 'The Creation and Application of Technology by MNEs' Subsidiaries in Europe', in F. Burton, M. Yamin and S. Young (eds), *International Business and Europe in Transition*, London: Macmillan, 207–30.

Papanastassiou, M. and R.D. Pearce (1997a) 'Technology Sourcing and the Strategic Roles of Manufacturing Subsidiaries in the UK: Local Competences and Global Competitiveness', *Management International Review*, 37 (1), 5–25.

Papanastassiou, M. and R.D. Pearce (1997b) 'Co-operative Approaches to Strategic Competitiveness Through MNE Subsidiaries: Insiders and Outsiders in the European Market', in P.W. Beamish and J.P. Killing (eds), *Co-operative Strategies: European Perspectives*, San Francisco: New Lexington Press, 267–99.

Pearce, R.D. (1989) *The Internationalisation of Research and Development by Multinational Enterprises*, London: Macmillan.

Pearce, R.D. (1992) 'World Product Mandates and MNE Specialisation', *Scandinavian International Business Review*, 1 (2), 38–58.

Pearce, R.D. (1993) *The Growth and Evolution of Multinational Enterprise*, Aldershot: Elgar.

Pearce, R.D. (1996) 'Creative Subsidiaries and the Evolution of Technology in Multinational Enterprises', paper submitted to special panel sessions, European International Business Association, Stockholm.

Pearce, R.D. and M. Papanastassiou (1996a) *The Technological Competitiveness of Japanese Multinationals*, Ann Arbor: University of Michigan Press.

Pearce, R.D. and M. Papanastassiou, M. (1996b) 'R&D Networks and Innovation: Decentralised Product Development in Multinational Enterprises', *R&D Management*, 26 (4), 315–33.

Pearce, R.D. and S. Singh (1992a) *Globalising Research and Development*, London: Macmillan.

Pearce, R.D. and S. Singh (1992b) 'Internationalisation of R&D Among the World's Leading Enterprises: Survey Analysis of Organisation and Motivation', in O. Granstrand, L. Hakanson, and S. Sjolander (eds), *Technology Management and International Business*, Chichester: Wiley, 137–62.

Roth, K. and A.J. Morrison (1992) 'Implementing Global Strategy: Characteristics of Global Subsidiary Mandates', *Journal of International Business Studies*, 23 (4), 715–36.

Taggart, J.H. (1993) 'Strategy Conflict in the MNE: Parent and Subsidiary', paper presented to 19th Annual Conference of European International Business Association, Lisbon.

Teece, D.J. (1976) *The Multinational Corporation and the Resource Cost of International Technology Transfer* (Cambridge, Mass.: Ballinger).

Teece, D.J. (1977) 'Technology Transfer by Multinational Firms: The Resource Cost of Transferring Technologic Knowhow', *Economic Journal*, 87, 242–61.

Vernon, R. (1966) 'International Investment and International Trade in the Product Cycle', *Quarterly Journal of Economics*, 80, 190–207.

4 Global Resource Flows and MNE Network Integration

Trond Randøy and Jiatao Li

INTRODUCTION

In 1995 the total sales of foreign-controlled affiliates of multinational enterprises (MNEs) exceeded the total world trade in goods and services of $6.1 trillion (WTO, 1996). Dunning (1993a) estimated that among major economies, such as Germany, the USA and the UK, MNEs account for approximately 80 per cent of trade in technology and managerial skills. In this chapter an attempt is made to identify and explain cross-border integration within established MNEs. Consideration is given specifically to the direction and the intensity of resource flows in goods and services, knowledge and capital that take place within the subsidiary network of an MNE. By examining the direction and magnitude of these resource flows, it is suggested, subsidiary strategy can be analysed along three major dimensions. This framework provides managers with greater understanding of global integration across subsidiaries.

The intra-firm relations of the MNE have been discussed with regard to a number of specific issues such as the transfer of managers (Edström and Galbraith, 1977), structural characteristics of industries (Kobrin, 1991), the structure of headquarters–subsidiary relationships (Hedlund and Aman, 1986), the role of subsidiary strategy (Jarillo and Martinez, 1990), entrepreneurship in MNEs (Birkinshaw, 1997), the transfer of technology (Cantwell, 1991; Kogut 1991), the transfer of knowledge (Gupta and Govindarajan, 1991, 1994), the governance of affiliates (Ghoshal and Nohria, 1989) and the transfer of financial resources (for example, Booth, 1982). This wide range of research adds to knowledge of integration within MNEs, although most of these studies are concerned only with single resource flows rather than with developing an overall framework of multiple resource flows.

Few studies have attempted to measure the degree of globalisation within the MNE, namely the extent of the transfer of capabilities and resources between affiliated organisational units across borders (Kobrin, 1991; Gupta and Govindarajan, 1994). Leong and Tan (1993) provide a broader empirical test of Bartlett and Ghoshal's (1989) typology of the MNE. Leong and Tan's results provide partial support for Bartlett and Ghoshal's classification of MNEs into multinational, global, international, and transnational organisations. However, by focusing on the corporate level, Leong and Tan are only able to capture inter-organisational differences, and not inter-subsidiary differences within the MNE. On the other hand, Jarillo and Martinez (1990) specifically examine the issue of subsidiary strategy.

This chapter addresses two research questions: first, what the key dimensions are of global integration within the MNE and, second, which factors influence the structure of global integration within the MNE, namely, the direction and intensity of resource flows. The chapter is organised as follows. Based on the existing literature, the first section discusses global integration in MNEs. A framework of subsidiary intra-MNE resource flows is next developed, which is then analysed in relation to the population of foreign-owned subsidiaries in the USA across twenty-five industries. Finally, we discuss resource flow patterns, identified as strategic industry groups, in relation to inflows and outflows of products, capital and knowledge.

GLOBAL INTEGRATION AND RESOURCE FLOWS

Several frameworks have been presented to analyse MNE strategy at, respectively, the industry (Porter, 1986), the firm (Bartlett and Ghoshal, 1987, 1989) and the subsidiary level (Birkinshaw, 1997; Jarillo and Martinez, 1990). These different levels of foci provide complementary perspectives on MNE strategy. Figure 4.1 extends the Bartlett and Ghoshal organisational typology as it relates to the intensity and direction of the overall resource flows within the MNE. Thus, Figure 4.1 provides an integrated model of international strategy at the overall *firm* level, while Figure 4.2 applies the framework at the *subsidiary* level in order to discuss the resource flows of product, capital and knowledge.

Figure 4.1 International strategy at the overall firm level

Outflow of resources from the subsidiaries to the rest of the MNE network	Inflow of resources from rest of the MNE network to the subsidiaries: Low	Inflow of resources from rest of the MNE network to the subsidiaries: High
High	Global	Transnational
Low	Multinational	International

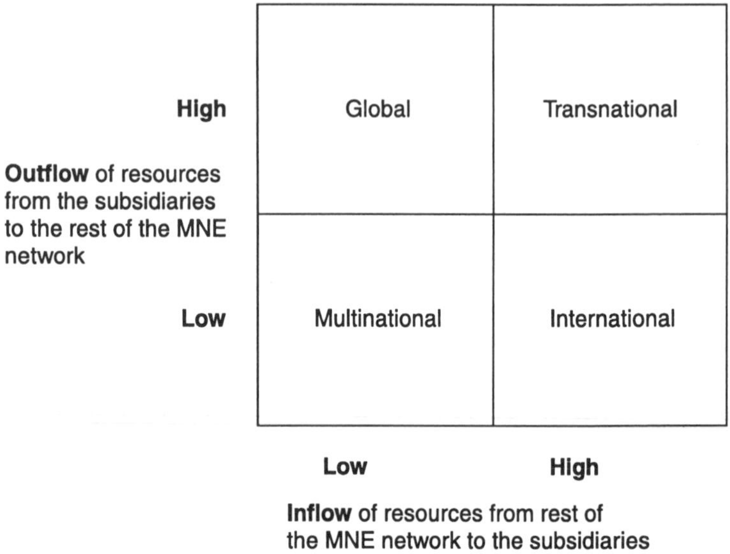

Figure 4.1 shows how 'multinational' and the 'international' MNEs transfer knowledge, capital and products that originate from their headquarters. There is a consistent pattern of one-way transfers, from the headquarters to the national subsidiary. The 'multinational' strategy reflects a decentralised organisation with distributed resources and delegated responsibilities. For example, Philips, the Dutch electronics firm, has historically belonged to this group. Prior to the Single European Market process, the company used to have a number of separate brand names and product lines in different European countries. The

'international' strategy reflects a much greater degree of integration, however, with a clear focus on foreign resource acquisition. A number of oil and mining companies fit into this category. An MNE with a 'global' strategy transfers a significant amount of resource to its subsidiaries, such as in the case of most car manufacturers. The 'transnational' strategy reflects two-way resource flows. A company with a 'global' strategy typically uses the corporate headquarters as the central hub whereby most resource flows are being transferred, or at least coordinated. This centralised function might provide an impediment to the degree of integration. The 'transnational' firm functions more as a network, so that multiple resource flows take place between a number of regional headquarters. The Swiss–Swedish ABB has been one MNE that has explicitly followed a 'transnational' strategy.

Porter (1986) argues that exports, and even foreign direct investment (FDI), are insufficient indicators of a truly global corporate strategy. A more appropriate measure focuses on the existence of integrated intra-firm transfers of finished and intermediate products. This observation motivated the research reported in this chapter in relation to MNE strategy at the subsidiary level.

The strategy literature has for some time discussed the advantages of moving from a system of loosely connected affiliates toward a global network of integrated entities within the MNE (for example, Bartlett and Ghoshal, 1989). One such example is 3M's reorganisation into pan-European product divisions. With its new subsidiary strategy, the company now significantly integrates personnel and expertise across Europe, building 3M's European operation into a network of cross-border linkages (*Financial Times*, 1993: 11). The message to managers is that a company can enhance its competitiveness by expanding the inflow and outflow of resources within the subsidiary network (for example, Bartlett and Ghoshal, 1991; Doz, 1986; Dunning, 1993b). The advantages of global integration are, however, limited by possible strong national product preferences and/or national regulatory restrictions (Prahalad and Doz, 1987). The above factors lead us to focus our attention in this chapter on analysing these intra-firm flows and the corresponding strategic trade-offs.

THREE DIMENSIONS OF INTRA-MNE RESOURCE FLOWS

Past research suggests that the major intra-MNE resource flows relate to capital, products, and knowledge (Bartlett and Ghoshal 1987, 1989; Gupta and Govindarajan 1991; Kobrin 1991). Kobrin (1991) focuses on product flows, but he also acknowledges the importance of considering all three kinds of flows. Gupta and Govindarajan (1991) discuss the three sets of flows, and their more recent research (1994) specifically analyses knowledge flows. Bartlett and Ghoshal's (1987, 1989) research attempts to discuss the three kinds of resource flows in rather fine-grained categorisations.

This research focuses on two aspects of the globalisation of capital, products, and knowledge flows, namely, the *extent* of integration and the *direction* of integration. The extent of integration is reflected in the intensity of the three resource flows. Rosenzweig (1993) measured the three flows within a sample of American MNEs. His analysis of US affiliates of foreign-based MNEs indicates that the various resource flows represent complementary aspects of global integration. His research looked into the first issue, the extent of globalisation, rather than possible two-way, or multiple, flows of resources.

The direction of resource flows within the MNE has apparently been given little attention, except in studies such as Hedlund and Kogut (1993). Most researchers have implicitly looked at the one-way transfer *from* the MNE centre *to* affiliates abroad. Porter's (1990) home-base concept is built around the premise that core resources are developed 'at home' and then transferred abroad, which was true for a number of industries in the 1970s and early 1980s (Dunning, 1993b). The transfer of knowledge from a subsidiary to the MNE centre, however, is a somewhat new phenomenon. Birkinshaw (1997) provides one rare example of research looking at initiatives taken by the foreign-owned subsidiaries. Franko (1976: 162) captured an early stage of this trend when he pointed out that, 'the desire to learn from the stimuli of the high-wage, high-income US market provided the motivation for some spectacular adventures (and misadventures) into American manufacturing'. The final stage of integration is one of multiple resource flows between nodes in the MNE network of affiliates and related companies. Dunning (1993b: 39–40) refers to the works of Hedlund and Kogut (1992) and Hedlund and Rolander (1990) as he points out that in

> MNEs like IBM, SKF and ICI, in which key resources and capabilities are geographically dispersed, cross-border flows of knowledge, information and ideas are multidimensional, communication is lateral, and there is a strong sense of shared values and mission among the different parts of the organization.

One such example is the world car concept developed by Ford. This concept implies integrated R&D, financing and production across a number of countries (United Nations, 1993).

Figure 4.2 shows how resource flows are conceptualised at the subsidiary level in this study. By combining a specific subsidiary's position in relation to the intensity and the direction of resource flows, four generic subsidiary roles are obtained in relation to product flows, knowledge flows, and capital flows. The 'network role' is the typical position of a subsidiary within an MNE that has a 'transnational' strategy. The 'resource-independent' subsidiary fits well within an MNE with a 'multidomestic' strategy. A subsidiary with a 'resource provider' role typically fits in with an MNE with an emphasis on 'global' or 'international' strategy. It is to be expected that a subsidiary role of 'resource user' is most prevalent among MNEs with an 'international' strategy.

Product Flows

Kobrin (1991: 19) focuses on measuring the product flows of MNEs, 'although an ideal index of integration would measure the entire range of resource flows'. His measure concerns only the extent of integration rather than the direction of such cross-border resource flows. Our framework distinguishes between the extent of outflow of products (including raw material and intermediate products) from the subsidiary to the rest of the MNE, and inflow of products from the MNE network to the focal subsidiary.

Figure 4.2 Alternative subsidiary roles related to different resources flows

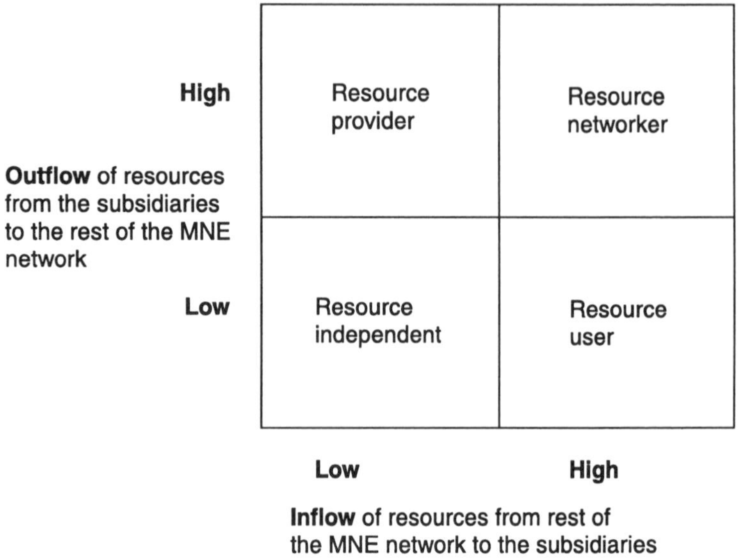

Outflow of resources from the subsidiaries to the rest of the MNE network		
High	Resource provider	Resource networker
Low	Resource independent	Resource user
	Low	**High**
	Inflow of resources from rest of the MNE network to the subsidiaries	

Four alternative subsidiary roles related to product flows have been identified. Commonly, the *product provider* (high outflow, low inflow) subsidiary role represents upstream FDI in raw materials or intermediate products. For the foreign-owned subsidiary, the MNE possesses unique complementary assets and competencies that enhance the productivity of its activities, in effect an ownership advantage controlled the MNE. The economic rationale for the role of the product provider is also to give the MNE access to lower-paid unskilled and semi-skilled labour, as well as secure access to vital raw materials. Ownership control (that is, FDI) is attractive when the motives of cost minimisation and supply security cannot be delivered in an open market of subcontracting (Dunning, 1993).

The *independent subsidiary* (low outflow, low inflow) operates rather autonomously from the MNE centre with limited economic gains from integration. The main economic rationale for such an independent subsidiary is to exploit certain firm-specific technologies, brand-names, or designs that the MNE possesses. These advantages are commonly based on the exploitation of economies of scale, scope and cross-country learning related to technology, brand names, or designs. The cost of transferring these resources or market positions to domestic firms prohibit such market exchanges. The ownership control (that is, internalisation) of key resources also provide the MNE with a potential to exercise some kind of cross-country market power (Kindleberger, 1969).

The *product networker* (high outflow, high inflow) fits in with the overall subsidiary strategy that Bartlett and Ghoshal (1987) describe as transnational. A product networker need not be the MNE headquarters, indeed in a typical MNE it is a divisional centre within a complex MNE structure. 3M's European organisation represents such an example, as does ABB's cross-national divisional centres. The product networker provides the MNE with the benefits of global economies of scale and scope. Pearce (1995: 1) points out that 'the emergence of this kind [rather autonomous subsidiaries with a global product mandate] of technological-creative-based independence at the subsidiary level provides enormous potential for MNEs'. The main advantage of the product networker subsidiary is its ability to be both global and local at the same time. Thus, it exploits both global scale economy as well as any unique industrial strengths of a host country. Kobrin's (1991) research on product flows suggests that the technological intensity of the industry is the most important structural determinant of global integration.

The *product user* (low outflow, high inflow) is the 'old-style' FDI that focuses on market access. This subsidiary role relates to what Jarillo and Martinez (1990) label the receptive subsidiary, or what Porter (1986) labels a 'multi-domestic' strategy at the firm level. It is reasonable to assume that economies of scale in manufacturing are an important determinant of global integration of product flow within the MNE.

Knowledge Flows

Gupta and Govindarajan (1991, 1994) relate knowledge flow patterns to subsidiary strategic roles. They point out that most research in the area of the management of subsidiaries has dealt with broad differences across entire MNE networks (for example, Prahalad and Doz, 1987). They address the need for a more complex approach that acknowledges variations across subsidiaries within the same MNE. Gupta and Govindarajan's research (1991, 1994) identified the existence of differentiated subsidiary roles in relation to knowledge flows. Gupta and Govindarajan specifically identified four generic roles a subsidiary can play within an MNE network.

The headquarters of the *knowledge provider* (high outflows, low inflows) serves as an overall knowledge supplier to the MNE. The knowledge provider, or *global innovator* as labelled by Gupta and Govindarajan, fits well with the original international product-lifecycle theory (Vernon, 1966). With this perspective, the host country subsidiary utilises unskilled or semi skilled labour in the international market, whereas the knowledge creation takes place somewhere else in the MNE-network. However, more recently there have been a number of examples of Japanese and European high-tech firms using their US subsidiary as a source of knowledge generation.

The *knowledge networker* role (high outflows, high inflows) implies a high degree of transfer of knowledge between the focal subsidiary and the rest of the MNE network. The economies of learning associated with developing, producing, and marketing international products is one determinant for the levels of inflows and outflows of products. Pearce (1995) argues that MNE's dispersion of centres for knowledge creation relates in particular to the way creative assets of countries can enhance the MNE's overall competitiveness (Pearce, 1995). These creative assets are location-specific, such that the MNE needs a significant host country presence in order to tap into these unique capabilities. Interestingly, Gupta and Govindarajan's (1994: 443) research reveals that 'innovation by foreign subsidiaries is more typically the result of autonomous initiative by subsidiaries rather than strategic directives issued from corporate headquarters.'

The *knowledge user* (low outflow, high inflow) focuses on utilising knowledge from the MNE network in the focal subsidiary. This type is the recipient of knowledge from either the parent company or other sister subsidiaries, which then have the role of a global innovator. In the early history of many

MNEs, the host country subsidiaries tend to serve as implementors (Gupta and Govindarajan, 1994).

The resource-independent subsidiary (low outflow, low inflow), or local innovator according to Gupta and Govindarajan, uses locally developed technology that has limited outside potential. The typical multidomestic MNE consists of a number of subsidiaries operating as knowledge independent entities.

Capital Flows

Capital flows within MNEs, both at the company and at the industry level, are extensively discussed by the well-established literature on FDI (for example, Dunning 1993a; Casson, 1987). FDI is by definition a transfer of capital from the parent company (or sister company) to the foreign subsidiary. One of the unique features of FDI is, however, the combined transfer of capital, skills and intermediate products. Rosenzweig (1993) shows how product flows and capital flows can be positively and significantly correlated, although the correlation was rather low. An MNE has the potential advantage of possessing both an internal and and international pool for project funding and evaluation, which might be restrained in the domestic market for funding (Stonehill and Dullum, 1990). Due to factors such as lower bankruptcy and agency costs, less of a problem with asymmetric information, and more efficient access to foreign equity markets, the MNE might outperform the domestic firm in terms of its ability to raise capital (Graham and Krugman, 1989; Froot and Stein, 1991).

This study identified four subsidiary roles related to capital flows. The FDI theory has mostly looked at how an MNE can be a *capital user* (low outflow, high inflow). The underlying assumption is that the subsidiary becomes profitable at a later point in time, and thus returns the invested capital as a *capital provider* (high outflow, low inflow). Another kind of capital provider is when the MNE can benefit from different national capitalisation rates on earnings. For example, Levi Strauss was able to sell shares issued by its Japanese subsidiary to Japanese investors at a share price above the one in the US market and this lowered the firm's overall cost of capital (Eiteman *et al.*, 1995: 335).

The relatively small capital flows of the *independent subsidiary* (low outflow, low inflow) might be caused by government restrictions, or by the fact that domestic capital can be tapped at an international rate. In contrast, the *capital networker* (high outflow, high inflow) subsidiary is both a capital provider and an extensive capital user. This role can be used as a motivational device, fostering internal competition for capital, as well as an instrument of project management, enabling the parent to manage cross-country liquidity. Such a role might be most applicable in complex matrix organisations, such as the Swiss–Swedish engineering company ABB. It is not predicted that a large number of subsidiaries will be found that are capital networkers, since the financing function is often one of the most centralised within an MNE.

DATA AND RESEARCH METHODS

This research analysed intra-firm resource flows for US foreign affiliates in twenty-five manufacturing industries in 1989 (see Table 4.1). The data was obtained from the 1989 Benchmark Survey of Foreign Direct Investment in the USA (Bureau of Economic Analysis, 1990). To ensure data comparability, only manufacturing industries were included. Each US affiliate was classified in the three-digit industry in which its sales were largest. Two related types of data for US affiliates of foreign companies are reported: first, financial and operating flows and, second, direct investment positions.

Using three-digit industry data allowed a data-driven specification of global integration. This approach facilitated cross-industry analysis, whereas most previous research has been industry-based or case-study-based, as pointed out by, among others, Kobrin (1991) and Doz (1987). However, it is recognised that the use of broad industry categories, as well as the obvious lack of measures for firm-specific effects, places considerable limitations on this exercise. The findings might be distorted by factors such as tax planning, economic cycles, and the characteristics of knowledge transfer in different industries, including the differences between, for example, tacit and non-tacit knowledge. The data employed therefore represent an industry aggregation of subsidiary resource flows. The published data makes possible the calculation of an index of product flows, knowledge flows, and capital flows for twenty-five industries at the three-digit SIC level, as shown in Table 4.1.

Since resource flows between a foreign parent and the US affiliate can move in two directions, both the extent and the direction are being considered here. From the US affiliate perspective, an inflow is the flow of resources from the foreign parent group, including the foreign parent firm as well as other foreign subsidiaries within the parent network, to the US affiliate. The outflow is defined as the flow of resources from the US affiliate to the foreign parent group. Definitions of measures are given in Appendix 4.A.

Measurement of Product Flows

Product flows are operationalised through intra-firm, or subsidiary, trade at the industry level, as in Kobrin (1991). Product inflows are measured as the total imports from the foreign parent group, including both the parent firm and other members of the parent group, adjusted for the subsidiary size. Similarly, product outflows are measured as the exports from the US affiliate to the foreign parent group, including both the parent firm and other foreign subsidiaries within the parent group.

Measurement of Knowledge Flows

Knowledge flows are operationalised through royalties and licence fees, as well as charges for other services between the US affiliate and the foreign parent. Direct investment royalties and licence fees are payments by US affiliates to, minus receipts by US affiliates from, their foreign parents and other members of the foreign parent group. These payments and receipts are fees for the use or sale of intangible property or rights, such as patents, industrial processes, trade marks, copyrights, franchises, designs, know-how, formulas, techniques, manufacturing rights, and other intangible assets or property rights. The measure for knowledge flows used here is naturally constrained by the fact that only explicit flows are measured.

Table 4.1 Patterns of resource flows

Industry	*Total sales of US affiliates Million US$*	*No. of US affiliates*	*Ave. size of affiliate Million US$*	*Product inflows (%)*	*Product outflows (%)*	*Knowledge inflows (%)*	*Knowledge outflows (%)*	*Capital inflows (%)*	*Capital outflows (%)*
Beverages	5 794	225	25.75	8.85	0.38	2.38	0.33	4.03	0.01
Other food	17 068	485	35.19	2.91	1.13	0.40	0.07	7.65	0.56
Industrial chemicals	48 398	500	96.80	4.29	4.71	0.36	0.20	5.26	0.22
Drugs	11 344	183	61.99	9.41	5.49	2.34	0.48	8.02	1.78
Soap, cleaners	9 144	147	62.02	1.25	0.77	0.25	0.11	22.48	0.25
Other chemicals	3 219	126	25.55	10.16	6.55	0.65	0.34	58.93	0.38
Ferrous metals	7 509	133	56.46	4.97	0.55	0.08	0.02	8.81	0.49
Nonferrous metals	10 524	234	44.97	16.77	3.24	0.18	0.09	11.10	0.23
Fabricated metal	8 626	342	25.22	4.78	0.73	0.36	0.52	46.09	3.78
Office machines	4 222	104	40.60	17.20	11.53	1.18	0.57	45.27	0.60
Other machinery	9 544	652	14.64	19.18	3.46	1.16	0.47	18.49	2.19
Audio/video equipment	12 768	220	58.04	12.95	2.76	0.21	0.84	10.17	0.01
Electronic components	4 332	183	23.67	24.52	7.80	0.39	1.04	49.49	2.72

Other electronic	9 477	183	23.67	24.62	7.80	0.39	1.04	49.49	2.72
Textiles	3 301	228	14.48	4.33	1.33	0.88	0.55	16.00	2.42
Lumber	1 796	96	18.71	10.97	4.90	0.11	0.29	10.23	0.72
Paper	6 699	152	44.07	3.82	3.63	0.16	0.01	13.14	0.08
Printing	8 303	391	21.24	0.87	0.51	2.65	0.19	51.77	0.40
Rubber	3 920	100	39.20	17.96	1.79	0.48	0.13	n/a	0.00
Plastics	2 677	144	18.59	6.50	2.05	1.08	0.45	12.34	1.02
Stone, clay, glass	13 377	670	19.97	2.65	0.29	0.34	0.03	7.85	0.04
Motor vehicles	5 503	106	51.92	26.24	2.98	1.80	0.02	25.14	0.34
Other transportation	2 881	94	30.65	24.92	2.12	0.17	0.14	13.88	0.16
Instruments	6 780	259	26.18	9.50	4.88	1.56	1.51	52.30	0.49
Other manufacturing	7 875	177	44.49	3.86	2.69	0.27	0.02	3.06	0.00

Source: Foreign Direct Investment in the US (1989), Benchmark Study, US Department of Commerce.

Investment service charges consist of fees for services, such as management, professional or technical services, rendered between US affiliates and their foreign parents or other members of the parent groups. These transactions are payments by US affiliates to (minus service charges by US affiliates) from their foreign parents and other members of the parent group. Knowledge inflows are measured by the payment of royalties and license fees and service charges by US affiliates to the foreign parent, whereas knowledge outflows are measured by the receipt of such charges by US affiliates from the foreign parent.

Measurement of Capital Flows

Equity capital inflows are the net increases in a foreign parent's equity stake in its US affiliates, whether incorporated or unincorporated. These inflows to US affiliates result from a foreign parent's establishment of new US affiliates, from its initial acquisition of 10 per cent or more ownership interests in existing US business affiliates, and from capital contributions to its US affiliates.

Equity capital outflows, conversely, result from the liquidation of US affiliates, from partial or total sales of ownership interests in US affiliates, and from the return of capital contributions. These outflows also include liquidated dividends, which are returns of capital to foreign parents. Equity capital outflows (decrease in equity) are netted against equity capital inflows (increase in equity) to derive the net inflow of (increase in) a foreign parent's equity in its US affiliates.

Finally, capital inflow is measured as the equity increase by the foreign parent group in the US affiliate, adjusted for the total equity of the affiliate. On the other hand, capital outflow is measured by the equity decrease in the US affiliate by the foreign parent group.

RESULTS AND DISCUSSION

Based on the framework presented earlier Figure 4.2, this section contains a discussion of industry groups (clusters) related to the three resource flows of products, knowledge, and capital. Four strategic roles are recognised to exist for each of the three resource flows. This research extends previous studies by Gupta and Govindarajan (1991, 1994), which emphasised the importance of knowledge flows, and that of Kobrin (1991) which focused on the significance of product flows. The implication for global managers is the strategic role of subsidiaries needs to be evaluated in relation to knowledge flows, capital flows and product flows. Table 4.2 sets the context.

As suggested by Hartigan (1975), and Punj and Stewart (1983), a combination of hierarchical (centroid method) and non-hierarchical (SAS FASTCLUS) clustering was used. The results of the cluster analysis are presented in Table 4.3.

Table 4.2 Means, standard deviations and correlation matrix

Variable name	*Mean*	*SD*	*1*	*2*	*3*	*4*	*5*	*6*	*7*
1. Product inflow	10.50	7.72	1.00						
2. Product outflow	3.25	2.69	0.44	1.00					
3. Knowledge inflow	0.79	0.78	0.01	0.01	1.00				
4. Knowledge outflow	0.38	0.37	0.22	0.44	0.18	1.00			
5. Capital inflow	22.25	17.81	0.16	0.40	0.23	0.48	1.00		
6. Capital outflow	0.81	1.01	0.09	0.12	0.04	0.42	0.31	1.00	
7. Subsidiary size	37.42	19.39	−0.09	0.09	−0.16	−0.24	−0.36	−0.35	1.00

Product Flows

Of the four subsidiary roles related to product flows, three of these can be clearly identified by the cluster analysis in Table 4.3a. The subsidiaries in cluster P2 have the role of *independent subsidiaries*, with meagre intra-firm product flows (low inflow, low outflow). Cluster P2 is represented by affiliates in industries such as soap/cleaners, printing, and ferrous metals. These industries provide limited opportunities for international economies of scale and scope produced by significant intra-firm product flows.

The *product user* (high inflow, low outflow) subsidiaries in cluster P3 are typically associated with industries with a high content of unskilled labour and/or scale sensitive specialised products. Such examples include motor vehicles, other transportation vehicles, and rubber. Motor and other transportation vehicles are typical examples of industries with significant economies of scale; whereas rubber represents an industry that utilises labour cost differentials.

Table 4.3 Clustering analysis

(a) Product flows = means

Cluster	*Frequency*	*Inflow*	*Outflow*	*Subsidiary role related to product flows*
P1	10	10.31	4.00	Product provider/independent subsidiary
P2	9	3.27	1.29	Independent subsidiary
P3	5	22.56	3.63	Product user
P4	1	17.20	11.53	Product networker

Pseudo $F = 37.48$; expected $R^2 = 0.88$.

(b) Knowledge flows = means

Cluster	*Frequency*	*Inflow*	*Outflow*	*Subsidiary role related to knowledge flows*
K1	4	2.29	0.26	Knowledge user
K2	8	0.69	0.65	Knowledge provider
K3	1	1.56	1.51	Knowledge networker
K4	12	0.29	0.12	Knowledge independent

Pseudo $F = 42.77$; expected $R^2 = 0.85$.

(c) Capital flows = means

Cluster	*Frequency*	*Inflow*	*Outflow*	*Subsidiary role related to capital flows*
C1	13	8.97	0.41	Independent subsidiary
C2	2	55.61	0.43	Capital user
C3	6	20.43	1.10	Capital provider
C4	4	48.16	1.87	Capital networker

Pseudo $F = 187.32$; expected $R^2 = 0.44$.

The *product networker* (high inflow, high outflow) subsidiary role in cluster P4 is represented by only one industry, namely office machinery. The international economies of scale and scope involved in producing such equipment make global specialisation necessary. At the same time, the international dispersion of creative assets motivates the MNE to seek to have strategic assets in a number of countries (Dunning, 1993b).

The average product flow of the subsidiaries in cluster P1 (low inflow, medium outflow) is positioned in the middle, with industries placed in both the *independent subsidiary* and the *product provider* category. Some of the subsidiaries in the product provider group, such as drugs, audio/video equipment and chemicals, are characterised by scale economy and innovation-based competition. These product provider industries are distinguished by global economies of scale and moderate demands for national product adaptation. Meanwhile, subsidiaries in the independent subsidiary group, represented by industries such as the beverages and plastics, show how globalisation can be significantly limited by the need for national localisation and expensive transportation. The beverage industry is a good example of the value of international brand-names, whereas the plastics industry represents a good example of the value of firm-specific technology.

Knowledge Flows

Four clusters of knowledge flows (Table 4.3b) that are parallel to the subsidiary roles suggested in Figure 4.2 have been identified. In line with Gupta and Govindarajan's research (1991, 1994), differentiated subsidiary roles also emerge. However, these conclusions are based on observations of industry averages. The subsidiary strategy of the *knowledge independent* (low inflow, low outflow), shown by cluster K4, is to produce knowledge for national market needs. Industries in this category include lumber, paper, ferrous metals, soaps and cleaners, and industrial chemicals. These represent industries with relatively low levels of knowledge content, as indicated by relatively low R&D expenditures.

The *knowledge networker* is represented by only one industry, namely instruments (cluster K3). This industry is particularly knowledge- and scale-intensive. The need for sufficient depreciation of high R&D costs, and the simultaneous need for innovation, makes two-way global integration important to it. Access to country-specific creative assets has been a major motivating force behind the major share of FDI flowing to the US (McClain, 1986; Randøy, 1994; Ågren, 1990).

The *knowledge user* (low outflow, high inflow) subsidiary role can be seen in cluster K1, represented by the four industries of beverages, drugs, printing and plastics. These industries heavily utilise technology from MNE subsidiary networks and knowledge generation within them is highly scale-sensitive, with limited demands for national adaptation.

The *knowledge provider* (high outflow, low inflow) subsidiary role is represented by cluster K2. Industries in this category include office machines, audio/video equipment and electronic components. In these industries non-US companies are drawn to the USA because of the competencies of American workers, the sophistication of its customers, and the competitiveness of its supplier industries. The global economies of scale make cross-border knowledge transfers a competitive necessity. In summary, it can be concluded that the four subsidiary roles related to knowledge provide further insight in order to develop an effective subsidiary strategy.

Capital Flows

The four subsidiary strategies related to capital flows are represented by the four clusters in Table 4.3c. The role of the *capital provider* (high outflow, low inflow) of cluster C3 is represented by subsidiaries in industries such as drugs, other machinery, motor vehicles and textiles. This partly reflects the mature nature of some of these industries and/or the attractiveness of the US as a source of funding for capital intensive industries. Two Scandinavian cases in the pharmaceutical industry provide ample evidence of the attractiveness of sourcing funds in the US capital market. Thus, Hafslund Nycomed of Norway and Novo of Denmark made successful stock issues in the US market in 1992 and 1981, respectively (Stonehill *et al.*, 1997). Another well-published illustration of the attractiveness of the US capital market is Daimler-Benz AG's decision to become listed on the New York Stock Exchange. Its stated objective was to be in a better position to raise capital.

The *independent subsidiary* role (low inflow, low outflow) revealed in cluster C1 consists of industries such as beverages, industrial chemicals, and paper. The small capital flows associated with these subsidiaries might reflect the mature state of these industries and the opportunities to tap capital sources within the USA. The capital-intensive innovations in these industries do not permit the MNE to transfer substantial amounts of cash from the US affiliates.

The *capital networker* (high outflow, high inflow) subsidiary role in cluster C4 consists of industries such as electronic components and fabricated metals. These tend to be rather mature, and are characterised by a modest amount of capital intensive innovation. The *capital user* (high inflow, low outflow) subsidiary role in cluster C2 includes industries such as chemicals and printing. These industries have a significant firm-specific know-how, and considerable growth potential. The large amounts of capital flowing from abroad to the US affiliates reflect the advantages associated with internalising the funding of the US activities with the MNE's network.

An Integrated Model

The final stage of the study included cluster analysis with data on all three dimensions of resource flows. Each cluster is examined in relation to the overall framework of subsidiary roles related to resource flows shown in Figure 4.2. The results show four clusters (Table 4.4), interpreted here as strategic industry groups. However, as argued initially, the combined analysis of resource flows reveals that each flow is somewhat independent from the others. The analysis in Table 4.4 is therefore an explorative attempt to identify any such overall subsidiary strategies. Even though both clusters K2 and K4 are high on resource inflow, these are recognised as two different groups. Thus, cluster K2 is high on capital and knowledge inflow (type I), whereas cluster K4 is high on product and knowledge inflow (type II).

Subsidiary strategy in cluster K1 corresponds clearly to the role of a *resource networker*, with high-intensity, two-way flows of resources on multiple dimensions. This typical 'transnational' subsidiary role is evident in the office machines and the electronic components industries. However, these industries are not 'transnational' (high outflow, high inflow of resources) on all dimensions. Thus the office machines industry is low on capital outflow, and the electronic component industry is low on knowledge inflows. The overall picture of the subsidiaries in these industries is still one of highly integrated MNE networks with significant resource flows. The overall corporate challenge in these industries is to build global efficiency and innovative capabilities at the same time (Bartlett and Ghoshal, 1989).

Table 4.4 Clustering analysis: overall resource flows = means

Cluster	*Frequency*	*Product inflow*	*Product outflow*	*Knowledge inflow*	*Knowledge outflow*	*Capital inflow*	*Capital outflow*	*Resource role of subsidiary*
#1	2	20.86	9.67	0.79	0.80	47.38	1.66	Resource networker
#2	4	6.33	3.17	1.31	0.64	52.27	1.26	Resource user I
#3	0	4.83	2.22	0.41	0.22	12.92	0.65	Resource independent
#4	9	16.36	3.01	0.98	0.31	12.63	0.60	Resource user II

Pseudo $F = 36.92$, expected $R^2 = 0.85$.

Cluster K2 represents subsidiaries with a mixture of predominately high resource inflows and moderate outflows, particularly in the areas of knowledge and capital. Cluster K2 fits in with what is labelled (Figure 4.2) as the subsidiary role of *resource user* type I. This cluster is represented by the industries of other chemicals, fabricated metals, printing, and instruments. The overall subsidiary strategy represented by cluster K2 is one that Bartlett and Ghoshal (1989) classify as an 'international' strategy. However, cluster K2 represents an interesting combination of an 'international' strategy in relation to knowledge and capital, and a 'multi-domestic' strategy in relation to product flows. This finding suggests that subsidiary strategy needs to be considered in relation to each of the three resource flows. The building of competitive advantages in these industries requires the MNE to build advantages in areas such as centralised R&D and efficient capital allocation.

Subsidiaries in cluster K3, which includes ten industries, display a *resource-independent* subsidiary strategy. This strategy corresponds to the focus of a 'multi-domestic' strategy (Bartlett and Ghoshal, 1989), competing in 'multi-domestic' industries (Porter, 1986). Typical examples of such industries are: paper; stone, clay and glass; foods other than beverages, soap, cleaners; and ferrous metals. With this subsidiary strategy the MNE seeks to build country-specific competitiveness, and the core of this strategy is to respond to national differences through resourceful and entrepreneurial domestic operations. Subsidiaries in this cluster have low intensity of resource flows within the MNE.

Finally, the nine industries in cluster K4 represent *resource user* (type II) subsidiaries. These affiliates have a primary focus on high inflows of products and or components and a secondary focus on knowledge inflows. Compared with Bartlett and Ghoshal's typology in Figure 4.1, cluster K4 represents a combination of a 'international' strategy in relation to products and knowledge flows, but a 'multinational' strategy in relation capital flows. In order to establish a competitive advantage in the cluster K4 industries, the MNE is required to build and exploit scale economies in manufacturing (utilise high product inflow) and knowledge creation (utilise high knowledge inflow).

CONCLUSIONS AND FUTURE RESEARCH

This chapter has analysed global integration by examining the cross-border resource flows between foreign MNEs and their US affiliates in twenty-five manufacturing industries. Whereas Bartlett and Ghoshal (1987, 1989) and Leong and Tan (1993) emphasise the existence of organisational typologies among the entire MNE organisation, this research argues that, in line with Birkinshaw (1997), various subsidiaries within the MNE can create specific subsidiary initiatives. This research also reveals that subsidiary roles can be categorised in relation to each of the resource flows of capital, knowledge and products. Furthermore, distinct strategic industry groups have been identified, and these are related to the direction and intensity of subsidiary network integration. The study as presented thus provides management with a framework for evaluating subsidiary strategy.

A word of caution is in order, however. Owing to data limitations, broad industry factors only can be identified as determinants of global integration. Further research needs to be undertaken both at the firm level and at the subsidiary level. This is especially relevant because Kogut (1991) argues that country capabilities, embedded in the national firm and its institutional relationships, are difficult to diffuse over national borders, except through intra-firm transfers. Future research should also consider the country effects, as they relate to both the host country and the home one.

References

Ågren, L. (1990) 'Swedish Direct Investment in the US', doctoral dissertation, Stockholm School of Economics, Institute of International Business.

Bartlett, C.A. and S. Ghoshal (1987) 'Managing Across Borders: New Organisational Responses', *Sloan Management Journal*, Fall, 43–53.

Bartlett, C.A. and S. Ghoshal (1989) *Managing Across Borders: The Transnational Solution*, Boston, Mass.: Harvard Business School Press.

Bartlett, C.A. and S. Ghoshal (1991) 'Global Strategic Management: Impact on the New Frontiers of Strategy Research', *Strategic Management Journal*, 12, 5–16.

Birkinshaw, J. (1997) 'Entrepreneurship in Multinational Corporations: The Characteristics of Subsidiary Initiatives', *Strategic Management Journal*, 18 (3), 207–29.

Booth, L.D. (1982) 'Capital Budgeting Framework for the Multinational Enterprise', *Journal of International Business Studies*, 13 (Fall), 113–23.

Bureau of Economic Analysis (1990) *US Direct Investment Abroad: 1989 Benchmark Survey Data*, Washington, DC: US Department of Commerce.

Cantwell, J.A. (1991) 'The International Agglomeration of Technological Activity' in M.C. Casson, (ed.), *Global Research Strategy and International Competitiveness*, Oxford: Basil Blackwell.

Casson, M.C. (1987) *The Firm and the Market*, Oxford: Blackwell.

Doz, Y.L. (1986) *Strategic Management in Multinational Companies*, Oxford: Pergamon.

Doz, Y.L. (1987) 'International Industries: Fragmentation versus Globalisation', in B.R. Guile and H. Brooks (eds), *Technology and Gobal industry*, Washington DC: National Academy Press, 82–94.

Dunning, J.H. (1993a) *Multinational Enterprises and the Global Economy*, Wokingham: Addison-Wesley.

Dunning, J.H. (1993b) *The Globalisation of Business*, London and New York: Routledge.

Edström, A. and J.R. Galbraith (1977) 'Transfer of Managers as a Coordination and Control Strategy in Multinational Organisations', *Administrative Science Quarterly*, 22, 248–63.

Eiteman, D.K., A.I. Stonehill and M.H. Moffett (1995) *Multinational Business Finance*, 7th edn, Reading, Mass.: Addison-Wesley.

Financial Times (1993) 'Here, There and Everywhere', 10 November.

Franko, L. (1976) *The European Multinationals*, New York: Harper & Row.

Froot, K.A. and J.S. Stein (1991) 'Exchange Rates and Foreign Direct Investment: an Imperfect Capital Markets Approach', *Quarterly Journal of Economics*, 106, 1191–217.

Ghoshal, S. and N. Nohria (1989) 'Internal Differentiation within Multinational Corporations', *Strategic Management Journal*, 10, 323–37.

Graham, E.M. and P.R. Krugman (1989) *Foreign Direct Investments in the United States*, Washington: Institute of International Economics.

Gupta, A.K. and V. Govindarajan (1991) 'Knowledge Flows and the Structure of Control within Multinational Corporations', *Academy of Management Review*, 16 (4), 769–92.

Gupta, A.K. and V. Govindarajan (1994) 'Organising for Knowledge Flows within MNCs', *International Business Review*, 3 (4), 443–57.

Hartigan, J. (1975) *Clustering Agorithms*, New York: Wiley.

Hedlund, G. and P. Aman (1986) *Managing Relationships with Foreign Subsidiaries*, Stockholm: Mekan.

Hedlund, G. and B. Kogut (1993) 'Managing the MNCs: the End of the Missionary era', in G. Hedlund (ed.), *TNCs and Organisational Issues, UN Library on Transnational Corporations*, London: Routledge, 343–58.

Hedlund, G. and D. Rolander (1990) 'Actions in Heterarchies: New Approaches to Managing the MNC', in Bartlett C.A., Y. Doz and G. Hedlund (eds), *Managing the Global Firm*, London and New York: Routledge, 15–46.

Jarillo, J.C. and J. I. Martinez (1990) 'Different Roles for Subsidiaries: The Case of Multinational Corporations in Spain', *Strategic Management Journal*, 11, 501–12.

Kindleberger, C.P. (1969) *American Business Abroad*, New Haven, Conn.: Yale University Press.

Kobrin, S.J. (1991) An Empirical Analysis of the Determinants of Global Integration, *Strategic Management Journal*, 12, Summer Special Issue, 17–32.

Kogut, B. (1991) 'Country Capabilities and the Permeability of Borders', *Strategic Management Journal*, 12, Summer Special Issue, 33–48.

Leong, S.M. & C.T. Tan, (1993) 'Managing Across Borders: An Empirical Test of Bartlett and Ghoshal's [1989] Organisational Typology', *Journal of International Business Studies*, 24, 449–64.

McClain, D. (1986) 'Direct Investments in the United States: The European Experience', in H.P. Gray (ed.), *Uncle Sam as Host*, Greenwich, Conn.: JAI Press.

Pearce, R.D. (1995) *Creative Subsidiaries and the Evolution of Technology in Multinational Enterprises*, University of Reading, Department of Economics, Discussion Papers in International Investment and Business Studies, no. 194.

Porter, M.E. (1986) 'Competition in Global Industries: A Conceptual Framework', in M.E. Porter (ed.), *Competition in Global Industries*, Boston, Mass.: Harvard Business School Press, 15–60.

Porter, M.E. (1990) *The Competitive Advantage of Nations*, New York: Macmillan.

Prahalad, C.K. and Y.L. Doz (1987) *The Multinational Mission*, New York: Free Press.

Punj, G. and D. Stewart (1983) 'Cluster Analysis in Marketing Research: Review and Suggestions for Application', *Journal of Marketing Research*, 20, May, 134–48.

Randøy, T. (1994) 'The Motives and Determinants for Foreign Market Involvement: A Survey of Norwegian Foreign Direct Investments', doctoral dissertation, Norwegian School of Economics and Business Administration, Bergen.

Rosenzweig, P.M. (1993) 'The Integration of MNC Affiliates: an Exploration of Patterns and Determinants', *American Academy of Management Proceedings*, 147–51.

Stonehill, A.I. and K. Dullum (1990) 'Corporate Wealth Maximisation and the Market for Corporate Control', *Nationaløkonomisk tidsskrift*, 79–96.

Stonehill, A.I, L. Oxelheim, T. Randøy, K. Vikkula, K. Dullum and K-M. Modén (eds) (1997) *Corporate Strategies to Internationalizing the Cost of Capital*, Copenhagen Business School Press.

United Nations (1993) *World Investment Report*, New York: United Nations Centre on Transnational Corporations.

Vernon, R. (1966) 'International Investment and International Trade in the Product Cycle', *Quarterly Journal of Economics*, 80 (May), 190–207.

WTO (1996) *Trade and Foreign Direct Investment*, www.wto.org/wto/Whats_new/chpiv.htm

APPENDIX 4.A DEFINITION OF RESOURCE FLOWS

The unit of analysis is the three-digit industry

X1	total sales
X2	total exports
X3	export to foreign parent
X4	export to foreign affiliates
X6	total imports
X7	imports from foreign parent
X8	imports from foreign affiliates
X14	total equity
X16	royalties and license fees, payments to parent X17, royalties and licensing fees, receipts from parent X18, service charge-payment to parent
X19	service charge-receipt from the parent
X20	equity increase – in the US affiliates
X22	equity decrease – in the US affiliates

Operationalisation of resource flows

Product INFLOWS	=	(X7 + X8)/X1
Product OUTFLOWS	=	(X3 + X4)/X1
Knowledge INFLOWS	=	(X16 + X18)/X1
Knowledge OUTFLOWS	=	(X17 + X19)/X1
Capital INFLOWS	=	(X20)/X14
Capital OUTFLOWS	=	(X22)/X14
Average affiliate SIZE	=	(X24/X1)

5 Between Headquarters and Subsidiaries: The RHQ Solution

Hellmut Schütte

CONCEPTUAL FRAMEWORK

Multinational Corporations as Complex Organisations

The multinational corporation (MNC) as a phenomenon of recent times differs from simpler organisations by 'the combined consequences of multidimensionality and heterogeneity' (Doz and Prahalad, 1991). Multidimensionality in this context is the result of multiple geographical markets, multiple product lines and multifunctional activities. Heterogeneity comes from the different economic and political characteristics that make an impact on the various countries, businesses and tasks in varied ways.

The literature on MNCs is relatively new and has evolved from various streams of research carried out over the last few decades. The academic field of international business was strongly influenced by economists, and focused on trade flows, direct foreign investment and comparative advantage. In parallel, two schools of thought in the area of international management concentrated on administrative and managerial issues (Bartlett and Ghoshal 1991). The first is represented by Stopford and Wells (1972) and Franko (1976), and built on Chandler's (1962) argument that the structure of an organisation follows strategy. Stopford and Wells (1972) argued that MNCs with a high number of products sold internationally would need an organisation based on product line; those with a high percentage of sales abroad would prefer an organisation based on geographical area, while those with both a large product diversity and important sales abroad would choose a matrix organisation.

The second school is represented by Prahalad, Doz, Bartlett, Ghoshal and Hedlund, and is termed the 'process' school. Prahalad and Doz (1987) describe the management of the MNC as a balancing act between two environmental influences, namely pressures for global integration and pressures for local responsiveness. While strategy is their departure point, Bartlett and Ghoshal (1989) focus on organisational issues, though in the sense of processes rather than structural forms and propose a new type of MNC, the transnational corporation. Hedlund (1986) has developed the idea of a heterarchical MNC, which is similar to this model.

Common to all representatives of the process school is the mistrust of unidimensional organisational structures, the search for flexible solutions and a preference for cultural control to unite the dispersed MNC. The use of more subtle mechanisms of coordination such as lateral relationships, informal communication and socialisation is recommended (Martinez and Jarillo, 1989). Ghoshal and Bartlett (1995) have recently emphasised this aspect by suggesting the replacement of the traditional strategy–structure–systems doctrine with a purpose–process–people doctrine.

Regionalisation between Globalisation and Localisation

In the mid-1960s, Heenan and Perlmutter (1979) had already observed a trend among MNCs towards regional integration. Consequently, they proposed adding regiocentrism to the earlier described ethnocentric, polycentric and geocentric orientations of top management in conducting business abroad. This approach characterised MNCs with a regiocentric orientation as organisationally highly interdependent on a regional basis, while authority and decision-making are concentrated within a regional headquarters and/or collaborating subsidiaries.

Only scant attention is paid to regional integration issues in the recent literature on MNCs. Neither Stopford and Wells, nor Franko, nor any of the representatives of the process school, have explored regional strategies or regional organisations as alternatives to the globalisation–localisation dilemma. This is somewhat surprising, because the dimensions of regional strategies and regional organisations could have helped to disentangle many of the global–local and centralisation–decentralisation dichotomies. Lehrer and Asakawa (1995) are among the few to pursue this avenue of research. They advance the idea of the integration–responsiveness grid of Prahalad and Doz by splitting it into two subgrids with a regional component. The first grid maps the pressures for global integration against those for regional, as opposed to local, responsiveness. The second grid maps the pressures for regional (rather than global) integration against pressures for local responsiveness.

While Heenan and Perlmutter describe regiocentrism as one option in structuring the operations of an MNC, Aoki and Tachiki (1992) – from a Japanese perspective – view regionalisation as a necessity for implementing globalisation. Morrison and Roth (1992) see regionalisation as a second-best solution to globalisation, especially for firms with a historical legacy of strong subsidiaries and difficulties in implementing global strategies. However, external pressure from regional competition and the formation of regional blocs can turn regionalisation into a feasible alternative to globalisation, thereby leading to 'a compromise between the traditional strategies adopted by miniature replica subsidiaries and the global strategies currently being advocated' (Morrison *et al.*, 1991).

THE STUDY OF REGIONAL HEADQUARTERS (RHQs)

Research Questions

Two trends have been observed that triggered the interest of the author in the study of the regionalisation attempts of MNCs and of RHQs, in particular. The first trend is internally driven and the result of the strategic and organisational shift in large, diversified MNCs towards global strategies and a more centralised organisation with the locus of power mainly, but not exclusively, at headquarters. After experiencing difficulties in implementing these more globally oriented strategies, MNCs have started to pay more attention to regional strategies, and this has in turn required an intermediate organisational solution – the establishment of regional headquarters.

The second trend is initiated by the environment, political forces in particular, and concerns the creation of geographic regions covering groups of countries bound together by preferential trade and investment regimes. MNCs have reacted to these signals by increasing regional trade and investment. This is accompanied by an increasing awareness of the similarities of markets within one region, and the need to exploit these similarities and geographic proximity in terms of marketing, manufacturing, finance and so on. To do this more systematically, regional headquarters are often established to integrate the diverse activities of the local subsidiaries whose influence, in general, is limited to the boundaries of the country in which they operate.

Initial interviews and in-depth case studies have showed that the creation of a RHQs is rarely a thoroughly planned undertaking with clearly defined responsibilities. This chapter therefore aims at shedding light on the managerial activities of RHQs, particularly with regard to the development of a regional perspective, the problems concerning the regional integration of the MNC's operations and the use of systems and culture by the RHQs in managing the regional operations. The analysis of these aspects will allow an overall assessment of the strength of RHQs. The perceived usefulness of RHQs and expectations of their role in the future are further explored.

Existing RHQs of large MNCs have been chosen for the study. They are defined as *organisational units concerned with and involved in the integration and coordination of activities of the MNC within a given geographical region, and representing the link between the region and the headquarters.*

This definition is, deliberately, very broad. It stresses the active managerial role taken by the RHQ and de-emphasises the locality of the regional headquarters. It includes a 'virtual RHQ', in which managers working in different national units are charged with regional responsibilities and work across borders without sharing the same office facilities. The definition, however, excludes holding companies set up for purely fiscal or financial reasons, representative offices, or R&D centres if they are not integrating and coordinating research and development activities across borders.

Sample of MNCs

Two groups of large multinational companies with existing RHQs have been selected for the non-random sample, namely 15 Western MNCs with regional activities in Asia and 15 Japanese MNCs with regional activities in Europe (see Table 5.1). In both cases the MNCs operate in regions far away from corporate headquarters. They are relatively new in the region and are exposed to increasing intra-regional activities.

Table 5.1 MNCs in sample

Company	*Sector*	*Company*	*Sector*
ABB (SWI/ SWE)	Engineering	NEC (JAP)	Electronics
Accor (FRA)	Hotels	Otis (USA)	Elevators
Asahi Glass (JAP)	Glass	Raychem (USA)	Electronics
BASF (GER)	Chemicals	Rhone-Poulenc(FRA)	Chemicals
BP (UK)	Oil	Schindler (SWI)	Elevators
Chugai (JAP)	Pharmaceuticals	Schneider (FRA)	Electricals/ electronics
Heineken (NED)	Beer	Seagram (USA)	Drinks
Henkel (GER)	Chemicals	Seiko (JAP)	Watches
Honda (JAP)	Cars	Shimizu (JAP)	Construction
ICI (UK)	Chemicals	Shiseido (JAP)	Cosmetics
Kao (JAP)	Toiletries/ chemicals	Sony (JAP)	Consumer electronics
Komatsu (JAP)	Construction Equipment	Toyota (JAP)	Cars
Matsushita (JAP)	Consumer electronics	Unilever (UK/ NED)	Food/toiletries
Mazda (JAP)	Cars	Volkswagen (GER)	Cars
Mitsubishi Electric (JAP)	Engineering	YKK (JAP)	Zippers

For the most part, MNCs in the manufacturing sector have been selected for study, because they tend to have tangible investments that require active management in the respective regions. (Trading firms were excluded because the Japanese '*sogo shosha*' have no Western equivalent. Financial institutions were also excluded because their operations are strongly influenced by regulatory forces that may distort organisational structures and systems.) All MNCs in the sample have billion dollar sales and large numbers of staff both at home and abroad. They are all among the leading global competitors in their specific industries. In absolute terms they have substantial operations in the region concerned, though not relative to the size of their operations in other parts of the world. European MNCs are at present less involved in Asia than in North America, while American MNCs are less involved in Asia than in Europe. Europe is less important than North America for Japanese MNCs.

This general observation of the geographic distribution of the activities of MNCs applies to all firms in the sample. It means that the region in question does not represent an area of prime importance for any of the MNCs in the sample, at least not at this moment. However, several of the Western MNCs are very ambitious so far as their growth targets for Asia are concerned. None of the Japanese MNCs in the sample sees Europe in a similar light or has announced ambitious targets for Europe.

Seven different home countries were found among the 15 Western MNCs and 26 MNCs of the total of 30 belong to 5 broadly defined groups of industries. Most of the MNCs are involved in several, though related, businesses. A low degree of diversification is shown by 4 of the Western and 5 of the Japanese MNCs. It can therefore be assumed that in terms of diversification no major differences exist between the two subsets in the sample.

Hypotheses

Five hypotheses about RHQs have been developed based on the literature and in-depth case studies. The first two hypotheses (1 and 2) concern the activities of the RHQ and test statements related to what RHQs do. The second set of hypotheses

(3 and 4) concern the structure and systems of the RHQ and seek validation of assertions on the way RHQs operate. The fifth hypothesis (5) deals with the perceptions managers have of the usefulness of RHQs and their future role in MNCs.

Role of RHQs

Prahalad and Doz (1987) assign responsibility for global integration to corporate headquarters, and for national responsiveness to national units. According to Heenan and Perlmutter (1979), RHQs are given the authority for bringing a regiocentric orientation into the MNC. They reduce the span of control, and provide for greater sensitivity towards an area and for better allocation of resources. Lasserre (1996) describes strategy development and regional integration as the core tasks of RHQs. This argues that RHQs are in charge of shaping the regional perspective in the sense of developing a strategy, initiating new business and setting and controlling targets.

However, any influence of the RHQ on the region will encroach on both the power of the headquarters and the national units, and may be opposed, as Morrison *et al.* (1991) and Blackwell *et al.* (1992) have pointed out. RHQs can therefore contribute to, but need not necessarily be strongly involved in, shaping a regional perspective. However, the decision to set up an RHQ as a special organisational unit can also be interpreted as a deliberate transfer of the leadership for the region to the group of managers assigned to it. Therefore the first hypothesis is set out as follows:

> Hypothesis 1: RHQs play a dominant role in shaping the regional perspective of an MNC.

Regional Integration

Functional activities such as marketing, finance and human resource development have to be carried out in each country within the region. With increasing integration of regions through external forces, pressure grows to bring these activities in line in order to reduce inconsistencies – which could lead, for example, to arbitrage between neighbouring countries in the case of different price levels or a confusing brand or company image through different advertising campaigns.

Reaction to such pressures leads in turn to greater integration across the region and businesses both in terms of the vertical and horizontal division of labour (Morrison and Roth, 1992). Combined activities and/or common platforms will result in lower costs through scale effects (Morrison *et al.*, 1991), and improved opportunities for benchmarking and the exchange of best practice. Such integration also leads to the bundling of scattered national activities, particularly when they are dispersed over a number of smaller businesses in smaller countries, and thus make HQ more aware of their needs. Aoki and Tachiki (1992) consequently consider RHQs as suitable vehicles for integrating and coordinating the activities of dispersed subsidiaries. For this reason, the second hypothesis is expressed in the following terms:

> Hypothesis 2:RHQs foster regional integration through the coordination of functional activities and the creation of synergies between different businesses.

Staffing and Mind-Set of RHQs

The staff for RHQs may be either drawn from among senior local managers in the region or assigned from HQs to the region. Nationals who come neither from the region nor from HQs may also become RHQ staff. In their day-to-day work they will be asked to act as the bridge between the region and HQ on the one hand, and to generate benefits from bringing dispersed businesses or country units closer together on the other. It is in the interest of HQ managers to assign regional tasks to staff who both know the HQ well and have a high degree of loyalty to the global centre of operations. For this reason, RHQ staff should not only come from HQ, but also be closely tied to it. Preferably they are dispatched for limited periods only and see their future career prospects lying at HQ rather than in the region. The head of the RHQ should remain closely integrated with the HQ organisation, while being responsible for a region far away from HQ.

This contrasts with the need to staff RHQs with managers who have accumulated experience in the region and in-depth knowledge of it. According to this argument, RHQs in Europe are to be staffed with Europeans, those in Asia with Asians. Unfortunately, the geographical proximity of countries does not necessarily result in cross-border knowledge. A French senior manager may be more familiar with Africa or Canada than with Germany or the UK, an Indonesian more with the Netherlands or the USA than with China or Japan. Thus, managers from a region are not automatically better qualified to take the role of RHQ staff than outsiders. On the contrary, strong loyalties to their home country may lead them to hold subconsciously biased views and to make decisions in favour of their home country rather than for the good of the whole region.

Finally, appointments to the more senior positions at RHQs are made by decision-makers at HQ. As they tend to trust their own colleagues more than those far away and from different cultures, the third hypothesis is formulated as follows:

> Hypothesis 3: RHQ staff are more closely linked with HQ than with the region.

Organisational Mechanisms

Coordination within the region can take different forms, ranging from central direction with line authority to informal cooperation based on exchange of information. The preferred level of coordination will vary not only from firm to firm, but also between business units in the same firm and between functions and tasks within the same business unit (Blackwell *et al.*, 1991). The 'one size does not fit all' approach is supported by Doz and Ghoshal (1994) in their survey of organisational changes in large, long-established American MNCs in Europe.

MNCs use both formal and informal mechanisms to coordinate their diverse activities (Martinez and Jarillo 1991). Heavy emphasis on formal mechanisms transforms the relationship between RHQ and local units into a strict hierarchy, in which the RHQ is the only unit with authority. This 'vertical' RHQ will suit power-conscious managers and depends on disciplined subordinates. It may also simplify complex decision-making processes.

In practice, it is impossible to treat the region as one single organisational unit, because of national legislation and the requirement that managers in charge of national units take care of the concerns of other stakeholders including, for example, local employees and national governments. Further complications are derived from functional and business managers with regional responsibilities, who will not only report to their immediate disciplinary superior, namely the head of the RHQ or of a national unit, but also to other managers in the organisation, normally located at HQ.

In contrast to the 'vertical' RHQ, the 'horizontal' RHQ is primarily driven by the will of the national units. The system operates on a consensus basis, with the authority of the RHQ dependent to some extent on the national units. This model comes close to what Handy describes as federalism in organisations, in which the autonomy of individual organisational units is combined with the scale benefits of coordination (Handy 1992). Applied to the regional organisation, the horizontal RHQ maintains the integrity of the national units, while at the same time unifying their activities for the common objectives of the region. It allows local directors to become local barons or local heroes, while moderating their individualism through mechanisms that demand collegial approval and enforce close cooperation. Long-established American MNCs in Europe tend to operate across the region in this way (Doz and Ghoshal, 1994).

The advantages and disadvantages of the two RHQ models are embedded in the classical centralisation–decentralisation dilemma. Too much centralisation strangles local initiative and entrepreneurship, while too much decentralisation leads to inefficiencies and a loss of control (Hungenberg, 1993). The dangers of demotivation are particularly critical, because managers in the national units tend to be local staff, while those in the RHQ are mainly expatriates. Any power dispute may deteriorate into emotional arguments between locals and expatriates, with all the attendant consequences on local recruitment, alienation of staff, and the ability of the MNC to become an insider. Further, managers from local units may feel marginalised and thus resist RHQ influence (Blackwell *et al.*, 1992). In view of these arguments, the fourth hypothesis states:

> Hypothesis 4: RHQs emphasise non-hierarchical organisational mechanisms in their relationship with national units.

Usefulness and the Future of RHQs

Despite 'global mania', Morrison *et al.* (1991) report widespread disenchantment among MNCs with global strategies, and instead argue in favour of a more regional approach. Not surprisingly, much of the empirical research on regional organisations therefore deals with the introduction of regional structures and management, thus indicating a trend towards organisational solutions such as RHQs. However, there is no lack of resistance to the transfer of power to such an organisational unit from either headquarters or the subsidiaries (Aoki and Tachiki, 1992; Blackwell *et al.*, 1991, 1992; Morrison *et al.*, 1991, 1992). Problems may also arise from a lack of commitment on the one hand, and from over-identification and regional myopia on the other (Heenan and Perlmutter, 1979). A perception survey by Lasserre (1993) among subsidiary managers in Asia reflects their uneasy feelings about RHQs. The respondents consider RHQs useful, but nevertheless want their role to be limited.

There is agreement, at least conceptually, among those in favour of regional strategies on the need for an RHQ as an organisational unit and on its usefulness in coordinating the MNC's activities in the region. It has, however, been argued that RHQs play a useful role only while the MNC is relatively new in a region; once the national units are sufficiently experienced they no longer need the support of an RHQ (Lasserre, 1996).

While internal arguments question the perceived usefulness of RHQs, external developments have an increasing impact on the need for RHQs. The trend towards further integration of the regional environment in Europe, Asia and the Americas is expected to continue and bring about ever closer political and economic interdependence. This in turn requires increased regional responses of the MNC to take care of regional particularities and regional competitors. Thus, an even greater need for and appreciation of a regional component in the organisation of the MNC is due. The fifth and last hypothesis therefore predicts as follows:

> Hypothesis 5: RHQs are perceived as useful, and will gain more weight, influence and power in future.

Research Design

Structured Interviews

Owing to the complexity of the issues for discussion, structured interviews were carried out. The interview guide is shown in Appendix 5.A. Preference was given to conducting a greater number of interviews in a limited number of firms, rather than opting for incomplete information from a larger number of MNCs. This facilitated the cross-checking of statements because the topics occasionally resulted in the expression of biased views by interviewees. Most of the managers interviewed were directly involved in regional tasks and considered to be the most knowledgeable and least biased with respect to the global–local dichotomy (Sullivan, 1992). Attention was, however, paid to balance their views with managers at headquarters and with those working in subsidiaries.

The interviews were carried out between summer 1994 and autumn 1995 in the thirty MNCs in the sample. Some intensive interviewing by the author related to RHQs in Henkel, Kao, Shiseido and Asahi Glass had preceded this larger survey and led to the writing and publication of a number of case studies by INSEAD and one article (Schütte, 1995). A total of 96 interviews took place in 17 different locations in 11 countries. The average interview lasted about two hours.

General Questions

All interviews commenced with a number of general questions. Three issues were explored in particular:

1. *The extent to which the RHQ is in charge of all or only some of the businesses of the MNC in the region.* In two-thirds of the cases the RHQ was in charge of all businesses of the firm in the region. The degree of diversification did not represent a differentiating variable. Cases of limited coverage of the region by the RHQ derived from a variety of firm specific reasons. In some cases the MNC ran some businesses on a regional, others on a global basis (Uni-

lever). In other cases a specific business was not pursued in the region at all (NEC), or else the different businesses were the responsibility of different RHQs (ICI and Rhône-Poulenc).

2. *The degree of change in regional organisation (either for Asia or for Europe) over the last five years.* Only 17 per cent of the MNCs in the sample had not seen a substantial change, while 57 per cent of the MNCs had undergone a dramatic change in their regional organisation. 'Dramatic' in this context refers to the establishment or dismantling of the RHQ during the last five years; to a major change in strategy with implications for the organisation; or to a major change in the world-wide organisation of the MNC concerned. It does not refer to changes of personnel, even if they had been dramatic. No significant difference between the Western and the Japanese MNCs could be detected. The instability of the RHQ reported by the majority of MNCs implies that their present regional organisation is relatively new.
3. *The organisational structure at board level as an indication of the dominant organisational logic.* Out of the thirty MNCs in the sample, twenty four had a clearly identifiable organisational logic. A third of them used a matrix structure, in which businesses and geographic regions carried more or less equal weight. Two-thirds preferred a divisional set-up. Almost all Japanese MNCs were organised by business divisions. Several of them assign profit responsibility to the businesses, but run sales and marketing divisions along geographic lines. The latter activities are considered cost centres. While this arrangement could be categorised as a matrix structure, it is apparent that the power resides within the product divisions.

Vertical and Horizontal Analysis

The following sections discuss the responses to most of the topics raised in the interviews. Four hypotheses will be tested in the process. The results give an in-depth, vertical view of how the thirty MNCs as a group manage certain aspects of their RHQs. This analysis will be followed by a horizontal approach which explores how specific MNCs have set up and/or operate their RHQs across all ten aspects researched. Available data will then be grouped in so as to indicate the strength of the specific RHQ according to a given definition. From there, a ranking is developed. Clusters will then be formed among MNCs with similar characteristics, and correlation analysis will be used to identify important relationships between variables.

Perception Survey

In September 1995 a short perception questionnaire was sent to all thirty MNCs included in the sample. For those MNCs in which several interviews had been conducted, the questionnaire was addressed to the manager in charge of the RHQs. The questions raised focus on the perceived usefulness of the RHQ at the global (headquarters), regional and local level, and on the future direction of the RHQ over the next three to five years. The fifth and last hypothesis will be tested against the results of this survey.

RESEARCH RESULTS

Hypothesis 1: Regional Perspective

The first group of issues raised during interviews deals with the influence of the RHQ on shaping the regional perspective, namely the MNC's long-term view of a specific region. The first aspect explored was the RHQ's influence in the development of the regional strategy. The responses in Table 5.2(a) show that the role or power of HQs and RHQs in the development of a regional strategy in this sample of 30 MNCs is divided relatively equally across five models of influence, though with a slight tendency towards 'some' HQ input. RHQs are, thus, not in the driver's seat – or at least not alone – when it comes to developing a regional strategy. In most cases, headquarters have kept alive their influence over the strategy development process despite the existence of RHQs.

Table 5.2 Interview results

(a) Regional strategy development ($n=30$)

	Main influence				
	RHQ with HQ consensus	*RHQ with some HQ input*	*HQ and RHQ equally*	*HQ with some RHQ input*	*HQ with limited RHQ input*
Percentage of MNCs	13	27	30	13	17

(b) New business initiatives ($n=21$)

	Initiative taken by		
	Mainly RHQ	*HQ or RHQ or national units*	*Mainly HQ*
Percentage of MNCs	43	43	14

(c) Target setting and control ($n=28$)

	Responsibility		
	Targets and control: RHQ	*Targets: HQ + RHQ* *Control: RHQ*	*Targets and control: RHQ + HQ*
Percentage of MNCs	43	25	32

(d) Staffing of RHQs ($n=30$)

	Total staff				*Percentage of expatriates*		
	Small 1 to 10	*Medium* 11 to 25	*Large* 26 to 75	*V. large* >75	*<33%*	*33–66%*	*>66 %*
Percentage of MNCs	20	30	40	10	17	30	43+(10[a])

[a]The RHQs of Unilever, Kao and Shiseido are located at HQs. They are not staffed with expatriates in the sense described here, but rather with Western and Japanese HQ staff delegated to a headquarters unit called RHQ. They represent 10 per cent of the sample.

(e)Reporting line for the head of an RHQ ($n=30$)

	Head of RHQs			
	Is a board member and Reports to		*Not a board member and reports to*	
	Board or CEO	*Other board member*	*Board member*	*One level below board*
Percentage of MNCs	17	30	33	20

Table 5.2 (*contd.*)

(f) Commitment to the region and/or HQ ($n=30$)

	Head of RHQ considers himself		
	Mentor, advocate, supporter	*Arbiter, Buffer*	*Controller, Enforcer*
Percentage of MNCs	57	23	20

(g) Reporting to the head of the RHQ ($n=29$)

	Who Reports to the head of RHQ		
	All units in the region	*Most units in the region*	*RHQ staff only*
Percentage of MNCs	69	21	10

(h) Linkages within the region ($n=30$)

	Linkages are considered		
	Strong, beneficial	*Limited, less beneficial*	*Weak, less beneficial*
Percentage of MNCs	27	43	30

As Western and Japanese MNCs are still relatively new and small in Asia and Europe, respectively, further expansion relies significantly on the development of new business. Therefore questions were raised regarding the degree of initiative for new business being taken by the RHQs. Only 21 valid responses were received to this question, because either the task of developing new business had never been specifically allocated or managers were not aware of any one unit's responsibility. The results are shown in Table 5.2(b). Overall, the MNCs indicated considerably greater involvement by the RHQ than the HQ. Often the answer was based on the fact that the RHQ is simply closer to the market than the HQ.

The role of the RHQ in shaping the regional perspective is also mirrored by the degree of its responsibility in setting targets for, and exerting control over the national units. The responses show that in 43 per cent of the MNCs, both targets and control are handled by the RHQ (see Table 5.2(c)). In another 25 per cent of the cases, the RHQs are fully in charge of control, though share responsibility for target-setting with HQ. This indicates an influential role for the RHQ. That target-setting is shared between RHQ and HQ in 57 per cent of all cases is due to the need for fit with corporate targets and budgets in the planning process.

Summing up, the findings regarding regional strategy, regional business development and target setting and control lend limited credibility to Hypothesis 1, that RHQs are not *dominant* in shaping their MNC's regional perspective. However, they do play an *important* role.

Hypothesis 2: Regional Integration

The second set of questions concerning the activities of RHQs deals with the role they play in moulding the various activities of the national units within a region into a single greater entity. In only 18 out of the total of 30 MNCs the regional coordination of functional activities is an important task. The 4 most prominent areas for coordination are marketing, human resource management, manufacturing, and product adaptation and development.

Marketing was mentioned as an important area of regional coordination mainly by those selling to consumers, particularly the coordination of advertising campaigns and the establishment of a consistent corporate image within the region. In the area of human resource management most efforts are concentrated on the development of common guidelines or of training programmes. Administrative affairs concerning expatriates are also dealt with by the RHQs.

Only two RHQs mentioned the regional coordination of manufacturing through some specialisation among their factories in their region. Japanese MNCs undertake efforts to streamline their manufacturing operations across Europe, but this is done within the framework of global manufacturing and sourcing, and often without involvement of the RHQ. Some product adaptation and development takes place in Western MNCs in Asia under the guidance of RHQs. No Japanese MNC claims to make the same product adaptation in Europe under the leadership of an RHQ.

The provision of services to the region represents a second aspect of regional integration. Many RHQs act as suppliers of a whole range of services. Others made no reference to this activity at all. The more important services in order of frequency are: human resource management, technical services, sourcing/logistics, finance/tax/legal services, information systems, marketing.

When the various businesses in the region are brought together, synergies may be created. This is the third aspect of regional integration and the role of the RHQ in fostering and facilitating exchange between the different product divisions. The response to this issue was rather negative. Only 6 out of the 30 MNCs confirmed the existence of closer links between the businesses in the region. Of these, 5 had a matrix as organisational logic at HQ. In many of the other MNCs the emphasis on businesses seems to work against achieving synergies at regional level.

Where links do exist between different businesses, they are based on common customers in the region who are supplied by different product divisions. Key account management can provide benefits to both the customer and the various product divisions involved. Sourcing from other manufacturing facilities in the region belong to another business of the same MNC is another means of reaping synergies. This requires the setting of priorities and of transfer prices: tasks better handled by RHQs.

Overall, the findings confirm the first part of Hypothesis 2, which states that RHQs foster integration through activities in functional areas across borders. However, RHQs play a negligible role in creating synergies between different product divisions in the region. The second part of Hypothesis 2 is therefore not confirmed.

Hypothesis 3: Staffing and Mind-Set

To find out the number of staff members who 'work at the RHQ office' or 'belong to the RHQ' is a difficult task, because quite a few managers are 'double-hatted', namely having both a regional and a business responsibility. Regional managers may also hold office in a location separate from the main RHQ. Adjusted to full-time equivalents of staff primarily concerned with regional affairs, the average RHQ has a staff of about 50.

Further, an attempt has been made to discover the distribution of expatriate and local managers on the RHQ staff, and in particular the percentage of expatriates among the total staff. (This question raised two issues. First, the expatriate/local alternative is generally only relevant for managerial positions or functions that require special expertise. Therefore a preliminary inquiry had to be made into the number of such qualified staff before asking for the number of expatriates. Second, the term 'expatriate' had to be given a precise meaning, as an increasing number of Asian managers work in countries in the region other than their own, i.e. *ex patria*.) An expatriate is defined as a person who is dispatched to the RHQ by HQ. In Western MNCs an expatriate was generally understood to be non-Asian, and in Japanese MNCs the term referred to Japanese staff.

In a majority of the RHQs (53 per cent), more than two-thirds of the staff were expatriates (see Table 5.2(d)). For most of them the assignment to the RHQ was their first posting in the region. In only 17 per cent of all RHQs was the percentage of expatriates lower than a third. Almost all of them had arrived directly or indirectly from HQ. None had made his career in a country of the region and then moved into this most senior regional position. Surprisingly, the RHQs of Japanese MNCs employed a smaller percentage of expatriates than the RHQs of Western MNCs. This result contradicts findings

(Kopp, 1994) and deep-seated beliefs that Japanese MNCs rely less on locals than comparable Western MNCs. Overall the staffing pattern shows a close linkage between RHQ staff and HQ and therefore supports hypothesis 3.

To determine how close or distant the heads of RHQs were from HQ the number of levels between them and the highest level of authority, the board or the head of the board, was taken into account. Unfortunately the terms 'board' and 'board members' do not have the same meaning in every country which makes comparisons difficult. (The Japanese board system allows for up to five different levels of hierarchy within the board and for a high number of board members. The most important decisions are in practice made by the Executive Committee of the board (Schütte, 1994). Western systems tend to be more collectivist and rely on a limited number of equally empowered board members. Board members in different countries therefore do not carry the same responsibility. For the sake of simplicity, it is nevertheless assumed here that board members are in general more powerful than those not on the board. In this survey we refer only to boards of managing directors and not supervisory boards.) Of the 30 RHQs surveyed a total of 14, or almost half, are headed by board members (Table 5.2(e)). Although almost all of them are stationed in the region, a number of them regularly attend board meetings at HQs. Others stay in very close contact with their board colleagues at HQ.

The degree of connectedness to HQ in terms of hierarchical levels, however, does not necessarily indicate where managers' loyalties lie. Asked about their personal objectives, 57 per cent of the heads of the RHQs considered themselves more committed to the causes of the region than to HQ concerns (Table 5.2(f)). These heads of RHQs can be called *mentors, advocates* or *supporters.* 20 per cent of the regional heads think of themselves as *controllers* or *enforcers* with strong allegiance to HQ and a weak commitment to the region. Some respondents, however, mentioned that their allegiance to HQ had been strongest when they arrived at the RHQ, but weakened over time. Therefore the possibility cannot be excluded that commitment to the region correlates more closely with the length of the tenure of the regional head than any other factor. Other heads of RHQs saw themselves as *arbiters* or *buffers* playing different roles at different times and in different locations, namely pushing HQ's views when in the region, and arguing in favour of regional concerns when at HQ.

Hypothesis 3 states that RHQ staff is more closely linked with HQ than with the region. Some findings support this claim, but not all.

Hypothesis 4: Organisational Mechanisms

The data on the rank of the head of the RHQ as described above show that most of them either belong to the board or are in a position one level below the board. This indicates that they are hierarchically very distant from the operating level in the national units. Arguably, this will make a non-hierarchical management style with mutual respect and some degree of egalitarianism less likely. To explore this hypothesis, further questions were asked about the extent to which the various organisational units in the region report to the head of the RHQ. The responses reveal that in 69 per cent of the RHQs, all units report to the head directly, or indirectly in cases where subregional offices exit. In an additional 21 per cent, most of the units in the region belong to the RHQ (Table 5.2(g)). This was the case in a number of Japanese MNCs, in which the head of their RHQ commands the sales and marketing operations in Europe while the factories and R & D centres report directly to relevant departments in Japan.

Where the heads of the RHQs have control and consequently also power over all or most of the units in the region, they have a choice between a more hierarchical or a more federalist style of management in coordinating the region. Where there is limited control, they have to use non-hierarchical approaches. As the majority of the heads are in powerful positions, the temptation to use authority rather than to seek consensus must be great.

Data were also collected on the attempts of RHQs to foster linkages between the various units in the region. The findings indicate that 27 per cent of all RHQs laid great emphasis on creating strong regional bonds and saw them as beneficial (Table 5.2(h)). These linkages were of a formal or an informal nature and established on a permanent basis or as temporary activities, as in the case of task forces or project teams. Frequent travel and communication, the holding of regional meetings, conferences and seminars, and the publication of regional newsletters were organisational mechanisms used to foster regional linkages. Some 43 per cent saw only limited benefits in these activities and undertook few efforts to build a regional network, while another 30 per cent did not pay very much attention to linkages and considered them less beneficial. Few RHQs had set up regional councils or committees other than temporary task forces. By and large they were staffed by expatriates, because it was felt that the task of linking the local units across borders is better left to the expatriates – acting as supra-nationals without any country bias.

Overall, no strong indications emerged that RHQs would use non-hierarchical organisational mechanisms to link up with their national units. Few RHQs were strongly committed to building a network across the region. Hypothesis 4, which states that RHQs emphasise non-hierarchical approaches in their relationship with national units, is therefore not supported.

Hypothesis 5: Usefulness and Future of RHQs

Of the 30 MNCs in the sample, 29 completed and returned the mailed perception survey. In achieving their goals in the region over the last 3 to 5 years, 41 per cent of these considered themselves very successful 52 per cent moderately successful. Regarding the extent to which the regional headquarters had contributed to the achievements in the region, 76 per cent of the respondents thought that the RHQ had contributed 'very much', 24 per cent answered 'not much'. On the basis that the large majority of MNCs in the sample consider themselves successful in the region, the RHQs may be indirectly judged to be performing well.

When asked about the extent to which the performance of the RHQ was appreciated in the organisation, the majority of the respondents reacted positively. Managers were then asked to respond for three different organisational levels (at the headquarters or global level, at the regional level and at the local level) as to whether the RHQ is beneficial; whether the RHQ is costly, but a must; or whether the RHQ is costly, and not useful. Positive perceptions of the RHQs were held widely among the regional managers themselves and at headquarters. However, the respondents – who were for the most part based in the regional organisation – felt that this view would not be entirely shared at the local level. The findings are broadly parallel with the perception survey carried out by Lasserre (1993) among European managers on RHQs in Asia.

The final questions enquired into the future of the RHQ in the respondent's MNC. Of the respondents 55 per cent felt that their RHQ would gain power and influence over the coming years, and another 41 per cent felt that the RHQ would at least maintain its present position. A very strong majority (83 per cent) expected their RHQ to become more involved in promoting regional integration. Nobody predicted a lesser degree of activity. There was also a prediction of greater profit responsibility of the RHQ (38 per cent of the respondents), although the majority of respondents expected no change. Nobody foresaw reduced profit responsibility.

Hypothesis 5 stated that RHQs are perceived as useful and will gain more weight, influence and power in the future. The results of the perception survey clearly support this hypothesis.

DATA ANALYSIS

Data Summary and Interpretation

In the previous section of this chapter the data for each aspect of the RHQ researched were reported and described separately. In this section the responses to the various research questions will be examined for each individual MNC. This approach is undertaken to identify consistencies, to detect correlations between variables and to find clusters of MNCs which exhibit similar patterns of characteristics and behaviour.

Determinants of the Strength of RHQs

A consistent numerical system is applied to all the data collected, based on the principle that aspects of the RHQs indicating strength have positive values and those indicating weakness have negative values. Whenever an aspect was considered neutral, a value of zero was allocated. The strength of the RHQ in this respect is defined by the role such an organisational unit may play in shaping and influencing its MNC's direction and activities in the region, and by the way its staff is positioned in terms of power and linkages within the overall organisation.

Of the various aspects of the RHQ explored, 10 have been selected as variables to measure the strength of the RHQ. The first 3 are derived from the development of a regional perspective (Tables 5.2 (a, b and c)). The next 2 aspects of the RHQ relate to regional integration: coordination of functions and the achievement of synergies (Table 5.2(b)).

The number of staff assigned to an RHQ has been considered an indicator of RHQ strength (Table 5.2(d)). Similarly, the position of the head of the RHQ in relation to headquarters has been included in the analysis (Table 5.2(e)). The commitment of the head to the region and to headquarters is also taken as a variable (Table 5.2(f)). The position of the head of the RHQ within the region (Table 5.2(g)) and the linkages which the RHQ tries to establish with the various units in the region (Table 5.2(h)) represent the other contributing factors for the measurement of the strength of the RHQ.

Variations of Strength Across the Sample

The values of the ten variables for each MNC in the sample have been totalled. A high value indicates a strong RHQ. A low or even negative value indicates a weak RHQ. A wide range of scores emerges from the survey. Otis has the strongest RHQ according to our definition, with a score of +9, while Seiko achieved a score of only –6. The full ranking can be seen from Table 5.3, which lists MNCs in descending order of strength.

Correlation Analysis

Three tests were undertaken to identify correlations between variables (called 'aspects' of RHQs in this survey). First, an attempt was made to see whether the answers given to one specific set of questions are related to the answers given to another question, namely whether linear regressions exist. Only one weak relationship could be identified, between the position of the head of the RHQ (Table 5.2(f)) and his commitment to the region (Table 5.2(h)). This relationship is negative or inverse. According to this finding, the more senior the head of an RHQ is, the less committed he appears to be to the region. This contradicts intuitive thinking, as well as the proposition by Aoki and Tachiki (1992) that a strong man would lend more weight to the concerns of the region. No specific tension at RHQ level related to this finding was observed. It should be stressed here that, while this relationship is statistically proven, it is nevertheless weak.

Table 5.3 Ranking of scores of MNCs

Score	*Western MNCs*	*Japanese MNCs*
9	Otis	
8		
7	Accor	YKK
6		Komatsu, Sony
5	ABB	Honda, Mazda
4	Heineken, Henkel, ICI	Asahi Glass
3	BASF, Schindler, Seagram	
2	Volkswagen	NEC
1	Rhône-Poulenc, Schneider	Chugai
0	Raychem, Unilever	Shimizu
–1		Matsushita
–2		
–3		Kao, Mitsubishi Electric
–4	BP	Toyota
–5		Shiseido
–6		Seiko

Second, the independent variables were tested with regard to their impact on the total score. The regression analysis shows that the active involvement of the RHQ in what has been termed here the development of a regional perspective through strategy building and formulation, the taking of new business initiatives, and the setting and controlling of targets are the most important criteria for creating a strong RHQ. Significantly contributing to RHQ strength are two other aspects, the development of linkages in the region and the position of the head of the RHQ within the region. Both of these aspects concern RHQ systems and culture.

Third, multiple regression analysis was used to determine the extent to which two selected variables could serve as predictors of the existence of a strong or a weak RHQ. For this purpose the total score was used as the dependent variable, and the development of a regional strategy (Table 5.2(a)) and the seniority of the head of the RHQ (Table 5.2(f)) were taken as independent variables. The result shows a close relationship between the two described aspects and the total outcome, explaining 80 per cent of the variation of the score. ($R^2 = 0.805$.) This indicates that further research on RHQs could be carried out by neglecting the other eight variables (aspects) of the survey without losing too much predictability with regard to the strength of the RHQ.

Clusters Across MNCs

Clusters by Country of Origin

Analysis of the various aspects of RHQs examined in the survey disclosed differences between the clusters of Western and Japanese MNCs, but only in a limited number of variables did major contrasts emerge. (These will be elaborated upon in a another publication.) The statistical summary in Table 5.3, however, reveals a clear distinction between the overall strength of the RHQs of Western and Japanese MNCs. With an average score of 2.8, RHQs of Western MNCs appear more powerful and more influential than those of Japanese MNCs, which achieved an average score of 0.93. However, the wide distribution of the scores across the two subsamples – and particularly across the Japanese subsample – renders the difference statistically insignificant.

With the exception of three outlying MNCs, the Western group is rather homogeneous. The same cannot be said for the subsample of Japanese MNCs. Their results are distributed across the whole spectrum. It may therefore be possible to make statements regarding the set-up of a typical Western

MNC's RHQ, but generalised statements about a typical Japanese RHQ cannot be made, at least not on the basis of the present findings.

Clusters by Industry

Of the total sample of 30 MNCs, 26 belong to five broadly defined industry groups or industry clusters. In allocating the total scores of the survey (Table 5.3) to the members of each cluster, an attempt was made to determine similarities of strength of the RHQs within the clusters and dissimilarities with other clusters. Although each cluster showed a different average score, the wide range of scores within each relatively small cluster renders any meaningful conclusion impossible.

In a second step, one single cluster of industries comprising consumer goods and cars (industries dealing directly with consumers) were compared with a second cluster of industries dealing with other businesses. The difference in average score between the clusters shrinks considerably, while the range of scores within the clusters remains high. As a result no significant differences between the two combined clusters emerge. On this evidence, industry characteristics therefore do not seem to have an impact on the strength of the RHQs.

Clusters by Maturity of RHQ

The maturity of an RHQ is the length of time the organisational unit has been in operation in its present form. In an earlier section the maturity of the RHQ was explored through discussion of how much the regional organisation had changed over the last five years. An attempt has been made to establish whether the three clusters of MNCs, which had either not experienced substantial change, had seen some change, or had undergone dramatic change, are consistent within themselves yet at the same time are different from each other. The results show that RHQ maturity cannot be used as a basis for clustering the MNCs in the sample. The differences in average score between the clusters are very small, while the range of scores among the relatively small number of MNCs in each cluster remains large.

Clusters by Organisational Structure

By definition, an RHQ represents the geographical dimension in the organisation of the MNC. It can be argued that its role and strength will therefore be influenced by the way the geographical dimension is dealt with at HQ. This issue was explored earlier through questions regarding the organisational structure of the MNC at the board level. The results revealed two distinct groups, each using a different organisational logic. The majority of the MNCs are primarily guided by the business divisions, while members in the smaller group utilise a matrix organisation where businesses balance geography or vice versa. It was further discovered that one half of the sample is rather diversified, the other not. Organisational logic and the degree of diversification of the RHQ are the determinants of what is called here the organisational structure.

Figure 5.1 Organisational structure matrix

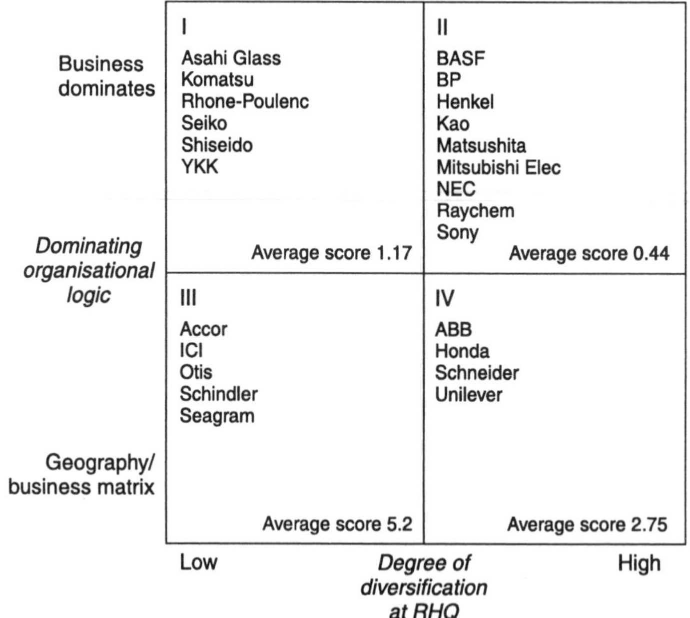

Coefficient of variation = standard deviation/Mean. The results of the clusters are as follows: coefficients of variation: 4.77

for cluster I; 7.9 for cluster II; 0.52 for cluster III; 0.96 for cluster IV. The MNCs are grouped together in clusters and the scores from the survey distributed between them. Figure 5.1 shows the distribution of the average scores of the MNCs across a matrix. The clusters in the four quadrants display distinctively different average scores, though again the significance of the differences is severely hampered by the small size of the sample and the wide range of scores within each cluster, particularly in quadrants I and II.

Aggregating the MNCs into two rather than four clusters, however, sheds some light on the influence of the organisational structure on the strength of the RHQ. In the first step, one combined cluster is formed among those RHQs that are less diversified (I + III), and another comprises those that are more diversified (II + IV). However, hypothesis testing of differences between the means of the two combined clusters using the *t*-distribution test again reveals no significant variation between these two clusters of RHQs.

In a second step, horizontal clusters are created, comparing all those MNCs with a dominant divisional or business logic with those organised according to a geography and business matrix. In contrast to the hypothesis testing in step one, here the differences were significant between the two combined clusters. (Coefficients of variation: 5.82 for combined clusters I + II and 0.68 for III + IV.) At a level of significance of 5 per cent, RHQs of MNCs that have adopted a geography and business matrix organisation at headquarters level are stronger than those of MNCs which are dominated by businesses, or where divisions play the most important role in the organisational logic. None of the MNCs with a matrix had a weak RHQ, while several of the business dominated MNCs did. In other words, MNCs in which businesses dominate run a high risk of ending up with weak RHQs.

CONCLUSIONS

This survey of thirty RHQs in Asia and in Europe has shed some light on the activities, structures and processes of these organisational units that stand between HQ and national subsidiaries. It was found that RHQs play an important, though not a dominant role in shaping the regional perspective of their MNCs. They are instrumental in integrating the region through the support of functional activities, but are rarely able or willing to create synergies between different businesses or divisions. The mind-set of the head and the staff of RHQs is more closely linked with HQ than the region, though not always. The organisational mechanisms used by the RHQ in dealing with the national units the region do not indicate a strong desire to seek consensus and to share power with them.

The perception survey revealed a very positive picture of the RHQs. The thirty MNCs in the sample were by and large successful in the region concerned, and attributed their success to their RHQs. These were perceived as useful and are expected to become more powerful and more active in future. RHQs were therefore seen not as temporary phenomena, but necessary organisational units.

Based on calculations of the strength of RHQs, a wide distribution of scores was found among the MNCs in the sample. Regression analysis showed that the active involvement of the RHQ in developing a regional perspective contributes most to the strength of an RHQ. Of the variation in the strength of an RHQ, 80 per cent can be explained by just two aspects: the development of a regional strategy, and the seniority of the head of the RHQ. Cluster analysis shows that the difference in strength between the RHQs of Western and Japanese MNCs is statistically insignificant. Equally, industry characteristics or the maturity of an RHQ have no impact on the strength of the RHQ. Significant differences were, however, discovered when taking into account the organisational structure of the MNC at headquarters level. Where businesses dominate the organisational logic, RHQs tend to be weaker than in those MNCs where a matrix organisation exists.

Assuming that a weaker RHQ means greater difficulty in pursuing regional strategies, and further assuming that MNCs may need a strategy in a given region which differs from their global one, MNCs with businesses as their overriding organisational logic are likely to show a weaker performance in that region. Therefore MNCs that want to emphasise a given region strategically should not only establish an RHQ, but also ensure that the geographical dimension is adequately supported by HQ.

Based on the results of this study, further research on RHQs and related issues is proposed in order to gain better insights into the complexities of large organisations. A questionnaire could be sent to a much larger sample of MNCs to cross-check and validate certain findings, and perhaps to identify significant industry clusters and differences between MNCs of different countries of origin. Alternatively, the sample could be broadened and rearranged in order to differentiate more clearly between external (or environmental) and internal (or firm) specific factors of influence.

Three approaches can help to clarify the interrelationships between the internal and external environments. First, holding constant the internal factors of influence, RHQs belonging to MNCs of a certain country of origin can be investigated in various regions of the world, and the differences between these various regions analysed. By design, any differences must derive from external factors of influence. Second, keeping constant the external environment, the RHQs of MNCs of different origin in the same region, such as RHQs of Japanese and American MNCs in Europe, can be explored. Differences between them should then be determined by internal factors.

Unfortunately, both approaches are difficult to realise. Few MNCs have set up comparable regional organisations in several regions of the world. Within the same region, MNCs of different origin will probably have a very different administrative heritage. (Studies comparing long-established American MNCs with relatively newly arrived Japanese MNCs in Europe suffer from this distortion.) These constraints would have to be taken into account in the research design.

A longitudinal study of the RHQs of a smaller number of MNCs would not suffer the same disadvantages. Such an investigation would be particularly valuable in view of the contradictory findings of this and other studies regarding the life expectancy of RHQs (Lasserre 1996). It could also provide deeper insights into the organisational responses of MNCs towards internal and external changes and their attempts to design an RHQ so that it represents a fit between the need for internal consistency within the MNC and the opportunities and threats of the environment. Contingency theory would provide a suitable framework for such studies (Miller 1992).

A very different idea for further research concerns the evaluation of the usefulness of RHQs, and suggests a more firm-specific approach. The present study has not dealt with the quantification of the costs and benefits of an RHQ, though this would be of great interest both from a theoretical and an empirical point of view, as it brings together issues from the areas of organisation and managerial accounting. MNCs themselves would be highly interested in a framework in which they can undertake cost/benefit analyses of their RHQs.

Instead of exploring in greater depth questions concerning the RHQ, research could also bring the study of this particular organisational unit into the broader context of research on the globalisation of the firm and the difficulties firms have in implementing global strategies. The principal question to consider is whether regional strategies and regional organisational structures and systems are able to substitute or replace those introduced on a global platform, and thereby improve the performance of the MNC. This raises exciting issues in a world in which, despite the existence of the WTO, regional institutions are being strengthened. (Note: During the later stages of the Uruguay Round (1990–4) which attempted to strengthen the global trade system, 33 new regional integration agreements were notified to the GATT as well as a deepening and widening of existing agreements, particularly in Western Europe. See World Trade Organization, *Regionalism and the World Trading System*, Geneva, World Trade Organization, p 1.)

References

Aoki, A. and D.S. Tachiki (1992) 'Overseas Japanese Business Operations: The Emerging Role of Regional Headquarters', *RIM Pacific Business and Industries*, 1, 29–39.

Bartlett, C.A. and S. Ghoshal (1989) *Managing Across Borders: The Transnational Solution*, Boston, Mass.: Harvard Business School Press.

Bartlett, C.A. and S. Ghoshal (1991) 'Global Strategic Management: Impact on the New Frontiers of Strategy Research', *Strategic Management Journal*, 12, Special Issue, Summer, 5–16.

Blackwell, N., J-P Bizet, P. Child and D. Hensley (1991) 'Shaping a Pan-European Organisation', *McKinsey Quarterly*, no. 2, 94–111.

Blackwell, N., J-P Bizet, P. Child and D. Hensley (1992) 'Creating European Organisations that Work', *McKinsey Quarterly*, no. 2, 31–43.

Chandler, A.D. (1962) *Strategy and Structure: Chapters in the History of the American Industrial Enterprise*, Cambridge, Mass.: MIT Press.

Doz, Y. and S. Ghoshal (1994) *Organising for Europe: One Size Does Not Fit All!*, Working Paper, INSEAD.

Doz, Y. and C.K. Prahalad (1991) 'Managing DMNCs: A Search for a New Paradigm', *Strategic Management Journal*, 12, Special Issue, Summer, 145–64.

Franko, L.G. (1976) *The European Multinationals: A Renewed Challenge to American and British Big Business*, Stamford, Conn.: Greylock.

Ghoshal, S. and Bartlett, C.A., (1995) 'Changing the Role of Top Management: Beyond Structure to Processes', *Harvard Business Review*, 73 (1), January–February 86–96.

Handy, C. (1992) 'Balancing Corporate Power: A New Federalist Paper', *Harvard Business Review*, 70 (6), November–December, 59–72.

Heenan, D.A. and H.V. Perlmutter (1979) *Multinational Organisation Development*, Reading, Mass.: Addison-Wesley.

Hedlund, G. (1986) 'The Hypermodern MNC – A Heterarchy?', *Human Resource Management*, 25 (1), 9–35.

Hungenberg, H. (1993) 'How to Ensure that Headquarters Add Value', *Long Range Planning*, 26 (6), 62–73.

Kopp, R. (1994) 'International Human Resources Policies and Practices in Japanese, European, and United States Multinationals', *Organizational Dynamics*, Winter, 33 (4), 581–99.

Lasserre, P (1993) *The Strategic Roles of Regional Headquarters in the Asia Pacific Region*, INSEAD, Euro-Asia Centre Research Series, no. 15, April.

Lasserre, P (1996) 'Regional Headquarters: The Spearheard for Asia Pacific Markets', *Long Range Planning*, 29 (1), February, 30–7.

Lehrer, M. and K. Asakawa (1995) *Regional Management and Regional Headquarters in Europe: A Comparison of American and Japanese MNCs*, Working Paper, INSEAD.

Martinez, J.I. and J.C. Jarillo (1989) 'The Evolution of Research on Coordination Mechanisms in Multinational Corporations', *Journal of International Business Studies*, 20 (3), 490–92.

Martinez, J.I. and J.C. Jarillo (1991) 'Coordination Demands of International Strategies', *Journal of International Business*, 22 (3), 429–43.

Miller, D. (1992) 'Environmental Fit versus Internal Fit', *Organization Science*, 3 (2), 159–78.

Morrison, A.J. and K. Roth (1992) 'The Regional Solution: an Alternative to Globalization', *Transnational Corporations*, 1 (2), August, 42–52.

Morrison, A.J., D.A. Ricks and K. Roth (1991) 'Globalization versus Regionalization: Which Way for the Multinational?' in *Organisational Dynamics*, Winter, 17–29.

Prahalad, C.K. and Y. Doz (1987) *The Multinational Mission: Balancing Local Demands and Global Vision*, New York: Free Press.

Schütte, H. (1994) *Corporate Governance in Japan*, INSEAD, Euro-Asia Centre Research Series No. 30, July.

Schütte, H. (1995) 'Henkel's Strategy for Asia Pacific', *Long Range Planning*, 28 (1), 95–103.

Stopford, J.M. and L.T. Wells (1972) *Managing the Multinational Enterprise*, New York: Basic Books.

Sullivan, D. (1992) 'Organisation in American MNCs: The Perspective of the European Regional Headquarters', *Management International Review*, 32 (3), 237–50.

APPENDIX 5.A INTERVIEW GUIDE

1. Regional Perspective

- Who is in charge of developing strategies for the region? How much influence do the HQ, RHQ and local units have in the process of strategy development?
- Who develops the ideas for new business initiatives in the region?
- Who sets the targets for the operational units and who controls their implementation?

2. Regional Integration

- Are functional activities within the region coordinated by the RHQs? To what extent? Which activities are more coordinated than others?
- Does the RHQ provide services to the operating units in the region? Which ones and to what extent?
- Where do synergies exist between the different businesses in the region? Does the RHQ actively foster the integration of businesses?

3. Regional Structure

- Of which countries does the region consist? Has the definition of the region changed recently? Does your firm divide the region further into sub-regions, each with their own sub-regional organisational structure?
- Where is the RHQ located? Have there been any recent changes? Are any changes planned?
- How many people are employed by the RHQ? How many in managerial functions? How many of them have been despatched as expatriates from HQ?

4. Culture and Communication

- Who reports to the head of the RHQ? To whom does the head of the RHQ report?
- What linkages exist between the various parts of the firm within the region and are such linkages being fostered by RHQ? Does the head of the RHQ see himself (or is he perceived) more as an HQ representative, or as an advocate of the region and its operational units against HQ?
- Does the RHQ carry profit responsibility? Who pays for the RHQ?

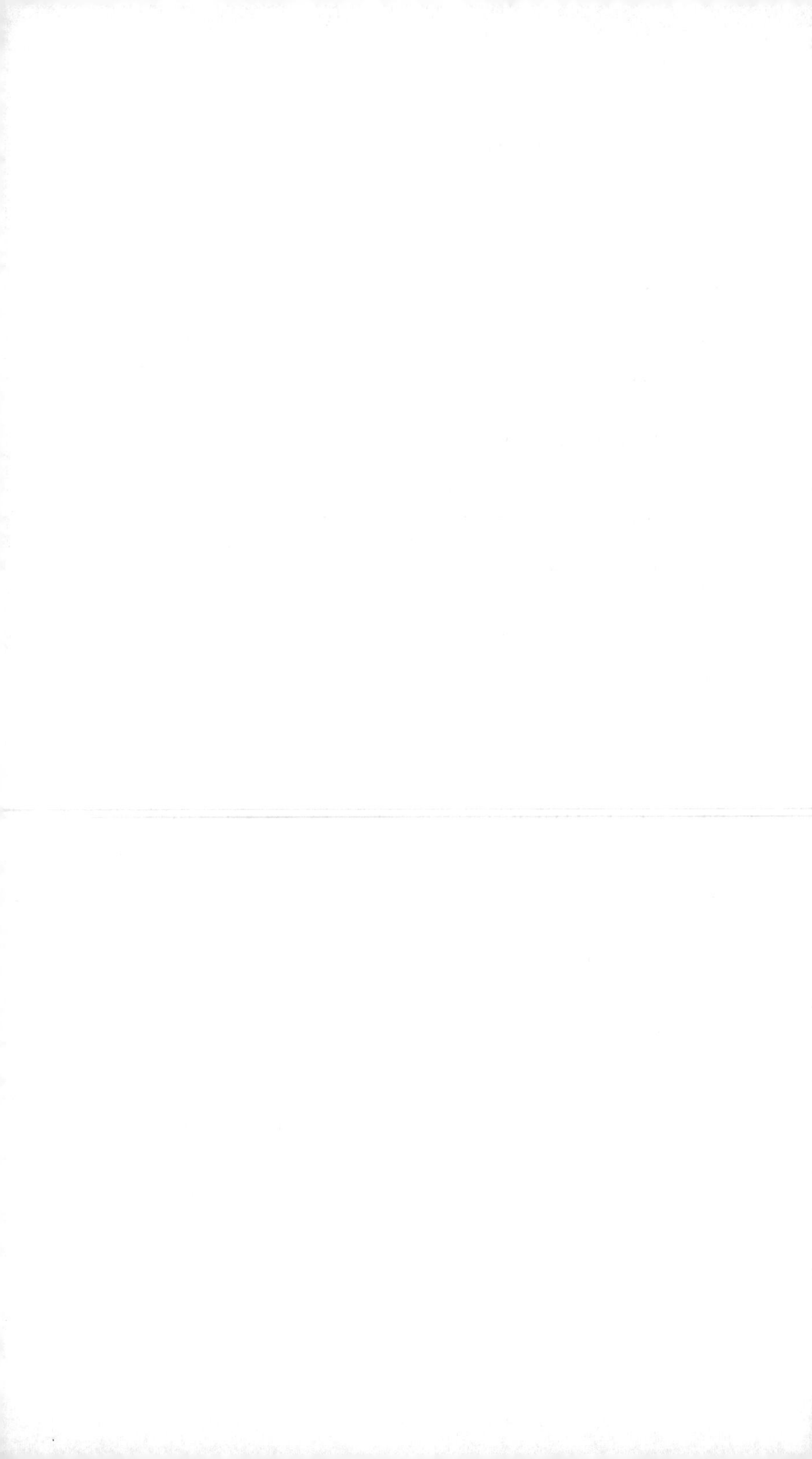

Part II
Centres of Excellence in Multinational Networks

6 Centres of Excellence in Multinational Companies: The Case of Denmark

Mats Forsgren and Torben Pedersen

INTRODUCTION

An important body of literature on multinational corporations (MNCs) relates to how they are organised, and especially the role of the subsidiaries within the organisation. (see Doz and Prahalad, 1981; Egelhoff, 1988; Bartlett and Ghoshal, 1989; Forsgren, 1989; Ghoshal and Nohria, 1989; Ghoshal and Bartlett, 1990; Gupta and Govindarajan, 1991, 1994; Forsgren and Johanson, 1992.) One theme in recent writings is the need to change from a situation of the firm as a bundle of headquarters–subsidiary relationships into a more complicated system with reciprocal interdependencies between units in different countries (Hedlund, 1986, Bartlett *et al.*, 1990). Connected with this view is the assumption that the competitiveness of the modern MNC is characterised by a shift away from the initial stage of proprietary knowledge and brand labels to the exploitation of international activities through economies of scale and scope, learning and operating flexibility (Kogut, 1990).

A common assumption in this literature is that some subsidiaries in the MNC will or should have a strategic role in the organisation, which goes beyond their local undertaking and is quite different from the traditional role of implementer of the parent company's decisions. But a closer look at this literature reveals that the models and perspectives, as well as the characteristics of this new type of subsidiary differs to a considerable degree.

The purpose of this chapter is twofold. First, the focus is on categorisations of subsidiaries based on the literature and product mandates about the network-based MNC. The aim is to highlight the decisive factors that open up the possibility of a subsidiary becoming what is sometimes called a 'centre of excellence' within the MNC. Second, data about foreign-owned firms in Denmark will be analysed in order to investigate the extent to which subsidiaries of these firms function as centres of excellence within MNCs in that country.

THE PRODUCT MANDATE SUBSIDIARY

The literature about product mandates was some of the first to deal with subsidiary roles. This literature originated from an interest among Canadian industrial organisation scholars in discussing the relevance of foreign-owned firms as sources of economic development in the host country (Dhavan *et al.*, 1981; Poynter and Rugman, 1982; Etemad and Dulude, 1986). Therefore, the main focus within this tradition is the extent to which the subsidiary can operate as a fully fledged unit within the MNC, with its own export and development activities. D'Cruz, for instance, identifies a product mandate as a mandate to sell the products anywhere in the world (D'Cruz, 1986). Although there is no clear and undisputed definition of what characterises a subsidiary with a product mandate (Fratocchi 1994), most of the literature seems to emphasise aspects of autonomy rather than interdependence *vis-à-vis* the rest of the MNC. The subsidiary with a product mandate should be able to operate as an independent unit with its own exports and also with a substantial degree of influence on the development of its products. The distinction often made in the literature between a product mandate and product rationalisation reflects the importance of autonomy as a prerequisite for a subsidiary having product mandate characteristics (Birkinshaw and Morrison, 1995). It is not primarily a question of specialisation *between* subsidiaries within an MNC, but rather a question of completeness of functions *within* one and the same subsidiary. Therefore, there is a striking similarity between how a product division is usually defined and how the concept of product mandate is treated in the literature. This does not imply that a subsidiary with a product mandate has no business relationship with the rest of the MNC, but rather that a certain degree of strategic autonomy is necessary.

The word 'mandate' implies something that is decided by the parent and given to the subsidiary, although some scholars have emphasised that a product mandate is earned, not given (D'Cruz, 1986). The discussion as to why certain subsidiaries will have product mandates is quite limited, but there seems to be a general assumption behind most writings that initiatives and decisions at headquarters are only one cause among others. The R&D function seems to play an important role in the discussion of the concept of product mandate. Many scholars stress that a product mandate implies that the subsidiary controls the development of products and production processes within a certain area. It is seen as one crucial factor that distinguishes a subsidiary with a product mandate from other subsidiaries (Roth and Morrison, 1992). Consequently, a product mandate requires more than the production and marketing of products. The subsidiary must have a substantial influence on the development of these products. Some scholars even argue that product mandate implies that the subsidiary becomes *de facto* the headquarters of development activities. This does not mean that the subsidiary has all the necessary R&D facilities, but it must be able to decide about innovative activities and delegate their realisation to other units within the MNC (Etemad and Dulude, 1986).

In summary, the literature about product mandates does not offer a precise definition of what constitutes a subsidiary with such a role. A common theme, though, is that a product mandate subsidiary fulfils a more advanced and independent role than subsidiaries that operate as the parent company's extended arm and implementer. It is a quasi-firm within the firm, somewhat as divisions are sometimes defined (Williamson, 1971). Two factors seem to be especially important. First, strategic autonomy rather than interdependence and integration with the rest of the MNC characterises a subsidiary with a product mandate (Roth and Morrison, 1992; Birkinshaw and Morrison, 1995). Second, this position is manifested through the degree of control over marketing and R&D. A subsidiary with a product mandate can market its product to countries outside the local country, which means that it has a dispersed configuration for sales and marketing (Roth and Morrison, 1992). It must also have a substantial degree of influence over the development process, either through its own R&D activities or through control of how these activities are carried out within the MNC.

THE SUBSIDIARY IN THE NETWORK MNC

During the 1980s another body of literature also discussed the advancement and complexity of subsidiary roles within the MNC. Today these writings are often classified very broadly as 'the network-based models, of MNC' (see for example Malnight, 1996), and in common with the literature about product mandates they include a rather heterogeneous body of perspectives and models. One group of models deals mainly with the 'network MNC' as a new ideal type of organisation that is radically different from the Weberian bureaucracy, and is based neither on hierarchical authority nor on market transactions (Nohria and Eccles, 1992), but rather on the assumption that an MNC today works under conditions that require more flexible, non-hierarchical organisational structures. MNCs are changing (or should change) from a bureaucratic organisation to an organic one consisting of personal networks rather than formal relationships. In such a multinational, the organisation is expected to be more efficient, because information about required changes is transmitted more easily through networks than through hierarchies (Hedlund, 1986; Bartlett and Ghoshal, 1989; White and Poynter, 1990; Marschan *et al.*, 1996).

The meaning of networks in these models is not quite clear, but networks in terms of communication channels between units within organisations seem to be an underlying theme. The keyword is integration rather than differentiation, but it is emphasised that subsidiaries have different roles depending on different contextual conditions (Ghoshal and Nohria, 1989). It is argued that the transformation into a network-like organisation is a strategic necessity in a world of the globalisation of industries and growing interdependencies across national markets (Kogut, 1990). But sometimes it is also linked to the discussion about the transition from an industrial to a post-industrial and post-fordistic society which requires new, more 'network-like' and flexible organisational forms (Miles and Snow, 1986; Nohria and Eccles, 1992). An MNC gives its subsidiaries different roles to achieve competitive advantage through integration, local responsiveness and learning (Malnight, 1996). As a consequence, it has to organise a world-wide flow of products and information within the firm. Some scholars have chosen to conceptualise the multinational corporation as a network of knowledge flows between the subsidiary and the rest of the corporation (Gupta and Govindarajan, 1994).

Compared with the product mandate literature, the basic difference seems to be that interdependence rather than autonomy is in focus. Even though subsidiaries can have different roles, they do not contribute primarily to the MNC's objective by generating profits, but rather by being a part of an overall corporate strategy in a learning organisation. Networks of information and knowledge flows *within* the MNC therefore become crucial. The initial question in the product mandate literature about how a subsidiary can contribute to the local economy through autonomy is replaced by the question of how the local subsidiary can contribute to the global competitiveness of the MNC through interdependence.

However, there is another body of literature that conceptualises the network MNC in a somewhat different way. It goes back to theories developed during the last two decades about relationships between industrial companies, especially the view of markets as a set of connected exchange relationships between actors controlling business activities. The model implies that exchange relationships are significant parts of the actors' assets that have been established and developed over time through the actors' investment of time and resources. Each business activity pursued by the actors is more or less dependent on the performance of other activities that must precede them or are expected to ensue from them. Such activity chains are important ingredients in all business networks. The existence and the role of business networks have received growing attention and have been the object of a number of empirical studies in Europe, the USA and Japan (for an overview see Håkansson and Snehota, 1995; Ford 1997).

Against this background, the subsidiaries within an MNC can be looked upon from two different angles. On the one hand the corporate headquarters uses different mechanisms, including information networks, to integrate the subsidiary into the rest of the MNC according to an overall strategy. On the other hand, subsidiaries are embedded in business networks that include other business actors. The role of the subsidiary in the network is shaped and developed in interaction with these actors, rather than through any specific decision by headquarters. Such a view of the network MNC emphasises that the role of a subsidiary within the MNC is dependent on the characteristics of the specific business network within which the subsidiary is embedded, and not just on the subsidiary itself (Ghoshal and Bartlett, 1990; Andersson and Forsgren, 1995, 1996). The role is developed over time and shaped by the position of the subsidiary in the business network. One aspect of this, for instance, is the link between the customer relationships of the subsidiary in terms of technological development and its role in the MNC's R&D (Andersson and Pahlberg, 1997).

If we compare this conceptualisation of the MNC based on theories about business networks with that of the MNC as an information network, at least three differences can be found. First, looking upon MNCs from a business network point of view does not imply that a 'network-like' organisation is considered more efficient than other organisational modes, including those that could be described as bureaucratic. The business network is there and has always been there, although changing over time. Therefore it is not a matter of replacing bureaucracy with networks, but rather of recognising the importance of specific relationships between the subsidiary and other actors. Bureaucracy and the business network coexist, and it is an empirical question which factor is the most important in a given case.

Second, networks are not primarily a question of organisation design, whether by the headquarters or by somebody else. The existing relationships between subsidiaries and other business actors are largely a consequence of a process of interaction between actors and successive investments made by them, rather than something designed and controlled by a single unit.

Third, while the internal network, in terms of product, knowledge and communication flows, is emphasised in the former 'network' perspective, the business network implies that relationships with specific external actors are in focus as well. Some scholars have argued that different attributes of the MNC can be explained by selected attributes of the external network (see, for example, Ghoshal and Bartlett, 1990). However, using the business network theory of the MNC implies that the network which a subsidiary considers important for its activities is not only a matter of business relationships with external counterparts, but with the whole network including other corporate units. The focus, however, is on the business activities underlying the relationships, not on the administrative or legal links as such. Therefore, one interesting aspect of the subsidiary role is its ability to function as a bridge between, for example, development activities in the external and internal business network (Forsgren *et al.*, 1996). Another related aspect is its role as a creator of value by linking resources and activities from different external and corporate members of the network. These have been described elsewhere as *strategic centres* (Lorenzoni and Baden-Fuller, 1995).

SOME CLASSIFICATIONS OF SUBSIDIARY ROLES

Without placing too much stress on the differences between the perspectives and models above, together they offer some basic dimensions that can be used to classify different subsidiary roles. The product mandate literature suggests that there are, above all, three variables that are important: own production, marketing outside the local market, and control of development resources relevant to the products produced. Characterising production subsidiaries accordingly gives us a simple two-variable matrix, as shown in Table 6.1.

The subsidiaries in the upper left quadrant in Table 6.1 have only local business, and are dependent on the rest of the MNC (parent company) in terms of R&D. In the lower left quadrant, the subsidiaries are allowed to sell outside the local market, but the products are developed somewhere else in the MNC. Therefore they do not fulfil the requirements of a product mandate. This is also the case for subsidiaries in the upper right quadrant, because the business is only local, although they carry out their own R&D. Only the subsidiaries in the lower right quadrant fulfil both requirements.

Table 6.1 Classification of production subsidiaries within an MNC with respect to export and R&D intensity

		Research and development	
		Low	*High*
Export	Low	Local supplier	Local developer
	High	International supplier	Product mandate

If the Network MNC models are applied with respect to R&D then it should be possible to distinguish between different combinations of R&D flows between the subsidiary and other actors in the network, both external and internal. For instance, subsidiaries that function only as local suppliers can have different patterns of relationships with other corporate units as well as with customers or suppliers in the local market. But in this case, as well as when the subsidiary is an international supplier of products developed somewhere else (lower left quadrant), it is reasonable to assume that its role in the R&D network is quite limited.

The other two quadrants are more interesting with respect to R&D. In the case of *local developers* as well as in the case of *product mandates*, the degree of corporate and external embeddedness will be interesting to study from a Network MNC perspective. For instance, the local developer can be analysed from several angles. One critical dimension has to do with the type of relationship the subsidiary has with other local actors of importance for its own R&D. For example, is it dependent on or does it have a mutual relationship with certain companies within its local network, or are the R&D flows primarily a matter of relationships with other corporate units? Does it act as a bridge between R&D activities going on at different places in the local environment and the MNC? Alternatively, does it function primarily as a developer of products for the local market with only limited R&D connections with other corporate units? These questions deal with the degree of corporate and external embeddedness of the subsidiary in terms of R&D and the balance between these two roles. The same type of analysis can of course be applied to the product mandate subsidiary, according to the criteria used above. Within a certain degree of completeness in terms of the marketing and R&D functions, different subsidiaries can play different roles, depending on their R&D relationships with other external and corporate units.

The dimension of embeddedness can be regarded as primarily reflecting the intensity of the knowledge exchange between the subsidiary and specific actors in terms of R&D. Basically, we can identify four different archetypes in connection with the degree of the embeddedness of a subsidiary. The first archetype is characterised by a low intensity of R&D flows, in relation both to the rest of the MNC and to external business actors. Such a subsidiary acts more as an isolated unit in terms of R&D. The second archetype is more involved in the exchange of R&D with external customers and suppliers than with corporate actors, while the third type has the opposite situation. The fourth archetype, finally, has a high involvement in R&D exchange with other corporate units as well as with external business actors.

The concept of a subsidiary as a centre of excellence within an MNC is a matter of degree rather than an absolute parameter. Therefore it would be possible to argue that the four different types of subsidiaries, at least to some extent, can have characteristics of a centre. But it is reasonable to assume that in order to be important for the strategy and development of the whole MNC – one important attribute of a centre of excellence – the exchange of R&D with other corporate units will be a crucial factor. Therefore, it would be expected that the two last-mentioned archetypes, both with a high degree of corporate embeddedness, are more in line with what is meant by a centre of excellence than the two first-mentioned types.

However, it is probably fair to say that the degree of external embeddedness also has an impact on a centre of excellence. If a subsidiary has a high degree of both corporate and external embeddedness, it seems to correspond to the 'ideal' type according to some of the network MNC literature (Doz *et al.*, 1990; Chakrawarty and Doz, 1992). The subsidiary is well integrated in both networks, which gives it a special position within the MNC. For instance, long-term cooperation with particular customers and suppliers in the local market concerning product development or production technology can be used by the subsidiary in its exchange with sister units to influence the future product policy within the MNC. Such a subsidiary has a more or less unique role as a bridge between R&D activities in the external business network and the demand for R&D within the MNC. The role is characterised by autonomy *and* interdependence *vis-à-vis* the MNC, and can be seen as a platform for developing and maintaining its position as a centre of excellence within the corporation.

The above analysis does not, however, tell us anything about how a subsidiary develops into a centre of excellence. One possible scenario is that the position of the subsidiary is shaped by a strategic process within the multinational company where the headquarters plays a decisive role in designing the organisation, in order to cope with competition on a global basis. Another scenario is that centres of excellence mirror the intra-organisational power exerted by some subsidiaries, based on control of critical resources including relationships with customers, suppliers and other counterparts in its business network. A third scenario could of course be some kind of combination between the other two. It is an empirical as to question which scenario is the most appropriate one. The primary objective of the next section is not to answer that question, but rather to investigate the extent and characteristics of product mandates and centres of excellence among foreign-owned firms in Danish industry.

EMPIRICAL ANALYSIS

The sample analysed in this study concerns foreign-owned production firms located in Denmark and is based on a survey conducted in 1991 among all foreign-owned manufacturing subsidiaries in Denmark. The database contains detailed information on a total of 141 firms, corresponding to 55 per cent of all foreign-owned manufacturing subsidiaries in Denmark with at least 20 employees. Among the 141 foreign-owned subsidiaries in Denmark, 40 were greenfield investments, whereas

101 were established as acquisitions (for a more detailed description of the survey, see Pedersen and Valentin, 1996). Table 6.1 shows some characteristics of the foreign-owned subsidiaries in Denmark at the time of the survey.

On average, the foreign-owned subsidiaries have a relatively high R&D intensity compared with other Danish firms. Their R&D intensity (measured as R&D staff as proportion of total staff) is 4.9, which is almost twice as high as the average in Danish industry. Almost 50 per cent of the total turnover is exported to other countries. The relatively high export intensity is probably due to the small Danish home market.

Table 6.2 Characteristics of the foreign-owned subsidiaries in Denmark (1991)

Characteristics	*Mean*	*SD*
Average turnover in millions, DKK	292	645
Sales in Denmark as share of total turnover	51.3	33.9
Export as share of total turnover	48.7	33.9
Internal export in MNC as share of total turnover	17.8	23.3
External export as share of total turnover	30.9	31.5
R&D expenses as share of total turnover	2.7	3.8
Average number of employees	238	336
Engineers as share of total staff	6.5	7.5
Skilled workers as share of total staff	17.3	18.2
R&D staff as share of total staff	4.9	5.8

The analysis of the subsidiaries now follows a two-step procedure. In the first step the extent to which the subsidiaries can be characterised as product mandates is investigated. This analysis follows the classification shown in Table 6.1. In the next step the subsidiaries identified as product mandates are further analysed to find out to what extent they can be characterised as centres of excellence within the MNCs.

The Autonomy Dimension

In order to identify those subsidiaries with product mandate characteristics, we used two variables: export intensity and

R&D intensity. A high export intensity should reflect the fact that the subsidiary has some kind of international competitive advantage, while a high R&D intensity indicates that the subsidiary is undertaking its own product development. Together, these two measures express the extent to which the firm has some kind of self-created international strength and responsibility, and thus reflects the autonomy dimension.

Export intensity is measured as a percentage of exports within total turnover (range from 0 to 100 per cent), and R&D intensity is measured as a percentage of R&D expenses of total turnover (range from 0 to 20 per cent). The correlation coefficients between these two variables is 0.21, indicating that there are no multi-collinearity problems among these variables. A cluster analysis was applied to classify all the foreign-owned firms according to their roles in the company. The cluster analysis is based on the two above-mentioned variables, and its purpose is to identify the foreign-owned firms that are similar, and group them together in clusters. As advocated by many experts, the cluster analysis was conducted in a two-stage procedure, using both hierarchical and non-hierarchical methods in tandem (Ketchen and Shook, 1996). A hierarchical algorithm is used to define the number of clusters and cluster centroids, and then these results serve as starting points for subsequent non-hierarchical clustering. In this case, Ward's method was used as the hierarchical algorithm to define the appropriate number of clusters and the related cluster centroids. The Ward method creates clusters, so that the distance between firms in the same cluster is minimised (Hair *et al.*, 1992). A common approach for choosing the appropriate number of clusters is to look for local peaks of the two statistics: cubic clustering criterion (CCC) and pseudo-*F* statistics. These are measures of within-cluster homogeneity relative to between-cluster heterogeneity.

Both the CCC and the pseudo-*F* statistics peak with four clusters, suggesting that a four-cluster solution was appropriate. The four-cluster solution will exhibit the highest internal (within-cluster) homogeneity relative to external (between-cluster) heterogeneity. To confirm this, solutions were developed with 2, 3, 4, 5, 6 and 7 clusters, and an evaluation made of the proportion of between-group variance. Thus, the two-cluster solution showed that 74 per cent of all variance was due to the between-groups element. The corresponding figure was 88 per cent for the three-cluster solution, and 93 per cent for four-cluster; after this the figure increased very slightly.

The next step was to conduct the actual cluster analysis. Here we applied a non-hierarchical method (SAS Fastclus) to classify all the foreign-owned firms in four clusters using the identified cluster centroids as starting points. Variable means for each of the four clusters are shown in Table 6.3.

Table 6.3 The average values for the three variables in the four clusters

	Cluster 1	*Cluster 2*	*Cluster 3*	*Cluster 4*
Export intensity	8.76	94.16	37.79	66.91
R&D intensity	1.93	3.47	2.25	3.32
Number of firms	43	35	35	28

In Table 6.3 a certain degree of polarisation of the data can be observed in the sense that the foreign-owned subsidiaries are of either a low-exporter–low-developer type or a high-exporter–high-developer type. This is an indication of a link between the export and R&D intensity, in the sense that if a subsidiary markets its products in several markets there will be a tendency that it will also have more R&D activities. It may also reflect the characteristics of Denmark as a small market. In such a market the MNC places a subsidiary either as a relatively small unit in order to exploit the product locally or as a tool for exploiting the product in several markets. In the former case, the relative size of the unit is too limited to conduct its own R&D, while in the latter case own R&D is a natural part of the role of the subsidiary as an exporter outside Denmark. Expressed in other words, either the Danish subsidiary has a product mandate or it has not.

Taking into account the fact that the majority (over 71 per cent) of the subsidiaries are acquisitions, the dual character seems plausible. It has been shown elsewhere that foreign acquisitions in Denmark are motivated either by the importance of the market or because of the capability of the acquired firm to produce and export a certain product (Pedersen and Valentin, 1996). It should also be noted that the difference in relative R&D and export cannot be explained by differences in size or industry.

The Interdependence Dimension

Even though product mandates by definition mean marketing outside the host country, and the subsidiary having its own R&D and therefore a certain degree of autonomy, the position in terms of knowledge flow with the MNC, and therefore the degree of interdependence, can differ between subsidiaries characterised as product mandates. In accordance with the discussion above, a first indication of interdependence, and therefore of corporate embeddedness, would be the coordination and exchange of R&D between the foreign subsidiary and the MNC. The more coordination and exchange of R&D (two-way flow of knowledge) between the subsidiary and other corporate units, the more interdependent is the subsidiary *vis-á-vis* the MNC. The corporate embeddedness with respect to R&D has a bearing on the question of a centre of excellence, in the sense that knowledge interaction between the subsidiary and other corporate units is an indicator of the possibility that the subsidiary has to play a distinctive role in the MNC's strategic process.

In order to measure the degree of corporate embeddedness with respect to R&D, the subsidiary managers were asked to indicate the level and importance of R&D coordination on a scale from 0 to 5 (not important at all) (very important). The frequency of the extent of R&D coordination is shown for the 63 product mandate subsidiaries in Table 6.4.

Among the product mandate subsidiaries it was possible to identify different strategic roles in terms of knowledge exchange with internal actors and the extent to which the degree of interdependence of these subsidiaries differs. In about 50 per cent of the product mandates (based on 30 firms reporting two or less on the scale of the importance of R&D coordination) the importance of other corporate units as sources for exchange of knowledge is limited. In that sense their integration with the rest of the MNC is low. However, 30 firms indicate that the coordination and exchange of R&D with the company is rather important (three or more on the scale). Only these 30 firms fit both criteria, namely being autonomous *and* interdependent.

Table 6.4 The extent of R&D coordination among product mandate subsidiaries

Value	*Frequency*	%
0 (not important at all)	12	20
1	6	10
2	12	20
3	14	23
4	10	17
5 (very important)	6	10
TOTAL	60[a]	100

[a] Three observations had missing value on this variable.

External Embeddedness Dimension

It was argued above that subsidiaries with high corporate and external embeddedness have a good platform for developing and maintaining a strong position within the MNC. Therefore, it would be interesting to identify to what extent these two variables correlate among the product mandate subsidiaries. Unfortunately, this survey did not include indicators, similar to the ones concerning corporate units, about the coordination of R&D with external counterparts. Consequently, it is not possible to measure external embeddedness in the same way corporate embeddedness was estimated.

However, the survey contains indicators about the strengths and weaknesses of the subsidiaries, as perceived by the subsidiaries themselves. The subsidiary managers were asked to indicate the strengths and weaknesses of various firm-specific properties for the foreign-owned firm on a scale from 0 (an obvious weakness) to 5 (an obvious strength). Two of these indicators concern important relationships with external customers and suppliers. If it is assumed, as in theories about business networks, that such relationships are crucial for technological development (see for example Håkansson, 1987; Lundgren, 1993), these indicators can be used as a rough estimation of the degree of external embeddedness of the subsidiaries.

A strong correlation was found between the two indicators, namely relationships with external customers and suppliers. The Cronbach alpha coefficient of 0.71 indicated that they were measuring the same relationship to external counterparts. Therefore, the two indicators were compressed into one variable measuring the external relationship. Table 6.5 shows the level of corporate and external embeddedness for all product mandate subsidiaries. It indicates that there are different positions among the subsidiaries. None of the combinations of low or high corporate and external embeddedness seem to dominate. Only in ten subsidiaries is there a positive correlation between corporate embeddedness and the extent to which the subsidiaries consider their relationships with specific external customers and suppliers of importance for their competitive strength.

Table 6.5 The level of corporate and external embeddedness for all product mandate subsidiaries

		External embeddedness		
		Low (0 to 3)	*High (3 to 5)*	
Corporate embeddedness	Low (0 to 3)	17	14	31
	High (3 to 5)	19	10	29
TOTAL		36	24	

CONCLUDING REMARKS

Although the present literature about MNCs emphasises that different subsidiaries have different strategic roles, there is no consensus about how these roles can be conceptualised. In this chapter it has been argued that the discussion about the role and characterisation of the subsidiary has followed two different strands. The first strand, mainly connected with the literature about subsidiaries as product mandates, has been occupied with the question of whether the subsidiary has a mandate, not only to produce and sell products on a more or less global scale, but also to carry out its own R&D connected with these products. One main concern within these writings seems to be the degree of autonomy of the subsidiary, that is to what extent it is able carry out its activities and investments without being too dependent on the mother company or other units within the MNC. This line of thought is a consequence of the fact that these writings are concerned with how the subsidiary can contribute to the host country's economic development by being a fully fledged operating unit.

The second strand is more related to the literature about the network-based MNC. In this heterogeneous literature, a common theme is that the subsidiary is more looked upon as a unit that should be integrated into the MNC in order to fulfil a specific corporate role. Interdependence rather than autonomy seems to be the crucial concept in these writings. One branch of the network MNC literature emphasises that every business actor's behaviour is shaped by his or her long-lasting relationships with customers, suppliers and other business actors in their business network. A subsidiary of an MNC, therefore, has a dual position. One component is its role as a actor in the business network, which has mostly been developed over a long time through interaction with specific business counterparts rather than imposed as a strategic decision by the headquarters or the subsidiary. The other component is the place the subsidiary is supposed to have in the MNC according to the overall strategy. Even though these two roles can coincide there is nothing a priori that tells us that they always will coincide. On the contrary, the subsidiary has to take its position in the business network into consideration when headquarters attempts to implement a corporate strategy.

In this chapter the conceptualisations above have been employed to discuss to what extent subsidiaries within an MNC can be characterised as centres of excellence. It has been argued that it is impossible to give this concept a precise definition, and therefore difficult to differentiate subsidiaries with respect to whether or not they are centres of excellence. But in most writings the concept seems to be linked implicitly to the importance of a subsidiary in shaping the future behaviour of the MNC in terms of strategic investments, and so on. Therefore this study has concluded that interdependence rather than autonomy is the crucial variable when assessing whether subsidiaries are centres of excellence. The possibility of a subsidiary having a fully fledged operation in terms of production, marketing and R&D, that is, a product mandate, is a necessary condition for a centre of excellence, but not a sufficient one. In order to be important for the MNC's strategic behaviour, the subsidiary has to be linked operationally to the rest of the MNC, that is, it has to have a certain degree of corporate embeddedness.

But it has also been argued above that the degree of external embeddedness matters. A subsidiary can use its relationships with important suppliers and customers in its business network to influence the strategic behaviour of the MNC. To express this another way, a subsidiary with strong relationships with both internal and external actors can be of specific strategic importance to the MNC. It can function as a bridge between the external and internal environment. Such a position is a good platform for developing and maintaining the role of a subsidiary as a centre of excellence within an MNC.

The empirical study of foreign-owned firms in Denmark was conducted on the basis of these arguments. Through a cluster analysis it was found that about 45 per cent of the investigated firms can be characterised as product mandate subsidiaries when export and R&D intensity are employed as discriminatory variables. By using data on the R&D flows between the subsidiary and the rest of the MNC, it was also possible to investigate whether the product mandate subsidiaries, together with their relative autonomy, also demonstrate a high degree of interdependence with the MNC. It was found that this is true in about 50 per cent of the product mandate subsidiaries. About 30 out of the original 141 foreign-owned subsidiaries not only have their own export and R&D activities but are also connected with the rest of the MNC with regard to product development, production technology, and so on. This can be considered as one important characteristic of a subsidiary as a centre of excellence.

The product mandate subsidiaries were further analysed with respect to how important they considered their external supplier and customer relationships to be for their competitive strength. If these indicators are used as a proxy for external embeddedness, it can be stated that among the subsidiaries with a high degree of corporate embeddedness there are subsidiaries with low as well as with high external embeddedness. It was argued above that productive and cooperative relationships with specific external customers and suppliers are an important resource for a subsidiary, which can be used to exert influence on the MNC's strategic behaviour. For instance, a subsidiary that has a productive cooperation with a demanding customer about the development of a specific product can use this to influence the MNC policy concerning that product through its relationships with sister units. If a high degree of embeddedness on both sides is the 'ideal' situation for a subsidiary that endeavours to be a centre of excellence then we can conclude that these situations are quite rare among foreign-owned firms in Denmark.

References

Andersson, U. and M. Forsgren (1995) 'Using Networks to Determine Multinational Parental Control of Subsidiaries', in S.J. Paliwoda and J.K. Ryans Jr (eds), *International Marketing Reader*, London: Routledge, 72–87.

Andersson, U. and M. Forsgren (1996) 'Subsidiary Embeddedness and Control in the Multinational Corporation', *International Business Review*, 5 (5), 487–508.

Andersson, U. and C. Pahlberg (1997) 'Subsidiary Influence on Strategic behaviour in MNCs: An Empirical Study', *International Business Review*, 6 (3), 319–34.

Bartlett, C.A., Y. Doz and G. Hedlund (eds) (1990) *Managing the Global Firm*, London and New York: Routledge.

Bartlett, C.A. and S. Ghoshal (1989) *Managing Across Borders. The Transnational Solution*, Boston: Harvard Business School Press.

Birkinshaw, J.M. and A.J. Morrison (1995) 'Configurations of Strategy and Structure in Subsidiaries of Multinational Corporations', *Journal of International Business Studies*, 26 (4), 729–53.

Chakrawarty, B.S., Y. Doz (1992) 'Strategy Process Research: Focusing on Corporate Self Renewal', *Strategic Management Journal*, 13, 5–14.

D'Cruz, J.R. (1986) 'Strategic Management of Subsidiaries', in H. Etemad and L.S. Dulude (eds), *Managing the Multinational Subsidiary: Response to Environmental Changes and to Host Nation R&D Policies*, London: Croom Helm, 75–89.

Dhavan, K.C., H. Etemad and R.W. Wright (eds) (1981) *International Business: A Canadian Perspective*, Reading, Mass.: Addison-Wesley.

Doz, Y., C.K. Prahalad (1981) 'Headquarters Influence and Strategic Control in MNCs', *Sloan Management Review*, Fall, 15–29.

Doz, Y., C.K. Prahalad and G. Hamel (1990) 'Control Change and Flexibility: The Dilemma of Transnational Collaboration', in C. Bartlett, Y. Doz and G. Hedlund (eds), *Managing the Global Firm*, London and New York: Routledge, 117–43.

Egelhoff, W.G. (1988) *Organizing the Multinational Enterprise – An Information-Processing Perspective*, Cambridge, Mass.: Ballinger Publishers Company.

Etemad, H. and L.S. Dulude (eds) (1986) *Managing the Multinational Subsidiary. Response to Environmental Changes and to Host Nation R&D Policies*, London: Croom Helm.

Ford, D. (ed.) (1997) *Understanding Business Markets*, London: Dryden Press.

Forsgren, M. (1989) *Managing the Internationalization Process. The Swedish Case*, London and New York: Routledge.

Forsgren, M. and J. Johanson (1992) 'Managing in International Multi-Centre Firms', in M. Forsgren and J. Johanson (eds), *Managing Networks in International Business*, Philadelphia: Gordon & Breach, 19–31.

Forsgren, M., U. Holm and P. Thilenius (1996) 'Network Infusion in the Multinational Corporation' in I. Björkman and M. Forsgren (eds), *The Nature of the International Firm. Nordic Contributions to International Business Research*, Copenhagen Business School Press, 475–94.

Fratocchi, L. (1994) 'The Role of Centre of Excellence within International Companies. Some Propositions to be Tested', University of Bologna (unpublished paper).

Ghoshal, S. and N. Nohria (1989) 'Internal Differentiation within Multinational Corporations', *Strategic Management Journal*, 10, 323–37.

Ghoshal, S. and C.A. Bartlett (1990) 'The Multinational Corporation as an Interorganizational Network', *Academy of Management Review*, 15 (4), 603–25.

Gupta, A.K. and V. Govindarajan (1991) 'Knowledge Flows and the Structure of Control within Multinational Corporations', *Academy of Management Review*, 16 (4), 768–92.

Gupta, A.K. and V. Govindarajan (1994) 'Organizing for Knowledge Flows Within MNCs', *International Business Review*, 3 (4), 773–57.

Hair, J.F., R.E. Anderson, R.L. Tatham and W.C. Black (1992) *Multivariate Data Analysis*, New York: Macmillan.

Håkansson, H. (1987) *Technological Development: A Network Approach*, New York: Croom Helm.

Håkansson, H. and I. Snehota (1995) *Developing Relationships in Business Networks*, London and New York: Routledge.

Hedlund, G. (1986) 'The Hypermodern MNC – A Heterarchy?', *Human Resource Management*, 25, spring, 9–35.

Ketchen, D.J. and C.L. Shook (1996) 'The Application of Cluster Analysis in Strategic Management Research: An Analysis and Critique', *Strategic Management Journal*, 17, 441–58.

Kogut, B. (1990) 'International Sequential Advantage and Network Flexibility', in C. Bartlett, Y. Doz and G. Hedlund (eds) *Managing the Global Firm*, London and New York: Routledge, 47–68.

Lorenzoni, G. and C. Baden-Fuller (1995) 'Creating a Strategic Center to Manage a Web of Partners', *California Management Review*, 37 (3), Spring, 146–63.

Lundgren, A. (1993) 'Technological Innovation and the Emergence and Evolution of Industrial Networks: The Case of Digital Image Technology in Sweden', *Advances in International Marketing*, 5, 145–70.

Malnight, T.W. (1996) 'The Transition from Decentralized to Network-Based MNC Structures: An Evolutionary Perspective', *Journal of International Business Studies*, 27 (1), 43–65.

Marschan, R., D. Welch and L. Welch (1996) 'Control in Less-Hierarchical Multinationals: The Role of Personal Networks and Informal Communication', *International Business Review*, 5 (2), 137–50.

Miles, R. E. and C.C. Snow (1986) 'Network Organizations: New Concepts for New Forms', *California Management Review*, Spring, 62–73.

Nohria, N. and R. Eccles (1992) 'Face-to-Face: Making Network Organizations Work' in N. Nohria and R. Eccles (eds) *Networks and Organizations*, Boston: Harvard Business School Press.

Pedersen, T. and F. Valentin (1996) 'The Impact of Foreign Acquisition on the Evolution of Danish Firms: A Competence-based Perspective', in N.J. Foss and C. Knudsen (eds), *Towards a Competence Theory of the Firm*, London: Routledge, 150–74.

Poynter, T.A. and A.M. Rugman (1982) 'World Product Mandates: How Will Multinationals Respond?', *Business Quarterly*, 47 (3), 54–61.

Roth, K. and A.J. Morrison (1992) 'Implementing Global Strategy: Characteristics of Global Subsidiary Mandates', *Journal of International Business Studies*, 23 (4) 715–35.

White, R.E. and T.A. Poynter (1990) 'Organising for World-wide Advantage', in C. Bartlett, Y. Doz and G. Hedlund (eds), *Managing the Global Firm*, London and New York: Routledge, 95–113.

Williamson, O.E. (1971) 'Managerial Discretion, Organization Form and the Multinational division Hypothesis', in R. Marris and A. Wood (eds), *The Corporate Economic Growth, Competition and Innovative Power*, London: Macmillan, 373–86.

7 A Typology of Centres Within Multinational Corporations: An Empirical Investigation

Bernard Surlemont

INTRODUCTION

The recent literature has witnessed an increasing interest in analysing a subsidiary within multinational corporations (MNCs) as a node within a network of interorganisational relationships (Ghoshal and Bartlett, 1990; Nohria and Eccles, 1992). This concern is motivated by the emergence of MNCs that wish to reconsider their conceptions of headquarters–subsidiaries relationships (Barham, 1992; Bartlett and Ghoshal, 1993; Borrus *et al.*, 1990; Hedlund and Ridderstrale, 1992; Maljers, 1992); the consequent changing role of subsidiaries within the MNC (Bartlett and Ghoshal, 1986; Ghoshal and Nohria, 1989) and increasing interdependencies between them (Bartlett and Ghoshal, 1993; Herbert, 1984; Prahalad and Doz, 1987).

As a consequence, more and more subsidiaries are qualified as a 'centre' in one form or another. In most cases, however, that notion of 'centre' remains undefined, is used in an *ad hoc* way and covers notions that can be completely different. The purpose of this chapter is to visit that notion of a centre. The chapter first proposes criteria to define a typology of centres. It then tests that typology and finally draws on a database to suggest different strategies to adopt in order to develop specific types of centres.

TOWARD A TYPOLOGY OF CENTRES WITHIN MNCs

The following examples show that reality is complex and that the notion of a 'centre', as it is used in research and practice, involves the overlapping of many different roles and can designate various phenomena. Thus the German subsidiary of Procter & Gamble, which coordinates marketing for a product line at the European level, is a centre (Bartlett, 1988). The Otis Elevator regional headquarters in Singapore, which centralises and controls activities, is also a centre (Lasserre, 1993). The Australian subsidiary of the Swedish MNC Erickson, which manages and develops group competencies in telecommunication stations, is again a centre (Bartlett and Ghoshal, 1989). The European entity of Toyota, which monitors European styling to originate and develop global design for the group (Miller 1993), the strategic centres of Sun Systems company, which develop and manage a web of alliances (Lorenzoni and Baden-Fuller, 1993), and the regional headquarters of Asahi Glass Cy in the Netherlands (Lehrer and Asakawa, 1995) – each is, some way or another, considered as 'a centre'.

'Influence' as the Key Characteristic to Qualify a Centre

The central theme of this chapter is that the extent to which a subsidiary is influential within its group provides a key criterion for associating that subsidiary with a specific type of centre. The proposition advanced relies on five arguments. First, increasing interdependencies among subsidiaries imply that they influence one another. That is, each subsidiary increasingly affects the way other subsidiaries operate their activities, so that the extent of influence provides a criterion by which to qualify as a centre. Second, in common language, the notion of 'centre' conveys the idea of prominence in a web of relationships. By this measure, a centre is characterised by the extent of the influence it exerts on other parties. Third, 'centre' and influence have a clear relational dimension. One is not influential in isolation, as one is not a centre in isolation. An organisation can only develop influence over another one, and this implies, consequently, a relationship between them. Thus, phenomenologically, influence is intimately linked to the notion of 'centre'.

Fourth, being influential and being a centre describe a state that is the result of past processes (Burt, 1977). In that respect, influence is a continuous variable. There is no discrete point at which a subsidiary becomes suddenly influential or, similarly, established as a centre. Each subsidiary can be more or less characterised as a centre that is more or less influential in its MNC network, so that the criterion of influence provides a measure of degree. For this reason, in the remainder of this chapter, 'subsidiary' and 'centre' are used interchangeably. In that respect, being influential is a notion that is deliberately chosen rather than the one of being powerful. Influence is a concept that is broader and more value-free than power, which is confined to situations where coercion is present. While manifestations of power are similar to those of influence, the driving forces of power are more restrictive. Power implies the involuntary submission of the influenced (Bacharach and Lawler, 1980). It relies on the exercise of either a legal or a moral authority, or on the exploitation of structural conditions that render the influence unavoidable (Bacharach and Lawler, 1980; Burt, 1982; Salancik and Pfeffer, 1978). While influence can be achieved through power, it can also be gained by persuasion, initiation, advice or manipulation.

Last, and most important, the manifestations of influence are not univocal. This is evident in the notion of a 'centre' as suggested by the above examples. Influence is indeed a multidimensional concept that cannot be grasped with one single indicator. The literature suggests different dimensions in order to assess the influence of a centre (Hinings *et al.*, 1974; Kaplan, 1964; Tannenbaum, 1968). These dimensions provide the basis to determine a typology of centres. They can be grouped in two categories: the depth and the breadth of influence.

The depth of influence addresses the question 'How much is the actor involved in the decision-making process?' It is characterised by ***participation power***, which is defined as the involvement of a centre in the four stages of the decision-making process related to the activities involving other subsidiaries: initiating the decision, providing information, choosing the course of action, and implementing action (Hinings *et al.*, 1974).

The breadth of influence addresses the question, 'How many actors or behaviours does an actor influence?' It is characterised by the domain and the scope of influence. The *domain* of influence is the number of units controlled (Kaplan, 1964; Lachman, 1989). In the context of MNCs it refers to the number of subsidiaries under the influence of a centre. The *scope* of influence is the number of activities or types of behaviour controlled (Hinings *et al.*, 1974; Kaplan, 1964; Lachman, 1989). The globalisation of business favours the emergence of centres in the management of any part of the value chain (Bartlett and Ghoshal, 1989; Porter, 1985). In this research, scope refers to the number of areas or activities in which a centre is active on behalf of other subsidiaries.

The Typology of Centres Within MNCs

It is possible to measure any subsidiary along each of these three dimensions of influence. If the consideration of each dimension taken in isolation provides an indication of degree in the extent to which a subsidiary is a centre, then the joint analysis of all three dimensions provides criteria to define a typology of centres.

Strategic Centres of Excellence (SCEs)

The concept of scope captures the number of activities a centre is managing for other group companies. It gives an indication of the specialisation of a centre. As its scope is reduced, a centre gets specialised on a narrow array of activities. For this reason, low-scope centres are likely to demonstrate expertise and knowledge of the latest techniques in some specific areas. These specialised low-scope centres emerge or are established for strategic purposes in MNCs. They are subsidiaries that, first, cultivate critical resources that are 'first class' according to their MNC standards (Dierickx and Cool, 1989; Rumelt, 1984; Rumelt, 1987) and, second, leverage these resources within their MNC for the benefit of other subsidiaries. Such an SCE allows the global leveraging of locally nurtured resources. This is the case, for instance, with the Siemens AG centre in Chicago, which specialises in medical electronics and operates as a world-wide centre, or for the global treasury management centre of Johnson & Johnson located in Beerse, Belgium. SCEs exploit their expertise to reap the economies of both scale and scope for their whole group. A subsidiary may be an SCE for one specific reason while being dependent on other SCEs for other resources. The concept of SCEs is not confined to technological areas. A centre may conceivably become excellent in any part of the value chain (Porter, 1985). A subsidiary with 'excellence' is one that masters the latest techniques in any one given area.

These centres that develop a reputation for expertise in specific areas are likely to cooperate with many subsidiaries that are seeking to improve their operations and global efficiency. As a consequence, the domain of SCEs is high because they develop products or provide services that are likely to be most useful for a large number of affiliated companies.

It follows from this discussion that SCEs are characterised by a low scope and a large domain. The SCE is an instrument of global decentralisation that requires the delocalisation of strategic decision-making from headquarters to the SCE and provides 'self contained manageable units with overview', as P Barnevik, CEO of ABB, puts it (Bartlett and Ghoshal, 1993).

Administrative Centres (ACs)

As it increases its scope, a centre becomes generalist and knows less and less about more and more. High-scope centres are thus less likely to be highly rated and to demonstrate specific competencies in technical areas. Such centres emerge or are established in MNCs for operational purposes. They often result from the structuring of the MNC into units, divisions or geographical areas (Stopford and Wells, 1972). The purpose of such administrative centres is to respond to the organisational needs of decentralisation, integration and differentiation (Lawrence and Lorsch, 1967). In that respect, they influence the management of a broad range of activities through coordination and control, but their influence is confined to a limited, and often fixed, number of subsidiaries. As a consequence, their domain of such a centre tends to remain low and constrained by structuring considerations within the MNC. The regional headquarters of Canon in Europe is a typical example. It follows from this discussion that an administrative centre is characterised by a high scope and a low domain.

Dormant Centres (DCs)

Some subsidiaries are 'dormant centres', which exert no influence within their MNCs. These centres are characterised by a low scope *and* a low domain. The first type of dormant centre is the subsidiary that neither masters any expertise useful for other affiliates nor plays any administrative role for other subsidiaries. Such subsidiaries are 'implementers' to exploit local markets and opportunities (Bartlett and Ghoshal, 1986), as, for instance, the Polish subsidiary of SAUR, a French multinational, which is managing local contracts in Gdansk for water cleaning. The second type of DC masters an expertise in specific areas, but for some reason does not exert any influence within its group It is a 'centre of lost opportunity' because its competencies are not globally leveraged and its potential rents are not properly appropriated.

Global Headquarters

Global headquarters complete the presentation of this typology. These centres concentrate in their hand most decisions, for most activities and for most subsidiaries. They correspond to the 'ethnocentric' MNC described by Perlmutter (Perlmutter, 1992). They are mainly present in the newly internationalised and highly centralised companies that keep most decisions in headquarters' hands. The tendency observed now, however, is that global headquarters are tending to disappear as more and more MNCs try to further decentralise their operations (Bartlett and Ghoshal, 1993). The central office of the French MNC, Bouygues, one of the largest construction companies in the world, fits that situation. This suggests that the global headquarters is characterised by a high domain and scope.

Table 7.1 summarises the typology of centres that is conceptually defined along the dimensions of scope and domain. Low-scope, low-domain centres are 'dormant centres'; low-scope, high-domain centres are 'strategic centres of excellence'; high-scope, low-domain centres are 'administrative centres; and high-scope, high-domain centres are 'global headquarters'.

Table 7.1 Typology of centres within MNCs

		Domain	
		Low	*High*
Scope	Low	*Dormant centres*	*Strategic centres of excellence*
	High	*Administrative centres*	*Global headquarters*

EMPIRICAL INVESTIGATION

Propositions

The purpose of this section is to test hypotheses regarding the relationships between the dimensions of influence, so as to validate the existence of different types of centres. The above discussion suggests that domain and scope are in conflict. It is hard for a centre to exert its influence over more and more subsidiaries and, at the same time, to extend the number of activities it manages on behalf of other subsidiaries. Hypothesis 1 follows from that analysis.

> Hypothesis 1: The scope and the domain of a centre are negatively associated.

It is hard to be excellent in multiple areas. Centres focused on a limited number of activities are more likely to develop a credible reputation of expertise. Credibility and expertise ease the delegation of the responsibility from subsidiaries to the centres that cultivate and manage activities for their group, so that the influence of SCEs on other affiliates should be deep As a corollary, coordination and control of a broad range of activities do not, in general, imply much depth of influence on the actual management of the activities. Depth of influence is also likely to be restrained by some resistance from affiliated companies. As a consequence, the administrative centre's influence on other affiliates should remain superficial. It follows from that discussion that the depth of a centre's influence is likely to be greater where it has a lower scope, while, as a corollary, a centre that develops domain should increase its depth of influence. Hence:

> Hypothesis 2: Scope and depth of influence are negatively associated.

> Hypothesis 3: Domain and depth of influence are positively associated.

Data Collection

In order to test these three hypotheses and to proceed with subsequent analyses, this chapter draws on a relational database of 662 relationships between centres from different MNCs and affiliated companies. The database provides information about each centre, affiliated companies within each group and about the relationships with each other. They have been collected in two large surveys, one addressed to centres and the other to the affiliated companies of each group so as to validate the information gathered from the centres.

The population of surveyed centres are Belgian coordination centres. These centres are entities of MNCs that are established according to Belgian Royal Decree 187. This Decree provides tax and financial advantages to multinationals that operate, from Belgium, activities such as cash management, funding of investments, netting, marketing, R&D and so on. To get accreditation, these MNCs must have a world-wide turnover of at least $350 million, possess a capital base of $35 million and operate in more than three countries outside Belgium. The Royal Decree states that coordination centres may develop only those activities that are exerted on behalf of other subsidiaries. That is, they cannot sell their activities outside their group. (This is known as the 'Intra Muros' legal requirement.) As at the end of 1996, more than 280 coordination centres were established in Belgium. This particular population of centres controls by design for three important aspects of influence that are relevant for this study:

- Since the law defines the activities that can be exerted by a coordination centre, centres are working in similar areas. This significantly reduces the sources of variance of influence due to the nature of activities (Woodward, 1958).
- Since all coordination centres operate from Belgium, the local environment is similar across firms. This reduces the possible variance of influence due to different environments (Lawrence and Lorsch, 1967).
- The research design also controls for the initial resource that can drive the extent of influence. Since, as a starting point, all coordination centres have access to the Belgian tax system, they can globally leverage their access, and that is not imitable by other subsidiaries in their organisations, not transferable and not tradable (Dierickx and Cool, 1989).

Also, all coordination centres were created after 1982, and 82 per cent of them between 1985 and 1990. This reduces the potential temporal distortion resulting from differences in date of establishment, since if centres were observed at development stages then they would significantly differ (Ring and Van de Ven, 1994; Van de Ven, 1992).

From a practical point of view, the survey was part of a large research project supported by the Federation of the Coordination Centres (FORUM 187), which facilitated the access to the study population. The survey was organised in May–August 1994, achieved a response rate of 54 per cent and investigated 581 variables. Since FORUM 187 covers about 95 per cent of existing centres, self-selection bias was not a major concern.

Measurement of Key Variables

Most questions were constructed on the Likert scale or summated rating scales. This method is a useful scientific instrument to evaluate questions of a subjective nature. Its robustness and reliability have been largely demonstrated in past research (Rossi *et al.*, 1982).

The Depth of Influence

The variable PARTPOW assesses the involvement of a centre in four postulated stages of decision for the management of activities: initiating, providing information, choosing the course of action, and implementing action (Hinings *et al.*, 1974). (The weight of the centre's influence was also measured (Hinings *et al.*, 1974). However, that (i) the correlation between that variable and PARTPOW is very high (0.49 with $\alpha = 0.0001$) and (ii) PARTPOW and WEIGHT demonstrate similar profile of association with other relevant variables, suggests that, in this specific research, they are but different indicators of the same underlying phenomenon. Hence, for the sake of simplicity, this chapter proceeds with only PARTPOW as the sole indicator of influence depth.) PARTPOW is a latent variable, the first principal component of a principal component analysis between the levels of the centre's involvement in each of these four stages (63 per cent of variance explained by the first factor).

The Breadth of Influence

The *domain* of influence refers to the number of units controlled (Kaplan 1964; Lachman 1989). In this research, the variable DOMAIN measures the ratio of the number of subsidiaries for which a centre operates over the total number of entities in its group This provides a criterion of comparison across centres that varies between 0 and 1. The *scope* refers to the number of areas of behaviour controlled (Hinings *et al.*, 1974, Kaplan 1964, Lachman 1989). With Forum 187, 28 activities were identified as potential areas for the development of the international influence of coordination centres. In this research, the variable SCOPE captures the number of areas in which a centre is active for other group entities among that list of 28 activities.

The analysis is conducted on the original database, and on each section of that database partitioned in four parts according to the types of centres (see Table 7.1). The median of scope and domain are the cutoff points to delineate the four types of centres. Since there is no cutting point where a centre suddenly changes its type, the procedure, as a first approach, is bound to be somewhat arbitrary. However, in this exploratory study, setting the cutting point at a level different from its 'true' value can still provide interesting insights.

Table 7.2 Correlation between the various dimensions of the influences of centres

GENERAL	DOMAIN	PARTPOW
SCOPE	−0, 25 [a]	−0, 27 [a]
PARTPOW	0, 34 [a]	
DORMANT	DOMAIN	PARTPOW
SCOPE	−0, 04 NS	−0, 11 NS
PARTPOW	−0, 10 NS	
GLOBAL	DOMAIN	PARTPOW
SCOPE	−0, 66 [a]	−0, 14 [c]
PARTPOW	0, 20 [b]	
ADMINISTRATIVE	DOMAIN	PARTPOW
SCOPE	−0, 06 NS	−0, 16 [b]
PARTPOW	−0, 19 [a]	
EXCELLENCE	DOMAIN	PARTPOW
SCOPE	−0, 25 [a]	−0, 29 [a]
PARTPOW	0, 59 [a]	

[a] = $A<0.0001$; [b] = $A<0.01$; [c] = $A<0.05$.

Results and Discussion

The top section of Table 7.2 shows that none of the hypotheses are rejected. This first result suggests that domain, scope and participation power provide relevant criteria to differentiate types of centres. The analysis conducted on the partitioned databases, however, shows interesting differences when the correlations are compared. The results pertaining to participation power show that the negative correlation with scope is invariant across the different groups. This confirms that centres have a hard time increasing their say in the decision-making process as they increase the number of activities in which they are involved.

With the exception of ACs, the results also suggest that as a centre increases its domain, it also increases its influence in the decision-making process. In that respect, the negative correlation between domain and participation power for ACs comes as a surprise. There is one possible explanation for that result. Since administrative centres coordinate many activities at a general level, they can control an increasing number of affiliated companies only at the expense of their lower involvement in the decision-making process and tend therefore to be more superficial.

Figure 7.1 Evolutionary paths of centres

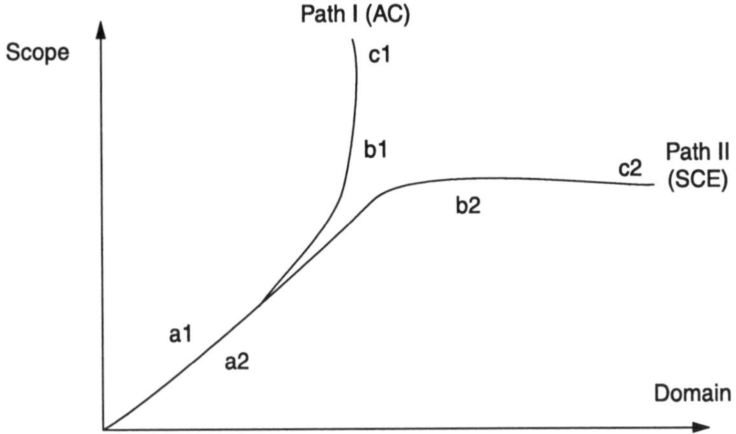

For dormant centres, all results are non-significant, indicating that there is no real tension between the development of any one dimension of influence. That a strong negative correlation shows up only for global headquarters suggests that there is a threshold where the development of domain is in tension with that of scope. In other words, these results bring up the interesting hypothesis that there may be two possible paths to develop an influential centre, as illustrated on Figure 7.1. Path I on this figure shows a centre that, at the early stage, develops simultaneously scope and domain (section a1 of path I). Such a centre is unfocused. As the centre matures, it reaches a point (b1) where it faces too many difficulties to increase the number of affiliates it is working with. This may be because, involved in too many activities, it lacks the credibility of a centre of excellence in order to convince more affiliates to collaborate with it. Here, it can develop its influence only by increasing the number of activities it manages for the companies it is already collaborating with (section c1 of path I). It is using these companies as a captive market to expand its influence (scope). Such a centre has the characteristics of an administrative centre, (ACs).

Path II in Figure 7.1 shows a centre that follows a direction similar to path I in the early stage, where it develops both domain and scope at the same time (section a2 of path II). This centre tends, however, to remain focused on a limited number of activities. As it matures, it reaches a point (b2) where it faces too many difficulties to increase the number of activities it is involved in without loosing the credibility as a centre of excellence that it needs to expand its domain further. At this point, the centre remains focused on a selection of activities to build up the credibility, expertise and reputation that it requires to expand its domain (section c2 of path II). Such a centre has the characteristics of a strategic centre of excellence (SCE).

This discussion suggests that the evolutionary path of centres will be completely different according to the growth strategy adopted in the early stage. This is, of course, but an interesting speculation, and needs to be confirmed by further research.

The absence of significant relationships for dormant centres may indicate that this category contains in reality different types of centres with different profiles. Centres that are not influential may be so for different reasons. It may be that they do not have the potential to become so, namely they do not master a key expertise to become a centre of excellence. It may be that subsidiary managers are not motivated to become influential, and have a local drive as opposed to global one (Prahalad and Doz, 1987). Alternatively, they are prevented by corporate managers from becoming so. This raises the important role of headquarters in favouring, or not favouring, the emergence of centres within the MNC. When the centre does not master any specific expertise, and can only become an administrative centre, then the decision of corporate management could be driven by the concern for adequate administrative structuring. In contrast, when the centre controls a key competence and is prevented from becoming a strategic centre of excellence that globally leverages a locally nurtured resource, then it is what is styled a 'centre of lost opportunities'. In this case, the role of corporate management is more questionable, because it prevents the extraction of all the potential rents of a resource

(Dierickx and Cool, 1989). It is also more likely that managements' attitude is driven by political reasons.

FURTHER STUDY OF ADMINISTRATIVE AND EXCELLENCE CENTRES

The paths presented in Figure 7.1 are opposed along the dimensions of scope and domain. The following analysis emphasises that scope and domain reveal the nature of the two major types of active centres, namely ACs and SCEs. The idea that there are two major distinct types of centres is indeed reinforced if additional data are analysed. In this section, some descriptive statistics and correlations collected in the survey are discussed to show that the distinction between SCEs and ACs is not only conceptually appealing but also empirically relevant. Statistical results confirm that there are two main strategies to develop an influential centre. On the one hand, centres that develop as SCEs operate for a major part of group companies, and tend to be strongly involved in the decision-making process of the focused activities they manage. On the other hand, centres that develop as ACs embrace and coordinate a broad range of activities for a limited number of affiliated companies, while they tend to be less involved in the decision-making process of the focused activities they manage.

Of course, understanding in detail the features of these strategies would require a fine-grained approach that could be achieved only by comparative clinical work. This section draws on the empirical results of the survey in order to characterise these strategies. Since previous results suggest a level of antagonism between developing a high-scope and a high-domain, this exercise is achieved by looking at Table 7.3, which shows the correlations between the variables SCOPE and DOMAIN and a selection of indicators measured in the survey. These indicators are grouped by eight themes.

Types of Headquarters

While the *raison d'être* of SCEs is the efficient management and leveraging of competencies, the purpose of ACs is coordina-

Table 7.3 Spearman correlation between descriptive variables and SCOPE and DOMAIN

LABEL	*MEANING*	*DOMAIN*	*SCOPE*
Types of headquarters			
REGHQ	Dummy variable for regional headquarters	–0.26***	0.20***
WWHQ	Dummy variable for world-wide headquarters	0.43***	–0.22***
(De)centralisation			
EASCENT	Easing centralisation of decision-making as centre contribution	NS	0.28***
EASDECEN	Easing decentralisation of decision-making as centre contribution	0.19***	NS
Structuring of the organisation			
OTHDIVIS	Affiliated companies in other divisions as barrier to initiation	–0.12**	0.20***
Resistance from other group companies			
RESAFCY [a]	Affiliated companies' resistance as barrier to cooperation	–0.19***	0.25***
RESHQCO	Headquarters resistance as barrier to cooperation	–0.25***	0.12**
FEARAFCY	Affiliated companies fear of losing relations with local community as barrier to cooperation	–0.18***	0.35***
RESHQINI	Headquarters as barrier to initiation	–0.21***	NS
PROBCONV [b]	Convincing affiliated companies as a key problem to handle for development	–0.28***	0.16***
Demonstration of competencies			
CONVAFCY	Convicing affiliated companies to keep coordination as barrier to move the centre abroad	–0.25***	NS

CONVHQ	Convincing headquarters to keep coordination as barrier to move the centre abroad	–0.16***	NS
KEEPTEAM[c]	Keeping the team of experts as barrier to moving the centre abroad	0.13**	–0.11**
LACKEXPR	Lack of coordination centre expertise as barrier to initiation	–0.14***	0.21***
LOCEFF[d]	Efficiency of the country as localisation factor	0.11**	NS
LOCGEOG[e]	Geography as localisation factor	–0.16***	NS
LOCLOBY[f]	Internal lobbies as localisation factor	NS	0.14***
Drive of fiscal opportunity			
FISCBAR[g]	Fiscal or legal issues as barrier to move the centre abroad	NS	0.12**
TAXADV	Providing tax advantages as centre contribution	NS	0.13**
Strategic choice of activities			
P_OUTSOUR	% of activities previously outsourced	0.11**	NS
Profile of personnel			
INPEROT	Rotation of personnel inside the centre	–0.19***	NS
OUTPEROT	Rotation of personnel between the centre and affiliated companies	–0.16***	0.17***
FUNCROT	Functional rotation of centre founder	–0.27***	0.24***
GEOROT	Geographical rotation of centre founder	–0.17***	0.18***
FONDTNR	Tenure of the centre's founder	–0.35***	NS
FONDSEN	Seniority of centre founder in the group	–0.32***	NS
Foundation of group			
FONDATE	Foundation date of the ultimate parent company	0.17***	–0.11**

Table 7.3 (*contd.*)

Spearman correlation between descriptive variables and scope and domain:
*** $=a<0.001$; ** $= a<0.01$; * $= a<0.05$; NS = not significant.

[a]RESAFCY is a latent variable expressing reasons coming from affiliated companies' resistance. It is the first principal component between the following indicators: (i) The centre faced too much resistance from affiliated companies' top management, (ii) affiliated companies were afraid of delegating activities, (iii) they did not understand the potential benefits of centralisation of activities and (iv) they were afraid of losing their independence (variance explained by the first factor = 75 per cent).
[b]PROBCONV is the first principal component between the following indicators for problems encountered: (i) To find allies in the group, to convince the ultimate parent company, and (ii) to convince headquarters or our direct parent company (variance explained by the first factor = 60 per cent).
[c]KEEPTEAM is the first principal component between the following indicators for problems to face in case of a move: (i) To find specialists and skilled people locally, (ii) to keep a team that is running well, and (iii) to train specialists and skilled people (variance explained by the first factor = 75 per cent). It is a latent variable for team skills related factors.
[d]LOCEFF is the first principal component between the following localisation factors: (i) The efficiency of the local finance community, (ii) the stability of the Belgian currency, and (iii) the efficiency of the Belgian financial markets (percentage of variance explained by the first factor = 70 per cent). It is a latent variable for efficiency related factors.
[e]LOCGEOG is the first principal component between the following localisation factors: (i) The central location of Belgium, (ii) the proximity with the EU authorities and (iii) the fact that Belgium being small is a neural choice compared to other bigger countries on the European market (variance explained by the first factor = 48 per cent). It is a latent variable for local opportunities related factors.
[f]LOCLOBY is the first principal component between the following localisation factors: (i) The influence of Belgian staff members at headquarters, (ii) the fact that top executives were posted in Belgium, and (iii) an existing presence of the group in Belgium (variance explained by the first factor = 63 per cent). It is a latent variable for management lobbying related factors.
[g]FISCBAR is the first principal component between the following indicators for problems to face in case of a move: (i) to find an equal legal stability and (ii) to find a status with similar legal/fiscal advantages (percentage of variance explained by the first factor = 68 per cent). It is a latent variable for fiscal or legal related factors.

tion and control. An administrative centre is a more generalist centre, likely to be associated with a high scope. These are, for instance, regional headquarters that control a broad range of activities managed by operational subsidiaries. This is suggested in Table 7.3 by the positive correlation between SCOPE and the dummy variable REGHQ indicating regional headquarters. Such control does not involve as much participation power in the decision-making process. Hence, administrative centres should have a lower weight and participation power than SCEs, as suggested by the negative correlation between these variables and SCOPE. This discussion suggests that there are two distinct types of centres and two separate avenues of growth; that is, developing scope or developing domain. The positive correlation between SCOPE and the dummy variable REGHQ (indicating regional headquarters) corroborates that high scope centres are administrative centres with the role of regional headquarters for the control of a broad range of activities managed by operational subsidiaries. In contrast, the negative correlation between the dummy variable WWHQ (indicating world-wide headquarters) and SCOPE suggests that low-scope centres are SCEs that globally leverage their competencies nurtured in focused areas and become the global headquarters of their group for the specific activities in which they excel.

(De)centralisation

The second interesting lesson of Table 7.3 concerns the centralisation/decentralisation issue. High-scope centres see one of their key contributions as 'easing the centralisation of decision-making in their group' (positive correlation between EASCENT and SCOPE) while high-domain centres consider, to the contrary, that easing the decentralisation of decision-making is one of their important added-value contributions (positive correlation between EASDECEN and DOMAIN). Thus, the coordination and control activities of administrative centres are driven by the concern of large groups to monitor and standardise a broad range of activities. The nature of this responsibility implies the reduction of the subsidiaries' autonomy in the management of these existing activities. So the development of administrative centres goes hand in hand with the increased centralisation of decision-making.

Instead, the 'SCE concept' builds on the idea that a subsidiary takes the global lead for the activities in which it masters the latest techniques. In other circumstances, this global lead would be taken by headquarters. This is the reason why SCEs associate their development with increased decentralisation since, in their case, it is the subsidiary, not head office, that takes the leadership In other words, SCEs will consider their greater involvement and responsibility in the management of focused activities as features of increased decentralisation within their group

Structuring of the Organisation

Table 7.3 also indicates that high-scope centres consider that affiliated companies belonging to other strategic entities or group divisions (positive correlation between SCOPE and OTHDIVIS) are a barrier to cooperation and to development. This association is negative for high-domain centres. These results suggest that high-scope centres are ACs that are finding it difficult to overcome such organisational barriers. In contrast, high-domain centres are centres of excellence that face fewer difficulties in overcoming these barriers, as suggested by the positive correlation between DOMAIN and the variable OTHDIVIS.

Resistance from Other Group Companies

The associations of SCOPE and DOMAIN with the items pertaining to barriers to cooperation provide other interesting insights. Barriers related to affiliated companies or headquarters attitudes are all negatively correlated with DOMAIN, but are positively correlated with SCOPE (see the variables RESAFCY, RESHQCO, FEARAFCY, and RESHQINI in Table 7.3). This pattern of association is similar for PROBCONV, which conveys the extent to which centres consider that convincing headquarters or affiliated companies to collaborate was a key problem to handle to enable their development. These results suggest that centres facing too much resistance from other subsidiaries opt for the extension of activities with those companies they are already working with. In other words, they develop scope because they face constraints in domain extension.

The Demonstration of Competencies

Developing an SCE supposes the ability to build up a strong reputation of expertise within the group. Centres developing too many activities are likely to lack the necessary reputation and credibility to convince affiliated companies. Some indications in the survey support the view that a centre's credibility and reputation is a critical issue in order to develop domain. For instance, the negative correlations between DOMAIN and the items 'convincing affiliated companies or headquarters as barrier to move the centre abroad' (CONVAFCY and CONVHQ) suggest that high-domain centres do not consider that headquarters or affiliated companies would object had they to move abroad. This indicates that they are confident about their stability and that their role as a centre does not tend to be questioned. The only problem that seems to worry high-domain centres in case of a move is to keep a team of experts that is running well (positive correlation with KEEPTEAM). This association contrasts the one with SCOPE that is negative. While mastering and keeping expertise is a key issue for SCEs moving abroad, it does not affect the ability of ACs to deliver their services, because their managers are more generalist and more likely to be interchangeable as compared to the experts of SCEs.

Additional evidence supports that high domain centres master special expertise. While the lack of expertise (LACKEXPR) as a reason for non-cooperating is negatively associated with SCOPE, it is not related with DOMAIN. This suggests that the lack of expertise is less of an issue for high scope centres to develop their influence, since in effect they do not need it. A look at the location factors provides indications in the same direction. Location factors related with efficiency issues (LOCEFF) are positively associated with DOMAIN, while more opportunistic localisation factors (LOCGEOG) are negatively associated with that variable. Also, internal lobbies (LOCLOBY), as drivers of localisation, are positively associated with SCOPE but not with DOMAIN. This suggests that internal lobbying plays an important role in the development of high-scope centres, while it is hard for centres to develop a high domain without efficiency-related arguments.

The Drive of the Fiscal Opportunity

The positive correlation between SCOPE and the items 'fiscal or legal issue as barrier to move the centre abroad' (FISCBAR) and 'providing tax advantages as centre's contribution' (TAX-ADV) corroborates the hypothesis that high-scope centres are more opportunistic to the extent that tax incentives provided by their special fiscal status are one of their driving forces.

Profile of Personnel

Other associations in Table 7.3 are worth mentioning. The negative correlation between DOMAIN and rotation of personnel (INPEROT and OUTPEROT) suggests that there tends to be little rotation in high-domain centres, while the positive correlation with SCOPE suggests the contrary for high-scope centres. As observed, managers in centres of excellence are highly skilled and specialised. The interest in rotating such specialists in the group is marginal. Groups are better to concentrate specialists in the centres in order to master a critical mass of the latest techniques and accordingly develop the overall expertise of the group (Zander and Håkanson, 1986). In administrative centres, however, the rationale is quite different. Rotation generates contacts that support control and coordination of activities (Doz and Prahalad, 1981; Edström and Galbraith, 1977; Otterbeck, 1981).

A look at the profile of the centre's founder corroborates the differentiated role of rotation. Functional and geographical rotation of the centre founder (FUNCROT and GEOROT) is positively correlated with SCOPE, while its association with DOMAIN is negative. In SCEs managers are more likely to be experts or specialists. Experts are less likely to rotate in a group than generalists. Also, if an expert rotated functionally or geographically, they would lack the necessary credibility *as* an expert to be trusted by affiliated companies. In ACs the needs are different. Managers who rotate a lot are more likely to be aware of affiliated companies needs and to identify potential areas of development (Gresov and Stephens, 1993). Rotation also contributes to building up ties that may constitute open doors for exchange and thus aid development. It is likely to set favourable conditions to encourage trust and contacts with affiliated companies, and hence favour the broadening of scope with those affiliated companies with which founders are well connected (Larson, 1991, 1992).

The negative correlation between DOMAIN and tenure and the seniority of the centre's founder (FONDSEN and FONDTENR) reveals another interesting insight. A reasonable prediction for this association would have been the opposite. High-tenure managers are better connected, well known in the group, probably respected and more likely to deal with subtle influences and political processes. These managers are well informed and know perfectly the routines and informal rules of their organisation. It should follow that such highly connected and respected managers are more likely to be aware of entrepreneurial opportunities to develop the centre (Burt, 1992). Results support the other view, that the more tenure a manager has, the more likely he has established his position and is committed to existing organisational routines (Salancik, 1977). It follows that tenure inhibits the bringing about of changes in the organisation and the development of new centres (Gresov and Stephens, 1993). Instead, younger managers may use every opportunity to develop centres and build up their careers based on them.

Foundation of the Group

A final association is worth mentioning. DOMAIN and foundation date of the group (ultimate parent company) are positively correlated (FONDATE), indicating that younger groups are more likely to nurture the development of SCEs. This suggests that, in recent groups, it is easier to reconfigure and organise so as to fully exploit competencies, while in older groups, inertia, commitment to the *status quo*, and the ossification of structures may prevent or inhibit the development of high-domain centres.

These results suggest that groups who able to benefit from the same fiscal opportunity of the Belgian coordination centre status, implement two different types of strategies, which lead to the development of two different types of centres. Some centres have taken the avenue of administrative centres, and have developed as many activities as they can in order to maximise the fiscal benefits. This avenue is preferred by groups that have had a pre-existing presence in Belgium, as suggested by the positive correlation with LOCLOBY. These centres operate, to a large extent, pure transfer of activities, and used the fiscal opportunity to reduce their operating costs, thus significantly affecting the actual management of the activities. Since these centres have a broad scope, they have had a hard time extending their domain, because they lack the reputation and the expertise to convince other affiliated companies to cooperate with them. These centres are also at the mercy of the fiscal advantages provided by their special status. They are exposed to the risk of losing their role as a centre if they have to move abroad, as is suggested by the positive association between SCOPE and FISCBAR.

Other centres have taken the route of becoming SCEs. The scenario for these centres seeking high domain development is somewhat different. Centre managers exploit the fiscal opportunity to build up and internally propose a specific project. They use the fiscal status as a good reason to develop new activities for their group and exploit that opportunity to build up real expertise in focused areas. The positive association between DOMAIN and the variable measuring the proportion of activities that were previously outsourced or non-existent (P_OUTSOUR) suggests that the strategy of high-domain centres is to develop very specific activities that were not already managed in the centre. In that way, they are able to create a good reputation, nurture new competencies and convince other affiliated companies to expand domain without too much resistance. As a consequence, the fiscal justification, as the initial impetus of the centre, progressively gives way to the competence justification. That is, the centre is recognised and its role becomes firmly established in its MNC. Its exposure to fiscal volatility is consequently reduced, as suggested by the absence of association between DOMAIN and FISCBAR and the negative ones between DOMAIN and the item 'convincing affiliated companies (CONVAFCY) or headquarters to keep the activities as barrier to move the centre abroad' (CONVHQ).

CONCLUSIONS

The objective of this chapter has been to identify criteria to characterise centres within MNCs. In that respect, the discussion has demonstrated that dimensions of influence are not only theoretically sound but also empirically relevant. The variables DOMAIN and SCOPE convey the idea of breath of influence, PARTPOW that of depth. Results also suggest that centres characterised by a high scope are more likely to be of different types than SCEs and driven by a different development logic. In particular, 'influence' is a key variable to characterise centres of excellence as 'strategic', because those subsidiaries that happen to control a key expertise or resource without actually leveraging these by influencing other subsidiaries are not 'strategic' but simply 'centres of lost opportunities'. In other words, to be strategic a centre of excellence must be influential within its group In that respect, the research raises an interesting hypothesis regarding the important role that corporate management could exert to block the growth of some *dormant* centres that could possibly become more influential within their group While this is not a key issue for potential administrative centres, it becomes a strategic one when corporate management prevents the leveraging of local resources of potential excellence centres.

As far as the role of subsidiary managers is concerned, the research suggests two antagonistic strategies if they want to develop cross-border influence over other subsidiaries. The first is to engage in a lot of activities in relationship with other subsidiaries. This means a lower involvement in the decision-making process related to the management of these activities. The other way consists of specialising in a limited number of activities and trying to operate for many group companies. This implies a higher involvement in the decision-making process pertaining to activities managed on behalf of other companies. This suggests that subsidiary managers willing to develop such a strategy will be better off by not running after too many horses. Focus, specialisation and expertise seem to be the preferable means to gaining credibility within the centre of excellence and to increasing its influence outside.

SCEs and ACs manifest, consequently, different patterns and strategies of development and display contrasting characteristics. High-domain centres of excellence are those with a team of highly trained specialists mastering the latest managerial or technological techniques. These centres tend to specialise in a limited and focused number of activities. They build up reputation on their expertise in order to extend their domain and operate for a large number of affiliated companies. These centres are *strategic centres of excellence* (SCEs). They are instruments to leverage competencies. Examples of such centres are the Hewlett-Packard office in Grenoble, France, which manages the personal computer business of its group, and the Jacob Suchard centre for protection of patents and trademarks located in Zug, Switzerland, away from headquarters. High-scope centres tend to manage a broad array of activities for a limited number of affiliated companies. These centres are only moderately involved in the decision-making process of the activities with which they are dealing. They are entities that control and coordinate activities for a geographical or strategic division. They are *administrative centres* (ACs). Mitsubishi Electric in London, which controls most activities of its group subsidiaries within Europe, is a good example of one.

References

Bacharach, S.B. and E.J. Lawler (1980) *Power and Politics in Organizations: the Social Psychology of Conflict, Coalitions and Bargaining*, 1st edn, Social and Behavioral Science Series, San Francisco: Jossey-Bass.

Barham, K. (1992) 'Overseas Assets', *International Management*, 47 (9), 56–9.

Bartlett, C.A. (1988) *Procter and Gamble Europe: Vizir Launch*, Harvard Business School, Case 384–139.

Bartlett, C.A. and S. Ghoshal (1986) 'Tap Your Subsidiaries for Global Reach', *Harvard Business Review*, 6, November–December, 87–94.
Bartlett, C.A. and S. Ghoshal (1989) *Managing Across Borders: The Transnational Solution*, Boston, MA: Harvard Business School Press.
Bartlett, C.A. and S. Ghoshal (1993) 'Beyond the M-Form: Toward the Managerial Theory of the Firm', *Strategic Management Journal*, 14, 23–46.
Borrus, A., W. Zellner and W.J. Holstein (1990) 'The Stateless Corporation', *International Business Week*, 14 May, 98–105.
Burt, R.S. (1977) 'Power in a Social Topology', *Social Science Research*, 6, 1–83.
Burt, R.S. (1982) *Toward a Structural Theory of Action*, New York: Academy Press.
Burt, R.S. (1992) *Structural Holes: The Social Structure of Competition*, Cambridge, Mass.: Harvard University Press.
Dierickx, I. and K. Cool (1989) 'Asset Stock Accumulation and the Sustainability of Competitive Advantage', *Management Science*, 1, 1504–514.
Doz, Y. and C.K. Prahalad (1981), 'Headquarters' Influence and Strategic Control in MNC', *Sloan Management Review*, Fall, 15–29.
Edström, A. and J.R. Galbraith (1977) 'Transfer of Managers as a Coordination and Control Strategy in Multinational Organizations', *Administrative Science Quarterly*, 22 (June), 248–258.
Ghoshal, S. and C.A. Bartlett (1990) 'The Multinational Corporation as an Interorganizational Network', *Academy of Management Review*, 15 (4), 603–25.
Ghoshal, S. and N. Nohria (1989) 'Internal Differentiation Within Multinational Corporations', *Strategic Management Journal*, 10 (4), 323–37.
Gresov, C. and C. Stephens (1993) 'The Context of Interunit Influence Attempts', *Administrative Science Quarterly*, 38, June, 252–76.
Hedlund, G. and J. Ridderstrale (1992) *Toward a Theory of the Self-Renewing MNC*, Working Paper presented at Insead Doctoral Consortium.
Herbert, T.T. (1984), 'Strategy and Multinational Organization Structure: An Interorganizational Relationships Perspective', *Academy of Management Review*, 9 (2), 259–71.
Hinings, R.C., D.J. Hickson, J.M., Pennings and R.E. Schneck (1974) 'Structural conditions of intraorganizational power', *Administrative Science Quarterly*, 19 (1), 22–44.
Kaplan, A. (ed.) (1964) *Power in Perspective. Power and Conflicts in Organizations.* London: Tavistock.
Lachman, R. (1989) 'Power from What? A Re-examination of its relationships with Structural Conditions', *Administrative Science Quarterly*, 34 (2), 231–51.
Larson, A. (1991) 'Partner Networks: Leveraging External Ties to Improve Entrepreneurial Performance', *Journal of Business Venturing*, 6, 173–78.
Larson, A. (1992) 'Network Dyads in Entrepreneurial Settings: A Study of the Governance of Exchange Relations', *Administrative Science Quarterly*, 37, 76–104.
Lasserre, P. (1993) *The strategic roles of regional headquarters in the Asia Pacific region*, Fontainebleau, France: Insead Euro-Asia Centre.
Lawrence, P.M. and J. Lorsch (1967) *Organization and Environment*, Boston, Mass.: Harvard Business School.

Lehrer, M. and K. Asakawa (1995) *Regional Management and Regional Headquarters in Europe: A Comparison of American and Japanese MNCs*, Fontainebleau, France: Insead Working Paper 95/01/SM.

Lorenzoni, G. and C. Baden-Fuller (1993)'Creating a Strategic Centre to Manage a Web of Partners, working paper presented at the Strategic Management Society's 14th Annual International Conference, Hautes Études Commerciales Jouy-en-Josas, France, September.

Maljers, F.A. (1992) 'Inside Unilever: The Evolving Transnational Company', *Harvard Business Review*, September–October, 46–51.

Miller, R. (1993), 'Recherche, développement et globalisation: le cas de l'industrie automobile', *Revue Française de Gestion* , Septembre–Octobre, 53–63.

Nohria, N. and R.G. Eccles (eds) (1992) *Networks and Organizations: Structure, Form, and Action*, Boston, Mass.: Harvard Business School Press.

Otterbeck, L. (ed.) (1981) *The Management of Headquarters–Subsidiaries Relationships in Multinational Corporations*, London: Biddles Limited.

Perlmutter, H.V. (1992) 'The Tortuous Evolution of the Multinational Corporation', in C.A. Bartlett and S. Ghoshal (eds), *Transnational Management: Text, Cases, and Readings in Cross-Border Management*, Boston, Mass.: Irwin, 93–103.

Porter, M.E. (1985) *Competitive Advantage: Creating and Sustaining Superior Performance*, New York: Free Press.

Prahalad, C.K. and Y.L. Doz. (1987) *The Multinational Mission: Balancing Local Demands and Global Vision*, New York: Free Press.

Ring, P.S. and A.H. Van de Ven (1994) 'Developmental Processes of Co-operative Interorganizational Relationships', *Academy of Management Review*, 19 (1), 90–118.

Rossi, P.H., J.D. Wright and A.B. Anderson (1982) *Handbook of Survey Research*, London: Academic Press.

Rumelt, R. (1984) 'Toward a Strategic Theory of the Firm', in R. Lamb (ed.), *Competitive Strategic Management*, Englewood Cliffs, NJ: Prentice-Hall, 556–70.

Rumelt, R. (1987) 'Theory, Strategy and Entrepreneurship', in D. Teece (ed.), *Strategy and Organization for Industrial Innovation and Renewal*, Cambridge, Mass.: Ballinger, 137–58.

Salancik, G.R. (1977) 'Commitment and the Control of Organizational Behavior and Belief', in B.M. Staw and G.R. Salancik (eds), *New Directions in Organizational Behavior*, Chicago: St Clair, 1–54.

Salancik, R. and J. Pfeffer (1978) *The External Control of Organizations: A Resource Dependence Perspective*, New York: Harper & Row.

Stopford, J.M. and L.T. Wells Jr. (1972) *Managing the Multinational Enterprise*, New York: Basic Books.

Tannenbaum, A.S. (1968) *Control in Organizations*, New York: McGraw-Hill.

Van de Ven, A.H. (1992) 'Suggestions for Studying Strategy Process: A Research Note', *Strategic Management Journal* 13, 169–88.

Woodward, J. (1958) *Management and Technology*, London: HMSO.

Zander, U. and L. Håkanson (1986) *Managing International R&D*, Stockholm: Mekan.

8 Centres of Excellence in the International Firm

Luciano Fratocchi and Ulf Holm

INTRODUCTION

In the last decade there has been increasing recognition that the international firm (in the strict sense of one with operations in both national and international markets) is organised as a heterogeneous entity built up of subunits with specific operative responsibilities and specific interrelated roles (Hedlund, 1986; Bartlett and Ghoshal, 1989; Nohria and Ghoshal, 1994; Malnight, 1996). Thus, certain subsidiaries within the international firm are regarded as being especially competent in one or several functional areas. For instance, because of its competence with a particular product, a foreign subsidiary can become globally responsible for production. Similarly, another subsidiary can be specialised in the development of a product, while a third can have responsibility for marketing and international sales. Having one or several operational competences – interrelated with the operational roles of other units of the firm – the specific subsidiary can become a strategic 'partner' of the firm's headquarters (Bartlett and Ghoshal, 1989), with potential impact on strategic decisions (Astley and Zajac, 1990; Ghoshal and Bartlett, 1990).

Labels for and definitions of such subsidiaries vary between authors, and can refer to different attributes of business. A widespread label is 'world product mandate' (Crookell and Caliendo, 1980; Poynter and Rugman, 1982), which refers to the autonomy and responsibility that a subsidiary has received for developing and selling a certain product on a world-wide basis. Other labels are 'strategic leader' (Bartlett and Ghoshal, 1989); 'centre of excellence' (Roth and Morrison, 1990); 'centre of competence' (Porter *et al.*, 1991); 'business centre'

(Lorenz, 1994); 'strategic centre' (Lorenzoni and Baden-Fuller, 1995) and 'strategic centre of excellence' (Surlemont, 1994). These concepts refer to the important position that a subsidiary has obtained in the international firm with regard to its particular competence or business position in the market. Another label is 'integrated player', which refers to the role a subsidiary has in the firm with regard to generating and distributing important business information (Gupta and Govindarajan, 1991, 1994).

One explicit, and sometimes implicit, implication in this literature is that the firm's international expansion into new markets increases the potential for new centres in the firm. At least two distinctions can be identified in the discussion: one has to do with the creation of foreign centres as a consequence of deliberate design or a choice made by headquarters. Thus, when the firm becomes geographically dispersed, there is a need to create new foreign centres and integrate them with the current structure of the firm (Hedlund, 1986; Snow *et al.*, 1992) A second distinction is that the foreign subsidiaries develop in a more or less unpredictable way and that some of them become centres, usually in a relatively mature stage of the firm's internationalisation process (Forsgren *et al.*, 1992).

However, independently of their origin, an important notion is that the existence of foreign centres implies a change in the driving forces of the firm's development, away from the home-based headquarters and in favour of foreign subsidiaries. Usually, the internationalisation of the firm is considered to be a matter of expansion away from the home country, with the parent firm or home-based units in focus (Johanson and Vahlne, 1977). Thus, if foreign centres are common, these authors believe that they represent an important dynamic aspect in the internationalisation of the firm.

In this chapter the focus is on centres of excellence (CoEs), that is, foreign subsidiaries that have become especially competent in one or several operational functions upon which other units in the firm are dependent for their activities. Although their importance has been pointed out (Surlemont, 1994), there is still relatively little empirical research on the existence of CoEs in international firms.

The main purpose of the chapter is, accordingly, to study the organisation of the international firm and identify the existence of foreign CoEs. In the next section the meaning of a CoE is discussed and related to the internationalisation process of the firm. This concept is then operationalised and applied to a sample of international firms. The sample and collection of data are described and the findings presented concerning the frequency of CoEs in 22 international Swedish firms. Two kinds of CoEs are investigated: *single-functional* and *multi-functional*. The chapter ends with concluding remarks.

THE CENTRE OF EXCELLENCE

The internationalisation of the firm is often described as being a relatively slow process (Johanson and Vahlne, 1977, 1990; Bilkey and Tesar, 1977). The main blocking factor for rapid expansion abroad has to do with the firm's lack of international business experience. For that reason, the starting up of large subsidiaries in unknown markets would mean a high risk to the firm. Instead, firms tend to start with relatively small steps abroad, often in neighbouring countries with a low 'psychic distance' from the home country (Johanson and Weidersheim-Paul, 1975; Nordström, 1991). And accordingly, the firm's limited formation of early greenfield establishments is often manifested through contacts with foreign agents or by starting up foreign sales subsidiaries, rather than by starting up large foreign production subsidiaries. Therefore, in this early stage of the firm's internationalisation, the foreign subsidiaries have generally a moderate capacity with regard to their level of activities. Their financial resources, technological and business competence are controlled and distributed to a great extent by the firm's headquarters. At this stage, the parent firm is usually the CoE of the firm to a great extent, while the subsidiaries are mainly local and operative, with a low degree of impact on the strategic development (Forsgren, 1989).

However, as the internationalisation process continues, the management relationship between the headquarters and the subsidiaries changes. In some cases subsidiaries start to adjust products received from the parent firm, and adapt them to the specific needs of the local market. Eventually, some subsidiaries become less dependent on headquarters for competence and more able to carry out their activities on the basis of the competence within their own organisations. In this way, the parent firm and the country of origin become less vital to the survival of the subsidiary. One conclusion is that when subsidiaries grow in their respective markets, the local business environments also become important for the subsidiary's development of competence (Porter *et al.*, 1991).

The business environment of an actor is sometimes described as a structure of business relationships with its customers, suppliers and other market actors. The development of competence of specific types has much to do with the depth in which an actor – a subsidiary – engages in such business relationships (Holm *et al.*, 1995). From a process perspective on a firm's internationalisation, a subsidiary's extensive or increasing interactions with local partners mean that headquarters declines as a centre relative to the subsidiary, because operational activities get configured around the subsidiary to a greater extent (Ghoshal and Bartlett, 1990). Thus, it is likely that the subsidiary develops certain kinds of operational competence in this business setting (Amit and Schoemaker, 1993; Grant, 1991; Mahoney and Pandian, 1992; Peteraf, 1993; Teece *et al.*, 1990). Further, to the extent that other units of the firm become dependent on the subsidiary, it will be the predominant link for the use of this competence within the firm. In fact, the more important the competence of the subsidiary, generated in its local network of business relationships, the more important the subsidiary will be for the whole international firm (Forsgren *et al.*, 1997).

Consider, for example, a subsidiary with exceptional competence in technological development. This was, for example, the case when the technology of the 'AXE-system' was developed. In that case, the Australian subsidiary of a Swedish telephone company played a crucial role since this technology was created in cooperation with a local customer. The knowledge – the excellence – developed and spread by the subsidiary made it a CoE and a new field of business originated from it. Today, the AXE-system has become a core business of the whole firm (Bartlett and Ghoshal, 1989).

So, in a way, the emergence of a new foreign CoE means a creation of a new role within the firm, more or less analogous to the role of the parent firm. In the same way as the parent firm, a foreign CoE has developed a capability that is needed by other units of the firm. Thus, a CoE has both strategic importance and an operative role outside its own undertakings. Therefore, to the extent that other units of the firm benefit from the subsidiary's capability, it should be considered to be a CoE. This can, among other things, embrace the ability to produce, develop and/or sell products in a more excellent or efficient way than other units of the firm are able to do. Being dependent on this ability means that the activities of others would be harmed if they no longer had access to the competence of the CoE (Yamagishi *et al.*, 1988).

As a consequence of the above, a CoE includes generating knowledge and carrying out activities which other firm units depend upon. Here a CoE is defined as a foreign subsidiary in the international firm that masters a high operational competence which other units of the firm depend for their activities. If this competence relates to a single function – such as marketing or production – it is called the subsidiary a *single-functional* CoE. If the competence relates to several functions within a single subsidiary, it is called a *multi-functional* CoE. This can be compared with what is called 'functional specialisation' between subsidiaries and/or within subsidiaries with world product mandate responsibilities (Birkinshaw and Morrison, 1995; see also the discussion by Forsgren and Pedersen in Chapter 6).

Even when acquiring foreign companies, there is at least one reason why it would take a long time before an international firm contains several foreign CoEs. This has to do with the fact that other units of the firm must first recognise a subsidiary as a CoE, which means the development of dependence between the subsidiary and the other units. Behind such a recognition lies a historical process in which the subsidiary's activities become increasingly linked to the activities of other units of the firm. This does not happen overnight. But the more that other units of a firm interact with the subsidiary the more they will become dependent on its activities if they are performed the high level of competence they desire. Sometimes, an effect of this dependence is that the other units may adapt their technology, organisations and business related to the functions of the

CoE, in order to coordinate their own activities and increase their own efficiency (Hallén *et al.*, 1991). This increases the dependence even further. It is therefore expected that before a subsidiary is recognised as a CoE it must have activity links with some other units of the firm and carry out its activities with a high level of competence over some time. Isolated occasions or situations where only a few units in the firm have a relatively limited dependence on the subsidiary should not be sufficient.

In conclusion, with regard to the internationalisation of the firm, the expectation is that the number of foreign CoEs will vary between firms. Of course, this has much to do with the size of the firm and number of foreign subsidiaries, but it also has to do with the possibilities of becoming interlinked with the activities of other units of the firm. It is likely that subsidiaries that must expand, owing to economics of scale, will develop large production facilities and create great technological competence when doing so. On this basis, they will expand into several markets and their competence is, *ceteris paribus*, more likely to be linked to the activities of other units of the firm than if they were only locally operating.

In general, it is expected that the level of internationalisation of the firm will be positively related to the number of foreign CoEs simply because it is, *ceteris paribus*, more likely that there will be foreign CoEs in the foreign organisation when the level of internationalisation is high compared with when it is low.

> Proposition 1: In firms with a high level of internationalisation, the number of single- and multi-functional CoEs is higher in comparison with firms with low level of internationalisation.

However, there is reason to expect that subsidiaries differ as to when they become CoEs depending on the function in focus. Owing to the lack of international business experience there is a risk involved in establishing, or acquiring, foreign subsidiaries that comprise activities with high costs. As the firm becomes more international, and larger, the international experience increases and the relative risk of establishing or incorporating a subsidiary abroad will decrease. Foreign investments in marketing and sales subsidiaries with CoE characteristics can be assumed to be associated with lower risk in comparison with production subsidiaries with CoE characteristics. Therefore, with regard to the level of internationalisation, it is to be expected that the proportion of marketing CoEs will be higher among firms with a low level of internationalisation in comparison with the proportion of production CoEs:

> Proposition 2a: In firms with a low level of internationalisation, the *proportion* of foreign marketing CoEs is higher than the *proportion* of foreign production CoEs.

Similarly, with regard to the level of internationalisation, the expectation is that the proportion of multi-functional CoEs will be higher among firms with a high level of internationalisation in comparison with the proportion of single-functional CoEs. If a multi-functional CoE is an acquisition then the relative risk of investment is lower when the internationalisation is high. Further, if the multi-functional CoE originates from being a relatively small greenfield establishment then it is not exposed to high risk in the same way, but such a foreign subsidiary is likely to have developed over a long time before reaching a CoE character. Therefore, even if the CoEs of a firm are acquired, or are the result of a long-term development, it is not likely that the firm will contain several multi-functional CoEs until the level of internationalisation is high:

> Proposition 2b: In firms with high internationalisation, the *proportion* of foreign multi-functional CoEs is higher in comparison with the *proportion* of single-functional CoEs.

In Proposition 2a the expectation is that marketing CoEs will occur before production CoEs as a firm undergoes internationalisation, and that they are associated with a lower risk to the firm. Therefore, it is to be expected that marketing CoEs will have reached 'further out' into geographical areas with high psychic distance (Johanson and Weidersheim-Paul, 1975; Nordström 1991) in comparison with production CoEs:

> Proposition 3: In countries with a high psychic distance, the *proportion* of foreign marketing CoEs is higher in comparison with the *proportion* of foreign production CoEs.

METHODS

In data collection an attempt was made to identify subsidiaries that fulfil a number of criteria associated with the above definition of a CoE. The search was for two kinds of CoE: single-functional and multi-functional. Note that the data originate from an earlier study of Swedish international firms in 1989. To identify foreign CoEs, information from that study has been used. A discussion of the sample and collection of data and of indicators chosen for the identification of foreign CoEs now follows.

The Sample and Collection of Data

The subsidiaries selected were, first, legally owned by the firm to at least 50 per cent. Thus, minority-owned units were not included, partly because their operations can be assumed to be more closely linked to a firm other than the one focused on, and partly because the parent firm may have only limited knowledge about those subsidiaries in which they have a low degree of ownership. Second, only foreign subsidiaries were studied. It is true that Swedish subsidiaries may have CoE characteristics, but they are left out because by the definition used here a CoE involves foreign subsidiaries only.

Further, since it was the intention to investigate as many international Swedish firms as possible, a task which includes more than a thousand subsidiaries, the study aimed to make it possible to collect data with the help of the parent firms in Sweden. But because firms are organised in variety of different ways, with different numbers of hierarchical levels and with the business organised in various formal and informal structures, it was especially important to identify the relevant people to interview. For instance, a very common organisational structure among international Swedish firms is the multi-divisional form. In this structure, each division consists of a number of subsidiaries with operational functions.

A further principle was that the sample should contain Swedish industrial firms with either a large proportion or a large number of employees abroad. The intention was to include as many of these international firms in Swedish industry as possible. All in all, 22 firms allowed access. The number of employees abroad in these firms, distributed in more than a thousand subsidiaries, was approximately 330 000 in 1989. This represented about 80 per cent of the total activities abroad of Swedish industry during that period (Swedenborg *et al.*, 1988). (See Appendix 8A concerning the main activities of the firms, their size and degree of employment abroad.) Among the largest firms, only three did not participate in the study, one being engaged in merging with another firm, and the other two preoccupied with large reorganisations and unable to find the necessary time for interviews.

The first problem encountered in collecting data was getting access to the firms, and the next was meeting respondents adequately qualified to answer questions about the international business of the firms. This procedure was arranged through contacts and discussions with a number of people at the firms' headquarters. Personal interviews were then conducted with managers mostly from information, administration and finance departments. In a few cases people at the top executive level were interviewed. In divisionalised firms this often meant interviewing two or three different managers before getting reliable information. Sometimes, when knowledge about the foreign subsidiaries' activities was limited, a recommendation was given to contact somebody at the divisional level. However, this was done only in a few cases because of the lack of time and the distance to some of the divisions abroad. Besides, the number of interviews would have grown considerably.

Less data were obtained from the firms' annual reports. Most came from interviews, though not without difficulties in some cases, over whether certain subsidiaries were to be classified as CoEs or not. This problem is understandable, given the size, complexity and international distribution of many firms, and the personal consultation between interviewer and respondent was therefore very important in solving it.

Indicators of Foreign CoEs

One important aspect of collecting data was avoiding the uncontrolled variations that could arise if managers in the different firms decided themselves whether subsidiaries were CoEs or not. Therefore, before approaching the firms some general measurements of functional CoEs were constructed that could apply to all industrial firms in the sample. This was important in order to compare the frequency of CoEs between firms in the analysis.

A number of subsidiary functions could have been included in the study. Principally, functions such as production, development, sales and marketing, purchasing and financing, could have been chosen for the analysis of the existence of single-functional CoEs. Then, a next step could have been to investigate the number of cases in which subsidiaries fulfil two or more CoE functions within the same organisation and so indentify multi-functional CoEs. Since the original data were collected with a slightly different purpose in 1989, all the data necessary for such an extensive analysis were not available. Therefore, this study of foreign CoEs will be restricted to two functions, namely production together with development and marketing together with sales. These two functions are traditional in firms, and they were well known to the responding managers, which is important for the quality of the data.

For both production and marketing three general aspects were measured to identify a subsidiary as a CoE. The first aspect is *specialisation*, which often is put forward in discussing centres in the international firm. The more specialised the roles of subsidiaries in the firm, the more they become interdependent as they need to link with each other and, for example, exchange information and products. Thus, it is to be expected that a subsidiary that is specialised in production or marketing related to a certain product will create a dependence among other units of the firm that relate to the same product (Birkinshaw and Morrison, 1995; Bartlett and Ghoshal, 1989; Hedlund, 1986).

A second aspect, the *internationalisation* of production or marketing related to a certain product, results in the subsidiary becoming larger and more important, not only for its own expansion, but also for the expansion of the whole firm. But internationalisation is also a matter of producing and selling to, or sharing business and technological competence with, other units of the firm in other countries (Andersson and Johanson, 1997). Thus, internationalisation of a subsidiary can reflect expansion on international markets, as well as linking business and competence with units of the firm in different countries.

A third central aspect when defining subsidiaries with important roles is whether they are responsible internationally for a product's development, production and/or marketing (Wolf, 1986; Rugman and Douglas, 1986; Beige and Stewart, 1986; Bonin and Perron, 1986).

These three aspects, namely *specialisation*, *internationalisation* and responsibility for *development*, were all included when formulating questions as to whether or not the firms had any production and marketing CoEs. To collect data, both a questionnaire and personal interviews were used. In the interviews, managers were asked to go through all the foreign subsidiaries of the firm. For each and every one of the subsidiaries they were asked to indicate if they fulfilled the criteria for production and marketing CoE as defined in the following terms.

First, to be identified in the study as a production CoE, a foreign subsidiary had to produce a certain product or line of products and conduct technological development for its own purpose and for the use of other units in the firm. This development could be conducted by the subsidiary itself, or done in cooperation with partners other than the parent firm. The production had to be exported to at least five countries other than the national market, and constitute at least 25 per cent of the subsidiary's turnover.

Second, to be identified as a marketing CoE, a foreign subsidiary had to be responsible for marketing at least 50 per cent of the product turnover within one division or business area. These products had to be sold and marketed in at least five countries other than the national market. The subsidiary had also to be responsible for market planning, the distribution channels and market research.

Third, to be identified as a multi-functional CoE, a foreign subsidiary had to combine the characteristics of both a production CoE and a marketing CoE within the legal borders of its own organisation.

Naturally, the fact that the number of countries was five was important when it came to the number of CoEs in the firm. This was for the reason that it needed to be higher than one or two to avoid domestic oriented operations with the risk of only cross-border business. At the same time, the number had not to be too high in view of the fact that some continents consist of relatively few countries. North America was, for that reason, excluded from the five-country rule. Subsidiaries in this region were instead given an alternative opportunity to meet with the measures formulated. In cases where they did not comply with the five-country rule, they were regarded as CoEs if they were responsible for at least 10 per cent of the business volume in their division.

EMPIRICAL FINDINGS

In the empirical investigation, the numbers of CoEs among firms were first identified. Then, in accordance with Propositions 1, 2a and 2b, the proportion of CoEs were investigated with regard to the level of internationalisation of firms. Finally, in accordance with Proposition 3, the proportions of CoEs were examined with regard to five geographical areas, representing increasing levels of psychic distance from Sweden.

Table 8.1 Number of CoEs in 22 Swedish international firms

Firm	*Production CoE*	*Marketing CoE*	*Multi-functional CoE*	*Firm*	*Production CoE*	*Marketing CoE*	*Multi-functional CoE*
AGA	0	0	0	Gambro	8	4	3
Alfa Laval	29	1	0	Modo	0	1	0
ASSI	0	0	0	NCB	1	0	0
Astra	0	4	0	Nobel	10	0	0
Atlas Copco	8	1	1	Perstorp	7	2	2
Dynapac	6	4	3	Pharmacia	3	2	2
Electrolux	65	1	1	Saab	3	2	2
Ericsson	5	5	5	Sandvik	8	3	0
ESAB	5	1	1	SCA	3	3	1
Esselte	9	6	2	SKF	26	1	1
Euroc	3	0	0	Volvo	7	0	0

Total numbers: production CoEs = 206; marketing CoEs = 41; multi-functional CoEs = 24.

As shown in Table 8.1, there were 206 production CoEs, distributed between 18 of the 22 firms. But there was a major variation in their occurrence. At one extreme are the classical Swedish engineering firms Electrolux, SKF and Alfa Laval. Together they account for almost 60 per cent of the total number of production CoEs. At the other extreme, with no or very few production CoEs are AGA, Astra, ASSI, MoDo and NCB. Although highly internationalised, and with a large number of subsidiaries, AGA only operates locally in each country. The production and transportation of its product, gas, cannot reach further than 300 kilometres and the number of CoEs is limited for that reason. Astra is a pharmaceutical firm and has most of its products produced and developed in Sweden and therefore has no production CoEs. The three other cases, ASSI, MoDo and NCB, are firms within the forest industry. Their business is characterised either by large exports of pulp and paper from Sweden or by local production and sales of paper products, such as container boards or boxes, and therefore they have few or no foreign CoEs. An exception within this industry is SCA, with three foreign production CoEs. This firm has diversified more into 'semi'-related paper products and, for that reason, has been able to develop more CoEs. Another interesting case is Volvo, which has only 29 per cent of its employees abroad (see Appendix 8.A), yet still has seven foreign production CoEs. This implies that their foreign investments in production reach a CoE level at an early stage of the firm's internationalisation. It can be explained by the fact that producing cars and trucks is strongly related to economies of scale, and accordingly there is a need for large production and efficient production technology, as well as for large volumes that can be distributed to several country markets.

There were 41 marketing CoEs within 16 of the 22 firms. Evidently, marketing CoEs are less common than production ones. But the distribution of marketing CoEs is slightly different. In 14 out the 18 firms with production CoEs, evidence is found of marketing CoEs, although not necessarily within the same foreign subsidiaries. Thus, there are 4 cases in which firms have production CoEs without having marketing CoEs, and two cases of firms having marketing CoEs without having a production CoE. The most prominent example of the latter is

Astra. Its production and development of pharmaceutical products in Sweden is marketed and sold by four CoEs. Further, CoEs were somewhat more common in 5 firms, Astra (4), Dynapac (4), Ericsson (5), Esselte (6) and Gambro (4). Together they account for 56 per cent of the 41 marketing CoEs. Another notion is that marketing CoEs are somewhat more evenly distributed among firms compared with production ones.

The study found 24 multi-functional CoEs distributed between 12 of the 22 firms. Eleven of these CoEs were identified in three firms; Ericsson (5), Dynapac (3) and Gambro (3). Somewhat surprisingly, none of these are firms with a very high number of production CoEs. The other 13 CoEs were found spread between 9 firms, while 10 of the firms had no multi-functional CoEs at all.

To test Propositions 1, 2a and 2b, the distribution of CoEs with regard to firms' level of internationalisation was investigated. The firms were divided into two groups, one with less and the other with more internationalisation than average. The average internationalisation was 57.6 per cent, measured as the foreign share of employees.

Table 8.2 Proportion of CoEs and level of internationalisation

	Firms in two groups according to level of internationalisation[a]	
	Group 1 (n = 11)	*Group 2 (n = 11)*
Type of CoEs	*Proportion of COEs*	*Proportion of CoEs*
Production CoEs ($n = 206$)	20%	80%
Marketing CoEs ($n = 41$)	46%	54%
Multi-functional CoEs ($n = 24$)	50%	50%

[a] Group 1 = below average internationalisation; Group 2 = above average internationalisation.

Evidently, there is a striking difference between the proportion of production CoEs and marketing CoEs. For the 206 production

CoEs, the group of firms with a high level of internationalisation accounts for 80 per cent of CoEs. Thus there seems to be a positive connection between the level of internationalisation and the relative number of production CoEs. Marketing CoEs have 46 per cent and 54 per cent in the respective groups. Thus they are almost equally distributed with regard to level of internationalisation. Further, although the vast majority of production CoEs, and slightly more than half of the marketing ones, are represented in the group with high internationalisation, the multi-functional CoEs are equally represented.

All in all, then, the analysis of the level of internationalisation of firms and the proportion of CoEs, in accordance with Proposition 1, shows a split picture. While there is support for the proportion in relation to production CoEs, it cannot be said that the internationalisation level matters for the occurrence of marketing CoEs or multi-functional CoEs, at least not in measuring internationalisation in terms of foreign share of firms' employees.

In Proposition 2a, it was stated that the proportion of marketing CoEs is higher in the early stages of internationalisation in comparison with production CoEs. This is supported by Table 8.2, in which 46 per cent of the marketing CoEs are distributed in firms with an internationalisation level below average, while there are only 20 per cent of the production CoEs in the same group. No support was found for Proposition 2b, because the proportion of multi-functional CoEs is not higher in a late stage of internationalisation. Instead, when the level of internationalisation is high, this proportion is less than for both production and marketing CoEs.

Next, to test Proposition 3, the distribution of CoEs with respect to psychic distance was investigated. In accordance with the indexes of increasing psychic distance, from the studies of Johanson and Weidersheim-Paul (1975) and Nordström (1991), the countries were divided into five groups. The first group contains Nordic countries (excluding Sweden), the second is Europe 1 (Germany, Great Britain, Belgium, Holland and Luxembourg), the third is North America (USA and Canada), fourth comes Europe 2 (all the other European countries) and fifth the rest of the world. Table 8.3 depicts the distribution of CoEs according to this procedure.

Table 8.3 Proportion of CoEs according to geographic areas with increasing psychic distance (%)

CoEs	*Proportion of CoEs*				
	Nordic Countries	*Europe 1*	*North America*	*Europe 2*	*Rest of the world*
Production CoE ($n = 206$)	9	29	20	34	8
Marketing CoE ($n = 41$)	5	29	27	17	22
Multi-functional CoE ($n = 24$)	8	29	29	21	13

Again, as shown by Table 8.3, the proportion of production and marketing CoEs differs to some extent. However, what is common for all CoEs is that they are relatively infrequent in the Nordic countries and, when distance increases to Europe 1, the CoEs are equally distributed (29 per cent). But for North America it emerges that the proportion of multi-functional CoEs and marketing CoEs is higher than for production CoEs. Then, in the next region, Europe 2, the pattern is reversed, and the proportion of production CoEs (34 per cent) is significantly higher.

In the group with the highest psychic distance from Sweden, the rest of the world, the relative distribution of marketing CoEs is higher (22 per cent) in comparison with production and multi-functional CoEs. It seems that production and multi-functional CoEs are more strongly represented in the relatively well-industrialised countries at a moderate distance from Sweden, while marketing CoEs can more easily be located at a greater distance. Thus, to some extent, Proposition 3 is supported, because the proportion of marketing CoEs is higher in geographical areas with the highest psychic distance from Sweden. But this conclusion is negated partly by the fact that production CoEs have the highest proportion in countries with the second highest distance: 'Europe 2'.

Another notion is that multi-functional CoEs are distributed in a similar way to marketing CoEs with the exception of their relatively low representation (13 per cent) in the most distant group of countries. Although there is no proposition for multi-functional CoEs with regard to psychic distance, it was found that the proportion with which they occur is highest among the subsidiaries in North America. Thus, it seems that this region tends to create subsidiaries with a CoE character for both production and marketing.

DISCUSSION AND CONCLUDING REMARKS

In this chapter the occurrence of foreign CoEs in Swedish international firms has been investigated. It can be clearly stated that production CoEs are a common phenomenon. They exist in all industries, although they seem to be less frequent in traditional exporting firms that base their production on raw material obtained in the home country. An example of this is provided by the firms within the forest industry. The engineering firms Alfa Laval, Electrolux and SKF can truly be regarded as being structured by production CoEs. Thus, the technological development and the firms' international expansion both depend highly on their foreign subsidiaries.

The relatively limited occurrence of marketing CoEs may have to do with the fact that marketing and sales are often local phenomena. Thus, there is a need for close contact with customers, and this restricts geographically the number of marketing CoEs among firms. The occurrence of multi-functional CoEs, here measured as foreign subsidiaries that combine both production and marketing CoEs, is even less. Still, they do exist. Thus, in Ericsson, Dynapac and Gambro there is evidence of foreign subsidiaries that are highly important for development and international business expansion.

Investigating the occurrence of CoEs is of course dependent on the measures used. In this study, managers in the parent firm were allowed to decide whether subsidiaries fulfilled the definitions of production and marketing CoE. One alternative could have been to approach the subsidiary managers directly instead. It is likely that this would change the picture of the number of CoEs in the firms, especially in large or highly international firms in which the knowledge of respondents in the parent firm can be assumed to be limited.

Also, one important aspect is that subsidiaries are CoEs partly because of the activity links to other units of the firm. The dependence on such links can be measured in more detail than in this study. For instance, measures on a specific relational level can be used in order to identify which and to what extent other specific sister units are dependent on a focal subsidiary. A future research issue would be to investigate the importance of specific business relationships for the emergence of CoEs. One specific topic in this area is to study the impact of subsidiary relationships with external market actors versus the impact of relationships with sister units within the international firm.

Thus, in this conception of the international firm, the subsidiary business relationships play an important role for the long-term strategy. But from a managerial point of view, this conception means that control by headquarters is limited. When the international firm consists of several CoEs of different kinds, each and every one with their own structure of specific business relationships, headquarters will not easily control the development of the firm. To maintain some control, the most important issue for the home-based headquarters is to continuously update their knowledge about the content and development of the business relationships of the most important subsidiaries in the firm, the CoEs.

References

Amit, R. and P.L.H. Schoemaker (1993) 'Strategic Assets and Organizational Rent', *Strategic Management Journal*, 14, 33–46.

Andersson U. and J. Johanson (1997) 'International Business Enterprise', in I. Björkman and M. Forsgren (eds), *The Nature of the International Firm – Nordic Contributions to International Business Research*, Copenhagen Business School Press, Handelshojskolens Forlag, 33–49.

Astley, W.G. and E.J. Zajac (1990) 'Beyond Dyadic Exchange: Functional Interdependence and Sub-Unit Power', *Organization Studies*, 11 (4), 481–501.

Bartlett, C.A. and S. Ghoshal (1989) *Managing Across Borders*, Cambridge, Mass.: Harvard Business Press.

Beige, C.E. and J.K. Stewart (1986) 'Industrial Adjustments and World Product Mandates: A Role for Public Policy', in H. Etemad and L.S. Séguin Delude (eds), *Managing the Multinational Subsidiary. Response to Environmental Changes and to Host Nation R&D Policies*, London: Croom Helm, 23–46.

Bilkey, W.J. and G. Tesar (1977) 'The Export Behaviour of Smaller Wisconsin Manufacturing Firms', *Journal of International Business Studies*, 8 (Spring/Summer), 93–8.

Birkinshaw, J.M. and A.J. Morrison (1995) 'Configurations of Strategy and Structure in Subsidiaries of Multinational Corporations', *Journal of International Business Studies*, (4), 729–53.

Bonin, B. and B. Perron (1986) 'World Product Mandate and Firms Operating in Quebec', in H. Etemad and L.S. Séguin Delude (eds), *Managing the Multinational Subsidiary. Response to Environmental Changes and to Host Nation R&D Policies*, London: Croom Helm, 161–76.

Crookell, H. and J. Caliendo (1980) 'International Competitiveness and the Structure of Secondary Industry in Canada', *Business Quarterly*, 45 (3), 58–64.

Forsgren, M. (1989) *Managing the Internationalization Process: The Swedish Case*, London: Routledge.

Forsgren, M., U. Holm and J. Johanson (1992) 'Internationalisation of the Second Degree – The Emergence of European Based Centres in Swedish International Firms', in S. Young (ed), *Europe and the Multinationals; Issues and Responses for the 1990s*, London: Elgar, 235–53.

Forsgren, M., U. Holm and P. Thilenius (1997) 'Network Infusion in the Multinational Corporation – Business Relationships and Subsidiary Influence', in I. Björkman and M. Forsgren (eds), *The Nature of the International Firm*, Handelshojskolens Forlag, Copenhagen: Copenhagen Business School Press, 475–94.

Ghoshal, S. and C. A. Bartlett (1990) 'The Multinational Corporation as an Interorganizational Network', *Academy of Management Review*, 15 (4), 603–25.

Gupta, A.K. and V. Govindarajan (1991) 'Knowledge Flows and the Structure of Control within Multinational Corporations', *Academy of Management Review*, 16 (4), 768–92.

Gupta, A.A. and V. Govindarajan (1994) 'Organizing Knowledge Flows within MNCs', *International Business Review*, 3 (4), 443–57.

Grant, R. (1991) 'The Resource-Based Theory of Competitive Advantage. Implications for Strategy Formulation', *California Management Review*, Spring, 114–35.

Hallén, L., J. Johanson and N. Seyed-Mohamed (1991) 'Interfirm Adaptation in Business Relationships', *Journal of Marketing*, 55, April, 29–37.

Holm, U., J. Johanson and P Thilenius (1995) 'Headquarters' Knowledge of Subsidiary Network Contexts in the Multinational Corporation', *International Studies of Management and Organization*, 25 (1–2), 97–120.

Hedlund G. (1986) 'The Hypermodern MNC – A Heterarchy?', *Human Resource Management*, 25 (1), 9–35.

Johanson, J. and J.E. Vahlne (1977) 'The Internationalization Process of the Firm – A Model of Knowledge Development and Increasing Foreign Market Commitment', *Journal of International Business Studies*, 8 (Spring/Summer), 23–32.

Johanson, J. and J.-E. Vahlne (1990) 'The Mechanism of Internationalization', *International Marketing Review*, 7 (4), 11–24.

Johanson, J. and F. Weidersheim-Paul (1975) 'The Internationalization of the Firm – Four Swedish Cases', *Journal of Management Studies*, 12, 305–22.

Lorenz, C. (1994) 'Cross Border Victory, National Causality', *Financial Times*, 6 May.

Lorenzoni, G. and C. Baden-Fuller (1995) 'Creating a Strategic Centre to Manage a Web of Partners', *California Management Review*, 37 (3), 146–63.

Mahoney, J.T. and R. Pandian (1992) 'The Resource-Based View Within the Conversation of Strategic Management', *Strategic Management Review*, 13, 363–80.

Malnight, T.W. (1996) 'The Transition from Decentralized to Network-Based MNC Structures: An Evolutionary Perspective', *Journal of International Business Studies*, 27 (1) 43–65.

Nohria, N. and S. Ghoshal (1994) 'Differentiated Fit and Shared Value: Alternative for Managing Headquarters-Subsidiary Relations', *Strategic Management Journal*, 15, 491–502.

Nordström, K.A. (1991) *The Internationalization Process of the Firm – Searching for New Patterns and Explanations*, Institute of International Business, Stockholm School of Economics.

Peteraf, M.A. (1993) 'The Cornerstones of Competitive Advantage: A Resource-Based View', *Strategic Management Journal*, 14, 179–91.

Poynter, T.A. and A.M. Rugman (1982) 'World Product Mandates: How Will Multinationals Respond?', *Business Quarterly*, 46 (3), 54–61.

Porter, M.E., Ö. Sölvell and I. Zander (1991) *Advantage Sweden*, Stockholm: Nordstedts Juridikförlag.

Roth, K. and A.J. Morrison (1990) 'An Empirical Analysis of the Integration-Responsiveness Framework in the Global Industries', *Journal of International Business Studies*, 21 (4), 541–64.

Rugman, A.M. and S. Douglas (1986) 'The Strategic Management of Multinationals and World Product Mandating', in H. Etemad and L.S. Séguin Delude (eds), *Managing the Multinational Subsidiary. Response to Environmental Changes and to Host Nation R&D Policies*, London: Croom Helm, 90–102.

Snow, C. C., R.E. Miles and H.J. Coleman Jr (1992) 'Managing 21st Century Network Organizations', *Organizational Dynamics*, 20, Winter, 5–19.

Surlemont, B. (1994) 'The Development of Strategic Centres of Excellence (SCE) in Multinational Corporations (MNCs): the Role of Organizational Context', paper presented at the Strategic Management Society's 14th Annual International Conference, Jouy-en-Josas, France, September.

Swedenborg, B., G. Johansson-Grahn and M. Kinnwall (1988) *Den Svenska Industrins Utlandsinvesteringar 1960–1986*, Stockholm: Industrins Utredingsinstitut.

Teece, D., G. Pisano and A. Shuen (1990) 'Firm Capabilities, Resources and the Concept of Strategy', Consortium on Competitiveness & Cooperation, working paper no. 90–8, University of California.

Wolf, B.M. (1986) 'World Product Mandates and Trade', in H. Etemad and L.S. Séguin Delude (eds), *Managing the Multinational Subsidiary. Response to Environmental Changes and to Host Nation R&D Policies*, London: Croom Helm, 207–19.

Yamagishi, T., M. Gillmore and K. Cook (1988) 'Network Connections and the Distribution of Power in Exchange Networks', *American Journal of Sociology*, 93, 833–51.

APPENDIX 8.A THE FIRMS STUDIED: TURNOVER, NUMBER OF EMPLOYEES AND MAIN ACTIVITIES IN 1989[a]

		Number of employees			
Firms	*Turnover*	*Total*	*Foreign*	*Proportion*	*Main activities*
AGA	9.805	13 501	10 801	80%	Gas, gas supplies
Alfa Laval	12.401	17 203	12 042	70%	Separators, farm machinery
ASSI	6.814	8 063	3 785	47%	Pulp, paper, paper products
Astra	6.278	6 981	3 770	54%	Pharmaceuticals
Atlas Copco	12.812	19 207	14 998	78%	Pneumatic drills, compressors
Dynapac	1.434	2 040	1 469	72%	Building machinery
Electrolux	73.960	148 214	117 089	79%	White goods, vacuum cleaners
Ericsson	31.297	67 910	33 276	49%	Tel. stations, exchanges equipmt
ESAB	4.550	5 712	3 770	66%	Welding equipment
Esselte	14.404	19 393	14 000	72%	Office equipment, printing
Euroc	9.403	8 012	4 086	51%	Cement, isolators
Gambro	2.853	3 748	2 998	80%	Dialyses, hospital equipment
MoDo	19.532	16 976	3 565	21%	Pulp, paper
NCB	4.014	3 743	2 845	76%	Pulp, paper
Nobel	21.328	22 040	6 612	30%	Defence materials, chemical prod.
Perstorp	5.146	6 012	2 946	49%	Chemical products, building products
Pharmacia	6.694	9 654	4 441	46%	Pharmaceuticals
Saab	42.448	48 400	9 680	20%	Cars, trucks, buses, aeroplanes
Sandvik	17.440	26 008	15 865	61%	Hard metal products, drills, saws
SCA	20 850	21 148	10 574	50%	Paper and allied products
SKF	21.248	43 416	38 206	88%	Roller bearings
Volvo	96.639	78 764	22 833	29%	Cars, trucks, buses

[a] Turnover in MSEK.

Part III
Corporate Process and Subsidiary Development

9 Using Technology as a Path to Subsidiary Development

William G. Egelhoff, Liam Gorman and Stephen McCormick

INTRODUCTION

Subsidiary development deals with the evolution and growth of foreign subsidiaries after they are established, or after initial foreign direct investment has occurred (Birkinshaw and Hood, 1997). Unlike the initial foreign direct investment decision, which necessarily is a HQ decision, subsequent subsidiary development decisions are open to both HQ and subsidiary influence. This chapter is primarily concerned with how subsidiaries attempt to influence their own development, and how they use technology as a path to further such development. Based on recent research in Irish subsidiaries, the view taken is that Irish subsidiaries are increasingly using technology to further subsidiary development within multinational corporations (MNCs).

Technology's rise to prominence in this case seems to have multiple causes. First, the traditional advantages of Irish subsidiaries, namely lower labour costs and tax preferences, have been waning as the Irish standard of living rises and the logic for tax preferences becomes stronger for nations other than for Ireland. Second, a good deal of first-class technology has been transferred into Ireland over the past decade, and the Irish infrastructure (universities and government research grants) increasingly supports local technology development capabilities. Foreign direct investment in Ireland has had to be globally competitive, because the local market tends to be small and most of the output is export oriented. Foreign direct investment that cannot be globally competitive in Ireland has little rationale for staying there. Hence, there is a growing desire on the part of many Irish subsidiaries to substitute more complex, technology-based advantages for the traditional low-cost advantages of the past.

This study examined technology development and strategy in sixteen Irish MNC subsidiaries. This chapter reports primarily on how Irish subsidiaries are developing technology-based advantages and using them to further develop or extend the strategic domain of the subsidiary within the MNC. Naturally, firms vary considerably in the extent to which they are doing this, and the interest in this study is more in understanding the nature and implications of these differences than in explaining why some subsidiaries are aggressively seeking technology-based advantages, while others are not. The next section reviews the literature associated with both subsidiary development and technology development and transfer in foreign subsidiaries. It uses this background as a framework for examining technology-based subsidiary development. Subsequent sections describe the research design, identify and describe three different levels of technology-based subsidiary development among the sample companies, and attempt to provide some preliminary conceptualisation for the most salient characteristics of technology-based subsidiary development.

LITERATURE REVIEW AND CONCEPTUAL FRAMEWORK

Given the subject, there are two literatures that need to be considered. The first deals with subsidiary development, and the second with technology development and transfer in MNCs. Subsidiary development is the subject of this book, and Chapter 1 has already presented a broad review of the existing literature. The key concepts borrowed from this literature in this context are: HQ assignments of subsidiary mission and resources, the company context or broader company environment within which subsidiary development occurs, subsidiary initiatives to extend mission and resources (Birkinshaw, 1997), and the manifestations or results of subsidiary development.

There is some debate as to whether HQ assignments or subsidiary initiatives exert the greater influence over subsidiary evolution. Empirical evidence seems to support the importance of both (Birkinshaw and Hood, 1997). Company context measures the growth and profitability of a company, and reflects the resources with which a company can provide a subsidiary (technology, investment capital, and demand for a subsidiary's output are the most important to Irish subsidiaries). The manifestations of subsidiary development are largely viewed in terms of the roles or mandates that subsidiaries can earn or capture within a company (Bartlett and Ghoshal, 1989; Birkinshaw *et al.*, 1998).

The traditional view has been that technology was developed largely in the home country (or some other central point) and then transferred, infrequently, and with various lags, to foreign subsidiaries (Behrman and Fischer, 1980; Cheng and Bolton, 1993), which faced the real problem of how to absorb and implement it locally.This may still be an accurate description for some companies, but the subsidiary's role in leading-edge technology companies has changed a lot (Gupta and Govindarajan, 1991; Hedlund and Rolander, 1990). Technology transfer is much more frequent. In some subsidiaries it is almost an ongoing activity. Increasingly the technology being transferred is the latest technology, rather than one with which the company has substantial experience. This necessitates locating more technology development capability in foreign subsidiaries. In this new environment, subsidiaries also transfer technology back to the parent and to other foreign subsidiaries,and engage in more collaborative technology development projects. As a result, specific subsidiaries often become specialised centres of knowledge for a technology (Ghoshal and Nohria, 1989). This is often associated with world mandates and centres of excellence. Clearly, it is this new view of technology in foreign subsidiaries that supports a model of technology-based subsidiary development.

The key technology concept that interacts with subsidiary development is the 'unique technical capability' that subsidiaries can develop and then leverage for purposes of furthering subsidiary development. There is growing empirical evidence that subsidiaries do possess unique technical capabilities in MNCs and that such capabilities are frequently the result of subsidiary initiatives (Ghoshal and Bartlett, 1988). This suggests that such unique technical capabilities probably mediate the causal relationship between technology-based subsidiary initiatives and the resultant manifestations of subsidiary development. These concepts create the conceptual framework that we want to use to measure and evaluate technology-based efforts at subsidiary development.

RESEARCH DESIGN

Semi-structured interviews were conducted with technology development managers in sixteen Irish MNC subsidiaries, which contained manufacturing and some technology development activity. On average, the interviews lasted about two hours per subsidiary and covered most aspects of technology development going on in the subsidiary, along with some contextual information. All of the subsidiaries had previously participated in a survey study, and data from this study allowed us to select firms where we knew some technology development or transfer was going on. Thus, the sample is representative, not of the population of Irish subsidiaries, but of the subpopulation that participates in some exchange of technical knowledge with other parts of the company. The content of the interviews varied, depending on the nature of technology development and transfer. The objective was to capture a full and hopefully rich picture of whatever technology development was going on in a subsidiary.

All of the interviews were taped and then written up soon afterwards.The research method resembled that of grounded research (Glaser and Strauss, 1967; Eisenhardt, 1989), where data collection and evaluation are intertwined and inform each other. This is appropriate methodology for an exploratory study that seeks to establish some early understanding and conceptualisation about technology-based subsidiary initiatives and the phenomenon of subsidiary development.

FINDINGS

When the sixteen sample subsidiaries were analysed in terms of the subsidiary initiatives being undertaken, the following three categories of subsidiary development emerged:

1. *Aggressive subsidiary development.* Initiatives are typically associated with the original development and exploitation of some unique technical capability in a subsidiary; they lead to a subsidiary becoming a recognised centre of excellence or obtaining a regional or global mandate for certain products or activities; they seek to directly set or influence the direction of subsidiary strategy.
2. *Incremental subsidiary development.* Initiatives are typically associated with the extension and routine development of subsidiary technical capability; they typically extend the subsidiary's position as a product centre; they seek to further advance or improve a subsidiary's strategy, but do not significantly change or set the direction of subsidiary strategy.
3. *Status quo subsidiary development.* Initiatives are typically operational and lie within the existing strategy of the subsidiary; they implement existing strategy, without changing it.

Five subsidiaries showed signs of aggressive subsidiary development. Another four showed incremental subsidiary development, and the remaining seven fell into the *status quo* category. The following subsections describe subsidiary development within the first two categories and attempt to understand what drives development and how development varies.

Aggressive Subsidiary Development

Of the five subsidiaries that pursued aggressive subsidiary development, two were in the pharmaceutical industry (P1 and P2) and three were in the electronics industry (E1, E2, and E3). The following paragraphs describe for each subsidiary the salient HQ assignments, company contexts, subsidiary initiatives, unique technical capabilities, and manifestations of subsidiary development. After this data has been presented, it is analysed and an attempt is made to draw some conclusions.

Subsidiary P1

This engages in the manufacture of bulk pharmaceuticals for a leading global pharmaceutical company. It possesses a relatively new plant, with modular, multi-purpose design. This mission and resource base were assigned to it by HQ. They provide the subsidiary with a unique technical capability, the flexibility to readily configure the plant for a wide variety of products. This is a capability not possessed by most of the other bulk manufacturing plants in the company. The company context has also been favourable to P1. Parent company research has produced a strong, sustained stream of new product technology that has driven strong company growth. From its inception, P1 has developed a strong technical staff of chemists and chemical engineers and a reputation for proficiency in transferring in new technology, improving processes, and solving technical problems.

Several years ago, P1 embarked on a major subsidiary initiative. It proposed and received HQ approval to build a small-scale production line (midway between a pilot line and a full-scale production line). This subsidiary initiative was justified by the subsidiary's technical capability,and track record, and the logic behind the proposal. The new facility allowed the subsidiary to economically manufacture low-volume products, which meant that it could transfer in new product technology (and its associated process technology) before full-scale commercial production was required or justified. In theory, this early transfer of new technology from R&D to manufacturing should reduce the time pressure associated with ordinary transfer and facilitate working out all the transfer and scale-up issues more carefully and thoroughly. More important than this technical benefit, however, has been the economic advantage the subsidiary has in attracting new products early and anchoring them to the site for subsequent scale-up. In order to maximise economies of scale, pharmaceutical companies are increasingly producing a bulk chemical at a single site, and P1's unique capability to economically produce both low and high volumes of a compound is a distinct subsidiary advantage. This and the manufacturing flexibility (a result of HQ assignment) have allowed the subsidiary to attract and produce more of the company's new products than any other site, and a major facilities expansion was recently approved.

Another potential subsidiary initiative was also discernible. The subsidiary formally transferred an engineer to the HQ process development department to work on a new technology, that was over a year away from transfer. While personnel overlap several months before transfer is common in the industry, this engineer actually became an integral part of the process development team and strongly influenced the process technology being developed (through his direct knowledge of manufacturing constraints and frequent communication with colleagues in the subsidiary). When the technology was ready, he became director of the transfer team (and subsequently resumed his career with the subsidiary).

If this practice becomes more frequent (as the subsidiary technical director intends), it could be viewed as another example of backward integration by the subsidiary. Thus, subsidiary initiatives appear to be successfully extending the subsidiary's domain horizontally (through a wide and growing range of products) and vertically (through the earlier transfer of new technology and more upstream participation in the development of new technology).

Subsidiary P2

This also engages in the manufacture of bulk pharmaceuticals for a leading global pharmaceutical company. The chemical processes it uses are unique in the company, and the products it manufactures cannot be made elsewhere. The subsidiary's global mandate for these processes was assigned to it by HQ. The wider company context has also been favourable to the subsidiary. Parent research has produced a strong, sustained stream of new product technology, which has provided new products and growing demand for the subsidiary. Like P1, P2 has also developed a strong technical staff and a reputation for proficiency in transferring in new technology, improving processes, and solving technical problems.

Some years ago the subsidiary requested and received approval for a new research facility and pilot plant. As with P1, this was justified by the subsidiary's track record and the recognised technical abilities of the staff. This subsidiary initiative has significantly strengthened the subsidiary's capability to solve technical problems and improve processes. As a result, the subsidiary has been transferring in new technology at an earlier stage of development, and debugging and improving the technology in the subsidiary.

This vertical extension, or backward integration, of the subsidiary domain into earlier stages of process technology development (in this case, the key manifestation of subsidiary development) may become increasingly important to P2. A new plant with the same technology as P2 is now being built elsewhere in the company. The new location will offer tax benefits greater than Ireland. P2 is providing a high level of technical assistance and technology transfer to the new sister plant (a HQ assignment). While P2 is losing its exclusive mandate for a certain technology, it will probably be able to remain the company's centre of excellence for this technology (a consequence of the earlier subsidiary initiative). It will probably be advantageous for the company to continue to transfer most new product and process technologies to P2, which can receive them early and improve them. P2 might then transfer more mature products and technologies to the new site.

Subsidiary E1

This is part of a global telecommunications equipment company and is principally engaged in technology development. The evolution of the subsidiary into its present domain has been a lengthy one, driven by many subsidiary initiatives. The company initially set up a local Irish subsidiary to sell equipment to the local telephone company. Some years later, the local subsidiary and government convinced the company to set up a local factory, which assembled mechanical switches for the local market and for export. In 1979, Ireland became one of the first countries to purchase an all digital telecommunications system. To support this shift, the subsidiary set up a training centre for digital systems. From its inception, the subsidiary management intended this to be a global business. This subsidiary initiative led to the early development of leading-edge digital systems training capabilities in the subsidiary. Today, this business has grown into one the largest of the company's global training centres.

Shortly after the training centre was established, the subsidiary developed a second initiative to extend its domain. It proposed and received approval to set up a software development group, the first outside the parent country. While modest at first, this initiative extended the subsidiary's domain vertically into the technology development area, where it aggressively grew its software development capabilities. When manufacturing was subsequently discontinued in the subsidiary, E1 was largely a technology development and training business serving global customers. During the late 1980s, another subsidiary initiative appeared. E1 took on important roles in maintaining older technologies, when the parent company decided to move these out of the home country. While none of the old technology roles exist today, they further developed the subsidiary's track record and reputation, and E1 was successful in converting them into new roles associated with new technologies. A couple of years ago, when the parent company decided to further decentralise technology development, E1 made a bid to take responsibility for a major subsystem of an important product line. This initiative was successful in further extending the subsidiary's domain when it obtained a global mandate for planning and maintaining the technology of this major subsystem. The justification for this latest manifestation of subsidiary development was the unique software capabilities of the subsidiary and its impressive track record. As was the case for the previous two companies, E1's company context was extremely favourable. The parent company emerged as a technology leader, with strong, sustained growth.

Subsidiary E2

This engages in a speciality niche of an industrial electronics industry and contains the European design, manufacturing, and marketing operations of the company. This European mandate is the HQ assignment to the subsidiary. The company context is quite different from the previous cases, in that E2 is not necessarily dependent on the rest of the company for its demand or technology inputs. The company has relatively similar businesses and operations in the USA, Europe and the Far East. While there is an increasing effort being made to exchange business and technology across areas, each area stands largely on its own. The subsidiary and company face significant competition, but are specialists in their niche and have been able to grow with it.

Some years ago, E2 installed the first surface mount technology in the company. This was an important subsidiary initiative, since it provided new design and manufacturing flexibility, and increased product differentiation. E2 has become the company centre of excellence for surface mount technology, doing some manufacturing for other regions and advising others on the technology. It is currently involved in another subsidiary initiative in this area, the acquisition of a fully automated surface mount line. This initiative was justified by the subsidiary's previous success with this technology. It will provide the subsidiary with leading edge surface mount technology and enhanced flexible manufacturing capability. Subsidiary development will proceed further along its present trajectory, and E2 will be the company's most flexible and competitive manufacturing site for low- to medium-volume products. As the company moves toward a global manufacturing strategy, E2 is clearly positioning itself to manufacture low- to medium-volume products, with short cycle times, for all three regions. High-volume products would be manufactured in the Far East.

A second area for strong subsidiary initiative has been the management of technology. A couple of years ago, E2 brought in consultants and worked with them to establish a strong concurrent engineering capability in the subsidiary. This increased design and manufacturing flexibility and significantly shortened cycle times. E2 became the company's centre of excellence for concurrent engineering and its associated benefits (flexible manufacturing, short cycle times). The subsidiary is presently leading the company's effort to globalise concurrent engineering, which is designed to support a more global manufacturing strategy. E2's general manager is the chairman of the company's engineering council overseeing the above effort.

It is interesting to notice that subsidiary development at E2 has not extended the subsidiary's domain either horizontally into other products or vertically into activities it was not already engaged in. Rather, it has been aimed at creating more unique technical capabilities that help to define a viable manufacturing and technology strategy for the long run. If it had not engaged in such development, it is doubtful whether manufacturing in Ireland would have remained a viable part of the subsidiary's domain. Several years ago the US operation shifted nearly all of its manufacturing to the Far East, and the rest to Ireland. E2's initiatives have positioned it as a relatively high-cost producer, offering flexible manufacturing, very short cycle times, and superior customer service. There is a demonstrated customer demand for this, and it is a position that appears differentiated and sustainable against lower-cost producers inside and outside the company. It is interesting to reflect on why this development occurred in Ireland instead of in the USA, the home country of its corporate parent. Subsidiary initiatives would appear to provide most of the explanation.

Subsidiary E3

This engages in designing, manufacturing, and marketing electronic products to the European market. When E3 was founded, its initial HQ assignment was to manufacture a single line of products for certain large customers who wanted a European source of supply. Soon an added assignment gave E3 responsibility for marketing related products, brought into Europe from the company's factories in the Far East. All of these products, including those manufactured in Ireland, had relatively low product differentiation and were price sensitive. This tends to be true of the company's products globally. A few years after E3's founding, subsidiary management concluded that the future would be bleak if the subsidiary simply stayed within its HQ assigned mission and domain. The subsidiary was meeting or exceeding HQ profit expectations, but subsidiary management did not believe there was a reliable future in manufacturing commodity electronics products in Ireland. They began a series of subsidiary initiatives to change the domain of the subsidiary.

The first initiative was to develop a new version of the existing product, designed to meet certain needs they had observed in the European market. Since the subsidiary didn't have any technology development group, 80 per cent of the effort was done by a design group in the parent country and 20 per cent was done locally by moving personnel from manufacturing to an *ad hoc* design group. This initial project served to establish a formal product development group and extended the subsidiary's domain into technology development. It was quickly followed by a much more ambitious second initiative. E3 attempted to develop new differentiated products through a self-described 'technology-driven' strategy. Two projects were launched using new forefront technology that neither the subsidiary nor the company had used before. The intended subsidiary development was to move the company into a new but related business, with the subsidiary having a *de facto* global mandate for the business. It is interesting to know that E3 did not have to get any HQ approval to undertake this initiative. As long as the budget was met, the subsidiary was free to engage in a variety of initiatives – and subsidiary management seemed more than ready to explore the limits of this policy. The first project produced a product that failed in the market, while the second was cancelled after development of a prototype. While this initiative failed to reach the intended objectives, it did provide the subsidiary with the technical capability to develop leading-edge technology products.

A third initiative soon followed. This time, the subsidiary pursued a 'market-driven' strategy of product development. Using knowledge gained from its own marketing efforts, E3 sought to design two very upscale and technologically differentiated products that are versions of its existing product line. Each was targeted at a specific industry and was designed to be first-to-market to meet the changing technology needs of customers in that industry. To support one of these product strategies, E3 even acquired a small European company that had some useful technology and was already selling a less sophisticated product. E3 retained the key technical people and moved production of the product to Ireland. The results of this third initiative are unknown, since neither of the new products had been launched into the marketplace at the time *our* research was undertaken. The intended subsidiary development is to move E3 into two new businesses, with sophisticated, differentiated technology, and much higher profit margins than the existing business. E3 designed the products to fit European needs, but believes it has adequately taken North American needs into account as well. It has shown the products to the company's North American and Asian operations, and believes they will become interested in selling the products if they succeed in Europe.

A fourth subsidiary initiative commenced about two years ago, when E3 set up a low-cost manufacturing operation in Eastern Europe. It has successfully transferred a number of low-end price-sensitive products in the existing product line to this facility. The parent HQ recently recognised this business as a wholly owned subsidiary reporting to the Irish subsidiary.

E3 is the most autonomous case of subsidiary development found among this sample of Irish subsidiaries. The subsidiary general manager reported to the head of an international division in the parent company. This manager permitted the Irish subsidiary a high degree of autonomy, as long as it met its budget. None of the subsidiary initiatives were really approved by the HQ, they were simply not opposed. HQ was aware that the subsidiary was moving into technology development and that it was developing products that were outside of the company's current domain. It did not fully understand or inquire about the subsidiary's strategy for these products. Nor did it attempt to coordinate or contribute to the development of these products, even though parent company had substantial technology development resources, albeit these were primarily devoted to designing cost-effective, low-differentiation products.

While E3 failed to receive any real support from the rest of the company, it clearly benefited from the high level of autonomy. It was attempting to move from an unexciting and probably dead-end manufacturing role to become, first, the recognised European HQ for the company's electronics business and, second,to achieve a global mandate for the two new businesses it was about to launch. The subsidiary had made a bold bid to expand its domain both vertically (into sophisticated product technology development and new business development activities) and horizontally (into new products and businesses). If successful, the subsidiary's initiatives would seemingly force the parent HQ to formally recognise the new role and status of the subsidiary. They would also appear to alter the parent company's strategy by putting it into some new upscale segments of the electronics industry that the company was not previously in, segments that had significant global potential.

Discussion

On the basis of the above, there is some scope to generalise from the five aggressive strategies for subsidiary development. The first four subsidiaries presently have strong HQ assignments. Only E3 at present has a limited HQ assignment, and it is currently taking bold initiatives to force HQ to assign it a stronger role. Subsidiary E1 also started with a limited HQ assignment, but through a number of successful initiatives succeeded in obtaining a strong role. The remaining three subsidiaries all began life with strong HQ assignments, and retain them today. This suggests that strong HQ assignments do not discourage subsidiaries from engaging in aggressive initiatives. In the cases of P1 and P2, it would appear that strong assignments even provided the resources needed to engage in aggressive initiatives that successfully pushed subsidiary domains upstream into process technology development. Limited HQ assignments, on the other hand, provide strong incentives for subsidiaries to engage in aggressive initiatives to force an improvement in their assignment. This is most evident in the actions of E3, where management seems obsessed with initiating such change before it is too late. In general, a limited assignment leaves a subsidiary more at the mercy of changes in technology, exchange rates, and tax preferences than does a strong one.

Company context appears to have a major influence on the direction and ultimate success of aggressive subsidiary initiatives. The first three subsidiaries all benefited from strong parent companies that possessed technological leadership and increasing global market shares and profits. Subsidiaries P1 and P2 directed their initiatives at integrating themselves more deeply into the very successful technology development part of the company value chain and riding the curve up. Subsidiary E1 started from a much weaker position, but also managed to engage in initiatives that ultimately integrated them with the rising technology development curve of the parent company. Subsidiaries E2 and E3, on the other hand, face less favourable company contexts. While E2 received some initial and on-going technology from the parent, it had to generate its own sales through competitive manufacturing and effective technology. E3 belonged to a successful company, but a company that largely pursued a low-cost, low-differentiation strategy. E3 did not believe an Irish subsidiary could succeed with this strategy over the long run. Both subsidiaries directed their initiatives at developing technical capabilities that they could deploy independent of the rest of the company. Thus, strong company contexts encourage subsidiaries to extend their domains deeper into the existing technology process, while weak company contexts encourage subsidiaries to either modify the existing technology process (E2) or develop a new technology process (E3).

Subsidiary initiatives vary in the extent to which they seek to tangentially extend existing subsidiary domain or more radically alter such domain. Extending process technology development capabilities by building strong process technology development groups and pilot lines in subsidiaries (P1, P2) is a tangential way of extending domain. So is building more flexible manufacturing capability (P1, E2). Both appear to be common initiatives in Irish subsidiaries, and they are probably relatively easy initiatives to get approved in MNCs. They do not directly threaten other parts of a company, and, since they are tangential extensions drawing from existing competencies, they are relatively easy to justify with the existing subsidiary reputation and track record.

Two of the sample subsidiaries (E1, E3) have employed more radical or discontinuous initiatives to alter domain. Both have strongly moved into product technology development, with the aim of establishing new businesses for a subsidiary. The two subsidiaries are at very different points in their subsidiary development processes. E1 appears to have successfully implemented most of its technology-based initiatives over the last few years, and it may, in fact, have already entered an incremental or *status quo* phase of subsidiary development. E3, on the other hand, is still in the middle of implementing its most crucial initiatives. These more radical initiatives that move subsidiary domain into product development should be more difficult to sell to HQ. In the case of E1, it appears that the subsidiary evolved through a sequence of related initiatives (setting up a software group, taking on the maintenance of older technologies, transitioning to newer technologies, gaining global responsibility for a major subsystem), which reduced the extent which each individual initiative was viewed as radical. The above process occurred over a period of 15 years. In the case of E3, the subsidiary is attempting a much more abrupt move into product development and a new business. There are a number of more radical initiatives, with less sequencing, occurring in a much shorter time period. The most important explanatory variable here would seem to be the unusually high degree of autonomy afforded the subsidiary by the parent company.

The general logic underlying subsidiary development is that the above initiatives lead to certain desired results or manifestations of development. The technology-based perspective taken in this chapter adds that this causal relationship is mediated through the creation of unique technical capabilities in a subsidiary. If an initiative does not produce some sufficiently unique technical capability then the desired manifestation of subsidiary development will not occur. The subsidiary initiatives aimed at extending a subsidiary's domain deeper into process technology development (P1, P2) have consistently produced a strong capability to solve technical problems and improve processes among the sample companies. In both cases, this capability appears to have been regarded as sufficiently unique by the parent HQ, that the subsidiary was receiving new technology at an increasingly early stage and was recognised as a centre of excellence for further improving such early technology. Perhaps it can be concluded that these are the two chief manifestations of subsidiary development. Similarly, the initiatives directed at improving the manufacturing flexibility of subsidiaries (P1, E2) have clearly resulted in P1 possessing the unique capability to efficiently manufacture both low-and high-volume products, and this is manifested in its receiving more new products than any other plant, as well as a major facilities expansion. While E2 also has achieved the most flexible manufacturing capability in its company and is regarded as a centre of excellence for this, it is less clear how much actual production will be transferred to the plant from the rest of the company – both of which are desired manifestations of subsidiary development. The answer to this question depends on how unique this capability turns out to be over the long run.

The subsidiary initiatives aimed at extending domain into product technology development (E1, E3) have in the case of E1 produced leading-edge software development capabilities for an important subsystem and leading-edge technical training capabilities. The respective manifestations of these are a global mandate for maintaining the subsystem and being one of the company's leading centres of excellence for training. As already discussed, the success of E3's initiatives are still uncertain. The intended consequences are leading-edge capability in two new product technologies,and global mandates for both of the resultant businesses. Thus, technology-based initiatives directed at product technology development lead frequently to global mandates for products or businesses, while initiatives directed at process technology development tend to result in a subsidiary becoming a centre of excellence for some activity. In both cases, a subsidiary aims by aggressive initiatives to create unique technical capabilities that are the basis for altering its strategy.

Incremental Subsidiary Development

Of the four subsidiaries that pursued incremental subsidiary development, three were in the electronics industry (E4, E5, and E6), and one was in the food-processing industry (F1).

Subsidiary E4

This manufactures several consumer electronics products for European markets. A number of engineering support groups that work on improving the yield and other short-run aspects of the process technology are also in the subsidiary. This is the HQ assignment, which the authors regard as limited because the subsidiary's products are also manufactured elsewhere in the company. Marketing and product and process technology development are located in another European country. The company context has been very favourable, with strong new product innovation and sales growth leading to several capacity expansions in the subsidiary. A couple years ago E4 took its first discernible technology initiative. It created a small advanced process technology group, which plans for new process technology a year or more in advance of its start-up. These groups typically exist only in the company's domestic operations. The group is providing E4 more control over the process technology it receives from the process technology development groups in the company. It does not develop any new technology, but its members sit on concurrent engineering teams along with the marketing, product development, process technology development, and procurement people, to ensure that, when new product and process technology is transferred in to E4, it better reflects their manufacturing constraints. The group has also turned its attention to European environmental policies, as they affect the company's products and manufacturing processes. It also coordinated the development of a new manufacturing capability by a local university, and this capability has since been transferred to other plants in the company. These appear to be the two best examples of unique technical capability in E4. The manifestations of this initiative are that E4 is increasingly regarded by the parent HQ as the expert on European environmental issues and E4's reputation for innovation is beginning to be established among the technical community in the company. One might argue that adding the small advanced process technology group to E4 has vertically extended its domain, to a small extent, into process technology development. However, this has occurred more through its influence on the planning of such development than by doing it. At the present time, E4 appears to be simply seeking a stronger product centre role within the assigned strategy.

Subsidiary E5

This is similar to E4. It also seeks a stronger product centre role within its assigned strategy. E5 manufactures the primary company products for the European market. Attached engineering support groups that work to improve yield and other short-run aspects of the process technology represent the local technical resources. All product and process technology are developed in the parent company and transferred to the subsidiary. On the surface, this HQ assignment appears to be the same as for E4, namely to be the European manufacturing plant, with responsibilities limited to operational matters. In the case of E5, however, the evidence suggests that the HQ assignment is strong, rather than limited, because it involved an extremely capital intensive technology and large capital-investment. This essentially makes it impossible for the HQ to withdraw its investment or reduce production in the subsidiary. The company context has also been strong, with a sustained stream of new product technology and strong company growth. E5 does not possess a lot of potential for technology-based subsidiary initiatives, but it has tried to innovate in the area of manufacturing safety procedures. This has resulted in some unique expertise on safety practices, and the site is beginning to be widely recognised as the company's centre of excellence for safety practices.

Subsidiary E6

This also was assigned the role of manufacturing electronic products for the European market. It was later assigned the task of doing certain systems testing for the entire company, when it became evident that it was more economical to do this activity in the subsidiary than in the parent country. This HQ assignment is limited, since it is also being implemented elsewhere in the company. A subsidiary initiative resulted when the system test engineers came in with some ideas for systems development and requested permission from HQ to do certain specific design jobs. In this manner the group grew into a small but formally recognised design activity. It developed one manufacturing system that is widely used throughout the company and also developed the product technology for a new and emerging product area in the company.

The subsidiary is not yet regarded as a centre of excellence by the rest of the company, but this is what it is trying to become. The design group was recently allowed to expand (the most evident manifestation of this initiative), but a relatively weak company context in recent years (with a variable record of new product development, flat sales, and downsizing) presents the most serious constraint on further subsidiary development. It is interesting to notice that E6 cannot attempt to develop its own technology-based strengths *vis-à-vis* the European marketplace, as E2 and E3 are doing under weak company contexts. E6 is very much a product centre for a business with a global product strategy. It has too little autonomy to be able to build a successful subsidiary strategy if the broader business continues to falter.

Subsidiary F1

This manufactures a variety of food ingredients that are shipped to a global network of plants that finish and package the final products for distribution to consumers in local markets. F1 is responsible for improving its process technology and the various support systems associated with it (for example, materials planning, inventory control). It also provides some technical support and training to the finishing plants. This is a limited HQ assignment, since the parent company provides similar support to a different set of global finishing plants and also does all of the new product development and more significant process technology development. The subsidiary has enjoyed a reasonably strong company context, with steadily increasing demand for its outputs.

The limited HQ assignment and relatively simple, mature manufacturing technology does not provide a lot of opportunity for technology-based initiatives, but F1 seems to be making the most out of those that are available. It has initiated a business process re-engineering programme, developed a new order fulfilment programme, and is working on a new quality agenda with some other company plants, this being a joint initiative taken by the plants. Thus, F1 is really working on the support systems for manufacturing and global logistics. The unique technical capability it is seeking to develop is expertise in technical and business systems improvement. To date there is some evidence that F1 is beginning to be recognised by the HQ and network of finishing plants as a centre of excellence for this kind of activity. The subsidiary objective is to continue to develop this kind of expertise and further extend F1's recognition as a centre of excellence.

Discussion

The aim of this section is now to generalise from the four incremental strategies for subsidiary development and, where possible, contrast them with the aggressive strategies for subsidiary development. Three of the four subsidiaries have limited HQ assignments,and only one has a strong assignment. This is a weaker assignment profile than that associated with the group of subsidiaries pursuing aggressive subsidiary development. But the most important difference is that none of the three incremental subsidiaries with limited HQ assignments is engaged in initiatives that might change the strength of this assignment. Both of the aggressive subsidiaries with limited HQ assignments engaged in initiatives that sought to change the assignment, while one had already succeeded in accomplishing this change.

Three of the incremental subsidiaries also have strong company contexts, which means that they can succeed and grow, even if they improve their position within the company only marginally . The single subsidiary with a weak company context, E6, appears unable to follow the pattern established by the aggressive subsidiary developers. This evidence suggests that weak company contexts encouraged subsidiaries to either modify the existing technology process or develop a new technology process. As already discussed, E6 is unable to do either. As the European manufacturing site for a global product strategy, its technology contribution is too small to influence the fate of the global strategy, and it has neither the autonomy nor the resources to support an independent subsidiary strategy. In fact, this lack of option seems to explain why a subsidiary continues to pursue incremental subsidiary development, even when its survival appears threatened.

While aggressive subsidiary initiatives vary in terms of whether they tangentially extend existing subsidiary domain or more radically alter such domain, incremental subsidiary initiatives are tangential in nature and moderate in terms of domain extension. The first three subsidiaries, E4, E5 and F1, all sought to increase their technical capability to improve some aspect of process technology. The initiatives ranged from having the existing engineering group target some limited aspect of process technology for improvement,(E5 and F1) to establishing a new group to accomplish this (E4), with the aim of both initiatives being to gain a company-wide reputation for possessing such technical capability. In the case of E6, there was an initiative to extend the subsidiary's domain into product development, but it was still modest and largely peripheral to the primary product development thrusts of the company. In only two of the subsidiaries did we see any real extension of subsidiary domain (E4, E6), and in both the extensions had a much lower impact on the overall strategic positions of the subsidiaries than in the case of the aggressive subsidiary developers. To a large extent, the incremental subsidiary initiatives led to technical capabilities and the establishment of reputations that were consistent with the existing HQ assignment and ensured that the subsidiary would be impressive, relative to other company subunits, in fulfilling that assignment.

Incremental initiatives tend to be relatively inexpensive, and in most cases can be approved at relatively low levels of the organisation. Initiatives in two of the subsidiaries (E5, F1) required no approval above the subsidiary level, and the initiatives in all four subsidiaries involved largely operating budget expenditures. All five of the aggressive subsidiary initiatives involved significant capital budget expenditures. The aggressive subsidiary developers tended to use strong track records (or in the case of E3, an unusually high level of local autonomy) to gain the necessary HQ approvals. In the case of the incremental subsidiary developers, E4 and E5 are relatively new subsidiaries that had not had time to build such track records – although both appeared intent on doing so. It is conceivable that both could seek to more aggressively extend their domains once supportive track records are established. In fact, the existing incremental initiatives are clearly consistent with and enhance such track record building. The other two subsidiaries are older. F1 has a strong track record, but it is not apparent how the subsidiary could develop beyond its present domain. Indeed, the track record appears to be an unused subsidiary resource. E6 has not had its track record recognised to the extent it desires (or believes it deserves), despite the development of some unique technical capabilities in the subsidiary. In this case, it would appear that a weak company context can frustrate the building of a strong subsidiary track record.

Status quo Subsidiary Development

The remaining seven subsidiaries were not pursuing any technology-based initiatives that sought to either change or improve a subsidiary's strategy, but were engaged in actions that fell within the routine implementation of existing subsidiary strategy. Of these subsidiaries, one was in pharmaceuticals, two were in food processing, two in chemicals, and two in other industrial products. The primary technical activity for all of the subsidiaries was improving process technology. Two subsidiaries were also engaged in some product development, and three transferred in new product and process technology on a fairly frequent basis.

Except for one subsidiary, all had a limited HQ assignment that involved manufacturing products that were also available from other sources. The pharmaceutical subsidiary had a strong HQ assignment. It possessed a technology and set of products that were unique within the company. Like E5, the lone incremental subsidiary that also had a strong HQ assignment, this subsidiary possessed a very advanced technology and was capital-intensive. It had a strong company context and appeared to be fully occupied in simply implementing its challenging assignment. Of the remaining six subsidiaries, three had strong company contexts, two had stable contexts (limited growth but not likely to decline), and one had a weak company context. None of the seven subsidiaries was engaged in any initiative that sought to develop a unique technical capability. In most cases, they were either satisfied with their present subsidiary strategy or perceived themselves as lacking the resources or autonomy to change it.

DISCUSSION AND CONCLUSIONS

The sample findings support the view that technology has become an important basis for subsidiary development. In the past, Irish subsidiaries might have sought to expand their strategic domains with initiatives based on lower factor costs (typically labour and taxes), but currently it appears that technology-based initiatives probably drive much of the subsidiary development in Ireland. This may not be the case for other host countries. The lack of a significant home market has undoubtedly concentrated Irish subsidiaries around technology-based subsidiary development, which makes it an ideal site for studying this form of subsidiary development.

The sample subsidiaries have engaged in a variety of technology-based initiatives. Most often these initiatives have sought vertical domain expansion, by backward-integrating the subsidiary deeper into process technology development. This is especially attractive when there is a strong company context, namely where the parent company has strong technology and growth. By backward integrating, the subsidiary attaches itself more firmly to a successful parent company strategy and becomes an integral part of the success story. Strong HQ assignments are preferable to weak ones, since they provide more favourable starting points for undertaking subsidiary development. But weak HQ assignments do appear open to change, especially if there is a strong company context and sufficient subsidiary autonomy.

Weak company contexts appear to be the major problem for subsidiaries that want security and growth. Deeper integration with the parent company's value chain does not provide either of these. Instead, the subsidiary needs to strike out on a new path that either leads the parent company into a more viable strategy or else makes the subsidiary more independent of the parent company's weak strategy. This requires an aggressive initiative by the subsidiary and radical or discontinuous domain expansion, which generally involves new technology or new products. Unfortunately, many subsidiaries facing this situation probably lack the resources and autonomy required to launch such an initiative.

This research study also has some implications for parent companies. A significant percentage of foreign manufacturing subsidiaries seem to engage in some form of technology-based subsidiary development. While the present research did not directly measure this, the impression gained is that subsidiaries actively involved in subsidiary development often tend to be the most productive and high-performing subsidiaries in a company. If this is so, then parent companies should mostly attempt to channel subsidiary development into constructive paths, rather than attempt to suppress or constrain it.

As discussed above, a strong company context principally encourages subsidiaries to compete for a bigger role in the company's value chain. This would seem to be largely backward integration into process technology development. This will lead to a greater diffusion of technology development in a company, which is something that needs to be planned for. Companies need to guard against loss of specialisation and economies of scale and at the same time exploit opportunities to transfer technology sooner and perhaps develop it at lower cost locations. Since most subsidiary domain expansion in a strong company context is likely to be tangential (and not discontinuous) with the existing domain, it should be relatively easy for an alert parent HQ to steer and integrate subsidiary initiatives into wider company initiatives.

While a weak company context is distressing at the subsidiary level, it is also difficult to manage at the parent HQ level. Consistent with the findings, a weak company context encourages radical or discontinuous domain expansion by subsidiaries. This generally involves products or technologies that are new to the company, as well as to the subsidiary. In the long run, this could lead to the renewal and improvement of a company's strategy. In the short run, it is likely to appear as a series of sub-optimised and questionable initiatives that are pulling company resources away from the existing strategy. It is doubtful how well the parent HQ can evaluate and decide when to encourage and when to discourage such subsidiary initiatives.

The above are some of the normative implications of technology-based subsidiary development, and they are attractive topics for future research to further explore. This exploratory study of the subject has uncovered a rich level of subsidiary activity and provided some preliminary understanding of what appear to be a number of the key constructs. Technology-based subsidiary development is a potentially important source of MNC change, which is both an alternative and a supplement to HQ-initiated technology change. It is a subject that needs to be better understood at both the subsidiary and the HQ levels.

References

Bartlett, C.A. and S. Ghoshal (1989) *Managing Across Borders: The Transnational Solution*, Boston, MA: Harvard Business School Press.

Behrman. J.N. and W.A. Fischer (1980) Overseas Research and Development Activities of Transnational Companies, Cambridge: MA: Oelgeschlager, Gunn and Hain

Birkinshaw J.N. (1997) 'Entrepreneurship in Multinational Corporations: The Characteristics of Subsidiary Initiatives', *Strategic Management Journal*, 18 (3), 207–29.

Birkinshaw, J.N. and N. Hood (1997) 'An Empirical Study of Development Processes in Foreign-owned Subsidiaries in Canada and Scotland', *Management International Review* 32 (4), 339–64.

Birkinshaw, J.N., N. Hood and S. Jonsson (1998) 'Building Firm-specific Advantages in Multinational Corporations: The Role of Subsidiary Initiative', *Strategic Management Journal* (forthcoming).

Cheng, J.L.C. and D.S. Bolton (1993) 'The Management of Multinational R&D: A Neglected Topic', *Journal of International Business Studies*, 24 (1) 1–18.

Eisenhardt, K.M. (1989) 'Building Theory from Case study Research', *Academy of Management Review*, 14 (4), 532–50.

Ghoshal, S. and C.A. Bartlett (1988) 'Creation, Adoption and Diffusion of Innovations by Subsidiaries of Multinational Corporations', *Journal of International Business Studies*, 19 (3), 365–88.

Ghoshal, S. and N. Nohria (1989) 'Internal Differentiation within Multinational Corporations', *Strategic Management Journal*, 10 (4), 323–37.

Glaser, B.G. and A.L. Strauss (1967) *The Discovery of Grounded Theory*, Chicago: Aldine.

Gupta, A.K. and V. Govindarajan (1991) 'Knowledge Flows and the Structure of Control within Multinational Corporations', *Academy of Management Review*, 16 (4), 768–92.

Hedlund, G. and D. Rolander (1990) 'Action in Heterarchies: New Approaches to Managing the MNC', in C.S. Bartlett, Y. Doz, and G. Hedlund (eds.), *Managing the Global Firm*, London and New York: Routledge, 15–46.

10 Strategic Development of Multinational Subsidiaries in Ireland

Ed Delany

IMPORTANCE OF FOREIGN DIRECT INVESTMENT TO THE IRISH ECONOMY

Ireland's economy is highly dependent on the activities of multinational subsidiaries. OECD (1991) data shows that over 45 per cent of manufacturing employment and almost two-thirds of manufacturing output is attributable to foreign-owned firms. These subsidiaries have been set up in Ireland in three basic time periods:

- Pre-1921: a small number of companies, including for example Guinness, pre-date the formation of the state in 1921.
- 1921–1960: a number, mostly of UK parentage, were set up to be located inside the trade barriers established by the Irish Government after the formation of the state.
- Since 1960: a large number of multinational subsidiaries have been established, many of which have been attracted by the range of incentives designed for mobile investment and actively marketed by the Irish Industrial Development Authority (IDA).

An IDA (1994) survey found that there were almost 1100 foreign-owned subsidiaries in manufacturing or IDA-supported international services. Ownership of these subsidiaries was spread across 29 different countries, but parent companies from three home countries – the USA, the UK and Germany – owned almost 70 per cent of the subsidiaries.

The emphasis of Irish industrial policy with respect to foreign direct investment since 1960 has been primarily on attracting in new investments. With the exception of some high-profile attempts to save closures of such subsidiaries, initiatives by the state and its agencies, specifically IDA, to strengthen and develop the subsidiaries once they have been located in Ireland have been limited. Yet, as attracting mobile investment becomes more difficult owing to the growing number of competing destinations, it is becoming more important to ensure the survival and development of the existing multinational subsidiaries. Consequently, in recent times, the development of these subsidiaries has attracted greater attention.

REVIEW OF SUBSIDIARY DEVELOPMENT LITERATURE

Parent Perspective Multinational Subsidiary Research

The output of management research tends to be centred on the larger economies, in particular, the USA. Because research tends to be 'problem-driven', a particular emphasis can develop within a research theme. Consequently, research on multinational subsidiaries has tended historically to be dominated by issues of how to find a role for them and how to control them from the perspective of head office. For example, Porter (1986) discusses the choices facing the multinational in terms of coordination and configuration of their activities. Egelhoff (1984) sets out two forms of control – output and behavioural control. Baliga and Jaeger (1984) use similar terms, namely bureaucratic and cultural control. Gupta and Govindarajan (1991) provide a contingency approach for the multinational in how it should control its subsidiaries. In defining roles for subsidiaries, there is a series of models such as those of Bartlett and Ghoshal (1986), Gupta and Govindarajan (1991) and Malnight (1995). What characterises this literature on control and on defining the roles of subsidiaries is that it is parent-centred. The world is viewed from the perspective of head office: the subsidiary is expected to obey parent company wishes and not to have an agenda independent of that the parent.

Subsidiary Perspective Multinational Subsidiary Research

In contrast, there is a relatively small amount of writing and thought given over to how the subsidiary should develop its own agenda or 'strategies'. The writers looking at the world of the subsidiary from this perspective have mostly been based in Canada, Scotland and Ireland – all countries that have a significant dependence on multinational subsidiaries and that have concerns about leaving their 'destiny' to head office decision-making. Those based in Canada were among the earliest contributors. White and Poynter (1984) provided a typology of subsidiaries and a set of imperatives for the subsidiary. Also in the early 1980s, there was much discussion among the Canadian academic community, owing to the impending arrival of NAFTA, about the need for Canadian subsidiaries to develop 'world product mandates' (D'Cruz, 1986; Rugman and Douglas, 1986). Crookell and Morrison (1990) extended earlier work in relation to how the subsidiary should act if it were to be successful. Morrison and Roth (1993) investigated the characteristics necessary for the subsidiary to develop 'global product mandates'. Birkinshaw in a joint article with Ritchie (1993) and a series of articles in 1995 (1995a, 1995b, 1995c, 1995d) focused on strategic initiative-taking by Canada-based subsidiaries, and identified four distinct value-adding strategies. He observed that strategy for the Canadian subsidiary had often to be set in the context of three 'markets' – global, local and internal corporate. He also discussed the specific role of the top management of the subsidiary. In Scotland, a number of pieces of research have sought to test the transferability of the White and Poynter (1984) typology to that country and to extend our understanding of subsidiary strategy-making in an EU context (Young *et al.*, 1989; Taggart, 1992, 1993, 1995). In Ireland, there have been a small number of action-learning studies carried out by general managers of Ireland-based subsidiaries in relation to extending their subsidiaries' mandate (McDonald, 1987; Lyons, 1995). In addition, Molloy (1992) provided a checklist of activities that a subsidiary should engage in order to strengthen its mandate. In particular, he neatly characterises the need for energy in the successful strategy initiating subsidiary by distinguishing between two types of subsidiary – 'boy scout' and 'subversive'. He recommends the subversive approach but he, in common with many other writers, believes that the 'subversion' involved is not about undermining the parent but rather is concerned with seeking out actions that benefit both the subsidiary and the parent. It is evident that all of this subsidiary-centred literature tends to emphasise the need for the subsidiary to take its own strategic initiatives and not to simply wait for orders from head office.

In conclusion, a key distinction between the two literatures – parent-centred and subsidiary-centred – is the use of the term defining a 'role' for multinational subsidiaries (which emerges from parent-centred literature) in contrast to development of 'strategies' or 'strategic initiatives' (which emerges from subsidiary-centred literature).

RESEARCH PROJECT INTO DEVELOPMENT OF SUBSIDIARIES IN IRELAND

The overall objective of the research project reported on in this chapter has been to understand through the eyes of the general manager or managing director of the subsidiary how they have sought to develop their subsidiary in Ireland both in terms of specific initiatives taken and the process by which that initiative was pursued within the corporation. Differences between subsidiary approaches and initiatives were also considered in terms of, *inter alia*, the type of subsidiary, its stage of development, its parent company of origin, size and the parent company context in terms of its strategy process and goals. While the research was started independently, it has a number of parallels with the work carried out by Birkinshaw (1995a, 1995b, 1995c, 1995d) in Canada.

For the research process, there were three strands of qualitative data collection.

Research by Interview of General Managers

General managers or managing directors from 28 multinational subsidiaries – 10 US, 9 UK and 9 Swedish parent organisations – were interviewed for about 1½ hours each. The interviews started with a structured questionnaire to gain some data about the subsidiary and proceeded to a taped interview that asked the interviewee to describe in their own words three strategic initiatives in which they were involved both in terms of the initiative and the process by which they sought to pursue that initiative. The subsidiaries, which excluded solely sales subsidiaries, were not sampled in a formal way but rather were chosen for the insight they might be able to give – in general, they were chosen as subsidiaries that had been successful in developing their mandate.

Workshop with Multinational Subsidiary Managers

A half-day workshop for multinational subsidiaries in the electronics industry, members of the Cork Electronics Industry Association, was led by the author and featured four case-studies of the development of subsidiaries. The conclusions and debate of this workshop were captured as another strand of the research.

Interviews with Industry Experts

Finally, a paper was drawn up as a result of the findings of the first two strands of research and circulated to twelve people chosen because of their wide understanding of multinational subsidiaries. These were subsequently interviewed and their reaction to the paper researched.

The data from the interviews and the workshop were subsequently analysed and conclusions drawn using techniques that closely followed the approaches recommended by Miles and Huberman (1994).

CLASSIFYING SUBSIDIARIES' STRATEGIC POSITION

Extending the White and Poynter Classification

The first task of the research analysis was to classify the strategic position of the subsidiaries whose general managers were interviewed. The typology of White and Poynter (1984) was used. This classified subsidiaries into five types:

Miniature Replica

This is a business that produces and markets some of the parent's product lines or related product lines in the local country. The business is a small-scale replica of the parent. It may not be engaged in all activities, such as product development. Historically, many UK subsidiaries in Ireland that existed behind tariff barriers were of this type. An example would be the cigarette manufacturing and marketing subsidiary of Imperial Group, which in turn is owned by Hanson.

Marketing Satellite

This is a business which markets into the local trading area products manufactured centrally. Operational activities locally will be confined to at most packaging, bulk breaking, some final processing and warehousing/distribution. Subsidiaries such as Lever Brothers, a subsidiary of Unilever, in Ireland are of this type.

Rationalised Manufacturer

This is a business producing a designated set of component parts or products for a multi-country or global market. Product scope and value-added scope is limited. Marketing of the output is done by the multinational organisation, often through marketing satellites. Development activities will usually be done in the parent country but sometimes some development takes place locally. Capacity and new product decisions tend to be controlled from head office. This is the classic situation of the start-up manufacturing subsidiary in Ireland. Intel's subsidiary in Ireland started off in this way.

Product Specialist

This is a business that develops, produces and markets a limited product line for global markets. Products, markets or basic technologies are similar to the parent company, but exchanges between the subsidiary and the parent are rare. The subsidiary is generally self-sufficient in terms of value added. The description in White and Poynter (1984) indicates the 'marketing independence' of the subsidiary. In the view of this author, there are few MNC subsidiaries in Ireland that conform totally to this description. This is due at least partly to the trends in terms of globalisation, which have accelerated since White and Poynter wrote their article. However, the Grand Metropolitan subsidiary that produces and markets Bailey's Irish Cream is an example of a subsidiary that is close to being a product specialist.

Strategic Independent

This is a business that has the freedom and resources to develop lines of business for either a local, a multi-country or a global market. The subsidiary is allowed unconstrained access to global markets and freedom to pursue new business opportunities. There are a small number of subsidiaries that would fit closely into this description, including Guinness Ireland and Tretorn.

The White and Poynter (1984) classification was developed in the context of Canadian-based subsidiaries that were experiencing a dismantling of traditional trade barriers. Many of the subsidiaries had started as miniature replica businesses behind trade barriers, and were anxious to find ways of 'protecting' their autonomy over all functions of the business. This is a very different scenario from that of the many manufacturing and operations subsidiaries that have set up in Ireland and are engaged in a gradual process of development of their operations into other parts of the value chain, such as customer service or product development. Consequently, in trying to use the model to classify the Irish subsidiaries researched, the author experienced difficulty in accurately fitting the subsidiaries to the White and Poynter (1984) typology. Three changes are therefore proposed to the classification to more accurately describe the sample of Irish subsidiaries. First, the term *rationalised operator* will be used to encompass both manufacturing and other activities in the subsidiary such as software or product development – a category of subsidiary that has become much more prevalent since White and Poynter developed their model. Second, the *product specialist* category will not require the subsidiary to have the total autonomy suggested above, but rather will indicate that it has substantial autonomy for its range of products. Third, a further category – *enhanced-mandate* – is used to extend the White and Poynter (1984) classification. An 'enhanced-mandate' subsidiary is defined as one that does not have control of the entire value chain of a business unit but has activities in a number of parts of the value chain. This might be a manufacturing organisation with product development activities or a regional logistics brief. A considerable number of subsidiaries were found to fit this description. By adding the additional enhanced-mandate category, the author has chosen a different approach to that used by the Scottish authors (Taggart, 1992, 1993, 1995) and Young *et al.* (1989). There are many similarities between the type of multinational subsidiaries in Ireland and Scotland, yet the Scottish authors would appear to have chosen to widen the definitional scope of the White and Poynter (1984) 'product specialist' category to include subsidiaries that have developed from the 'rationalised manufacturer' category but may not have any significant marketing responsibilities. In this author's view, this lessens the usefulness of the classification and, consequently, the additional category is proposed.

Applying the Extended Classification to the Research Sample

Using the 6 categories described above, the sample of 28 subsidiaries was classified in terms of their start-up classification and their present classification. The summary results of this classification are shown in Table 10.1.

The following points can be made. All except 1 of the 10 US companies that set up were started as rationalised operators; 7 of the 9 Swedish companies started as rationalised operators; only 4 of the 9 UK companies started out as a rationalised operators.

This is in line with expectations. While over 16 per cent of the subsidiaries on the Industrial Development Authority's (1994) database were of UK parentage, the vast majority of these were principally marketing satellite businesses exploiting the Irish market with goods made in UK or elsewhere. The advantages to a UK company in setting up a rationalised operation (that is a manufacturing operation) in Ireland for supplying countries outside Ireland are usually less than they are to a US parent. In contrast, subsidiaries from non-UK locations are more likely to have been attracted by incentives for mobile investment and the Irish market is usually of only minor concern. This has important implications for the development of the subsidiary, because there are very different 'start points' for UK and US or Swedish subsidiaries.

Table 10.1 Strategic positions of subsidiaries at start-up and current parent nationality

Start-up strategy	*Current strategy*	*US*	*UK*	*Sweden*	*Total*
Rationalised operator	Rationalised operator	1	4	0	5
Rationalised operator	Enhanced mandate	7	0	4	11
Rationalised operator	Product specialist	2	0	3	5
Miniature replica	Miniature replica	0	1	1	2
Miniature replica	Product specialist	0	2	0	2
Miniature replica	Strategic independent	0	1	0	1
Marketing satellite	Marketing satellite	0	0	1	1
Strategic independent	Strategic independent	0	1	0	1
Total		10	9	9	28

Of the 28 that started, 27 were either rationalised operators, miniature replicas, or marketing satellites. These can be considered the 'basic mandates' for start-up operations of investments in Ireland. The exception started out as a strategic independent – an Irish start-up business later acquired by a UK parent. In the case of two of the companies that are described as miniature replicas, they started as being owned by Irish-based investors, but under an arrangement with an overseas 'licensee' who subsequently acquired them. If the subsidiary is to develop beyond its basic mandate, it can move into the trio of 'development mandates' – enhanced mandate, product specialist, or strategic independent. In developing, the subsidiary extends the scope of its activities by extending the number of operations it has under its control and increases the responsibility it gets from the parent. It should of course be noted that the subsidiary can grow without moving to a development mandate. For example, a marketing satellite can double its sales volume in Ireland. However, in such cases, the subsidiary is increasing its scale but not its activity scope. Figure 10.1 illustrates the conclusion that there are basic mandates and development mandates.

Figure 10.1 Basic and development mandates using extended version of White and Poynter (1984)

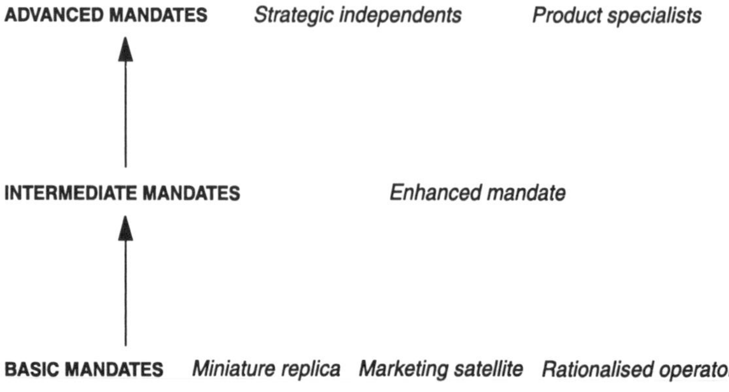

It is important to note that there are different patterns of development among the different parent nationality subsidiaries. UK subsidiaries in the sample appear to be the least successful in developing their mandate beyond that originally granted to them. A reason for this may be the existence of a much larger parent company organisation in a neighbouring country with much greater opportunities for scale. The data shows that 19 of the 28 subsidiaries have extended their mandate since they were started up. This is, however, unlikely to be a generalisable finding, because the sample was deliberately selected to reflect subsidiaries that had developed their mandate. Of the 19 subsidiaries that have developed their mandate, 11 have moved from being rationalised operators into enhanced mandates. In many cases, these have not taken on the marketing mandate but have added functions such as product development and customer service. While most groups have taken a few steps away from being rationalised operators, the sample includes some subsidiaries that have moved considerably from their original basic manufacturing mandate. For example, Tretorn Ireland moved from being involved in a single labour-intensive step of the manufacturing process for tennis balls to having full business responsibility for that product line, including world-wide marketing and all product development activities.

STRATEGIC INITIATIVES BY SUBSIDIARIES

Extending the Birkinshaw (1997) Classification of Initiatives

Birkinshaw (1997) is one of the few researchers on MNC subsidiaries to seek to classify strategic initiatives taken by subsidiaries. The initiatives were classified under the four categories explained below by reference to an example from the present author's research:

Pursue a New Business Opportunity in the Local Market

Subsidiary 16, a UK-parented software development subsidiary, was in charge of developing the local market in Ireland as well as some operational activities. It set up a marketing alliance in Ireland with one of the largest world-wide companies in a complementary sector. This had a major benefit on sales and became a model for the parent company in developing other markets.

Bid for Corporate Investment

Subsidiary 17, a US-parented manufacturing subsidiary, had a large manufacturing plant in Ireland and bid successfully for a new plant investment that was going to be placed by the US parent in Europe.

Extend Mandate

Subsidiary 1 was involved in manufacturing a specific consumer product range for the European market on behalf of its

US parent. It sought to move into the manufacture of a complementary product range, which it believed would be marketable through the country market business units of the parent.

Reconfigure Operations

Subsidiary 6, a Swedish-parented manufacturing and marketing subsidiary, had a plant in South America as well as the Irish plant and others located world-wide. The South American plant was small-scale and inefficient, and the Irish plant sought to absorb its production into the Irish manufacturing unit.

These four categories are a useful classification of strategic initiatives, although the third category, 'extend mandate', often also encompasses the 'bid for corporate investment' because corporate investment can be required to extend a mandate. However, in the author's research on subsidiaries in Ireland, each subsidiary manager was asked to discuss three strategic initiatives that they had been engaged in over the previous years. The researcher deliberately did not define a 'strategic' decision in precise terms, and so the respondents tended to discuss issues which varied in their apparent impact. However, the important issue from the research perspective was that the decisions were perceived as strategic to the respondents. This gave rise to 83 strategic initiatives – of which 71 were viewed by the general managers as successful, 10 as failed, and 2 were inconclusive. The high proportion of examples of success is in line with other research findings (Huber and Power, 1985) in that managers prefer to discuss successes in order to project a positive image and, consequently, are often reluctant to raise events where they are not seen in as good a light. However, when Birkinshaw's classification was used, it was found that only 49 of the initiatives (59.0 per cent) fitted into the four classifications. This was because Birkinshaw's classification only considers initiatives where the end objective was to develop the domain of the subsidiary. However, the general managers also described taking strategic initiatives aimed at defending the subsidiary, as well as initiatives aimed at consolidating or building the credibility of the subsidiary. As a result of the finding noted above, a classification of strategic initiatives was developed, using Thompson's (1967) domain theory, under three 'master categories' – domain building, domain defending, and domain consolidating (credibility building).

Domain Building

- Pursuing new business opportunity in local market.
- Bidding for corporate investment.
- Extending mandate.
- Reconfiguring operations.

These restate the four categories drawn up by Birkinshaw (1997) and described above.

Domain Defending. Three categories of domain-defending initiatives were found, as follows:

Retain Operations Irish subsidiaries face corporate pressure in times of downsizing and other changes. Subsidiary 2, a manufacturing subsidiary of a US company, was involved in a series of initiatives aimed at ensuring the Irish unit's survival.

Retain Reporting It is critical for Irish subsidiaries, if they are to maintain influence, to be reporting into influential parts of the organisation. Subsidiary 4, a software development subsidiary of a large US parent, had to fight to retain a direct reporting relationship for its subsidiary into head office.

Find New Patron Irish subsidiaries are frequently dependent on getting business from a specific division within their corporation or from the success of a specific product line. If these run into difficulties, the subsidiary must seek a new patron. An extreme case was subsidiary 18, a manufacturing subsidiary of a Swedish parent that was seeking to withdraw from basic manufacturing, which eventually sought to establish an MBO of the Irish unit as an alternative to closure by its parent:

Domain Consolidating. Initiatives under this heading were generally seeking to ensure that the subsidiary carried out its existing activities in a superior and competitive fashion. Two categories were found:

Performance Improvement Cost competitiveness, quality and TQM-type initiatives have been important in building the relative advantage of one plant over another. Subsidiary 23, a recently acquired subsidiary of a Swedish parent, sought a major investment in capital equipment for the Irish plant to substantially improve the cost per unit of output.

Input into Corporate Decisions As well as improving the performance of the local operations, the subsidiary can gain credibility and consolidate its contribution by making constructive inputs into corporate decisions. Subsidiary 19, a major processing subsidiary of a UK parent, has been involved in a substantial world-wide review of the parent's activities and would be seen to have been one of the main drivers for change.

Applying Extended Birkinshaw (1997) Classification of Initiatives

The above categories were used as a basis for classifying the strategic initiatives raised by the general managers. There were some classification difficulties, because an initiative might have been classified as in either of two categories, in particular to make the distinction between 'bidding for corporate investment' and 'extending mandate'. Table 10.2 sets out the results by parent country.

The results highlight a number of important issues. Subsidiaries from all three parent nationalities had most initiatives classified as 'domain building', but those from US ones had a substantially higher percentage in this category. The UK subsidiaries had a higher percentage of their initiatives in the combined category 'domain consolidating' and 'pursuing new business opportunities in local market'. The reasons for this difference between UK and US subsidiaries may have been related to parent nationality, but a more likely explanation is the nature of the subsidiaries. More UK parented subsidiaries are

Table 10.2 Classification of strategic initiatives from research

Classification of strategic Initiative	*Subsidiary parent nationality*			*Total*	*Failed initiatives*
	US	*UK*	*Sweden*		
Domain building					
Pursuing new business opportunity in local market	2	4	0	6	0
Bidding for corporate investment	1	2	6	9	
Extending existing mandate	13	5	5	23	5[a]
Reconfiguring operations	5	3	3	11	1
Subtotal	21	14	14	49	6
% of Total initiatives of parent country	*70*	*52*	*54*	*59*	
Domain defending					
Retain operations in Ireland	4	1	3	8	3
Retain Existing Reporting Relationship	1			1	0
Find New Patron	0	2	2	4	0[b]
Subtotal	5	3	5	13	3
% of Total initiatives of parent country	*17*	*11*	*19*	*16*	
Domain consolidating					
Improving Performance	2	8	6	16	0
Input into Corporate Decisions	2	2	1	5	1
Subtotal	4	10	7	21	1
% of Total Initiatives of Parent Country	*13*	*37*	*27*	*25*	
Total	30	27	26	83	10

[a] +1 inconclusive.
[b] 1 inconclusive.

miniature replicas, which have been found to have lesser opportunities to develop their business mandate internationally. Consequently, initiatives may be local-market-related or designed to ensure competitiveness.

The findings showed that US subsidiaries were more likely to be involved in extending their mandate than were those from UK. This may be due to the fact that the US subsidiary starts off with a very limited functionality and managers are anxious to move away from a 'recipe-following' mode. There is a significant difference between the US and Swedish subsidiaries in the proportion of 'extending mandate' initiatives. However, Swedish subsidiaries had a high proportion of 'bidding for corporate investment' initiatives, which make up this difference. This may highlight an important difference in corporate culture. US subsidiary managers appeared to be more often engaged in covert or highly political attempts to develop their business. In contrast, while competition between subsidiaries was also acknowledged in the Swedish case, they appeared to be encouraged to engage in 'open' behaviour concerning their aspirations, and mandate extension opportunities were bid for in an open, competitive way.

Classifying Strategic Initiatives with Respect to Value Chain

Domain-developing initiatives can, in value chain terms (Porter, 1984), come from four different types of moves:

- increasing the scale of existing activities;
- increasing business by similar activities such as manufacturing a new but similar product, or selling existing products to new markets;
- developing upstream activities – moving into design and development;
- developing downstream activities – moving into customer service and marketing.

The 49 'domain-developing' strategic initiatives were classified under these four headings, providing the results in Figure 10.2. There is a surprisingly even spread among the various initiatives. Just over 50 per cent involved moving along the value chain of the organisation. As an example of a downstream move, subsidiary 14, a US-owned manufacturing plant of large-scale electronic products, took on the responsibility for transport and delivery of the product to the European sales subsidiary and, subsequently, used the credibility of experience in logistics to make a successful play for a much wider role in world-wide logistics.

Figure 10.2 Classifying the 49 domain developing strategic initiatives by value chain moves

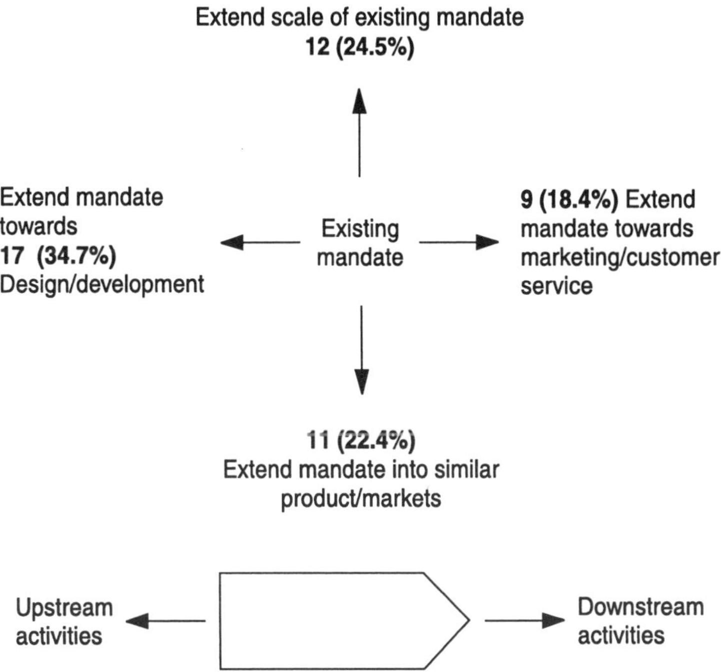

PHASES OF SUBSIDIARY MANDATE DEVELOPMENT

Performance and Its Perception – Building Credibility

The issue of 'building credibility' was found to be particularly important in terms of the ability of the subsidiary to engage in the successful development of its strategic mandate. The subsidiary had to have a high level of perceived competence in its current mandate to be taken seriously. Influence was seen by the interviewees as a function of this perceived credibility. The general manager of subsidiary 7, a UK-owned software development operation, said that the credibility provided by satisfactory performance within the current mandate gave the subsidiary 'its strategic degrees of freedom'. Other general managers used such colourful phrases as 'credibility comes out of the barrel of performance' and 'freedom is earned from high standards of performance'. The bottom line is that inadequate performance in one's current mandate excludes the subsidiary from setting out a proposal for any type of development; average performance will fail to adequately capture the parent's attention; superior performance is required to provide a credible platform for proposing that the subsidiary extends its mandate. Furthermore, it is not sufficient to perform in a superior fashion. The subsidiary must also be perceived as performing in a superior fashion by the key head office managers. In short, the message must be sold internally.

Phases of Development – Evidence from Research

Having achieved credibility within the current mandate, the subsidiary is then in a position to develop its mandate. The workshop with multinational subsidiaries in the electronics industry concluded that there was a phased development of the strategy of the subsidiary and that there were three such phases:

- Phase 1 – building credibility of the subsidiary.
- Phase 2 – gradual build-up of competence of the subsidiary.
- Phase 3 – strategic development.

It concluded that development should be in terms of mandate development and not purely a scale-of-activity development. The issue of scale is returned to below. The case studies and the subsequent debate with managers highlighted a need to establish credibility within the current mandate, and to move gradually into higher level mandates, and confirmed the broad thrust of the workshop conclusions. Evidence for this staged development was seen earlier in the move to advanced mandates on the part of successful subsidiaries when White and Poynter's (1984) classification was applied. Some direct evidence from the interviews is also worth setting down. The general manager of subsidiary 12, a financial services subsidiary, explicitly discussed the start-up success as the first strategic initiative, its success leading into the other initiatives that were progressively 'more strategic'. The general manager of subsidiary 17, a US-owned manufacturing plant, had his first strategic initiative as the turnaround of a subsidiary that was performing so poorly in its basic mandate that it was in danger of closing. It was only when the management had succeeded in this task that it had opportunities to develop its mandate. Subsidiary 1, a US-owned consumer goods manufacturing plant, talked of the development of its operational performance prior to its success as a beneficiary from a succession of more complex operations reconfigurations at corporate level. Subsidiary 3, a US-owned healthcare manufacturing plant, had developed its manufacturing performance prior to absorbing production from sister sites, after which it developed its activities by mandate extensions along the value chain. Within the literature, Malnight (1995) had also noted an evolution of the successful subsidiary. Sargeant (1990) had also postulated a three-phase development of the sales subsidiary of multinationals, which he termed 'childhood', 'adolescence' and 'adulthood'.

Phases of Development – an Eight-Stage Model Hypothesis

Drawing together the classification of initiatives, the classification of subsidiaries' strategic position and the phasing issue leads to the 'model hypothesis' of stages of development of multinational subsidiary in Figure 10.3. A series of eight steps, broken into three higher-level classifications, in the development of the subsidiary are set down and are now explained.

Stages 1–3: Basic Mandate

The first step will involve the establishment of the subsidiary as either a 'rationalised operator', a 'marketing satellite', or a

Figure 10.3 Stages of development of multinational subsidary

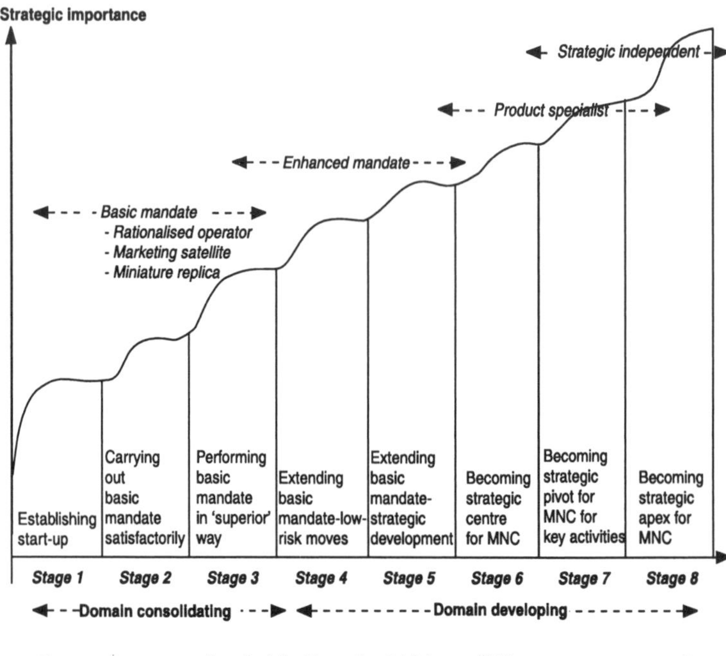

'miniature replica'. These are the entry strategic positions for the subsidiary. The initial three stages are associated with carrying out the basic mandate only.

Stage 1: Establishing Start-up This involves simply getting the subsidiary into operation. It may require some level of basic technology transfer, premises identification, training of staff and carrying out of the functions to a 'recipe' provided by the parent. Frequently, the start-up stage is under the direct supervision of parent company managers. One of the general managers referred to this experience as 'spoon feeding' of the subsidiary by the parent.

Stage 2: Carrying Out the Basic Mandate Satisfactorily This requires the subsidiary to start meeting the original goals set for it in terms of efficiency and quality in the case of a rationalised operator or sales and budgets in the case of other start-up modes. The teething problems associated with stage 1 have to be overcome and the subsidiary starts to be able to operate with fewer parent inputs. However, viewed from the parent, the subsidiary will still be 'recipe following'. While this stage is only just beyond start-up, it is evident that some subsidiaries fail to really reach even this basic stage. Their performance remains inferior both to the goals set for it and to those of the parent model.

Stage 3: Performing Basic Mandate in a 'Superior Way' This is a crucial stage if the subsidiary is to develop. The subsidiary must start being perceived as doing more than simply meeting basic goals. It needs to go beyond simply 'meeting the recipe' and start performing in ways that are perceived as superior to other comparable sites. A first-level move is to simply start sourcing material locally in a more effective manner than buying from the parent. Beyond that, subsidiary 28, a US-owned healthcare manufacturing subsidiary, installed superior quality systems that became an important focus of attention as the parent plant started to encounter quality problems.

An outcome of this stage may be an increase in the scale of manufacturing as volume increases are directed to the 'superior performer'. A rare outcome is the absorption of the parent plant's operations into the Irish plant, as happened in the case of subsidiary 3, a US-owned healthcare manufacturing plant.

Stages 4–5: Moving Beyond the Basic Mandate

In these stages, the subsidiary moves beyond the basic mandate to gain an enhanced mandate. It is not that it necessarily increases its scale, but that it actually moves into different activities. A key prerequisite to any move into stages 4–5 is that the subsidiary has demonstrated superior performance, and gained credibility, in its original mandate.

Stage 4: Extending Basic Mandate – Low-Risk Moves The parent is unlikely to simply grant the subsidiary an extension to its mandate. A considerable canvassing effort is required from subsidiary management. However, just as in start-up businesses customers like to make 'low-risk' decisions, so parents do not want to give mandate extensions that involve high risk. One general manager referred to 'having to move through corridors of indifference', meaning that one has got to look for opportunities to extend one's mandate in areas that are of low significance both in terms of risk and in terms of perceived loss of mandate to sister sites or other parts of the organisation. Subsidiaries 5, UK-owned, and 12, Swedish-owned, were both subsidiaries established in the Irish Financial Services Centre for a specific purpose. However, they sought out extensions of their remit in areas where others found the activities a 'nuisance' and of little strategic significance.

Because the subsidiary cannot fully develop a competence in the new activity prior to obtaining the mandate, there is often a need for the 'skunkworks' type of activities that allow it subsequently to demonstrate its ability. This requires the subsidiary to develop a level of slack within its organisation to take on development of 'unallocated' activities. Subsidiary 10, a US-owned manufacturing plant, started its product development mandate by recruiting development engineers in the place of approved manufacturing engineers and then getting them to work on unapproved product development activities.

Stage 5: Extending Basic Mandate – Strategic Development Having shown the ability to carry out activities outside the basic mandate, the subsidiary has the credibility to take on a bigger challenge in terms of extending their mandate. It is in a position to compete for 'mandate extensions' with sister sites. Subsidiary 14, a US-owned manufacturing subsidiary, moved from a basic manufacturing role to a minor role in European logistics (a stage 4 move) but, having demonstrated success in this new role, it was then in a position to canvass for the world-wide logistics function. A succession of the companies in the sample moved from basic manufacturing to taking on product development functions. Others moved into customer service functions.

Stages 6–8: Growing Strategic Significance of Subsidiary within the Parent

In these stages, the subsidiary increases its strategic role by becoming either a product specialist or a strategic independent.

Each stage differs in the degree of strategic importance of the subsidiary.

Stage 6: Becoming a Strategic Centre for the MNC In this stage, the subsidiary ceases to be simply a subsidiary and starts to become a differentiated centre for corporate activities. The term 'centre of excellence' is frequently used. The subsidiary starts taking on a world or regional mandate, which gives it a unique role within the organisation. A US-owned healthcare subsidiary that had established itself as a product development centre from a previous pure manufacturing base has now become a technology centre for a range of products within the corporation. It has become a strategic site for the corporation as opposed to one that is duplicating activities elsewhere.

Stage 7: Becoming a Strategic Pivot for the Organisation The distinction between stage 6 and stage 7 is one of the degree of strategic importance. Subsidiary 19, a UK-owned consumer goods manufacturer, has become one the world centres of excellence for manufacturing and product development in its corporation. It has a specific product range responsibility, which includes a key brand for the corporation. In addition, the international marketing centre for that brand has also been located in Ireland. Consequently, the Irish subsidiaries have responsibility and control of the key functions of the business. This is in contrast to subsidiary 23, a Swedish-owned healthcare plant, which is also the world-wide centre for a specific range of products for the corporation. However, the range is peripheral to the corporation's main business, and the Irish subsidiary does not have control of marketing. Consequently, it would be positioned as a Stage 6 subsidiary.

Stage 8: Becoming a Strategic Apex for the MNC In this final stage, the subsidiary has a very high level of autonomy and is a standalone 'strategy-making' unit of the corporation. Subsidiary 9, a UK-owned consumer goods subsidiary, is a very major company in Ireland. The Irish operation is a very major contributor to the division's profitability. It is a full-line business, with significant linkages and business outside Ireland. It has a significant world-wide role and contains the division's R&D unit.

Moving through the Phases – a Case-study

Subsidiary 20 started as a Swedish-owned manufacturing subsidiary carrying out a single, labour-intensive activity within the value chain. It made significant progress in its original mandate and gradually outperformed its sister site in Sweden because of lower costs in Ireland and higher levels of efficiency. After about five years of operations in Ireland, a dynamic Irish general manager was recruited. The new manager lobbied the Swedish parent managers hard to extend its manufacturing scope. It eventually succeeded through a series of phases to take over all manufacturing activity for its product line, thus causing the Swedish manufacturing plant to close. The general manager then focused on taking on product development activities, and argued that there was no business logic in having product development activities in Sweden if the manufacturing was to be carried out in Ireland, given that manufacturing had to get involved at a very early stage of the product development process. The product development manager eventually relocated from Sweden to Ireland. At about the same time, the parent company went through a series of corporate changes and moved to a holding company structure. This presented the Irish plant with an opportunity of bidding for the sales and marketing activity to be headquartered in Ireland. It was unsuccessful in achieving this initially, but it still gained a more active customer interfacing role. After a year, business problems due to poor sales performance presented the Irish plant with a second chance to bid for the sales and marketing functions and it was successful. Finally, a further series of corporate level changes in Sweden has allowed the corporation's centre for the entire business area controlling all activities for that business – product development, manufacturing, marketing and selling, finance – to be located in Ireland. While luck played a part in providing the Irish subsidiary with the opportunities for extending its business mandate, the dynamism of local Irish management was a key factor.

Subsidiary Development 'Snakes and Ladders'

While Figure 10.3 indicates a ladder of development, 'snakes and ladders' is a better analogy. Regardless of where a subsidiary has arrived at in terms of its stage of development, it can slip back through lack of performance, environmental change or organisational restructuring. Subsidiary 19, a UK-owned consumer business subsidiary, is a very successful stage 7 subsidiary, which owed its origins to an ambitious and progressive miniature-replica business in Ireland. This miniature-replica business sought to develop a product which would have market potential outside Ireland and was very successful leading to the creation of the subsidiary 19 unit, which, however, reported into the Irish business. Effectively, the miniature-replica business developed to a stage 7 or stage 8 subsidiary. However, a world-wide corporate restructuring caused this corporation to be reorganised along global functional lines, leaving subsidiary 19 to report into the manufacturing division and the original Irish business reporting into the marketing organisation as a marketing satellite (effectively as a stage 2 or stage 3 subsidiary). From a position of controlling one of the key products in the group, it found itself as a sales subsidiary of a minor European market.

The 'snakes and ladders' analogy indicates the potential precariousness of the developed subsidiary. It points to the need to consolidate gains at each new stage of development before seeking to further broaden the mandate. Furthermore, regardless of how advanced the subsidiary becomes, there is a need to continuously reinforce and consolidate the subsidiary's credibility by performance improvements within the current mandate. This is the reason that the bottom of Figure 10.3 indicates that domain-defending and domain-consolidating initiatives may be required at any stage of the subsidiary's development through the eight stages.

SCALE INCREASES – A DIFFERENT TYPE OF DEVELOPMENT

The model of stages of development illustrated and discussed focuses on the development of the functional scope of the business, namely adding new activities to the existing mandate. While increased functional scope may lead to a larger Irish operation to man the new functions of the organisation, it is a different type of development to the increase of scale associated with expansion of current operations. Subsidiary 20, our earlier case-study of a successful stage 8 subsidiary business, has a much lower employment level in Ireland than do many subsidiaries of MNC companies. All the three strategic initiatives discussed by the general manager of subsidiary 20 concerned adding to the subsidiary's strategic breadth. In contrast, the general manager of subsidiary 22, a UK-owned food ingredients plant, described three initiatives that all concerned the increase in scale of the Irish operations due to corporate reconfigurations involving the closure of plants in other countries. However, it would still be described as a stage 3 subsidiary – performing its original, albeit expanded in scale – manufacturing mandate in a superior fashion. It has not succeeded in increasing its strategic importance in terms of adding new critical mandates. The concerns over describing such simple scale development as a strategic development for the subsidiary stem from what the scale increase does for the perceived position of the subsidiary within the parent corporation. On the one hand, many subsidiaries can extend scale but remain weakly positioned relative to their parent, because their activities are non-strategic from the parent's perspective. The subsidiary may have no increase in decision-making autonomy or in its power–dependence relationship with the parent. There is therefore little progress in 'tentpegging' the subsidiary into the parent company's critical heartland. On the other hand, an increase in scale of the subsidiary is positive, and may signal a growing importance of the subsidiary in the parent's overall operations. Where it is accompanied by further investment, the subsidiary has clearly raised the commitment level of the parent to, and hence the parent's dependence on, the Irish operation.

Resolving the question of whether the increased scale of a subsidiary can be termed as development of the subsidiary's strategic importance may come from measuring the relative scale of the Irish operation. If the scale increase, either in capital investment, value added, profitability or employment terms, has increased the subsidiary's relative importance in the corporation then it is clearly increasing its strategic importance. Relative scale can be measured by the scale of the subsidiary as a proportion of the total corporate entity on that measure.

CONCLUSIONS

This chapter has sought to set down some of the more important findings from research into strategic initiative taking by multinational subsidiaries in Ireland. The principal contributions referred to involve, first, an extension of the White and Poynter (1984) classification of subsidiaries by changing the 'rationalised manufacturer' category to 'rationalised operator' and, more importantly, the creation of the category 'enhanced mandate'. This allowed sorting of the categories into higher-order categories of basic, intermediate and advanced mandates. Second, the findings led to an extension of Birkinshaw's (1995a) classification of development initiatives to include a classification also including 'defending' and 'consolidating' initiatives based on Thompson (1967) domain theory. Third, this research makes the case for the establishment of a eight-stage model hypothesis of the development of the multinational subsidiary, building on earlier work of Sargeant (1990) and Malnight (1995). It is hoped that this model will contribute to the important issues relating to subsidiary development considered throughout this volume.

References

Baliga, B.R. and A.M. Jaeger (1984) 'Multinational Corporations: Control Systems and Delegation Issues', *Journal of International Business Studies*, 15(4), 25–40.

Bartlett, C. and S. Ghoshal (1986) 'Tap Your Subsidiaries for Global Reach', *Harvard Business Review*, November–December, 64(6), 87–94.

Birkinshaw, J. (1995a) 'Taking the Initiative', *Business Quarterly*, 59(4), Summer, 97–102.

Birkinshaw, J. (1995b) 'Entrepreneurship in Multinational Corporations: the Initiative Process in Foreign Subsidiaries', unpublished doctoral thesis, University of Western Ontario.

Birkinshaw, J. (1995c) 'Encouraging Entrepreneurial Activity in Multinational Corporations', *Business Horizons*, 38(5), May–June, 32–37.

Birkinshaw, J. (1995d) 'Entrepreneurship in Multinational Corporations: Characteristics of Subsidiary Initiatives', Draft Working Paper, University of Toronto.

Birkinshaw, J. (1997) 'Entrepreneurship in Multinational Corporations: The Characteristics of Subsidiary Initiatives', *Strategic Management Journal*, 18 (3), 207–29.

Birkinshaw, J. and W. Ritchie (1993) 'Balancing the Global Portfolio', *Business Quarterly*, 57(4), Summer, 40–49.

Crookell, H. and A. Morrison (1990) 'Subsidiary Strategy in a Free Trade Environment', *Business Quarterly*, Autumn 1990, 33–39.

D'Cruz, J. (1986) 'Strategic Management of Subsidiaries' in H. Etemad and L.S. Dulude (eds), *Managing The Multinational Subsidiary: Response to Environmental changes and to Host Nation R&D Policies*, London: Croom Helm, 75–89.

Egelhoff, W.G. (1984) 'Patterns of Control in US, UK and European Multinational Corporations', *Journal of International Business Studies*, 15(4), Fall, 73–83.

Gupta, A.K. and V. Govindarajan (1991) 'Knowledge Flows and the Structure of Control within Multinational Corporations', *Academy of Management Review*, 16 (4), 768–92.

Huber, G.P. and D.J. Power (1985) 'Retrospective Reports of Strategic Level Managers: Guidelines for Increasing their Accuracy', *Strategic Management Journal*, 6, 171–80.

Industrial Development Authority (1994) *Overseas Companies in Ireland*, Dublin: Industrial Development Authority.

Lyons, P. (1995) 'Subsidiary Survival Through Turbulence', MSc thesis, Trinity College, Dublin.

Malnight, T.W. (1995) 'Globalisation of an Ethnocentric Firm: An Evolutionary Perspective', *Strategic Management Journal*, 16, 119–41.

McDonald, D. (1987) 'Strategies to Increase the Dependence of a Multinational on its Irish Subsidiary', MSc thesis, Trinity College, Dublin.

Miles, M.B. and A.M. Huberman (1994) *Qualitative Data Analysis* (2nd edn), Thousand Oaks, Calif.: Sage.

Molloy, E. (1992) 'Strategic Agenda for a Subsidiary', unpublished consulting notes and handouts, Advanced Organisation and Management Development Limited, Naas, C. Kildare, Ireland.

Morrison, A.J. and K. Roth (1993) 'Developing Global Subsidiary Mandates', *Business Quarterly*, Summer 1993, 104–10.

Organisation for Economic Cooperation and Development (1991) *Economic Surveys: Ireland 1990/91*, Paris: OECD.

Porter, M. (1986) *Competition in Global Industries*, Boston, Mass.: Harvard Business School Press.

Rugman, A.M. and S. Douglas (1986) 'The Strategic Management of Multinationals and World Product Mandates' in H. Etemad and L.S. Dulude (eds), *Managing The Multinational Subsidiary: Response to Environmental changes and to Host Nation R&D Policies*, London: Croom Helm, 90–101.

Sargeant, Lee W. (1990) 'Strategic Planning in a Subsidiary', *Long Range Planning*, 23 (2), 43–54.

Taggart, J.H. (1992) 'Coordination Versus Globalisation: The Multinational's Dilemma, *Multinational Business*, no. 3, 1–12.

Taggart J.H. (1993),'Multinational Subsidiaries and Host Country Impact', Strathclyde International Business Unit Working Paper 93/14, Glasgow: University of Strathclyde.
Taggart J.H. (1995) 'MNC Subsidiary Strategy in Scotland', Strathclyde International Business Unit Working Paper 95/3, Glasgow: University of Strathclyde.
Thompson, J.D. (1967) *Organisations in Action*, New York: McGraw-Hill.
White, R.E. and T.A. Poynter (1984) 'Strategies for Foreign-Owned Subsidiaries in Canada', *Business Quarterly*, 48(4), Summer 1984, 59–69.
Young, S., N. Hood and S. Dunlop (1989) 'Global Strategies, Multinational Subsidiary Roles and Economic Impact in Scotland', *Regional Studies*, 22 (6), 487–97.

11 Foreign-Owned Subsidiaries and Regional Development: The Case of Sweden

Julian Birkinshaw

INTRODUCTION

There continues to be a high level of interest in academic circles regarding the roles of subsidiary companies in multinational corporations (MNCs). This interest has been directed primarily towards the implications of subsidiary companies taking ever more strategic roles within their corporate system. As subsidiaries become 'strategic leaders' and gain 'world product mandates', it is argued, their relationship with headquarters shifts from one of subordination to equal partnership. This suggests a higher level of strategic discretion and opportunities for initiative on the part of the subsidiary (Birkinshaw, 1995), and a wholesale shift in the organisational logic of the MNC (Hedlund, 1994).

This chapter is another contribution to the literature on subsidiary management, but it examines a relatively underexplored dimension, namely *the relationship between the MNC subsidiary and the host country*. (To clarify, the economic impact of FDI on host countries is very well researched (for example. Dunning 1993), but the managerial dimensions, particularly as they relate to the subsidiary, are not.) It has long been recognised that one of the distinctive features of the MNC subsidiary is its dual 'allegiance' to its host country and its parent company. The use of institutionalisation theory in the international context, for example, is built on the observation that the subsidiary faces competing 'isomorphic pulls' from host country and parent company (Westney, 1994), and the research of Ghoshal and Nohria (1989) sees the MNC as a 'differentiated network' in which each subsidiary unit is both differentiated according to its immediate task environment and integrated into its corporate system. Moreover, a number of subsidiary typologies explicitly consider the host country environment as a key distinguishing variable (for example, Bartlett and Ghoshal, 1986; Ghoshal and Nohria, 1989).

The nature of the relationship between the subsidiary and its host country environment is seldom spelled out, however. The most common approach is to adopt the simplifying assumption that the host country environment is more or less given, and that the subsidiary has to somehow adapt to it. This is seen most obviously in the work of Ghoshal and Nohria (1989) mentioned above, as well as in a variety of empirical studies of human-relations practises in subsidiaries (for example, Rosenzweig and Nohria, 1994). A second approach, which to some degree overlaps the first, is to see the subsidiary as tapping into or drawing from the host country environment. Examples of this approach are Porter's (1990) view that foreign-owned subsidiaries typically tap into local clusters in order to keep their parent company informed about leading-edge thinking in that cluster, and studies by Frost (1996) and Almeida (1996) that show how subsidiaries draw from local sources in their innovation processes.

A third approach, which has not been argued to any great extent in the academic literature, is to see the subsidiary as a *contributor* to the host country environment. This approach is conceptually and intuitively straightforward, in that many national economies, including Canada, Singapore and Ireland, appear to rely to a large degree on foreign-owned subsidiaries to provide employment, investment and exports. At the same time, though, most models of regional development (for example, Ozawa, 1992; Dunning, 1993; Porter, 1990) are still based on the implicit assumption that an economy's principal firms are indigenous. This, it is argued is a limiting assumption, and there is therefore need for research that looks explicitly at the impact that foreign-owned subsidiaries have on their host country economy. This author's expectation is that foreign subsidiaries do, to an important degree, contribute to the host country economy, but that the nature of that contribution will be substantially different from and probably lower than the contribution of indigenous firms. Such factors as the level of decision-making autonomy, the presence of R&D activities, and the relationships with local suppliers, are all likely to be lower in foreign-owned subsidiaries, which will have a corresponding negative influence on the development process in the host country.

The three approaches to modelling the relationship of the subsidiary with its host country environment are, of course, all partially true. When superimposed on one another, they suggest an ongoing process of development, whereby the subsidiary reacts and draws from the local environment at the same time as contributing to the local economy as a whole as well as to specific business partners. Over time, it is argued, the subsidiary co-evolves with its environment and gradually plays a more and more important role in the local economy. The subsidiary itself typically goes through a development process where it gains enhanced value-added scope and greater decision-making autonomy (Birkinshaw and Hood, 1997), and this process is both driven by and a source of benefit to the local economy.

The purpose of this chapter is to report on an empirical study of the issues discussed here. More specifically, the focal interest is in the process of subsidiary development over time, and the extent to which that process impacts on the host country in a positive way. The research, then, has a dual focus, in that it is straddling the perspectives of subsidiary managers *and* host country policy-makers. While the empirical analysis is all based on the activities of subsidiaries, the discussion will lean towards understanding the implications of such activities for policy-makers.

The research was conducted on the body of foreign subsidiaries in Sweden. The selection of Sweden is based partly on convenience, but also on the fact that country represents an interesting experimental setting. For decades, Swedish policy-makers were negatively disposed towards foreign direct investment, for the simple reason that Sweden's prosperity had been built on heavy *external* investment, namely, by Swedish MNCs abroad. Over the last five years, however, there has been an acceptance that both internal and external investment are important. Reasons for this change include entry into the European Union, hence the removal of curbs on inward investment; a slowing of Sweden's GDP growth, hence some questioning of past policies; a number of large acquisitions of Swedish MNCs; and the increasing transfer of high-value-added activities out of Sweden by its larger MNCs. The result of these changes is that Sweden now has a significant level of foreign ownership in its industrial sector and, perhaps more important, a will to do more, in terms of both attracting new investments and enhancing the activities of existing subsidiaries. The study reported here was commissioned by the recently created Invest in Sweden Agency to help them understand the prospects for subsidiary development in Sweden.

THEORETICAL BACKGROUND

The basic concept underlying this research is that of *subsidiary development*, defined here as the process through which the subsidiary company adds increasing levels of value to the multinational corporation to which it belongs (Birkinshaw and Hood, 1997). Research from other countries has shown that subsidiaries typically evolve along a number of trajectories. In Scotland, for example, many American- and Japanese-owned subsidiaries began as low-cost assembly operations, exporting foreign-designed products throughout Europe. As these factories became established they gradually took on more value-adding functions, which in some cases extended back into engineering and development work and forward into logistics and distribution activities (Hood and Young, 1983; Hood *et al.*, 1994). In Canada, by contrast, many subsidiaries were established as 'miniature replicas' of their parent companies, with manufacturing, marketing and sales operations all focused on the national market. Some of these operations lost their manufacturing and ended up as sales-only subsidiaries; others developed leading-edge expertise in a single product line and went on to gain a mandate to develop, manufacture and market that product on a world-wide basis (Birkinshaw, 1995; Etemad and Dulude, 1986; Safarian, 1966; White and Poynter, 1984).

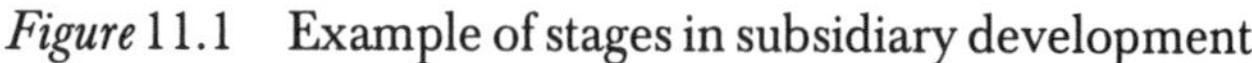

Figure 11.1 Example of stages in subsidiary development

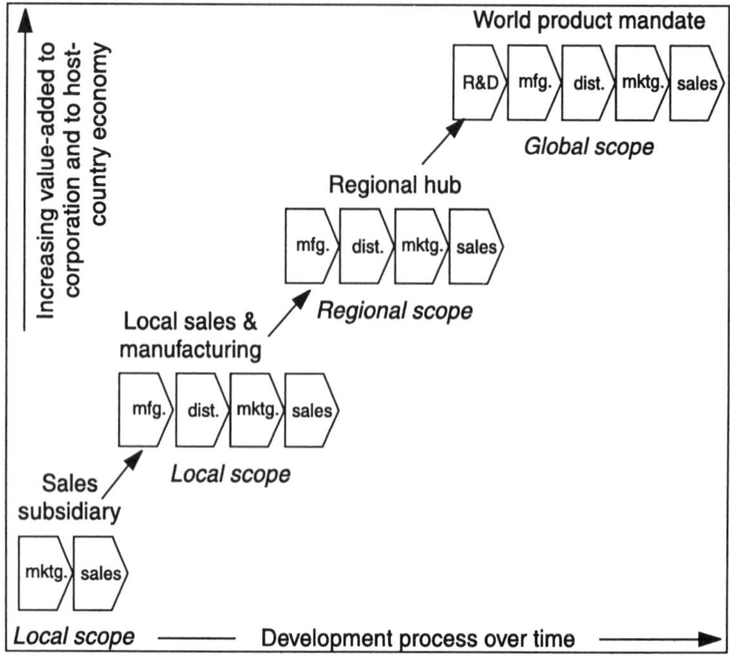

Figure 11.1 depicts a spectrum of foreign-owned subsidiary types according to their level of value added. Value added here is defined along two dimensions: the extent of the value chain that is undertaken by the subsidiary (sales, sales and manufacturing, etc.), and the geographical scope for which the subsidiary has responsibility (local, regional, global). Value-added has both tangible aspects, such as the number of jobs or the level of investment in the operation, and intangible aspects, such as the quality of the work undertaken.

The lowest level of value-added is provided by the sales subsidiary, which simply distributes and sells the parent company's products or services in the local market. Such a subsidiary may also undertake some local marketing and after-sales service. Second is the local sales and manufacturing subsidiary that undertakes production just for the local market, and perhaps some related development or engineering work. The next level of value added is provided by a regional hub subsidiary with some level of international responsibility, typically exporting of products to nearby countries or perhaps marketing or distribution responsibility for a region such as Scandinavia. (Note that the term 'international responsibility' is used to refer to any activity undertaken by the subsidiary that extends beyond the boundaries of its country of operation.) Finally, the highest value added is provided by subsidiaries with leading-edge international responsibilities. These subsidiaries typically have R&D, manufacturing, and business management activities for an entire business or division, and are recognised for their technological and commercial leadership. They are often referred to as strategic leaders or world product mandate subsidiaries (Etemad and Dulude, 1986).

Two points of clarification are important in terms of Figure 11.1. First, the subsidiary development process is by no means guaranteed. Many subsidiaries will never change their roles, and some may actually move backwards, for example, through the divestment of a manufacturing operation. Second, while value added is defined in terms of the subsidiary's contribution to the parent company, it should be clear that the level of subsidiary value added is also related to the strength of the relationship with the host country economy. The sales subsidiary provides local employment, a small amount of investment and imported products for local sale; the world product mandate subsidiary provides high levels of employment and investment, sourcing opportunities for local suppliers, export sales, technological innovation, and so on. Expressed slightly differently, low-value added subsidiaries are 'exploiters' of the local environment, whereas high-value added subsidiaries are 'contributors' to the environment. There are exceptions of course, but as a general rule the subsidiary development process represents an enhancement of value added to both the parent company *and* the host country environment.

How does subsidiary development occur? The process is the result of a complex interplay between the actions of subsidiary managers, the actions of parent company managers, and the characteristics of the local marketplace. Subsidiary-driven development is a bottom-up, entrepreneurial process. It is characterised by the creation of new business opportunities within the subsidiary that are nurtured and gradually built up by subsidiary managers and eventually brought forward to parent management for funding. Parent-driven development is a top-down process. It involves the allocation of investment funds or new responsibilities to the subsidiary on the basis of strategic decisions taken at head office. Finally, both subsidiary- and parent-driven processes are to some extent a function of the host country marketplace. The subsidiary needs to receive stimuli from local customers, competitors and suppliers in order to identify entrepreneurial opportunities; and the parent company has to perceive the local marketplace as being an attractive or strategic location in which to invest.

Developing a Typology of Subsidiaries

The focus in this study on subsidiary roles *vis-à-vis* the host country economy meant that it was necessary to develop a new categorisation of subsidiaries. Most subsidiary typologies focus on the contribution the subsidiary makes to the MNC, for example, using words such as 'implementer', 'contributor', 'strategic leader' and 'world mandate' (Birkinshaw and Morrison, 1996). The few that consider the host country environment make a point of distinguishing between the strategic importance or dynamism of *different* host countries (Bartlett and Ghoshal, 1986), which is clearly inappropriate in a study of a single host country. It was decided therefore to use a very simple categorisation that was also relevant to the host country situation.

Subsidiaries were categorised according to the mode of formation, acquired or greenfield; and the value added scope, namely, sales/marketing only, or sales/marketing plus R&D or manufacturing. The mode of formation proved to be critical in the Swedish context, because Sweden's history of export-led growth meant that most large subsidiaries arose through acquisition of formerly Swedish companies. There is also a theoretical reason to expect different characteristics in acquired and greenfield subsidiaries, namely that acquired operations are likely to have long-standing and hence strong relationships with other entities in the host country economy (Woodcock, 1994).

The value added scope is a simple measure of importance to the host country (White and Poynter, 1984), both in terms of the number of jobs created and in terms of possible exports to other parts of the MNC. Value-added scope is also the most accessible measure of subsidiary development (Figure 11.1), so categorising subsidiaries in this way allows us to induce the extent to which development has occurred in the body of Swedish subsidiaries. The analysis in the rest of this chapter builds on this typology. Specifically, the following research questions are addressed:

1. What differences exist between the four types of subsidiaries (in terms of their sales profile, their relationship with the parent company, and the relationship with the host country)?
2. What are the prospects for subsidiary development and for a significant economic impact on the host country for each group?

RESEARCH METHODOLOGY

This research was undertaken in two distinct parts. First, a questionnaire was administered to a sample of foreign-owned subsidiaries in Sweden. Second, six case studies of subsidiaries were undertaken. The questionnaire allowed the examination of the validity of the typology and identified the specific differences between the four types. The case studies allowed the development of a more detailed understanding of the development prospects for one particular group of subsidiaries.

In the first phase of research, a questionnaire requested descriptive information about Swedish subsidiaries (for example, revenues, ownership, percentage exports, acquired or greenfield) and perceptual measures of various aspects of subsidiary management, relationships with the parent company, and aspects of the local marketplace. This questionnaire was mailed to a sample of five hundred foreign-owned subsidiaries. Companies were identified from lists compiled by Veckans Affär, Compass, and the American Embassy. (Note that none of these sources provided a comprehensive listing. Thus, the sample polled in this research cannot be said to be the entire population of foreign-owned subsidiaries above 100 m kr. in Sweden, though it is believed to be close.) The survey attempted to sample all subsidiaries with revenues greater than 100 million Swedish kronor m kr. However, the American Embassy list did not include information about size, so there are some subsidiaries in the sample, some of which are smaller than 100 m kr. A total of 137 subsidiaries responded, with a mean size of 990 m kr.

In the second phase of research, subsidiaries were approached that were greenfield investments with manufacturing and/or R&D activities. The logic was that these subsidiaries represented the best evidence for subsidiary development, in that they had moved along the trajectory indicated in Figure 11.1. Ten of these subsidiaries were approached. Six were positive towards the research and allowed the write-up of case-studies of their development process; a further two agreed to shorter telephone interviews.

The case-study interviews were semi-structured. The senior managers of the subsidiaries were invited to describe how they had come to develop R&D or manufacturing operations in Sweden, and from this description the specific factors that were of interest in this study were examined in greater detail. Each case-study was written up separately, and sent back to the subsidiary managers to verify the accuracy of our write-ups. The accounts in this chapter are brief summaries of four of the longer case-studies.

Construct Measures

All constructs were measured using multi-item scales. Where possible these scales were taken from previous studies. The precise wording of questions can be found in Appendix 11.A.

FINDINGS: QUESTIONNAIRE RESPONSES

The 137 responding subsidiaries had average sales revenues in 1995 of 990 m kr. However, this reflects an enormous range from 10 million kronor up to 20 billion. The vast majority (130) of these subsidiaries were wholly owned by their parent companies; only three had minority owners, and four were joint ventures. Parent companies originated from eighteen different countries. The most common parent country was the USA, but this is in part a reflection of the bias in the sample towards American-owned subsidiaries. Other common parent–company nationalities were Switzerland (largely ABB companies), Denmark, Finland, France, Germany and UK.

In terms of the key variables used in the typology, 77 of the subsidiaries had only sales and marketing activities. However, it should be observed that this group included a number of service firms. The remaining 60 had either manufacturing (48), R&D (39) or both. Regarding mode of formation, 68 were acquired and 69 were formed as greenfield operations. The resulting distribution of subsidiaries between the four types is therefore as shown in Figure 11.2.

Figure 11.2 Typology of Swedish subsidiaries

Functional scope:	Mode of formation Greenfield site, organic growth	Acquisition
Downstream activities only (sales, marketing, professional service)	Group 1 Organically grown sales subsidiaries 48 cases	Group 2 Acquired sales subsidiaries 29 cases
Upstream activities (manufacturing, R&D) and some downstream activities	Group 3 Organically grown manufacturing and R&D subsidiaries 21 cases	Group 4 Acquired manufacturing and R&D subsidiaries 39 cases

Assessing the Typology

In order to establish the validity of the chosen typology, the mean values of certain descriptive variables such as sales revenues, levels of international sales and so on were examined. Table 11.1 lists these figures for the four groups, and indicates

Table 11.1 Basic characteristics of the four groups

	Group 1 Organic growth, sales subsidiary	*Group 2 Acquired sales subsidiary*	*Group 3 Organic, manufacturing and R&D*	*Group 4 Acquired, Manufacturing and R&D*	*ANOVA F-value Significance level*
Number in sample	48	29	21	39	
Number with international responsibility	13	12	12	24	5.29, $p < 0.01$
Average international sales	12.2%	6.5%	**15.5%**	**41.8%**	14.53, $p < 0.001$
Average annual revenues	419 m. kr	987 m. kr	809 m. kr	**1854 m. kr**	2.44, $p < 0.05$
Average R&D expenditure	0.5%	0.3%	2.8%	**4.6%**	11.60, $p < 0.001$
Number selling in Sweden	24	15	8	9	
Number selling to Nordics	24	18	12	9	
No. selling beyond Nordics	4	4	5	31	

Numbers refer to mean responses on 3-point, 5-point and 7-point scales.
Statistical significance tested for using ANOVA. Where differences between pairs are significant they are shown using *italic* and **bold** face type.

the results of the ANOVA analysis that was used to detect significant differences between the groups. The results indicate a high level of difference along most key variables. Group 1 subsidiaries are much smaller on average than the other groups. They have virtually no R&D, and sell almost exclusively in Sweden and the other Nordic countries. Group 2 subsidiaries are similar to group 1 in market scope and level of internationalisation, but almost twice as large. Group 3 subsidiaries are only slightly more international than the first two groups, but they have much more R&D and are similar in size to the second group. Finally, group 4 subsidiaries are typically much larger, much more international and conduct more R&D than any of the other groups.

Differences between groups

Table 11.2 lists the group means for the various characteristics of the host country environment and subsidiary. The strength of local suppliers was predictably greater in groups 2 and 4, namely in those subsidiaries that had been acquired. Interestingly, however, it was also relatively high in group 3, suggesting that this group has built strong relationships with local supplier companies as its own operations have developed. The number of subsidiaries that were members of leading-edge clusters also showed a high level of variance – 25 per cent and 27 per cent in groups 1 and 2, versus 57 per cent and 49 per cent in groups 3 and 4. Again, this is more or less as one would expect, in that foreign multinationals are more likely to establish manufacturing or R&D if the host country environment has a leading-edge cluster. With regard to the level of local competition there were no significant differences. Groups 1 and 4 registered the highest mean responses, which is as one would expect for group 4 but not for group 1. It can only be surmised that the high perceived local competition in group 1 reflected the local orientation of these subsidiaries (relative to other groups with more international orientations).

In terms of the characteristics of the subsidiary and its corporate system, group 4 had the highest level of autonomy, significantly higher than group 1 and marginally higher than the other groups. This ordering was also reflected in the level of communication with the parent, in that group 4 had rather lower levels of communication than the other three. The level of subsidiary initiative was also examined, which was approximately the same in groups 2, 3 and 4 but significantly lower in group 1. This finding is somewhat surprising, in that it was not expected that group 2 would reveal such a high level of initiative. It is perhaps symptomatic of the previous existence of the subsidiaries in this group as independent companies.

Table 11.2 Distinctive characteristics of the four groups

	Group 1 Organic, sales Subsidiary	*Group 2 Acquired sales subsidiary*	*Group 3 Organic, manufacturing and R&D*	*Group 4 Acquired, Manufacturing and R&D*	*ANOVA F-value Significance level*
Strength of suppliers	4.00	**4.65**	4.47	**4.63**	4.46, $p < 0.005$
Number with presence in cluster	12 of 48	8 of 29	12 of 21	19 of 39	
Level of local competition	5.14	4.97	4.63	5.13	1.10, ns
Level of subsidiary autonomy	2.08	2.24	2.38	**2.53**	9.41, $p < 0.001$
Level of communication with parent	4.40	4.58	4.49	4.19	0.89, ns
Evidence of subsidiary initiative	1.85	**2.51**	**2.88**	**2.70**	5.50, $p < 0.01$

Numbers refer to mean responses on 3-point, 5-point and 7-point scales.
Statistical significance tested for using ANOVA. Where differences between pairs are significant they are shown using *italic* and **bold** type.

Description of the Four Groups: Prospects for Development

The analysis thus far has been closely based on the data. In order to address the second research question, namely in terms of prospects for development and impact on the Swedish economy, the next section is somewhat more speculative. While based on the data above, it also draws on only the author's general understanding of subsidiary companies and on the specific understanding of the situation in Sweden.

Group 1. Organically Grown Sales Subsidiaries

This group consists primarily of subsidiaries that were set up to serve the Swedish marketplace. It includes many well-known names such as Microsoft, Honeywell, Nike, Fujitsu and Gillette. These subsidiaries appear to be more closely tied into their corporate system than to the Swedish industrial system.

In terms of their impact on the host country economy, the future prospects for this group of subsidiaries are somewhat limited. The only obvious opportunity for such subsidiaries is to broaden their sales and marketing responsibility to the Nordic region or similar. Some of this group are already responsible for sales throughout the Nordic region (often using distributors in the other countries). As multinationals move to consolidate their activities further in Europe, such 'sub-regional' responsibilities will only increase. However, at the same time there is a risk for some of these subsidiaries, because they can themselves be eliminated as European operations are rationalised. One common approach, for example, is to pair the British Isles with Scandinavia and to run the entire portfolio out of England.

Group 2. Acquired Sales and Service Subsidiaries

This group is rather heterogeneous, consisting of some pure sales subsidiaries (of manufacturing multinationals) but also a large number of subsidiaries of service multinationals. It includes, for example, Burger King, Nyman & Schultz, Svenska Statoil and Scandinavia Seaways. All these subsidiaries arose through acquisition of Swedish companies, often quite a long time ago. However, the legacy of Swedish ownership is to some extent still visible, in comparison with the group 1 subsidiaries, because this group has much stronger links to the Swedish economy, more autonomy, and greater average sales volume. However, its members do tend to be very Sweden-focused, with only 6.5 per cent of their sales on average coming from outside the country.

In terms of their impact on the Swedish economy, the prospects for this group are much stronger than for the group 1 subsidiaries. As acquired companies, they are likely to have unique expertise in certain areas that may be valuable to the parent company. If this expertise is made known to the parent company, then it may over time lead to the development of a centre of excellence on which other parts of the corporation draw. (The latter part of this chapter provides a full discussion of the centre of excellence concept.) Furthermore, another facet of this group's independent heritage is that there is much more likelihood of entrepreneurship from management. The evidence suggested that there were sporadic cases of initiative from subsidiaries in this group, for example bidding for new corporate investments and suggesting new acquisition targets in Sweden. However, it seems there is very little prospect of subsidiaries in this group attracting investments in manufacturing or R&D. They do not have existing manufacturing operations that can be used as justification for further investment, and they are mostly not in leading-edge clusters that would make them attractive locations for greenfield investments. It may be that the centre of excellence approach is the most promising for these subsidiaries.

Group 3. Organically Grown Subsidiaries with Manufacturing and/or R&D

In many ways the subsidiaries in this group are the most interesting, because they arose from nothing to a status where they have manufacturing or R&D or both. However, this group is also the smallest of the four, with only 21 subsidiaries (out of 137). There are a number of well known names in this group, including 3M, Johnson & Johnson, Glaxo Wellcome and Mobil Oil.

As a matter of definition, this group has undergone a relatively high level of development. Most appeared to start as sales subsidiaries, but they subsequently gained manufacturing and/or R&D, in large part through their own entrepreneurial effort. The process through which such responsibilities were gained is interesting, and it forms the basis of the latter part of this chapter. Currently, the subsidiaries in this group have a wide variety of responsibilities. Many are focused on the Nordic market (international sales only average 15.5 per cent), but they have high average R&D expenditure (2.8 per cent) and they have relatively high autonomy. Just over half of these subsidiaries are in leading-edge clusters, predominantly health care, and they typically have relatively strong links with local suppliers. Despite their organic origins, these subsidiaries are now strong contributors to the Swedish economy, and have considerable potential for further growth.

The prospects for this group are mixed, however, because the opportunity for growth is high but the threat of closure is also high. The reason for this is simply European rationalisation: because the plants attracted by these subsidiaries were often small, one-product operations, they were also the first victims of consolidation programs. (See the Johnson & Johnson case-study below for an example of this point.) Thus, the challenge for manufacturing subsidiaries in this group is, in the first instance, to retain their current operations.

Group 4. Acquired Subsidiaries with Manufacturing and R&D

This group consists of many well-known names such as Akzo Nobel, Avesta Sheffield, Siemens Elema, Svenska Nestle (Findus), and various ABB companies. Not surprisingly, subsidiaries in this group are on average much larger than those in the other groups. They are also much more international in their outlook, more autonomous, better connected to the supplier network, and predominantly members of leading-edge clusters.

Because of their size and proven strengths, it seems that subsidiaries in this group are not seriously threatened by the process of consolidation that is underway in many large multinationals. Indeed they may gain additional investment, because one of the strong arguments for investing in Sweden is to become an active participant in some of the leading-edge clusters such as the forestry, metals and telecommunications industries. Put another way, these subsidiaries have mostly attained the 'critical mass' necessary to be judged as major operations in their own right within their multinational network.

The prospects for further investment in group 4 subsidiaries are strong – but they *should be*, given that several of Sweden's better-known multinational companies now fall within this group. Perhaps their greatest responsibility, with regard to the Swedish economy, is to actively support their industry clusters by making greater use of local suppliers and by encouraging spin-off firms to start up in the vicinity. There is an important lesson here from Silicon Glen in Scotland. While Silicon Glen has a very high concentration of semiconductor and computer manufacturers, it has failed to some degree to build either a comprehensive supplier network or a significant body of start-up companies. As a result, there is not a sufficiently well-developed supporting cluster, which means that the industry does not generate leading-edge ideas in the same way that Silicon Valley and other high-tech areas are able to.

FINDINGS: CASE-STUDIES

The case studies provided some important insights into the development process. There were very few cases of 'traditional' investments, in terms of capital flows or job creation. Instead, initiatives directed towards every possible activity were identified, ranging from pure research to logistics to customer service. These initiatives had several positive impacts on the subsidiaries in question. They typically enhanced revenues, they created a few jobs, and they enhanced the standing of the Swedish subsidiary in the multinational network. The following paragraphs provide brief descriptions of some of the case-studies that were followed in this research. The key issues from these case studies are drawn together at the end of the section.

Baxter Medical AB

Baxter International is an American health care and pharmaceutical company specialising in renal, cardiovascular, hospital products and biotechnology products. Baxter Medical AB is responsible for the sales, marketing and distribution of Baxter products in Sweden and the other Nordic countries. Yvonne Petersson, Managing Director of Baxter Medical AB, is responsible for about 150 people and $100 million in sales revenues.

The interesting development here was the formation of a renal research facility in Sweden that is legally part of Baxter Medical AB, but operationally part of Karolinska Institute, a large research hospital. The origins of this research facility can be found in Baxter's commitment to long-term, university-based research programs. Baxter has for many years funded an 'extramural' research program open to researchers anywhere in the world. Through this program Baxter developed links with several top European medical research establishments, among them Karolinska. This led to Baxter's attempt in 1994 to recruit professor Bengt Lindholm, a leading authority on renal medicine at Karolinska. He declined the proposed move to Baxter's main research facility in Belgium, but he suggested that he work for Baxter while remaining at Karolinska. While there was some scepticism about how such an arrangement would work, a deal was structured that allowed Lindholm to be employed full-time by Baxter, but for him to continue to work with a group of 15 renal researchers at Karolinska. Lindholm is now the director of scientific affairs for the renal division in Europe, but his Baxter colleagues are based mostly in Belgium.

This case-study emphasises the importance of Sweden's leading-edge research capabilities as a magnet for corporate investment. Clearly, Bengt Lindholm was the key individual in this case, but his desire to stay at Karolinska owed a lot to the level of excellence in renal research in Sweden, as well as to his personal preference not to move to Belgium. A related factor is that Baxter's strongest world-wide competitor in renal products is Gambro, a Swedish multinational.

While the structure of the deal between Lindholm and Baxter was somewhat unusual, and built heavily on mutual trust, it nevertheless represents an interesting way of retaining Sweden's strong position in certain areas of research while also attracting foreign investment. Moreover, the prospects of Sweden attracting additional investment in cases such as this appears to be strong, because centres of excellence tend to attract top quality researchers who can then further promote the reputation of the institute. On the negative side, however, it should also be noted that Baxter is relatively unusual in its desire to fund R&D in such a decentralised manner.

Johnson & Johnson AB

Johnson & Johnson (J&J) is a well-known American healthcare company, with interests in consumer products, pharmaceuticals and professional equipment. Johnson & Johnson AB was established in 1956 as a sales and marketing subsidiary, but it developed two manufacturing operations in the 1970s. The rise and subsequent fall of these manufacturing operations provides some interesting insights into subsidiary development.

The first plant was established in 1972 as a local source for sutures, because Swedish surgeons were requesting some adaptations of the standard J&J product. By 1990 there were five suture plants in Europe, and the Swedish plant was producing a tenth of the volume of the Hamburg plant at greater unit cost. J&J, like every other large multinational, was looking for ways to consolidate its European operations, so the decision was made to close the Swedish and Italian plants.

The second plant was built in 1979 to manufacture 'nursing pads' for breast-feeding women. In marked contrast to the suture plant, this was the only one of its kind in Europe. The product had been developed from scratch by a couple of Swedes, and in true entrepreneurial style they had generated enough interest in the product to build a dedicated manufacturing operation. Approximately 60 per cent of output was exported. Unfortunately, this plant too became a victim of J&J's European rationalisation program. Despite recent investments that made the product cheaper in Sweden than it would be elsewhere, the decision was made in 1995 to close the factory and shift production to a large plant in France. As Ragnar Svensson, Managing Director of J&J AB, explained, this decision was harder to accept than the decision to close the suture plant, because the nursing pad plant was profitable and efficient, and Sweden represented a large part of the market for nursing pads.

The rise and fall of these two plants has worrying implications for manufacturing investments in Sweden. Most multinationals are still rationalising their European operations, and a common approach is to concentrate production in a small number of locations that are either geographically central or low-cost. This means that small factories in Sweden, such as the two described here, are very vulnerable. Thus, for many Swedish subsidiaries with manufacturing, the challenge in the years ahead may be simply to retain what they have, rather than to look for new investments. This can best be achieved by being proactive. If a plant appears vulnerable then Swedish management have to look for ways of adding value (for example, through product upgrading) to make it attractive as a long-term investment for the parent company.

There is one important postscript to the J&J story. Following the decision to close the second manufacturing plant, top management shifted their attention to the distribution and logistics operations in the Nordic countries. Manual procedures were superseded by an EDI system that allowed products to be ordered directly from computers installed in hospitals. Many independent distributors were eliminated, and a central warehouse was established at Viskafors. The result of these changes was both more rapid fulfilment of orders *and* reduced distribution costs. J&J AB is now recognised as the leader within J&J Europe on issues of distribution and logistics. The ideas carried out in Sweden are now being transferred elsewhere in Europe. (It is interesting to note that Baxter Medical AB has recently made some similar changes to its distribution and logistics system. Perhaps the challenge of distributing products in the Nordic countries provides unusually high opportunities for cost-saving that companies such as J&J and Baxter are beginning to exploit.)

3M Svenska AB

3M is a well-known American corporation producing a wide range of industrial and consumer products including abrasives, tapes, office products, and healthcare products. 3M's data recording and imaging businesses were recently spun off as an independent company called Imation. 3M established a Swedish operation in 1962, with responsibility primarily for marketing, distributing and selling 3M products. In the late 1980s changes were made to the European operation, leading to the establishment in 1991 of a Nordic region, based in Stockholm and headed by Erik Moe.

3M Nordic performed poorly in 1991 and 1992, resulting in a small round of layoffs. Faced with a soft economy and low morale among the workforce, Moe embarked on a series of initiatives directed at fundamentally rethinking 3M's relationships with its customers in the Nordic region. While none of these initiatives resulted in significant new investments in Sweden, they were enormously successful, both with regard to the market share and profitability of 3M in the Nordic region, and with regard to the enhanced stature of the Swedish organisation in the rest of the 3M world. Again, the term 'centre of excellence' can best describe the current status of 3M Nordic.

Two initiatives will be mentioned here, though it should be emphasised that these are just the most prominent elements of a complete renewal of 3M's Nordic operations. The first was *customer days.* Inspired by a 3M promotion at the Lillehammer Olympics, Moe and his management team recognised the possibility of putting on a large promotional event that would display a broad range of 3M products and provide seminars on a variety of topical business issues. The dual objective was to attract a lot of potential customers and to involve a large number of 3M employees. The first customer days event was held in Göteborg in October 1994, and subsequently 35 others have been held in Sweden. The results have been impressive: 44 000 visitors led to 17 800 sales leads and significant enhancements to sales in Sweden. Moreover, customer days have now been established in other parts of Europe, and Swedish management are frequently called on to provide advice on how best to apply the concept.

The second initiative was *key account management.* This originated from Moe's experiences in managing 3M in the Netherlands, but it lent itself particularly well to the Swedish market, where there are a small number of large customers such as ABB and Ericsson. Key account management was built on the recognition that large corporations are moving towards close relationships with a relatively small number of lead suppliers. 3M Svenska assigned high-potential people to work with these companies, in order to coordinate the sales efforts of the thirty business units. These key accounts have averaged 23 per cent annual growth over the last three years.

As with customer days, 3M Svenska's initiative in key account management is leading the way within 3M Europe, and attracting interest from other regions that are interested in replicating their success. The turnaround in performance has been impressive: 10 per cent growth annually in the Nordic region and pre-tax profits of around 15 per cent. The important insight from the 3M case-study is that it is possible to be entrepreneurial, even if the subsidiary is focused on sales and marketing operations. These initiatives did not lead to any major capital investments, but they did enhance 3M's sales in the Nordic region and they led to an enhanced stature for the Swedish subsidiary in Europe.

Datapoint Svenska AB

Datapoint is one of the large American companies that dominated the computer industry back in the 1970s. As the computer industry evolved from its focus on mainframes towards personal computers, network solutions, and open standards, so did Datapoint's services. However, they were slow to change, and at the beginning of the 1990s the company lost money for six consecutive quarters.

Terry Morris became president of Datapoint Svenska in July 1993, and was faced with the challenge of returning a technically bankrupt subsidiary to profitability. Like its parent company, Datapoint Svenska was selling IT solutions in a variety of areas such as networking, personal computing, telephony and videoconferencing. However, they did not have the size and installed base of large companies such as IBM or Fujitsu.

Morris reduced the workforce at Datapoint Svenska from 120 to 75, and imposed strict financial targets. More importantly, he gave his employees great latitude to achieve these targets however they saw fit, including selling competitors' products if necessary. This led to a major contract with the Swedish Statskontoret to install a network of several thousand machines. Hewlett-Packard machines were used, which presumably was not appreciated by the parent company but led to a major change in philosophy within Datapoint Svenska. From that point on, employees began to search for innovative ways of satisfying customer demands, rather than sticking to the approach of selling traditional Datapoint solutions. Recent contracts have included the provision of electronic tags to the Stockholm police, hand-held terminals to hospitals, and the development of an international computer network for a major law firm. Datapoint Svenska is now the most profitable subsidiary in the corporation, and a centre of excellence in the areas of data networking and communications.

The turnaround at Datapoint Svenska can be attributed to many factors, including Terry Morris's inspiring leadership, an upturn in the demand for computer services, and the freedom to pursue any sort of business because the financial situation was so bad. From the point of view of this research, however, two important factors should be mentioned. First, the Stockholm area is a sophisticated market for information technology, with a variety of state-run institutions prepared to invest heavily in state-of-the-art technology. Datapoint Svenska's informal centres of excellence can be attributed to their early involvement with technologies that are only now becoming common practice in other European markets. The second key factor is simply one of entrepreneurship. Terry Morris felt that all the necessary capabilities existed before he took control. He provided the freedom for the employees to apply their expertise where it was needed, and this resulted in sales in areas that the company had never previously considered.

As with the 3M case, this case-study suggests that subsidiary development can be achieved through internally driven growth that is focused on customer service. Datapoint Svenska is now a very profitable operation, with plans to hire additional staff and with a strong reputation at head office. Datapoint Svenska is also beginning to engage in international projects. Further, the case-study hints at the importance of demanding customers as a stimulus for the development of a leading-edge cluster.

Common Themes from the Case Studies

The four case studies were deliberately selected to shed light on some of the more interesting cases of development among subsidiaries that were not formed through acquisition. Bearing in mind that they cannot be said to be representative of the population of Swedish subsidiaries, there are nevertheless some interesting themes that emerged when the cases are considered collectively.

Figure 11.3 Centres of excellence in Swedish subsidiaries at the different stages of the value chain

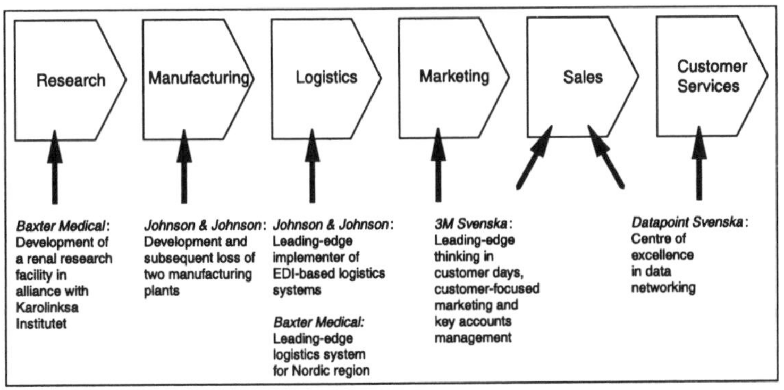

The first common theme is the emerging concept of a 'centre of excellence' as a desirable form of recognition for subsidiary development. In all cases there was some sort of centre of excellence, defined as an area of expertise for which the subsidiary is recognised by the corporation, and which other parts of the corporation draw on. Moreover, it was apparent that centres of excellence can be gained at every stage of the value chain, from research (Baxter) through to sales and services (Datapoint). Figure 11.3 illustrates this point. Centres of excellence do not represent major investments by the parent company, but they do show that the subsidiary is thriving in at least one area, which is typically good for the parent company and for the Swedish economy. If, as some claim, we are moving to a world where knowledge management is imperative to success, then centres of excellence will become a much more common phenomenon because they represent the wellsprings of knowledge on which others draw.

The second point, which was made very clear in the Johnson & Johnson case, is that manufacturing responsibilities are as likely to be lost as won given the continuing rationalisation of operations underway in most large multinationals. It seems that for a manufacturing operation to be sustainable in the long term, it is not enough just to be cost competitive. In addition, it must either have unique capabilities that cannot be easily replicated elsewhere, a critical mass that makes it a survivor in the consolidation process, or local factors (for example, presence in a leading-edge cluster) that make Sweden an attractive location for manufacturing.

The third point, which came out in the Baxter and Datapoint cases, is that there are certain leading-edge aspects of the Swedish business environment that can have an important impact on subsidiary development in Sweden. These can be research institutes (Karolinska), demanding customers (The Statskontoret), competitors (Gambro), and related industries (IT, software, telecommunications). Of course, the industry cluster concept is now well understood, but the original study by Porter (1990) never really considered the role of foreign-owned subsidiaries in cluster development. This research shows that at the very least foreign subsidiaries do develop in response to existing clusters. It may even be that large foreign-owned subsidiaries, such as those in group 4, also contribute to the development of such clusters.

Finally, these cases illustrate the point that subsidiary initiative is critical to the development process, but that it also depends on a high level of acceptance of initiative by the parent company. The cases of Baxter, 3M and Datapoint all suggest that the subsidiary was given a lot of freedom by the parent to pursue opportunities in directions it saw fit. Essentially the parent company acts as the facilitator, so that the subsidiary can actually drive the initiative process. If the parent company is not cooperative, or if the subsidiary does not respond to the opportunity it is given, then initiative will obviously fail to transpire.

CONCLUSIONS AND IMPLICATIONS

In this chapter an argument has been advanced that a process of subsidiary development has positive ramifications for both parent company and host country. Using evidence from Sweden it is evident that those subsidiaries with broader value-added scope had greater levels of international sales, higher levels of initiative, and stronger relationships with local suppliers than those with more narrow value-added scope. Furthermore, it is clear that subsidiaries that have come about through acquisition generally have stronger relationships with local suppliers, higher revenues sales, and higher levels of initiative than those that were established as greenfield operations. Using case-study evidence, it was demonstrated that there is a subsidiary development process in evidence in Sweden, though it is probably less established than that observed in other countries (for example, Canada, USA, UK).

Why do we see a less-developed body of foreign-owned subsidiaries in Sweden than in many other countries? Several reasons are apparent. First, Sweden is a small market that until recently was not even part of the European Union. It is also relatively high-cost and geographically peripheral. Most foreign MNCs therefore saw Sweden as a market for their products, but not as an appropriate site for manufacturing or development. Second, Swedish policy-makers were neutral or even averse to inward investment until recently. Given the high level of effort made by many other European countries towards attracting inward investment, it is hardly surprising that Sweden ended up in the late 1980s with a relatively underdeveloped body of subsidiaries. Third, there is only limited evidence for subsidiary initiative, which is one of the major drivers of subsidiary development (Birkinshaw and Hood, 1997). The highest levels of initiative were observed in acquired subsidiaries, many of which were rather recently acquired.

One important conclusion, then, is that the process of subsidiary development varies significantly from country to country. In Sweden the strong manufacturing development of Ireland or Scotland is not evident; nor is the emergence of world product mandates, such as are frequently seen in Canada and the USA. Instead, occasional large R&D or manufacturing operations are found (typically in acquired operations) and then a large number of centres of excellence at all parts of the value chain. Furthermore, these centres of excellence are focused in a few leading-edge clusters and/or in some of the more entrepreneurial MNCs, for example, 3M and Johnson & Johnson. Much of the rest of the foreign owned subsidiaries in Sweden are, and will remain, market access operations with minimal local value added.

A second important conclusion is that the centre of excellence model identified in Swedish subsidiaries may be part of an emerging trend. Many MNCs are looking for ways of utilising their geographically dispersed operations more effectively, and the centre of excellence approach is simply a way of recognising the pockets of expertise that exist all over the place, and inviting other operations around the world to make use of that expertise.

So what are the implications of this study for the recently created Invest in Sweden Agency? It is perhaps obvious that Sweden has a difficult job ahead of it in attracting investment, both because it lacks the low-cost or large-market advantages that many countries in Europe can offer, and because it is a very late into the inward-investment game. Nevertheless, a number of broad suggestions can be made. First, the four groups have very different prospects for development, and each requires a tailored strategy. Second, Sweden's leading-edge clusters, including telecommunications and healthcare, represent a clear selling point, which probably needs to be the focus of most future investment efforts. Third, Sweden has not only to sell its benefits: it needs to counteract the mostly incorrect negative perceptions about the country's high taxes and negative attitude towards foreign investment. Finally, it is important for the selling process not only to target parent company managers who are thinking about making investments in Europe, but also to raise the awareness of existing subsidiary managers of the issues raised here. These individuals often make better spokespersons for inward investment than do government officials.

References

Almeida, P. (1996) 'Knowledge Sourcing by Foreign Multinationals: Patent Citation Analysis in the US Semiconductor Industry', *Proceedings of the Academy of International Business Annual Meeting*, Banff, Canada.

Bartlett, C.A. and S. Ghoshal (1986) 'Tap Your Subsidiaries for Global Reach', *Harvard Business Review*, 64 (6), 87–94.

Birkinshaw, J.M. (1995) *Entrepreneurship in Multinational Corporations: The Initiative Process in Canadian Subsidiaries*, unpublished doctoral dissertation, Western Business School, London, Ontario, Canada.

Birkinshaw, J.M. and Morrison, A.J. (1996) 'Configurations of Strategy and Structure in Subsidiaries of Multinational Corporations', *Journal of International Business Studies*, 26 (4), 729–53.

Birkinshaw, J.N and N. Hood (1997) 'An Empirical Study of Development Processes in Foreign-owned Subsidiaries in Canada and Scotland', *Management International Review*, 37 (4), 339–64.

Dunning, J.H. (1993) *Multinational Enterprises and the Global Economy*, Wokingham: Addison-Wesley.

Etemad, H. and L.S. Dulude (1986) *Managing the Multinational Subsidiary*, London: Croom Helm.

Frost, T. (1996) 'The Geographic Sources of Innovation in the MNE: US Subsidiaries and Host Country Spillovers, 1980–1990', *Proceedings of the Academy of International Business Annual Meeting*, Banff, Alberta, Canada.

Ghoshal, S. and N. Nohria (1989) 'Internal Differentiation within Multinational Corporations', *Strategic Management Journal*, 10, 323–37.

Hood, N. and S. Young (1983) *European Development Strategies of MNCs in Scotland*, Edinburgh: HMSO.

Hood, N., S. Young and D. Lal (1994), 'Strategic Evolution within Japanese Manufacturing Plants in Europe: UK Evidence', *International Business Review*, 3 (2), 97–122.

Ozawa, T. (1992) 'Foreign Direct Investment and Economic Development', *Transnational Corporations*, 1, 27–54.

Porter, M.E. (1990) *The Competitive Advantage of Nations*, New York: Free Press.

Rosenzweig, P. and N. Nohria (1994) 'Influences on Human Resource Management Practices in Multinational Corporations', *Journal of International Business Studies*, 25 (2), 229–52.

Roth, K. and A.J. Morrison (1992) 'Implementing Global Strategy: Characteristics of Global Subsidiary Mandates', *Journal of International Business Studies*, 23 (4), 715–36.

Safarian, E. (1966) *Foreign Ownership of Canadian Industry*, Toronto: McGraw-Hill.

Westney, D.E. (1993) 'Institutionalization Theory and the Multinational Corporation', in S. Ghoshal and D.E. Westney (eds), *Organization Theory and the Multinational Corporation*, New York: St Martin's Press.

White, R.E. and T.A. Poynter (1984) 'Strategies for Foreign-Owned Subsidiaries in Canada', *Business Quarterly*, 48(4), Summer, 59–69.

Woodcock, P. (1994) *The Greenfield vs. Acquisition Entry Mode Decision Process*, unpublished doctoral dissertation, Western Business School, London, Ontario, Canada.

APPENDIX 11.A STUDY QUESTIONS

Strength of Suppliers

Two questions were adapted from Woodcock (1994) to assess the strength of relationships with local suppliers.

> Indicate how characteristic each of the following statements are in describing your business environment:
>
> 1. Capabilities of suppliers are very high.
> 2. Relationships between suppliers and buyers are very strong.
>   (1 = strongly disagree; 7 = strongly agree.)

Reliability was acceptable (Alpha = 0.71).

Level of Local Competition

Two questions were adapted from Roth and Morrison (1992) to assess the level of local competition.

> Indicate how characteristic each of the following statements are in describing your business environment:
>
> 1. Competition in this country is extremely intense.
> 2. Domestic competition is intense.
>   (1 = strongly disagree; 7 = strongly agree.)

Reliability was high (Alpha = 0.92).

Subsidiary Autonomy

Three questions were used from Roth and Morrison's (1992) measure of subsidiary autonomy. The reliability of the scale was acceptable (Alpha = 0.78). Wording as follows:

> Which level in your business unit has authority to make the following decisions? Circle the most appropriate decision level based on the following:
>
> 1. decision-made in the subsidiary company;
> 2. decision-made at the sub-corporate level;
> 3. decision-made by corporate headquarters:
>
>   a. changes in product design;
>   b. subcontracting out large portions of the manufacturing instead of expanding the subsidiary's own facilities;
>   c. switching to a new manufacturing process.

Parent–subsidiary Communication

Two questions were used on communication patterns from Ghoshal (1986):

> How often do senior managers in your subsidiary communicate with their counterparts and bosses in head office?
> (1 = daily; 5 = less than once a month.)
> How often do senior and middle managers in your subsidiary make business trips to head office?
> (1 = twice a month or more; 5 = less than once a year.)

Reliability was acceptable (alpha = 0.68)

Subsidiary Initiative

Questions were put together which asked respondents to indicate the extent to which they had pursued initiatives of various types. The questions were based on an interview study, described in Birkinshaw (1997). Eight items were used, with a high level of inter-item reliability (alpha = 0.87). Items were worded as follows:

> To what extent have the following activities occurred in your subsidiary over the past 10 years?

1. New products developed in (for example) Sweden and then sold internationally.
2. Significant extensions to existing international responsibilities.
3. Successful bids for corporate investments in Sweden.
4. Proposals to transfer manufacturing to Sweden from elsewhere in the corporation.
5. New international business activities that were first started in Sweden.
6. Enhancements to product lines which are already sold internationally.
7. New corporate investments in R&D or manufacturing attracted by Swedish management.
8. Reconfiguring of Swedish operations from domestic to international orientation.
   1 = never; 5 = plentifully.

Number with Presence in Cluster

The description of clusters used was that in Porter's (1990) *Competitive Advantage of Nations* to identify the five major clusters in Sweden. These are:

1. Transportation and logistics.
2. Forestry, timber, pulp and paper.

3. Ferrous metals and fabricated metals.
4. Health-related products.
5. Telecommunications.

Using the descriptions of the industries provided by questionnaire respondents, we assessed whether each subsidiary was a member of a cluster or not. This analysis allowed us to identify the percentage of each group that were members of leading-edge clusters.

12 Functional and Line of Business Evolution Processes in MNC Subsidiaries: Sony in the USA, 1972–95

Sea-Jin Chang and Philip M. Rosenzweig

INTRODUCTION

An important development in recent years has been the increasing interest in the evolution of multinational corporations (MNCs). Rather than examining questions of MNC strategy and structure in a cross-sectional fashion, a number of scholars have focused their attention on the developmental trajectory by which firms undertake foreign investment, configure their world-wide activities, and achieve coordination among them.

This growing interest in MNC evolution is welcome for both theoretical and practical reasons. (The term 'evolution' has more than one meaning and it is important that we be clear about our usage. Van de Ven (1992) makes the distinction between life cycle, teleological, dialectic, and evolutionary processes, with the last being reserved for a continuous process of change through variation, selection and retention. The authors take a broader definition of evolution in this chapter, taking the view of Barnett and Burgelman (1996: 5) that evolution involves a 'dynamic, path-dependent model' which may exhibit variation and selection within organisations. This use is consistent with earlier authors on MNC evolution, notably Perlmutter (1969), Kogut and Zander (1993) and Malnight (1995).) From a theoretical standpoint, it is important not merely to assert that MNCs can be viewed as heterarchies (Hedlund, 1986) or as inter-organisational networks (Ghoshal and Bartlett, 1990), but also to understand the process by which they evolve. From a practical standpoint, understanding the process of MNC evolution is important because firms that develop strong multinational positions can more fully take advantage of operational flexibility (Kogut, 1985) and tap the capabilities of each subsidiary (Bartlett and Ghoshal, 1986).

This chapter presents findings from a case-study of Sony Corporation's United States subsidiary. Sony undertook its first foreign direct investment in 1972, with a small television assembly operation in San Diego, California. At the beginning, the plant employed fewer than 50 people and performed only final assembly. Over the next two decades, Sony expanded its television activities at the San Diego plant, eventually performing fully integrated television manufacturing, and also branched into related products such as video display monitors for air traffic control. In addition, Sony entered the United States in several other lines of business, ranging from magnetic tape to audio equipment, and eventually records and motion pictures. In many of these businesses, Sony's activities underwent their own evolution, from a limited initial position to often undertake fully integrated manufacturing and product design. By 1996, Sony had a complex and multi-business presence in the USA, with more than 20 000 employees.

This study of Sony in the USA sheds light on the processes by which a foreign subsidiary develops from initial entry to a position of high complexity. It differs from previous research on MNC subsidiaries in a few ways. First, Sony's US subsidiary is examined along two dimensions: initially by showing the process by which Sony added functions within a given line of business, describing in depth the evolution of its television business, and then by depicting the process by which Sony later entered into other lines of business. Second, rather than describing evolution as a series of stages, this study seeks to capture the various organisational actors who initiated, facilitated, and impeded this evolution. By focusing on the interplay of different forces within the organisation, a process model is developed that is adaptive in nature, depicting subsidiary evolution as a series of loops, each involving action, feedback, and evaluation for further action. Furthermore, by examining the interplay of forces that shape evolution, and by conceiving of the process in terms of sequential loops, this research identifies many of the factors that facilitate or impede evolution, both in terms of functional migration and also line of business diversification, showing how the relative importance of these factors may shift depending on the stage. The result is a more complete understanding of the organisational processes involved in MNC evolution than previously extant.

ANTECEDENT RESEARCH ON MNC EVOLUTION

Of the vast literature on MNCs, a few streams of research are particularly important as antecedents for this chapter. First, a great deal of research has focused on the ways firms expand abroad, known as foreign direct investment (FDI). Numerous studies have examined the conditions that lead to FDI (Dunning, 1988; Magee, 1977); patterns of FDI by industry (Caves and Mehra, 1986; Kogut and Chang, 1991) and by host country (Ajami and Ricks, 1981); the choice of entry mode (Hill *et al.*, 1990); and the choice of subsidiary ownership structure (Gatignon and Anderson, 1988). These studies have identified many factors that explain the initial occurrence and mode of FDI, but they have not examined the challenges of managing foreign subsidiaries following entry.

A second avenue of research has examined the management of MNCs as complex organisations. These studies have identified the varying roles played by national subsidiaries (Bartlett and Ghoshal, 1989; Jarillo and Martinez, 1990); knowledge flows among subsidiaries (Gupta and Govindarajan, 1991); headquarters–subsidiary governance structures (Ghoshal and Nohria, 1989); diffusion of innovation among subsidiaries (Ghoshal and Bartlett, 1988); and inter-unit communication (Ghoshal *et al.*, 1994). This body of research mainly includes cross-sectional studies of firms that are already multinational, but does not shed light on the process by which they became differentiated networks.

A third avenue of research has taken an explicitly temporal perspective, focusing on the sequence of steps in MNC development. This research has often gone under the heading of internationalisation. Most influential in this regard has been the so-called Uppsala School, based initially on the work of Johanson and Weidersheim-Paul (1975) and Johanson and Vahlne (1977), who showed that MNCs tend to expand from lesser to greater commitment, usually beginning with sales and marketing organisations, and building toward fully integrated manufacturing. This line of research, while important, has usually focused on a single line of business at a time, and has tended to describe the stages of internationalisation rather than the process by which such change takes place.

To these three avenues of research a fourth is added, namely that of the evolution of the MNC. Much of this recent thrust can be traced to the initial conception by Kogut (1983) of foreign direct investment as a sequential process, with initial investments providing the basis, or serving as a platform for subsequent investments. In a later empirical study, Kogut and Zander (1993: 640) noted that 'the sequential expansion of a firm's activities after first entry is a expression of the evolutionary acquisition and recombination of knowledge'. They showed that the nature of knowledge was significantly associated with the mode of foreign entry and the means by which knowledge was transferred, yet their research design did not permit them to examine the intra-organisational process by which the evolution took place. Malnight (1995) noted the dearth of process models to explain MNC evolution, and presented a case-study of Eli Lilly to describe how an ethnocentric firm evolves into a more fully globalised position. He identified four stages of functional development, describing them as first as appendages, later as participators, then contributors, and eventually becoming fully integrated within the MNC network.

This evolutionary perspective is embraced in this chapter and an effort is made to extend it. Like Malnight, MNC evolution is studied at an intra-organisational level, yet the approach differs from his in two ways. First, it is not limited to a single line of business, but explicitly considers the addition of multiple lines of business as a dimension of subsidiary evolution. This inclusion is critical because most MNCs are multi-business firms, and their foreign subsidiaries often begin with one or a subset of their lines of business, adding others over time. Chang (1995) provided empirical support that MNCs enter foreign markets in their core lines of business, then expand sequentially into other businesses for which they have less competitive superiority versus local firms. Chang did not, however, examine the intra-organisational processes by which MNCs decide to add further lines of business to an existing foreign subsidiary. By incorporating this dimension, the present study seeks to capture an important but often overlooked aspect of MNC subsidiary evolution. Second, the hope is not merely to identify the stages of evolution, but to capture the interaction among key actors that may drive or impede the evolutionary process. Simply identifying stages of evolution can unwittingly suggest that evolution is inevitable, rather than adaptive in nature. It may also result in the portrayal of the organisational as implicitly monolithic, acting as a unitary rational actor (Allison, 1971), and not as the product of interactions among different actors, each with their own perspectives and interests.

METHOD AND DATA

In order to study the process of subsidiary evolution at an intra-organisational level a case-study was conducted. As described by Yin (1989), a case-study is an appropriate design for research that seeks to capture the complex interaction among organisational actors. This use of a case-study approach to understand the dynamics of organisational processes is in the tradition of a number of examinations of the strategy process (see, for instance, Aharoni, 1966; Bower, 1970; Burgelman, 1983 and 1996; Malnight, 1995 and 1996; Noda and Bower, 1996).

As a first step, the United States was selected as the host country. The search was for an MNC whose US subsidiary was complex and had a multi-business presence, so that it was possible not only to study the functional migration of a given line of business but also to examine entry by line of business. A subsidiary was chosen whose evolution had taken place relatively recently, so that managers who had been directly involved could be interviewed.

Based on these criteria the selection was Sony Corporation, the Japanese-based electronics and entertainment firm. Sony was a mature global firm, with world-wide sales in 1993 distributed almost equally among North America (30.4 per cent), Europe (26.0 per cent), and Japan (25.8 per cent). In the United States, Sony Corporation operated at many sites and in a variety of business, including televisions, magnetic tape, semiconductors, and precision audio equipment, as well as music and entertainment. A summary of Sony's US activities is shown in Tables 12.1 and 12.2. A study of Sony in the United States promised to shed light on the key questions of interest for this

Table 12.1 Sony Corporation: activities in the USA, 1995

Sony Corporation of America
Financial, tax, and administrative services for Sony's subsidiaries
Sony Capital Corporation
Financing for business operations for Sony Corporation of America and its subsidiaries
Sony Electronics Inc.
Business planning and public relations for US electronics operations
Sony Sales and Marketing of America
Sale and service of Sony electronic products in the United States
Sony Software Corporation
Coordination of entertainment services
Sony Music Entertainment Inc.
World-wide recording operation, including manufacture and sale of CDs, MDs, laserdiscs, audiocassettes, videotapes, and video software
Sony Pictures Entertainment
Production and world-wide distribution of motion pictures, television programs, and theatrical exhibition of motion pictures.
Sony Electronic Publishing Company
Development, manufacture, and sale of game software and multimedia products
Sony Trans Com Inc.
Manufacture, sales, and service of airborne audio and visual entertainment systems; distribution of audio and video programs
Materials Research Corporation
Manufacture of thin film processing equipment and high purity metal targets

Source: Sony Annual Report.

study, namely: what was the process by which Sony increased the functionality of its US activities?; what was the process by which Sony added lines of business to its US subsidiary?; and for each of these, what factors facilitated and impeded further evolution?

Table 12.2 Sony Engineering and Manufacturing of America, 1995

1. *Administrative headquarters*, Park Ridge, NJ
2. *Product divisions*

   Picture tube, colour television, and display products activities
   San Diego, Calif. Est. 1972
   Tijuana, Mexico Est. 1987
   Pittsburgh, P. Est. 1990

   Audio Manufacturing Division, hi-fi speakers and audio racks
   Delano, P. Est. 1975

   Sony Magnetic Tape Division, manufacture of audiocassettes and MFDs
   Dothan, Aa. Est. 1977

   Sony Professional Products Company, manufacture of broadcast and professional use VTRs and audio products
   Boca Raton, Fla. Est. 1982

   Factory Automation Division, factory automation solutions
   Orangeburg, NY Est. 1989

   Sony Microelectronics, manufacture of semiconductors
   San Antonio, Tex. Est. 1990
3. *Research and development centers*

Monterey, Calif.	Advanced Computer Architectures Research Laboratories
San Jose, Calif.	Sony Microelectronics Design Center
	Semiconductor and Systems Laboratory
	Sony Intelligent Systems Research Laboratory
San Diego, Calif.	Display Systems Television Business Group of America
Boulder, Co.	Data Storage Laboratory
Boca Raton, Fla.	Sony Professional Products Company
Orangeburg, NY	Factory Automation Division

Source: Sony company documents.

Data Gathering

Archival, documentary, and interview data were gathered. The researchers began by collecting and reading publicly available data, including company annual reports, press articles, case studies, and books. Once an understanding of the milestones in Sony's evolution in the USA had been developed, interviews were conducted at several Sony divisions including San Diego, California; Tijuana, Mexico; Pittsburgh, Pennsylvania; and San Antonio, Texas. To provide a critical complementary perspective on the evolution of the US subsidiary, additional interviews were conducted at Sony Corporation headquarters in Tokyo.

Table 12.3 Interviews conducted at Sony Corporation

SEMA Headquarters, New Jersey

1. President and COO, SEMA
2. Vice-President, Human Resources, Sony Corporation of America
3. Vice-President, Business Planning, SEMA
4. Manager, Human Resources, SEMA

San Diego, California

5. President, Televison Business Group of America
6. Senior Vice-President, Sony Display & Components Products Company, Sony Electronics Inc.
7. Manager, Business Planning and Development, Display Systems, Sony Electronics Inc.
8. Business Planner, SEMA
9. Director, Business Planning, SEMA
10. Manager, Display Systems, SEMA
11. Director, CTV Division, Sony Display & Components Products Company, Sony Electronics Inc.
12. Director of Manufacturing & Engineering, Sony Display Tube Company, Sony Electronics Inc.
13. Manager, Total Quality Management, Sony Display Tube Company, Sony Electronics Inc.
14. Director, Site Engineering/Facilities Maintenance, Sony Electronics Inc.
15. Director, Planning & Control, Data Storage Systems, Sony Electronics Inc.

16. Vice-President, Personal Telecommunications Division, Sony Electronics Inc.
17. Director, Product Design & Development, Personal Telecommunications Division, Sony Electronics Inc.

Tijuana, Mexico

18. Director General, Video Tec de Mexico, SA de CV

Pittsburgh, Pennsylvania

19. Vice-President, Sony Display Device Pittsburgh
20. Manager, Sony Display Device Pittsburgh
21. Director, CRT Manufacturing, Sony Display Device Pittsburgh
22. Engineering Director, Sony Display Device Pittsburgh
23. Director, Materials CTV, Sony Display Device Pittsburgh
24. Manager, Mask Engineering, Sony Display Device Pittsburgh

San Antonio, Texas

25. Executive Vice-President and General Manager, Sony Microelectronics
26. Director of Quality Control, Sony Microelectronics
27. Director, Finance and Administration, Sony Microelectronics
28. Manager, Manufacturing Science Research Center, Sony Microelectronics

Tokyo, Japan

29. Executive Vice-President, Consumer A&V Products Company
30. Senior Vice-President, Consumer A&V Products Company
31. General Manager, Planning and Control Department, Consumer A&V Products Company
32. Manager, Business Planning Sector, Planning and Control Department, Consumer A&V Products Company
33. Senior General Manager and Vice-President, Recording Media and Energy Company
34. Manager, Business Planning Sector, Recording Media and Energy Company
35. General Manager, Strategic Planning Department, Semiconductor Company
36. Vice-President, InfoCom Products Company
37. Assistant Manager, Business Strategy Sector, InfoCom Products Company

---

In total, 37 Sony managers were interviewed, some more than once. They included a cross-section of managers: Japanese, American and Mexican managers; senior executives, division managers and technical professionals; and managers from a variety of functions, including R&D, manufacturing, human resources, finance and business planning. A list of interviews is presented in Table 12.3.

SONY IN THE UNITED STATES: A CASE-STUDY OF SUBSIDIARY EVOLUTION

Sony Corporation was founded in 1946 as Tokyo Tsushin Kogyo (TTK), a start-up electronics company that emerged from the ashes of Tokyo. The founding partners were Masaru Ibuka and Akio Morita. Among the earliest products were audio tape and tape recorders. In 1958 the company's name was changed to Sony – an easier name for Westerners to pronounce which combined the Latin word for sound, *sonus*, and the English-language term of endearment, sonny. In 1959, Sony introduced the first transistor television, followed in 1961 by the first solid-state video tape recorder. (Data about Sony's history prior to 1972 came from several sources: interviews conducted with Sony managers, company publications, reference publications and books (Morita, 1986).)

During the 1950s and 1960s, Sony Corporation designed and manufactured audio and electronic products in Japan, and exported them around the world. With labour costs much higher in the USA than in Japan, Sony and other Japanese firms manufactured at home and pursued an export strategy. By 1960, more than half of Sony's sales were generated outside of Japan, with the US market playing an especially important role. Under the guidance of Akio Morita, Sony established a US sales office in 1960, and in 1970 became the first Japanese firm to be listed on the New York Stock Exchange. Morita served as president of Sony Corporation of America from 1960 to 1971, building the company's US presence.

In the late 1960s, Sony introduced the Trinitron, a breakthrough colour television with superior technology that established the company's reputation for high quality. Sales in the US continued to expand rapidly. Soon, however, Sony became concerned about its dependence on US sales. In the early 1970s, Japanese TV makers were charged with 'dumping' in the USA, prompting a Department of Commerce investigation, and raising the spectre of import restrictions. Morita was successful in arguing for Sony's exemption from any import restrictions, but remained deeply concerned about Sony's vulnerability to future disputes, since company revenues relied heavily on sales in the United States.

Initial Direct Investment: Final Assembly of Colour Televisions in San Diego

Largely to minimise Sony's vulnerability to future trade frictions, Morita explored the possibility of setting up a manufacturing operation in the USA. In August 1972 Sony established a small manufacturing plant at the Rancho Bernardo Industrial Park north of San Diego, California. Locating on the West Coast was particularly attractive, because Sony planned to import all parts from Japan. Although the company had no experience managing a manufacturing operation in the USA, it was assured that Rancho Bernardo was an excellent site and that hiring high-quality local employees would not be difficult.

At first, Sony managers determined that the San Diego plant would perform only final assembly of colour televisions (CTVs) from kits imported from Japan. There were at least two reasons for limiting San Diego's activities to final assembly. First, the yen–dollar exchange rate made it more economical to incur costs in Japan than in the United States. Second, there were serious doubts as to whether American workers could perform activities at the desired level of quality. Sony did not want to jeopardise its new-found reputation for quality with poorly manufactured CTVs assembled in the USA.

Rather than hire people with experience in appliance manufacturing, Sony hired thirty Americans with no related experience and trained them directly by a team of Japanese expatriates. The assembly line layout was an exact replica of the CTV assembly line in Japan. The plant built just one product – CTVs – and performed just one function – final assembly. In fact, at the outset San Diego merely reassembled CTVs that had already been assembled, adjusted, then disassembled, in Japan. So concerned were Japanese managers about the quality of manufacturing in the United States that they wanted to make sure that Americans, working under the supervision of Japanese managers, could properly put back together a working television! The quality of CTVs at the San Diego plant were carefully monitored by Japanese managers on-site, and detailed reports were scrutinised in Japan. Once it was determined that American workers could satisfactorily reassemble televisions, they began to build CTVs without previous assembly in Japan.

Initial Functional Migration: From Final Assembly to Minimal Local Sourcing

By 1974, with two years of successful experience in CTV final assembly at San Diego, managers at Sony's CTV headquarters in Japan began to consider whether additional functions should be performed in the United States. Certain parts that were bulky and 'non-critical', such as cartons, cushions and cabinets, were henceforward sourced locally, saving on shipping costs. More importantly, Sony managers examined the possibility of assembling cathode ray tubes, or CRTs, in the United States. Of all the parts that Sony shipped from Japan, CRTs were the heaviest and most expensive to ship, and also the most brittle. Local final assembly of CRTs, known as 'finishing', would avoid a considerable shipping expense, and also minimise losses from breakage. Accordingly, in 1974 Sony began to finish CRTs in San Diego, triggering a new round of knowledge transfer from Japan, with engineers and technicians experienced in CRT manufacturing travelling to San Diego to train American employees. Additional plant space was prepared and additional employees hired to handle CRT finishing. Sony's San Diego plant now performed both final assembly of CTVs and finishing CRTs, yet otherwise continued to receive all inputs from Japan.

Entry in Additional Lines of Business

Based on the initial success of CTVs in San Diego, managers of Sony's other businesses began to explore the possibility of setting up plants in the USA. In 1975, Sony's audio equipment business built a factory to manufacture high-fidelity audio equipment in Delano, Pennsylvania. In 1977, a magnetic tape plant was built in Dothan, Alabama. Audio equipment and magnetic tape, like colour televisions, were lines of business where Sony enjoyed a competitive superiority, and, as with televisions, the firm transferred product technology and manufacturing process technology to the USA, where it combined these resources with others sourced locally. Both of these plants reported to their respective line of businesses in Japan, just as the managers in charge of the CTV and CRT operations in San Diego reported to the head of the television business in Tokyo. By the end of the 1970s, Sony Corporation of America included three plants, located in different parts of the country, in three separate lines of business.

Functional Migration in Televisions

During the late 1970s and early 1980s, the San Diego plant grew in size, with new buildings being erected to contain the growing number of CTV production lines. All parts other than packaging materials were still imported from Japan, and all decisions about product design, product strategy and business planning were taken in Japan. After 1974, when CRT finishing had been added to final assembly of CTVs, no further upgrading of activities in San Diego took place. The reasons for this lull were several. First, there was no obvious economic benefit associated with further functional migration. Second, additional functional migration would call for local sourcing of parts, and managers in Japan were doubtful whether US vendors could meet Sony's exacting standards for quality and delivery. It was better, they reasoned, to continue purchasing parts from reliable vendors in Japan. Third, it became clear from several interviews that there was a reluctance on the part of numerous managers in Japan to allow the US subsidiary to perform key functions such as product design. It was one thing to allow it to perform activities such as final assembly that replicated activities in Japan, but it was something else entirely to shift activities from Japan to the USA. For reasons described benignly as risk aversion, or more pointedly as organisational politics, a number of Tokyo-based managers opposed shifting further functions to the USA. For more than a decade, Sony's CTV business unit in Japan performed R&D, product design and strategic planning, while assembly from imported products and a minimum of local procurement were performed in the USA.

In the late 1980s, however, a number of factors changed. Following the Plaza Accord in September 1985, the value of the US dollar fell from 240 yen to 140 yen in just over a year, making it critical for Japanese firms to incur costs in local currencies rather than in yen. Akio Morita, Sony's CEO, articulated a policy of 'global localisation', in which 'each region makes its own autonomous operational decisions, while maintaining and reflecting the corporate policy developed at a global level'. (This quotation is from Sony company documents.)

For televisions, 'global localisation' meant that additional functions needed to be performed in the USA. Yet as one manager commented, 'We couldn't just say, "Let's move everything at once to the US", Instead, there followed over the next years a continuing process of functional migration, in which one activity after another was shifted to San Diego. A sequential approach was necessary, one manager indicated, because business planning could not be performed in the USA until products were designed there, and product design could not be conducted in the USA as long as the parts in those designs were procured in Japan. The first step therefore was local parts procurement. Under an initiative called PLP, or procurement of local parts, Sony managers in San Diego began to work actively with US vendors to determine the specifications, quality standards, and delivery schedule for key inputs. Once these inputs could be reliably procured in the USA, certain design functions were then shifted to San Diego. This shift, managers recalled, was a sensitive matter politically, as it involved a net transfer of responsibilities from Japan to the USA, not merely a replication of existing activities.

While several activities were shifted to San Diego, certain labour-intensive activities were moved out. In 1987, Sony built a plant in Tijuana, Mexico, to perform the assembly of its smaller televisions, which were relatively labour-intensive and price-competitive. (The Mexican operation first went under the name of Ynos, a Spanish-sounding term that was the reverse of Sony.) This time, managers and technicians from San Diego set up the new plant in Mexico, putting in place the assembly line and training local workers. In time, production of the smallest CTVs, which sold for the lowest price and required the lowest costs, as shifted from San Diego to Tijuana.

Entry in Further Lines of Business

Sony's first three entries to the USA – CTVs, audio equipment and magnetic tape – had been in lines of business where it enjoyed a technical superiority over local firms. In each instance entry had taken place through greenfield investment, and key product and process technology had been transferred from Japan. By the 1980s, Sony's confidence about managing in the USA had grown to the point where it could enter in additional lines of business, some of which offered little or no competitive superiority over local firms. In these instances, Sony often entered through acquisition as a way to bolster its capabilities. In 1982, Sony Professional Products, specialising in advanced audio equipment, was created from the acquisition of Music Center Inc. in Florida. In 1989, Sony acquired Materials Research Corporation, a producer of thin metal film and etching equipment. In 1990, Sony acquired one of AMD's semiconductor fabrication plants in San Antonio, Texas. In each of these instances, Sony extended its position in existing lines of business through acquisition, something it had not dared to undertake in the 1970s. It also sought to tap expertise resident in the employees and processes of the acquired firms, rather than exclusively to transfer resources from Japan.

Reorganising Sony Corporation of America

Until 1990, each of Sony's numerous lines of business in the USA was managed directly by its respective business headquarters in Japan. Sony Corporation of America, with headquarters in New York, was limited to administrative functions, including legal, tax, and public affairs, but made no effort to coordinate the upstream activities of Sony's many businesses. Only sales and marketing were coordinated on a national level. By the 1990s, with Sony's activities in the USA reaching a critical scale, a reorganisation was effected, establishing a new entity, Sony Engineering and Manufacturing America, or SEMA.

SEMA was intended to provide an umbrella organisation over all of Sony's US manufacturing activities, allowing them to share engineering expertise. The first president of SEMA, Masaaki Morita, not only sought synergies across lines of business but also advocated further localisation of activities in the USA. His successor, Kunitake Ando, also acted as a strong proponent of localisation, pulling for greater decision-making responsibilities in the USA.

By 1990, Sony's CTV activities in the USA had taken on considerable responsibility for local procurement and product design, yet responsibility for business planning remained in Japan. Managers in San Diego, not only Americans but also the senior CTV managers, who were Japanese expatriates, sought to more fully localise operations, and argued for shifting business planning responsibility to the USA. Most important in this regard was the '*seihan*' process, which matched marketing requirements and factory allocations on a world-wide basis, and was a vital component of strategic planning. In Japanese '*seihan*' literally means 'make-sell', and describes the process of identifying production ('make') and sales ('sell') volumes. SEMA management, notably Kunitake Ando, strongly advocated shifting seihan to the United States, yet could not decree such a change. At first, two Japanese managers responsible for the seihan process moved to San Diego, from where they now continued to run the process.

Over time, it became accepted throughout the company that key strategic decision-making could be located in the USA, marking a profound event in the maturation of the US subsidiary. Sony's CTV activities in the USA were now a fully fledged business unit, or '*jigyobu*', with responsibility for all strategic decisions. Sony's world-wide CTV business, until now run from Japan, was divided into three regions: TVJ managed Japan and Asia; TVA handled the Americas and was located in San Diego; and TVE took on responsibility for the European market, which had also grown during the 1980s.

Expansion of Related Businesses

In the late 1980s, Sony's San Diego plant not only took on more functions in the design and manufacture of CTVs, but also expanded into related businesses, largely driven by specific local demands. The explosion in personal computer sales in the 1980s led to a surge in demand for monitors. IBM, one of the largest makers of PCs, approached Sony to supply its monitors, which resulted in an expansion of capabilities in the design and manufacture of computer display monitors. As San Diego's display tubes activities flourished, the US Federal Aviation Authority (FAA) approached Sony to develop sophisticated wide-screen monitors for air traffic control. Again, demand for a specific product stimulated new activities in the US subsidiary. The San Diego plant was no longer merely replicating activities performed in Japan, or even taking on activities that had been shifted from Japan, but was now developing unique capabilities owing to the specific demands of local customers. By the early 1990s, the San Diego site housed the headquarters of TVA as well as the Sony Display & Components Products (SDCP) and the Sony Display & Tube Company (SDTC).

In addition, new lines of business were being added at the San Diego plant. In 1991, Sony established the Data Storage Systems Division, which manufactured floppy disk drives, CD-ROM drives and computer mass storage systems. This division had at first been set up to avoid import duties, and, much as had been the case with CTVs in the 1970s, it had been limited to final assembly based on parts imported from Japan. Yet as technology changed and Sony's data storage products needed to draw on the latest advances, managers both in Japan and in the USA recognised that the leading technology for data storage was in the USA, not Japan. The Data Storage Division was swiftly developed into Sony's world-wide leader, with R&D labs established in San Jose, California, and Boulder, Colorado, where other major computer and information systems firms were located. By 1994, just three years after its establishment, Sony's Data Storage System Division in San Diego was responsible for R&D, product design and manufacturing, and was expecting soon to become a full business unit, or jigyobu.

In 1994, Sony established a Personal Telecommunication Division at the San Diego plant, seeking to gain a share of the rapidly growing digital personal communications market. Since 1991, Sony had produced analogue cellular phones in

Japan and imported them to the USA. By 1994, however, it was clear that digital technology was becoming dominant, and again it was recognised that leading technology was in the USA. Accordingly, the Personal Telecommunications Division was established, not as an offshoot of a dominant Japanese business unit, but with the expectation of spearheading Sony's world-wide personal telecommunications business. As with Data Storage Division, the Personal Telecommunications Division was groomed to quickly assume *jigyobu* status.

A Second Television Site: Pittsburgh, Pennsylvania

In 1992, TVA opened a major new television plant near Pittsburgh, Pennsylvania. San Diego had been an ideal site for television assembly when all parts were imported from Japan, but it was far from ideal as the site for a fully localised US operation. San Diego was, after all, in one corner of the USA, far from the geographic population centre, no small consideration for products that were relatively heavy and expensive to ship. After searching extensively, Sony selected the Pittsburgh site.

By the 1995, Sony's CTV operations were managed out of San Diego as TVA, and included plants in San Diego, Tijuana and Pittsburgh. TVA was responsible for engineering and product development, and while a few key parts were still purchased from vendors in Japan, more than 70 per cent of the dollar value of inputs was purchased locally. ('Global localisation' did not imply that 100 per cent of inputs would eventually be sourced locally, as some components and other inputs were most efficiently sourced from South-East Asia. The implication was that Sony would gravitate towards sourcing as many inputs as efficient in each country where it operated.)

MODELLING THE PROCESSES OF SUBSIDIARY EVOLUTION

Many aspects of Sony's evolution in the USA are consistent with previous research. Initial entry with a small greenfield investment, over time giving way to larger entries and entries by acquisition, is consistent with patterns of foreign market entry described by Root (1994). The gradual commitment of resources and the migration of functions, from sales and marketing to manufacturing, and eventually to business planning, is consistent with models of progressive commitment in internationalisation theory (Johanson and Vahlne, 1977; Forsgren *et al.*, 1995). The increasing role of the USA in Sony's world-wide network is consistent with the typology of Bartlett and Ghoshal (1986, 1989), in which subsidiaries often begin as implementors of a global strategy, over time become important contributors, and may eventually play a role of world-wide strategic leadership. Finally, the evolutionary process we observed resembles that of Eli Lilly, with specific functions such as assembly and product design first acting as appendages to the home-country operations, later making unique contributions, and finally playing a globally integrated role (Malnight, 1995).

As for entry by line of business, Sony first entered the USA in core businesses of televisions, audio equipment and magnetic tape. In each of these it had a competitive and technological edge over American firms and leveraged these strengths by entering through greenfield investments, where it could specify the plant layout, train local employees and ensure the exact replication of activities. Over time, Sony entered in lines of business where its superiority was less clear, such as semiconductors; and in related lines of business where it sought to tap US technological leadership, such as advanced data storage and digital personal telecommunications. This pattern of sequential entry by line of business according to decreasing competitive advantage, and from core to non-core businesses, is consistent with the findings of Chang (1995). Many of Sony's later entries took place in industries, such as personal telecommunications, that did not exist in 1972, and therefore could not have preceded or been concurrent with entry in televisions.

It is reassuring that the broad patterns of Sony's experience in the USA conform to existing theory, yet what is most noteworthy about this case-study is that it provides an understanding of the process that shaped its evolution. As a result of the interviews, combined with archival and documentary data, it was found that Sony's evolution was neither inevitable nor automatic, but reflected the interplay of forces, both internal and external, which stimulated and impeded evolution. In the following section both evolutionary processes observed are modelled, the first involving functional migration in a given line of business, and the second involving sequential entry by lines of business.

Modelling the Process of Functional Migration

Based on this study of Sony in the USA, functional migration can be modelled in MNCs as a series of loops, each consisting of distinct steps and involving multiple actors. The basic process model is depicted in Figure 12.1.

Figure 12.1 A process model of functional migration

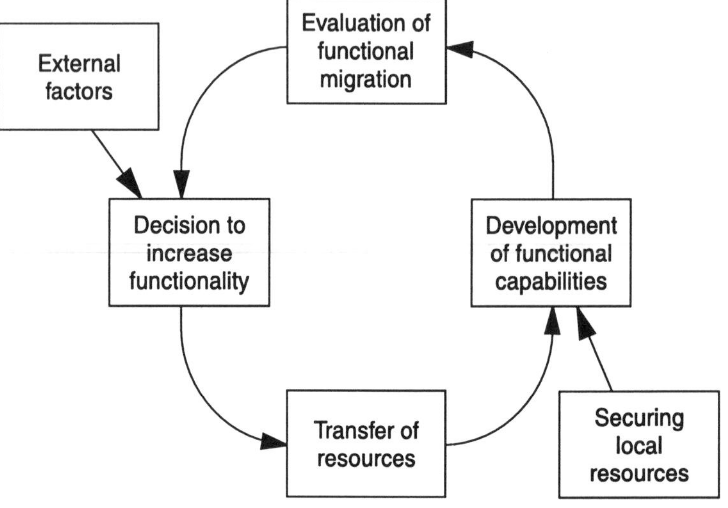

A combination of external and internal factors combine to motivate foreign direct investment, leading to an initial determination of which activities should be performed in the subsidiary. For Sony, the key factor was external: the fear of import restrictions that would hamper television sales in the USA. For other firms, of course, a wide variety of external factors may be decisive, including location advantages, access to low-cost inputs of materials or of labour, or distinctive country capabilities (Dunning, 1988). Depending on these motivations, and on internal confidence or scepticism regarding the performance of activities abroad, initial functionality may be limited to final assembly or may involve more extensive and vertically integrated activities such as local sourcing or even product design.

Once it was determined that final assembly of CTVs would be performed in San Diego, there followed a transfer of resources from Japan. Sony transferred not only financial resources but also equipment to build the assembly line in an exact replica of that in Japan, and dispatched a team of Japanese expatriates who taught local employees how to assemble televisions. Other firms may transfer a greater extent and variety of resources, including knowledge-intensive resources such as patents and formulas, proprietary processes or proprietary equipment, and managerial practices.

In addition to resources transferred internally, the new subsidiary also secures resources locally. For Sony, only minimal local resources were initially required: rental of a factory site at Rancho Bernardo, consumption of utilities such as power and water, and the hiring of small number of American employees. It is by combining resources from the MNC parent with resources secured locally that the subsidiary begins operation. For Sony, it was the combination of a local factory site and local employees, trained according to Sony's techniques, and building kits entirely imported from Japan, that produced the first CTVs built in the USA.

Once San Diego began to carry out these initial functions, its performance was carefully monitored both on-site and in Japan. Through frequent communication with expatriate managers at the subsidiary, through a direct examination of output and through discussions with customers, managers at headquarters evaluated the quality and quantity of output. Once Sony's CTV managers in Japan were satisfied that final assembly was performed at a sufficient level of quality, a first loop as shown in Figure 12.1 was complete.

Once a first loop of functional migration has been completed, MNC managers may begin to evaluate further functional migration. Such evaluation involves two elements: an identification of potential gains from greater functionality, and an assessment of whether the subsidiary can successfully carry out additional functions. Again, both external and internal factors contribute. If the MNC decides to increase the functions performed by the subsidiary then a second loop of development begins, repeating the steps in Figure 12.1 but this time at a new level of functionality. Additional resources are transferred, and additional resources are secured locally, so that the subsidiary can take on greater functionality, perhaps in a more complex manufacturing process or local product development. In Sony's case, a second loop was undertaken in 1974, this time involving the finishing of CRTs, as a way to save on shipping costs and reduce breakage. Once again, resources were transferred and combined with additional resources sourced locally, and performance was evaluated carefully.

Functional migration can undergo any number of loops. The process may cease after one or a few loops, or it may continue for several loops. In the case of CTVs at Sony's San Diego plant, there was a lengthy pause after two loops, from 1974 until the late 1980s, San Diego handled CTV final assembly and finishing of CRTs, but all other functions – including product design, the sourcing and basic manufacture of all kits, and all strategic decision-making – were performed in Japan. Neither internal nor external forces triggered a new round of functional migration.

The shift in the yen–dollar exchange rate proved to be the external factor that triggered the policy of 'global localisation', leading a series of further loops. Undertaking local parts procurement was a new loop, again involving the transfer of resources, mainly knowledge of product specifications and the process of vendor development, and securing additional local resources, in this case inputs from local vendors. Once it had been ascertained that this function was performed satisfactorily, it was agreed that product design could be carried out in the USA, triggering another loop of resource transfer. Successful local design led to a further loop, the shifting of business planning functions including the *seihan* process, which again involved the transfer of resources, in this instance two key managers who embodied the *seihan* process and could conduct it in the USA. The creation of a self-sufficient business unit, or *jigyobu*, represented a further loop. Thus the functional migration of Sony's television activities in the United States can be understood as a series of loops, each one involving a transfer of resources, the securing of additional local resources, combining them to develop local capabilities, and an evaluation to determine if further migration should take place.

Facilitators and Impediments of Functional Migration

The process of functional migration at Sony involved many factors, some external and some internal. Two external factors, mainly the threat of import barriers in 1972 and the shift of exchange rates in 1985–6, were critical in instigating the process. Other important external factors included technological developments in the host country, notably in data storage and personal telecommunications technology, which pushed those lines of business to take on responsibility for R&D, product design, and even strategic leadership; and the demands of local firms, notably IBM in personal computers, which stimulated the development of Sony's display business. In addition to acting as a stimulus to functional migration, external factors may also slow or impede the process. Thus perceptions about the dearth of local manufacturing talent made Sony at first unwilling to increase or raise functionality, while perceptions about the unavailability of adequate vendors and local suppliers made the company reluctant to source local parts until the shifting exchange rates made 'global localisation' a necessity.

As for internal forces, these again acted both to facilitate and impede functional migration. To a large degree, the external factors that argued for greater functional migration were offset by internal factors that slowed the process. Often these internal factors consisted of a concern that the US subsidiary could successfully take on greater functions. Managers in Japan often worried: 'Do we have confidence that the subsidiary can perform at a desired level?' 'Are we willing to let a key function such as product design, or an important management process such as *seihan*, be performed in the USA?' In several interviews, such concerns were described in terms of trust – not trust as in integrity or honesty, but trust in terms of confidence that actions would be appropriately undertaken.

A number of internal factors helped to overcome internal resistance. First was the active desire on the part of managers in the USA, both Americans and also Japanese expatriates, to take on greater responsibility and autonomy. The interviews also revealed the critical role played by specific managers who had the vision and confidence to extend the organisation into new domains. The role of champions was apparent at several instances. First, of course, was the role played by Akio Morita, whose sense of the importance of the US market led to the establishment of a sales company in 1960 and then to the establishment of CTV assembly in San Diego in 1972. Later, Morita's pronouncements of 'global localisation' in the late 1980s once again pushed the firm toward expanding the activities of its US subsidiary. In addition, Kunitake Ando, head of SEMA in the 1990s, continued to advocate continued functional migration, not only in CTV but in other lines of business as well. If Morita could be described as pushing for greater responsibility in the US, Ando's role could be described as one of pulling.

The Shifting Relative Importance of Facilitating and Impeding Factors

One of the most interesting findings is that the factors that facilitate and impede functional migration may be different in early and later loops, as shown on Table 12.4. At early stages, which may often involve the location of assembly or manufacturing activities in the new subsidiary, the most important impediments involve the transfer effective of technical know-how and the systems by which to evaluate the performance of initial functions. Migration would be successful if technical resources could effectively be transferred within the firm, and if managers at the parent company could be persuaded of the performance of initial activities. The challenges at this stage were exclusively internal and technical. There was as yet little concern about external factors such as local vendors, since all parts were imported from Japan, and little political resistance from managers in Japan, since they did not stand to lose any power.

In subsequent loops, as Sony sought to source more inputs locally, the ability to secure resources locally became more critical. Later loops encountered impediments that were different once again – and in some instances quite severe – as the objective is not merely to replicate existing functions in a foreign market, but actually to shift functions from the home country to a foreign subsidiary. Such a shift may trigger resistance from home country managers, making evolution to higher functions a very difficult matter. The main impediments at this point were no longer technical, but political.

Table 12.4 Impediments and facilitators in functional migration

Stage of functional migration	*Key impediment*	*Key facilitator*
Replication of assembly or manufacturing	Inadequate training of local employees	Effective transfer of knowledge
	Uncertainty about performance of subsidiary	Effective information systems to communicate high level of performance Trust-building: technical
Local sourcing of inputs	Lack of confidence regarding local vendors	Effective vendor development
Transfer of strategic functions, inc. product design and business planning	Political resistence to transfer Trust among managers	Strong advocate or champion Trust building: personal

Modelling the Process of Entry by Line of Business

Sony's US subsidiary not only evolved in terms of functions performed, but also in terms of line of business. As shown above, Sony did not enter the USA with all of its lines of business at one time, nor even in a few waves, but in a gradual sequence over many years. The process of sequential entry by line of business can also be modelled as a series of loops, as shown in Figure 12.2.

As with the process of functional migration, each new line of business entry involves a decision to enter, a transfer of

Figure 12.2 A process model of line of business addition

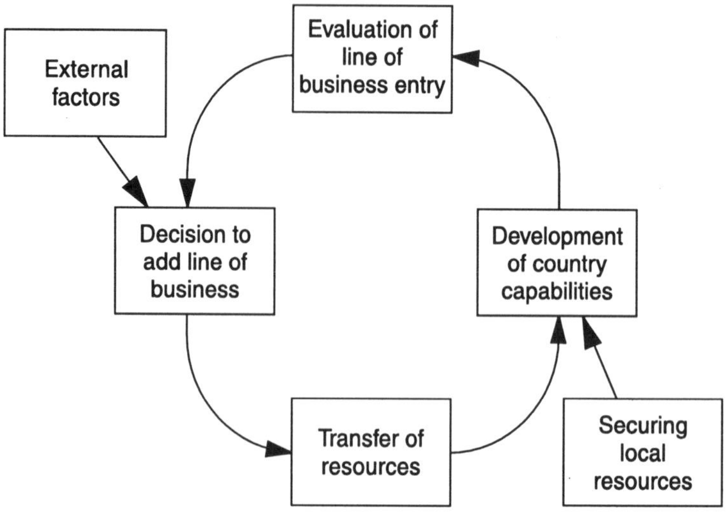

resources and the sourcing of local resources, and an evaluation of performance. Based on this evaluation, other lines of business may decide to enter, triggering a new loop. Yet the process of line of business entry differs from the process of functional migration in a few important respects. First, each new loop involves a new line of business, not the increased functionality in a given business. Second, Figure 12.2 stresses that in addition to the development of functional capabilities, the subsidiary develops country-specific capabilities, by which we denote expertise about doing business in the host country, and that it is these country-specific capabilities that can facilitate entry by successive lines of business.

The development of country-specific capabilities can be understood by reviewing Sony's early experience in the USA. As of 1972, Sony had no experience managing a manufacturing site in the USA, nor had it any reputation as an employer or experience managing a local workforce, no network of local suppliers, no experience as a manufacturer working with local regulatory bodies. Sony did, of course, have a general level of experience doing business in the USA, thanks to its strong commitment to a US sales company and to the direct experience of Akio Morita, but it was inexperienced as a direct investor and as a locally based manufacturer. It was in part thanks to the support and encouragement of local firms that Sony began operation at Rancho Bernardo.

Over the next two years, as it was building up capabilities specific to television assembly in the USA, Sony also built capabilities that were more broadly related to running a manufacturing plant in the USA. As its experience in the USA grew, Sony developed a strong reputation as an excellent employer and customer for local suppliers, learned about local regulations, and generally developed capabilities that could serve other lines of business as well. In the 1990s, with the creation of an organisation, (SEMA), that served as an umbrella to coordinate and share experience among all manufacturing activities, Sony found a way to accumulate and leverage expertise across lines of business. Some additional lines of business, such as display systems, were related to the CRT business, and drew on Sony's existing capabilities. Other entries, however, were in lines of business where Sony did not have a strong advantage over US firms, but sought to tap local expertise, as with the Data Storage Division and Personal Telecommunications Division. These recently founded divisions would never have been attempted in the 1970s, when Sony concentrated on exploiting its competitive advantages. They were subsequently possible only because of the existence of a strong country organisation and the abundance of Sony capabilities, including management support, financial infrastructure, and engineering talent, that could be shared across units. In addition, Sony entered the USA in completely new lines of business, since its forays into records and movies represented not only diversification at the subsidiary level, but diversification at the corporate level.

Facilitators and Impediments of Line-of-Business Entry

The various factors shown in Figure 12.2, both external and internal, may facilitate or impede the process of line-of-business entry. External factors include some that were important for functional migration, import restrictions, currency shifts and so forth. Other external factors speak more to line-of-business entry, namely actions by competitors in that business that demand a local presence, technological advances in a given business that prompt a need to locate in the country. External factors may also impede entry by a specific line of business. Internal factors include the development of country-based capabilities, both operational and administrative, which may facilitate additional entry. The more that resources can be shared, the more economies of scale in plants, or scope in terms of marketing mix, the greater the advantages of further entry. In addition, in some MNCs successful foreign investment by one line of business can lead to investment by others in a sort of follow-the-leader effect, analogous to what Knickerbocker (1973) identified as oligopolistic reaction.

DISCUSSION

This study of Sony in the USA from 1972 to 1995 depicts two dimensions of subsidiary evolution: not only functional migration but also line-of-business entry. Along both dimensions a process of incremental evolution was observed, and this was carried out with several discrete loops. Sony's experience is clearly not typical of all MNCs, since many undertake functional migration in a more compressed fashion, or even enter a foreign market by acquisition and effectively capture all functions at a single stroke. Many MNCs also add lines of business more swiftly than did Sony, developing a diversified position in just few years rather than over several.

Yet if the evolution of Sony's US subsidiary is not typical, it is prototypical, in that it illustrates clearly the basic processes and dynamics of MNC evolution. Precisely because an observer can detect several distinct steps in functional migration, and can discern the roles played by external and internal actors, not only in a single loop but also as it changes over time, the Sony case allows the development of a process model of subsidiary evolution. In that respect, Sony's experience in the USA serves as a baseline against which the evolution of other subsidiaries can be compared.

The contributions of this case-study, and the models of functional migration and line of business entry that have been induced, are several. First, the analysis shows subsidiary evolution along both dimensions to be a dynamic and adaptive process, with actions, feedback, evaluation and further actions. Far from being an automatic process, the continual adaptation of the subsidiary is evident, both in terms of lines of business and functions performed in a given line of business, to both external factors and internal factors. The vital role played by external factors to stimulate the evolutionary process is evident, as in the threat of import barriers and currency exchange rates. Worthy of note is also the essential role played by individual champions whose vision and persistent managerial action helped to guide the process, overcoming the inertia, scepticism and lack of trust which characterised the organisation.

Managerial Implications

This chapter points up several practical implications for managers of MNCs. First, it underscores that evolution is not inevitable or automatic, nor is it steady, nor is it symmetrical across lines of business. Rather, it is a dynamic process that responds to a variety of external and internal factors. More important, for managers, is that subsidiary evolution calls for concerted efforts at all stages, and that the necessary skills differ sharply depending on the level of functional migration. At the early levels, when the firm seeks mainly to replicate relatively simple and self-contained functions, the key is effective transfer of technical skills, careful training of employees in the host country, and the elaboration of adequate information and control systems to properly assess the performance of subsidiary functions. At intermediate stages, where local sourcing becomes more important, the major stumbling block may involve vendor development. For many firms this step represents an increase in complexity, as it involves not merely internal actors but firms that are outside the company. At later stages, where the objective is not merely to replicate activities that are performed in the home country, but actually to transfer activities, functional migration may trigger substantial resistance for political reasons. Ensuring a successful and efficient process of functional migration is therefore a complex managerial task, calling for a variety of skills, ranging from technical to political.

DIRECTIONS FOR FURTHER RESEARCH AND CONCLUSIONS

This study of Sony not only sets out two process models, but also helps to identify a number of questions merit further study. One question involves the advantages and disadvantages of undertaking subsidiary evolution – functional migration or line of business addition – in terms of many small loops or a few big ones. Sony, as shown, undertook many loops, each of which involved a small increase in subsidiary functionality or an incremental line of business addition, and monitored the results of each loop carefully before beginning a next loop. Other MNCs may be relatively more ambitious, expanding the activities of their subsidiaries by taking a fewer number of large steps. Although either approach can be understood in terms of resource transfer, subsidiary capability development, feedback and possible further transfer, the causes and effects of many small loops or a few large ones are likely to be very different. In the former instance, many loops may reflect a careful and deliberate approach, as in the case of Sony, or could suggest an unnecessarily lengthy and protracted process, and providing many invitations for impediments. In the latter instance, attempting to compress evolution into just a few large steps runs the risk of asking the subsidiary to undertake a role for which it is not fully ready, or of triggering major resistance from within the MNC.

The number and extent of loops may also reflect national differences. Indeed, it is not surprising that this case-study of evolution, involving many small evolutionary steps, involved a Japanese-based MNC. As noted by Kagono and colleagues, Japanese firms are known for taking an 'inductive, gradual adjustment approach' to their strategic development (Kagono *et al.*, 1985: 83). Driving this evolutionary process is the 'continuous accumulation and development of in-house resources' through 'learning and accumulated expertise' (1985: 151), again very much in keeping with the model set forth here. By contrast, it has been suggested that European firms are more likely to take a few bold steps, rather than a gradual approach. Whether there are important national patterns in the process of MNC evolution is a topic worthy of study, and a natural extension to this single case-study of a Japanese-based firm.

Finally, it is to be hoped that further research will attempt to empirically test aspects of the process models set out in this study. Figures 12.1 and 12.2 identify a number of variables that may facilitate or impede the evolutionary process. Future studies could combine the focus on intra-organisational level variables with the rigours of large-sample empirical testing, not looking in depth at a single firm. Such an approach would collect data about MNC evolution in a number of firms, and use those data to test the relationships among independent and dependent variables. In such a study, the extent and speed of functional migration, and the extent and speed of line of business entry, could serve as dependent variables. Independent variables would include many of those shown in Figures 12.1 and 12.2: external factors such as currency shifts and technological advances, and internal factors such as effective resource transfer mechanisms, perceptions of trust among organisational actors, and the presence of a champion.

Pending the results of further studies, this study has sought to contribute to the growing research on MNC evolution in a few important ways. First, the study of Sony Corporation in the USA depicts evolutionary processes along two dimensions simultaneously: functional migration within lines of business and sequential entry by additional lines of business. These dimensions are guided, in turn, by two distinct processed of capability development and accumulation, one involving capabilities within the line of business, and one involving country-capabilities. Furthermore, interviews with managers at Sony make clear that along neither dimension is evolution linear, but that it involves a series of loops, each one involving actions, evaluations, and further actions. This study also argues that subsidiary evolution is not inevitable, and is not the same for all lines of business, but is shaped by the interplay of internal and external factors.

References

Aharoni, Y. (1966) *The Foreign Investment Decision Process*, Boston, Mass.: Division of Research, Graduate School of Business Administration, Harvard University.

Ajami, R.A. and D.A. Ricks (1981) 'Motives of Non-American Firms Investing in the United States', 12,1 *Journal of International Business Studies*, Winter, 25–34.

Allison, G.T. (1971) *Essence of Decision*, Boston, Mass.: Little, Brown.

Barnett, W.P. and R.A. Burgelman (1996) 'Evolutionary Perspectives on Strategy', *Strategic Management Journal*, 17, 5–19.

Bartlett, C.A. and S. Ghoshal (1986) 'Tap Your Subsidiaries for Global Reach', *Harvard Business Review*, November–December, 87–94.

Bartlett, C.A. and S. Ghoshal (1989) *Managing Across Borders: The Transnational Solution*, Boston: Harvard Business School Press.

Bower, J.L. (1970) *Managing the Resource Allocation Process*, Boston, Mass.: Harvard Business School Press.

Burgelman, R.A. (1983) 'A Process Model of Internal Corporate Venturing in the Diversified Major Firm', *Administrative Science Quarterly*, 28, 223–44.

Burgelman, R.A. (1996) 'A Process Model of Strategic Business Exit: Implications for an Evolutionary Perspective on Strategy', *Strategic Management Journal*, 17, 193–214.

Caves, R.E. and S.K. Mehra (1986) 'Entry of Foreign Multinationals into US Manufacturing Industries', in M.E. Porter (ed.), *Competition in Global Industries*, Boston, Mass.: Harvard University Press, 449–81.

Chang, S-J. (1995) 'International Expansion Strategy of Japanese Firms: Capability Building Through Sequential entry', *Academy of Management Journal*, 38(2), 383–407.

Dunning, J.H. (1988) *Explaining International Production*, London and Boston: Unwin Hyman.

Forsgren, M., U. Holm and J. Johanson (1995) 'Division Headquarters Go Abroad: a Step in the Internationalization of the Multinational Corporation', *Journal of Management Studies*, 32 (4), 475–491.

Gatignon, H. and E. Anderson (1988) 'The Multinational Corporation's Degree of Control over Foreign Subsidiaries: An Empirical Test of the Transaction Cost Explanation', *Journal of Law, Economics, and Organization*, 4, 304–36.

Ghoshal, S. and C.A. Bartlett (1988) 'Creation, Adoption and Diffusion of Innovations by Subsidiaries of Multinational Corporations', *Journal of International Business Studies*, 19, 3 Fall, 365–88.

Ghoshal, S. and C.A. Bartlett (1990) 'The Multinational Corporation as an Interorganizational Network', *Academy of Management Review*, 15 (4), 603–25.

Ghoshal, S., H. Korine and G. Szulanski (1994) 'Interunit Communication in Multinational Corporations', *Management Science*, 40 (1), 96–110.

Ghoshal, S. and N. Nohria (1989) 'Internal Differentiation within Multinational Corporations', *Strategic Management Journal*, 10, 323–37.

Gupta, A.K. and V. Govindarajan (1991) 'Knowledge Flows and the Structure of Control within Multinational Corporations', *Academy of Management Review*, 16 (4), 768–92.

Hedlund, G. (1986) 'The Hypermodern MNC: a Heterarchy?', *Human Resource Management*, 25, 9–35.

Hill, C.W.L., P. Hwang and W.C. Kim (1990) 'An Eclectic Theory of the Choice of International Entry Mode', *Strategic Management Journal*, 11, 117–28.

Jarillo, J.C. and J.I. Martinez (1990) 'Different Roles for Subsidiaries: the Case of Multinational Corporations in Spain', *Strategic Management Journal*, 11, 501–12.

Johanson, J. and J-E. Vahlne (1977) 'The Internationalization Process of the Firm: a Model of Knowledge Development and Increasing Foreign Market Commitments', *Journal of International Business Studies*, 8, 23–32.

Johanson, J. and F. Weidersheim-Paul (1975) 'The Internationalization of the Firm – Four Swedish Case Studies', *Journal of Management Studies*, 12 (3), 305–22.

Kagono, T., I. Nonaka, K. Sakakibara and A. Okumura (1985) *Strategic Versus Evolutionary Management: a US-Japan Comparison of Strategy and Organization*, Amsterdam: North-Holland.

Knickerbocker, F.T. (1973) *Oligopolistic Reaction and Multinational Enterprise*, Boston, Mass.: Harvard University Graduate School of Business Administration.

Kogut, B. (1983) 'Foreign Direct Investment as a Sequential Process', in C. Kindelberger and D. Audretsch (eds), *The Multinational Corporation in the 1980s*, Cambridge, Mass.: MIT Press, 35–56.

Kogut, B. (1985) 'Designing Global Strategies: Comparative and Competitive Value-added Chains', *Sloan Management Review*, Summer, 15–28.

Kogut, B. and S-J. Chang (1991) 'Technological Capabilities and Japanese Foreign Direct Investment in the United States', *Review of Economics and Statistics*, 73, 401–13.

Kogut, B. and U. Zander (1993) 'Knowledge of the Firm and the Evolutionary Theory of the Multinational Corporation', *Journal of International Business Studies*, 24 (4), 625–45.

Magee, S.P (1977) 'Information and the Multinational Corporation: an Appropriability Theory of Direct Foreign Investment', in J. Bhagwati (ed.), *The New International Economic Order*, Cambridge, Mass.: MIT Press, 317–40.

Malnight, T.W. (1995) 'Globalization of an Ethnocentric Firm: an Evolutionary Perspective', *Strategic Management Journal*, 16, 119–141.

Malnight, T.W. (1996) 'The Transition from Decentralized to Network-Based MNC Structures: an Evolutionary Perspective', *Journal of International Business Studies*, First Quarter, 27 (1), 43–65.

Morita, A. (1986) *Made in Japan: Akio Morita and Sony*, New York: Dutton.

Noda, T. and J.L. Bower (1996) 'Strategy Making as Iterated Processes of Resource Allocation', *Strategic Management Journal*, 17, 159–92.

Perlmutter, H. (1969) 'The Tortuous Evolution of the Multinational Corporation', *Columbia Journal of World Business*, 4, 9–18.

Root, F.R. (1994) *Entry Strategies for International Markets*, New York: Lexington Books.

Van de Ven, A. (1992) 'Suggestions for Studying Strategy Processes: a Research Note', *Strategic Management Journal*, 13, Special Issue, 169–88.
Yin, R.K. (1989) *Case-Study Research: Design and Methods*, Newbury Park, Calif.: Sage.

13 Organisational Learning in Japanese MNCs: Four Affiliate Archetypes

Schon Beechler, Allan Bird and Sully Taylor

INTRODUCTION

For much of the history of international business, academics have focused on the foreign direct investment decision. While the decision to expand overseas is an important one, it is only the first step in a long journey for multinational company (MNC) managers. Setting up the necessary systems for managing the overseas affiliate and ensuring that it contributes to organisational goals are much longer-term, more complicated issues that have only recently received the scholarly attention they deserve.

This chapter examines one particularly important and complex issue in this domain: organisational learning from overseas affiliates. As organisations expand overseas, they must, by necessity, establish new systems for managing that operation. These events present an occasion for organisational learning.

In the case of newly-established operations in the company's home country, the determination and implementation of those systems is usually straightforward, namely a simple replication of systems currently in effect at existing operations. Because the operating environment is generally the same in a domestic expansion, the fundamental assumptions underlying the organisation's design and processes are seldom called into question and, as a result, learning is minimal. However, because overseas operations face different contexts from domestic operations, there are higher levels of uncertainty and the question of what systems to implement overseas becomes more problematic. Consequently, setting up overseas operations provides many challenges, but also a significant opportunity for learning as organisations are forced to examine systematically each system's components for their applicability in the new environment.

In this chapter, attention is specifically focused on how Japanese firms learn from their overseas operations – specifically, what they learn with regard to their management systems. The focus in this study is on the management system, for several reasons. First, of the various activities an overseas affiliate engages in, the management of people appears to be the one most sensitive to variations in environmental conditions and factors. It also appears to be the most complex and uncertain. Second, as national barriers to the flow of capital and technology continue to fall, the importance of the human factor to the value-adding activities of the firm rises, further emphasising the importance of effectively managing its human resources (Pfeffer, 1994). Third, when compared with their US and European counterparts, Japanese firms are often perceived as relying far more extensively on management systems as a means of achieving competitive advantage (Abo, 1994). Finally, with the simultaneous rise in the value of the yen, the longest Japanese recession in the postwar era, and keen competition globally, the overseas operations of Japanese MNCs (JMNCs) have become critical to firm survival. Consequently, today more than ever, the future of JMNCs hinges on their ability to learn from their overseas affiliates.

The next section describes the research methodology, outlining the reasoning behind the chosen approach. Then, the theoretical foundations of the study are set out, delineating a model of learning that best fits the phenomena observed as well as describing factors identified as influential in the process. This is followed by a generalised description of the archetypal patterns of decisions pursued by the firms selected for the study. The fifth section considers the similarities and contrasts among the four learning types found in the JMNCs studied. In the concluding section the implications of the findings are discussed to show how Japanese MNCs should approach learning in their foreign operations. In addition, the question of the importance of these findings for non-Japanese MNCs is also addressed.

METHODOLOGY

Over the past eight years, the authors have designed a series of studies to explore how Japanese MNCs manage human resources in their overseas affiliates. By employing questionnaire surveys and semi-structured, open-ended interviews conducted in person as well as over the telephone, data were collected as part of a comprehensive, multi-method project to understand the nature of management systems – philosophies, policies and practices – in Japanese overseas affiliates. The goal was to track how management philosophies were transferred from parent companies, how policies were developed and implemented, and what the effect of specific practices were on affiliate performance in terms of a variety of outcomes (cf. Bird and Beechler, 1995).

The project began in 1989 with a questionnaire survey of 64 seniormost American personnel managers and their immediate Japanese superiors in USA-based affiliates. Simultaneous to the US study, a parallel study of four Japanese maquiladoras was carried out in Mexico. Interview and survey data from the four Mexican affiliates was pooled with that of the US study. Data was also included from interview surveys with 26 Japanese affiliates located in 5 countries in South-East Asia, which had been undertaken in 1987. In 1991, interviews and a questionnaire survey of 38 additional Japanese affiliates based in the USA were carried out. These were followed in 1992 by field interviews with Japanese affiliates in Europe – 8 in the UK and 7 in Spain. Thus, a total of 147 Japanese affiliates comprise the database from which the observations are drawn.

This analysis employed a 'grounded research' approach in which notes from earlier rounds of interviews were examined to guide in the development of questions for subsequent rounds of data collection. As part of this iterative process, 'working theories' were induced and these were explored and tested as the project moved forward.

THEORETICAL FOUNDATION

Adaptation and Adjustment as Learning

Before discussing the study results it is important to first define what is meant by organisational learning in this context. As Hedberg (1981) points out, organisations are not individuals, and hence organisational learning must differ from individual learning, not simply constitute an aggregate of individual learning. More than thirty years ago, Cyert and March (1963) addressed this issue by noting that organisation routines, standard operating procedures, and policies change over time in response to changes in the environment. They argued that these changes, in and of themselves, constitute 'learning' by the organisation. Labeled 'stimulus–response' learning, this perspective frames learning as an adaptive–manipulative response by a system to its environment: 'learning results when organizations interact with their environments: each action adds information and strengthens or weakens linkages between stimuli and responses' (Hedberg, 1981: 9).

This model of learning is predicated on Campbell's (1959) suggested mechanism of 'variation → selection → retention'. Changes in the environment provide the variation stimuli perceived by the organisation, which then assembles responses to match the perceived stimuli. If the organisation concludes that a particular response assembly matches perceived stimuli, then that assembly is retained for future use, that is, a change is made in the organisation's routines.

Weick (1969), however, noted that it is not the variation of environmental stimuli *per se* to which organisations react, but rather organisations' perceptions of stimuli. Stimuli pass through perceptual filters, so that when an organisation responds, it is not a response to what is, but rather to what is perceived. In this sense, organisations *enact* their environments. Consequently, the organisational learning process is more accurately conceptualised as 'enactment → election → retention'.

The distinction is particularly important with regard to establishing management systems within overseas affiliates. MNCs have pre-existing routines and theories of 'how the world works', which serve as perceptual filters enacting the overseas environment. Management and other operating systems within the overseas affiliates may be viewed as *selected* response assemblies which, if perceived to match stimuli, will be *retained.*

The perspective on organisational learning in this chapter is consistent with that of Cyert and March (1963) and Campbell (1965), in that the authors believe the very process of establishing a management system in the overseas affiliate and then making adjustments to the system – fine-tuning or overhauling – constitutes the initiation and continuance of an ongoing organisational learning process. As shown in Figure 13.1, the process of organisational learning is initiated with the decision by the parent firm to establish an overseas affiliate. At that time, the parent enacts a picture of reality that includes an interpretation of the local environment in the host country, as well as the firm's own capabilities. Using this picture, it makes an assessment as to how well existing systems fit with the host country environment. To the extent that the newly installed system or some of its parts suit the local environment, they are retained in the affiliate and become institutionalised in the ongoing system. Information about what is retained feeds back to influence subsequent perceptions of the local environment and firm capabilities. In the meantime, those aspects of the system that do not suit local conditions serve as stimuli in the enactment phase of the subsequent learning cycle that iteratively continues.

Figure 13.1 A basic process model of the Japanese MNC parent–affiliate management learning cycle

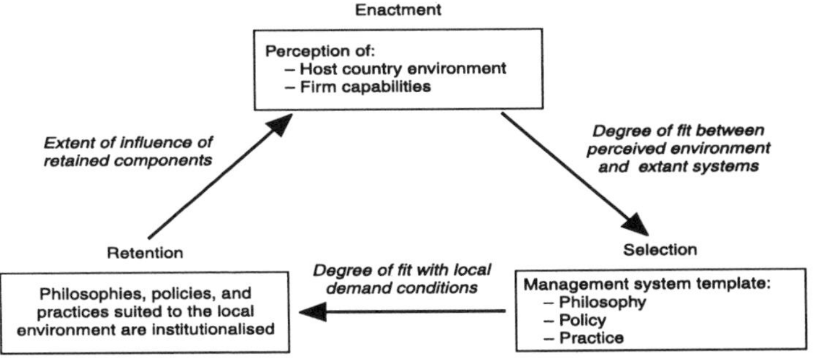

It is important to note that the learning process occurs at two levels of the organisation and involves two sets of actors. The process is initiated by the parent firm through decisions made by headquarters personnel, but directly involves the overseas affiliate and its personnel as the process moves forward into the selection phase. Retention then takes place at the affiliate level, but feedback subsequently influences both affiliate and parent perceptions.

Imprinting and the Start of Learning

If organisational learning is an ongoing, cyclical process consisting of phases of enactment, selection and retention, then it is important to identify at what point the learning begins. In the case of JMNCs and their overseas affiliates, this research concluded that learning begins with the selection and implementation of the affiliate's management template. Attributes imprinted at the founding of an organisation shape its subsequent trajectory of development (Stinchcombe, 1965). As outgrowths of an existing organisation, affiliates are born with particular predilections and orientations. At the same time, they encounter specific conditions and chronologies in the host country not previously experienced by the parent, which may impose new constraints and apply unanticipated pressures. The imprinting of the affiliate, both genetically and environmentally, signals the start of the learning process.

Selecting Management Templates

The genetic code of the affiliate is located in the philosophies, policies and practices of its various operating systems. The specific interest in this research is in the management system, by which is meant those aspects of the operating system directly related to the treatment of human resources. This definition extends beyond the notion of human resources management, as focused solely on planning, staffing, training, compensation and performance appraisal, by including such other activities as the moulding of corporate culture, communication and control systems.

To guide them in the development of an affiliate's management system, parent firms often employ a template, that is, a pattern or mould, on which the new system can be modeled. A critical decision, then, involves the selection of the basic template to be used in guiding subsequent decisions about the management system design. Variation in template selection occurs along two lines: the origin of the template and the level at which the template is established. The first dimension involves choosing between two possibilities. On the one hand, the parent may adopt an internal template, choosing to pattern the affiliate's system on that of the parent and making minor adjustment to accommodate local variances. The second is to opt for an external, host country template, often making major adjustments from the system to which the parent is accustomed.

The second aspect of the template decision involves the level at which the template is established. It can operate at one of three levels: philosophy, policy or practice. A philosophy is a set of beliefs about 'how the world works'. In the case of a management system, beliefs pertain to the best way to allocate, enhance, and utilise the human resources of an organisation. Policies can be thought of as the decision rules designed to guide actions in a manner consistent with beliefs about how the world works. In short, they are procedures that organisation members are expected to follow based on a belief that following them will lead to success. Practices, on the other hand, are members' responses to policy and can be thought of as the actual decisions taken and behaviours engaged in.

The relationship between philosophy, policy and practice is analogous to the distinction Schein (1985) makes regarding culture as operating at the level of assumptions, values and artifacts. As a template, a philosophy serves as a 'theory-in-use' (Argyris, 1976) that the parent employs in constructing the affiliate's management system. If, for example, the parent uses its home country philosophy as a template, it does not necessarily make a commitment to transferring specific sets of home country policies. Rather, it leaves itself open to examining the suitability of specific home country policies for the host country environment as well as to the possibility that some widely accepted policies in the host country may also be congruent with its chosen philosophy. The basic mold into which policies will fit is defined by the philosophy. For example, a widely accepted Japanese management philosophy is that of resource accumulation (Beechler and Bird, 1994; Kagono *et al.*, 1986; Schuler, 1989). Predicated on a belief that successful organisations endure over time as a result of their ability to exploit human capital, such a philosophy would emphasise building maximum involvement and a pool of skilled workers by providing on-going training and development that develops the latent potential of members. Policies consistent with such a philosophy need not necessarily be drawn solely from those already in effect in Japan.

In contrast, when the parent seeks to apply a policy template, in addition to a particular philosophy, it also intends to implement specific sets of policies. In such cases, the belief is that particular policies represent the best possible fit to a philosophy. Building on the example above, a Japanese MNC may employ an accumulator philosophy and then select a parent policy as being the best fit. For example, when Kyocera announced the opening of its San Diego facility in the mid-1980s it also announced a policy of no layoffs. In doing so Kyocera imposed a policy template, applying not only a resource accumulation philosophy, but also a specific employment policy adopted from its Japanese operations deemed consistent with that philosophy.

Finally, a practice template focuses on eliciting specific types of behaviour. The concern of a practice template is on actual behaviour, not necessarily attitude or intention. A firm adopting a parent practice template is interested in having host country employees behave in ways similar to Japanese employees back home. The philosophy and specific policies of the affiliate are of less importance than whether or not host country employees act in a desired fashion. When a chemical processing facility in North Carolina paid its employees overtime to stay after hours to work in quality control circles its primary concern was in having US workers engage in the same sort of small-group activities as its Japanese employees in Osaka. The fact that Japanese employees stayed after work voluntarily, without pay, reflected differing policies and differing philosophies between the two sites. A critical point here is that similarity with respect to some practices (QC circles) could only be achieved through differences in other practices (compensation), thus drawing attention to the parent's assessment of certain *practices* as being essential to the effective operation of the affiliate.

Japanese Management as a Template

In the following discussion of management systems in Japanese overseas affiliates, generalisations are made regarding parent company templates and Japanese management as a general system. In doing so, it is recognised that there are wide variations among Japanese firms (Beechler and Bird, 1994). Nevertheless, as a whole, the JMNCs studied in this project exhibited commonality in their Japan-based systems with regard to work organisation, labour relations and employee development. Therefore, when Japanese management is referred to, the authors are designating a system possessing an underlying philosophy of resource accumulation and development characterised by the following types of policies and practices: work organisation is team-based and relies on a sense of unity and a sharing of information; job classifications are few and job descriptions ambiguous; wages are person-centred (Abo, 1994), that is, focused on personal criteria such as tenure, work experience, and so on; staffing is from within and promotions are predicated in large measure on years of service; training takes place through job rotation and ongoing educational activities both on and off the job; and loyalty to the organisation is valued.

It should be noted that in recent years much debate has arisen over the extent to which the above-mentioned attributes remain typical of Japanese firms. Increases in labour mobility rates, corporate downsizing and organisational restructuring have been cited as evidence that the Japanese management system is in a state of transition. While changes are occurring, the authors believe that such a conclusion is premature. Whether such actions constitute a fundamental, lasting shift or a short-term response to economic exigencies remains unclear. Consequently, this discussion of the Japanese management system takes the stance that it is still possible to talk about a 'Japanese' style of management.

A DECISION TREE AND FOUR LEARNING ARCHETYPES

The outcome of this analysis was the identification of a typology of learning patterns experienced by Japanese firms in the establishment and ongoing management of their overseas affiliates' management systems. This typology is comprised of four distinct archetypes, each of which follows a different path in its development. These four archetypes are presented in Figure 13.2 in a decision tree diagram that describes the specific sequence of decisions and set of influencing factors that characterise each of the four types.

In the following subsections the starting-point common to all of the types is described and the factors leading to differentiation into each of the archetypes are discussed. This is followed by a comparison of the four types and the ways they differ from one another.

Tactical Decisions and Emergent Learning Strategies

The decision to set up an overseas affiliate creates, in turn, the need to make a large number of other decisions, most of them viewed as tactical in nature. For these purposes, 'tactical' is defined as being concerned with the act of implementing a strategy – in this case, a specific strategy for setting up operations overseas. The first of these decisions is how to staff the new affiliate. In the case of greenfield investments, for example, most of the employees were hired locally, but key managerial positions were filled by Japanese personnel. In these studies, the actual number of Japanese expatriates installed in new overseas affiliates ranged from a low of 3 per cent up to a high of 30 per cent. Although constraints of space do not allow for elaboration (see Beechler and Bird, 1994, for a more thorough discussion), initial staffing decisions were guided by ownership structure, method of establishment (greenfield, joint venture, takeover, and so on), whether the company saw Japanese management as one of its core competencies, and by the overarching corporate strategy (Taylor *et al.*, 1996).

The most important tactical decision involved the selection of a basic template to be used in guiding subsequent decision-

Figure 13.2 Diagram of tactical decisions and influences in the development of subsidiary HRM system

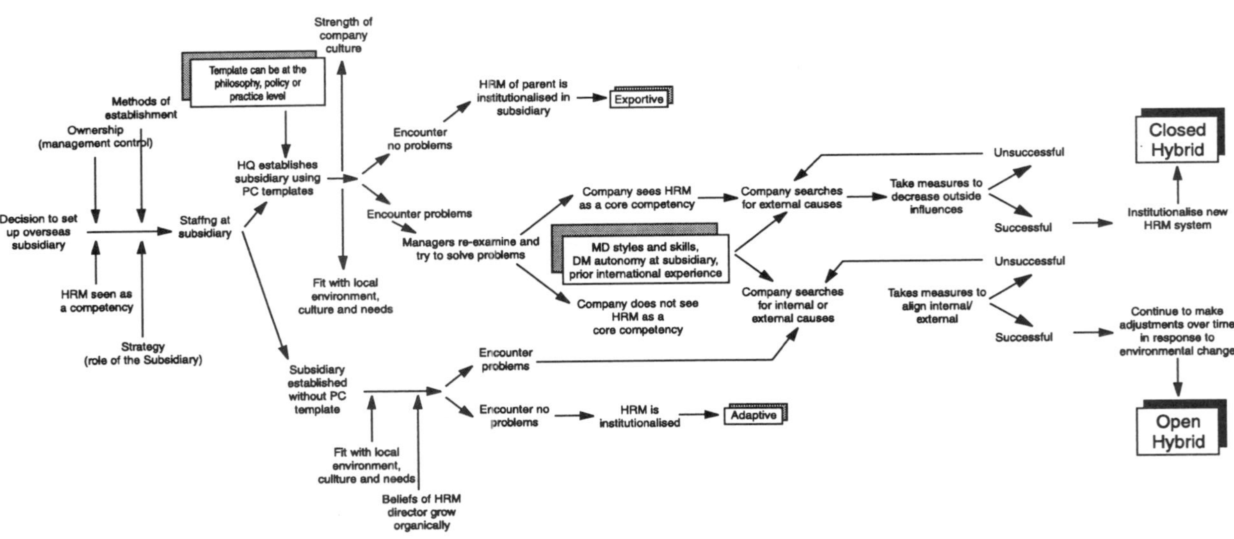

making about the specifics of the affiliate's management system. Some firms in the study sought to transfer the parent template at the level of management philosophy. That is, they endeavoured to transfer an underlying set of values that were to be used in defining how and what policies to establish. For example, one firm had a well-defined corporate philosophy that valued both the development of human capital and a long-term relationship between employee and company. When it established its first overseas affiliate in the USA it emphasised these values in delineating specific HRM policies. By contrast, other firms studied sought to implement a template at the policy level, spelling out in great detail the specific procedures to be followed. For instance, one consumer electronics firm sought to transfer the entire parent company template to its US operations. To do so, it had its entire set of work rules and personnel manuals translated into English and then made the modifications required by the US legal system. Finally, a third set of firms were less concerned with philosophy or policy, but instead focused specifically on how they wanted employees to behave. These firms sought to establish a template at the practice level, seeking to elicit specific types of behaviour. Typical of this type of affiliate was a copy machine manufacturer in southern California that provided employees at each work station with a sequence of Polaroid photographs detailing each step of that station's task in lieu of OJT or other methods of employee training and development. The essential behaviour was the 'correct' sequence of steps, even though a supervisor admitted that at some stations the task could be completed by following a different order, 'but this is the way it is done in Japan'.

One finding was that decisions by JMNCs about whether to adopt a parent or host country template and the level at which the template was to be applied were strongly influenced by two factors: the company's perception of its own management approach as a core competency and the perception that the parent's management system fit with the host country environment. In instances where management was perceived as a core competency or when the parent system's fit with the local environment was perceived to be high, Japanese MNCs were more inclined to select a fully elaborated parent template that included philosophy, policies and practices. While there was some variation at the practice level, all of these companies employed a philosophy and policy template based on the parent.

The role of the affiliate in the JMNC's overall strategy also appears to exert some influence on the choice of template. Beechler *et al.* (1993) suggest that the need for fit between a firm's overall business strategy and its HRM system may create pressures for consistency between parent and affiliate HRM systems. This is reflected in a preference for imposing a parent company template. Interview data from managers in the US-based set of affiliates support this thesis. One human resources manager in a New-Jersey-based electronics affiliate confessed that he had little control over policy decisions because they were often dictated from Tokyo, owing to the affiliate's tight linkages with Japan-based facilities.

As the affiliates studied moved forward with the implementation of their chosen template they usually found it necessary to make adjustments in their management system. The types of adjustments they made were guided by their perceptions of the causes of problems inevitable in any implementation, the degree of autonomy granted to them by the parent, and the amount of international experience key personnel possessed. For some firms the adjustments were straightforward and easily made. Typical of this type was a photochemical processing firm that, in an effort to adapt to US labour norms, had decided not to ask local employees to wear company uniforms, even though Japanese expatriates wore them on the shop floor. This being the company's first overseas facility, corporate planners in Japan had assumed that the Americans would not want to wear uniforms and had instructed the US plant manager not to issue them. However, local workers expressed discomfort at being treated differently from their bosses and their counterparts back in Japan. Once the manager became aware of local employee concerns, he instituted a policy requiring that uniforms be worn in the plant and morale immediately improved.

For others, adjustments followed an iterative, experimental process whereby managers would try first one solution and then another. For example, a copier manufacturer in the UK sustained levels of labour turnover higher than any local firm. Believing that turnover was due to low wage rates, the company implemented a pay increase for line workers. When turnover rates remained high, quality circles were established and a team-based bonus system was installed. When turnover still remained high the company shifted attention away from manipulations in the compensation system and undertook a more rigorous selection procedure designed to eliminate candidates with career profiles similar to those who had left the company.

It is important to point out that during the course of these observations, not all problems were resolved and adjustments were ongoing. Changes in the local environment as well as shifts in strategy and fluctuations in parent operations require that the affiliate management system undergo continual adaptation. In the case of another UK-based affiliate, for example, a no-layoff policy became problematic when one of the two products it assembled was discontinued. Layoffs were avoided, but only as a result of revamping work schedules and redefining a full work week in terms of fewer hours.

Although each affiliate's experiences were unique, common themes and patterns recurred as the sample of firms grew. As reflected in Figure 13.2, it was possible to classify each of the affiliates learning process into one of four types, which are now examined in turn.

The Exportive Model

In establishing the overseas affiliate's management policies and practices, some Japanese firms seek a wholesale transplant of the management template from the parent company in Japan. Referring back to Figure 13.2, this approach is labelled for this purpose as exportive because of its implicit assumption that parent company ways of doing things are inherently the most appropriate, if not superior to other approaches. Hence, the parent exports its way of doing things to the new site. Firms following this model are inclined to view their management of human resources as a core competency that is a source of competitive advantage and are also inclined to see it as something universally applicable. These firms also perceive the gap between local environmental conditions and those back home in

Japan as relatively small, subsequently concluding that significant modification of the parent template is not required.

What distinguishes the exportive model from the other learning types on this particular branch of the tree is that, indeed, the management system does seem to work reasonably well, and at the first attempt. Japanese firms in the exportive category are characterised by successful management systems that closely mirror the philosophy and policies of the parent. While the initial inclination was to think that firms adopting this model would experience significant difficulty in establishing effective HRM policies and practices in their overseas affiliates, such a sweeping conclusion proved inaccurate. The exportive model seemed to work reasonably well when affiliates were located in countries that were legally and socioculturally similar to Japan. Consequently, only minor adjustments in the parent template were necessary. The most successful examples of this type were found among affiliates in South-East Asia.

Figure 13.3 indicates how the exportive learning type varies around the basic model. The affiliate enacts by perceiving the host environment as similar to Japan's and also perceives its own capabilities in management as a core competency. Given the perceived match between home and host country environments and the perceived strength of its existing management system, it selects a parent management template in the overseas affiliate. The selected template roughly suits the local environment such that only minor adjustments are required for it to work well there. Early on the affiliate concludes that its experience with the parent template is successful and so it is retained. This is viewed by both the affiliate and HQs as a confirmation of the parent template as an appropriate way to manage the affiliate's HRM function. Consequently, learning for both the affiliate and the parent is in the form of a confirmation of the original assumption. Hedberg (1981) points out that learning derived from success often focuses on fine-tuning the existing system. We found this to be true for thos Japanese firms in the study that were convinced of the correctness of their systems as well as their systems' widespread applicability. Moreover, since the experience confirmed what was already believed, there was little attempt by the parent at disseminating this particular affiliate's experiences to its other foreign affiliates. Any minor adjustments made to the template were seen as idiosyncratic to the host country and therefore irrelevant to both the parent and to other affiliates.

Figure 13.3 A process model of the Japanese MNC parent– affiliate management learning cycle for exportive firms

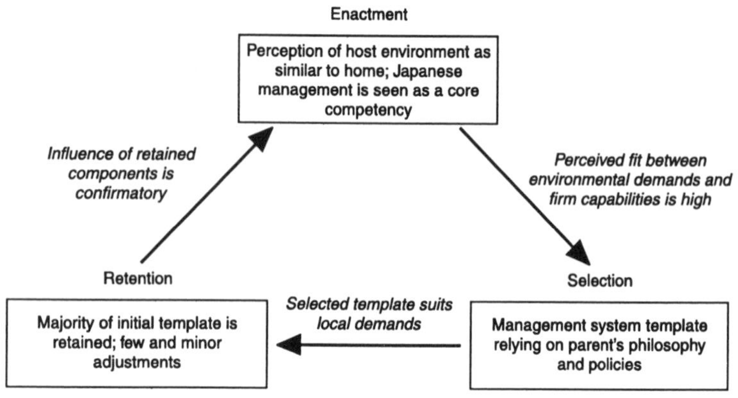

The Closed Hybrid Model

A second group of firms adopted a variant of the learning model labelled for this purpose as 'closed hybrid'. As was the case with exportive learners, this type is characterised by the affiliate's reliance on a parent company template in the development of the initial management system. However, early on the affiliate encountered problems indicating that the fit was not good, and that substantive changes were required. At this point, if the affiliate and the parent had strong beliefs in their management as a core competency, modifications to the system were based on a belief that the cause of problems was external. This included such attributions as the belief that the local workers were poorly trained or had a bad attitude, that local competitors were able to pay higher wages or that government regulations interfered with management policies. Consequently, modifications to the system tried to buffer it from outside influences. The earlier example of the UK-based affiliate experiencing high turnover falls into this type. When several adjustments designed to adapt policies to local conditions failed to achieve the desired decrease in turnover, it moved to a highly selective hiring process aimed at protecting the rest of the management system by screening out potential leavers. In other words, selection would buffer the exported system from the 'failure' of the local environment to produce loyal, motivated workers.

How the closed hybrid learning type varies around the basic learning model is shown in Figure 13.4. The affiliate perceives the host environment as similar to that of Japan and it perceives its own capabilities in management as a core competency. Given the perceived match between home and host country environments and the perceived strength of its existing management system, it opts for a parent template in the overseas affiliate. The closed hybrid differentiates itself from the exportive type as a result of its initial lack of success in adapting and functioning effectively in the local environment. Hedberg (1981) notes that failure often encourages a re-evaluation of assumptions and beliefs. As illustrated in Figure 13.4, closed hybrid firms, faced with failure, recognise that the parent template does not fit the local environment. However, because they hold strong beliefs about the efficacy of their own approaches, their problem search is externally directed, as is their learning. They acquire more information about the local environment, recognise how their system needs to be modified to function well within it, and make changes accordingly. Dissemination of what they learn, however, is limited to themselves. Because of the perception that local conditions are exceptional, the parent learns very little, judging suitable adjustments for this affiliate inapplicable to other settings. This is the reason these firms are labelled closed hybrid learners: experience leads to the creation of a hybrid system, but learning is closed off from the larger organisation.

The Adaptive Model

In contrast to an approach that assumes the superiority and efficacy of Japanese parent company ways of managing, some

Figure 13.4 A process model of the Japanese MNC parent–affiliate management learning cycle for closed hybrid firms

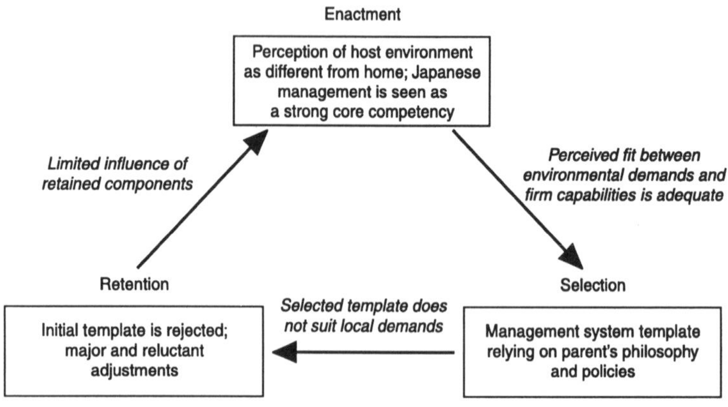

firms focus on adapting as much as possible to the local situation, eschewing the notion that parent-company approaches might be useful except in limited areas. Because this approach leads to a relatively disparate set of policies and practices across overseas affiliates, this was named the 'adaptive' learning type. Firms employing this model downplay the importance of the HRM function in their overseas operations. They hold the position that human resources ought to be managed as effectively as possible and that, while they might possess considerable expertise in this area, parent-company policies should not be imposed on overseas affiliates which face considerably different conditions.

When these firms confront problems in the course of establishing HRM policies, their inclination is to search for the cause of the problem internally, seeking to discern in what ways their approach or the actions that flowed from that approach are flawed. One consequence of doing so is that these firms learn a great deal, not only about the local environment and local actors, but also about themselves. Unfortunately, because of their belief that local conditions are so different, they also believe that what is learned cannot be extended beyond their own situation. Instead, their perception is that each affiliate has to learn on its own, with little if any transfer between them or between affiliate and parent.

These characteristics are reflected in Figure 13.5, which describes the adaptive version of the learning cycle. Perceiving a host environment dramatically different from that of Japan and possessing no strong attachment to parent's management system, the overseas affiliate begins with a template customised to fit with the demands of the local environment. Because the template fits reasonably well, few adjustments are made and the system is viewed as successful in terms of its responsiveness to local demands. Again, the success of the initial implementation effort in conjunction with a perceived misfit with the parent management system discourages attempts to share what is learned beyond those associated with fine-tuning the process. Viewed in this way, both the affiliate and the parent are inclined to conclude that learning is not easily transferred, so diffusion is limited.

Figure 13.5 A process model of the Japanese MNC parent–affiliate management learning cycle for adaptive firms

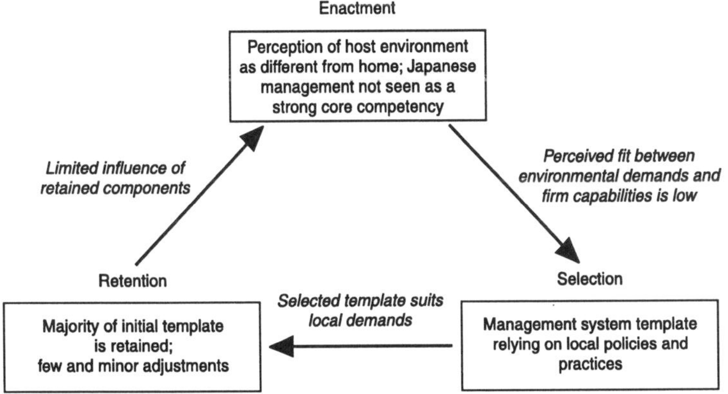

The Open Hybrid Model

The final type, here styled as the 'open hybrid' learning model, encompasses firms that approach the development of a management system for their overseas affiliates from a variety of starting-points. Firms adopting this model may or may not have originally begun with a parent company template as the basis for their system once they confronted difficulties. Rather, unlike the other three types, they tend to move very quickly to a position that sought a duality in outlook – a simultaneous emphasis on parent and local perspectives. Almost invariably, this shift is the result of problems they encounter that are much greater than anticipated and cause them to re-evaluate their initial assumptions and beliefs. As a sidenote, only firms not strongly wedded to a belief in their management as one of their core competencies seem able to undergo such transformations. For instance, one consumer electronics sales operation in the UK best typified this pattern. The initial managing director had sought to create a bridge between the parent's strong corporate culture and the British work ethic. After almost a year of struggling with bad morale and low productivity, nearly the entire system was jettisoned and a new one developed. Changes addressed both internal and external factors. For example, greater time was spent in socialising new local employees into corporate and Japanese ways of doing and thinking. At the same time, several of the policies relating to compensation and work assignments deemed most objectionable by British employees were modified to conform more closely to the norms in effect among British competitors.

Figure 13.6 illustrates the learning cycle as experienced by open hybrid learners. Firms in this category perceive the host environment as substantially different from that in Japan, and do not see their corporate strength or competitive advantage as lying in the management of their human resources, although this does not mean that they do not believe they do a good job in this area. They subsequently initiate their affiliate management system using a customised template, modified from the parent or local models, and open themselves up to change once they encounter difficulties. They make revisions to the template involving both adjustment to local conditions and modification from parent positions. They closely monitor the application of adjustments and are cautious in the acceptance of success. This is not to suggest that they are timid in identifying what is working – quite the opposite. When they do discover successes, they are inclined to disseminate them quickly and widely within the company. Rather, what is noteworthy is their recognition that the system requires continual adjustment. They are humble regarding what they know, and hence make themselves open to learning. Moreover, they seek ways to connect what they are learning locally with applications to other situations in the larger organisation.

Figure 13.6 A process model of the Japanese MNC parent–affiliate management learning cycle for open hybrid firms

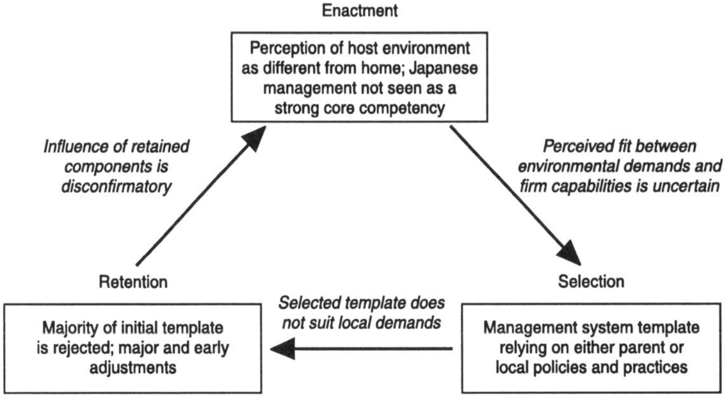

The greater flexibility of the open hybrid, brought about as a result of a dual focus and a willingness to relax assumptions about the superiority of the parent company's management system, enables these JMNCs to search for the source of problems both internally and externally. One consequence of this is that firms in this group tend to identify problems more quickly, while problems are still in gestation and before they have time to develop into fully grown crises. Change is incremental and continuous.

The orientation of the open hybrid toward change is also highly proactive, characterised by a constant fine-tuning of the system. Open hybrid firms exhibit a willingness to learn from local sources or from other parties within the organisation. In similar fashion, they are willing and often enthusiastic about sharing what they have learned with others in the local community, but more frequently with the parent company and with other affiliates within the organisation. One UK affiliate in the study demonstrated this through its active membership in a local business association that met monthly to share insights about HR issues and how to resolve various management problems. Within the larger organisation, they met quarterly with HR managers from others affiliates in Europe, again using the occasion to share information and trade insights.

The openness of affiliates in this grouping was also reflected in interviews. Often interviewees sought the observations and evaluations of the researchers as to the policies they had developed. They seemed genuinely interested in exploring such events from different perspectives so as to better understand and learn from them.

Comparing the Four Learning Types

A consideration of the similarities and differences among the four models highlights several important distinctions between them. Contrasts across the models are presented in Table 13.1 in terms of the three stages of the learning cycle: enactment, selection, and retention.

Enactment

The most critical decision point in the process of establishing the Japanese overseas affiliate's management system is that of the initial template to be used. This choice sets the direction and tone of subsequent decisions. Exportive and closed hybrid firms opt for a parent management template, thereby establishing what will subsequently become barriers to locally responsive adaptations. By contrast, adaptive and open hybrid firms emphasise host country responsiveness and put into place local templates. The template decision is influenced by a variety of organisational factors mentioned previously, most particularly their perception of the gap between host country and Japan as well as the belief that management was a core competency. Just as critical as these, however, is the staffing decision, that is, who is selected to install the template. Specifically, the general manager of the affiliate serves as the primary 'carrier' of the template. In the case of exportive and closed hybrid models, the carrier is a Japanese expatriate from headquarters, quite often working in close connection with staff in the parent company. In contrast, adaptive and open hybrid firms are more likely to use a host-country national. When the affiliate general manager of adaptive and open hybrid firms is a Japanese national, then it is common to find that the executive responsible for HRM is a local person who has been given substantial autonomy in the design of the management system.

Table 13.1 A comparison of four learning cycle models

	Exportive	*Closed hybrid*	*Adaptive*	*Open hybrid*
Enactment	Parent template	Parent template	Local template	Customised, temporary template
Selection	Minor adjustments	Major adjustment	Minor adjustment	Major adjustment
Retention	Verification of fit; fine-tuning	Identification of success consistent with self-image	Local success	Cautious success

A second distinction between the exportive/closed hybrid types and the adaptive/open hybrid firms is the level of template selected. The former are much more inclined to establish a parent template that includes management philosophy and policies than are the latter. Although adaptive/open hybrid firms select a local or highly customised template, with rare exception these are predicated upon a management philosophy borrowed from that of the parent. Typical of this was a US affiliate of an electronics company, which was classified as open hybrid. The US manager assigned the responsibility of designing the management system was given free rein to do what he thought best. His chose to visit the parent company in Tokyo and spent several months talking with headquarters personnel in order to get a feeling as to why they did things the way they did. Upon his return he set about developing a US version of the parent philosophy and then elaborated a set of policies, many of which on the surface bore little similarity to those back at the parent company. Nevertheless, the underlying aim of the policies was consistent with the philosophical values of the parent.

Selection

The defining difference between the four learning types in the selection stage centres on the extent of adjustments required. Both open and closed hybrid types experienced substantial difficulties early on in the development process. These difficulties forced firms to re-evaluate their initial assumptions about the system and develop new ways of doing things. What differentiates the two from one another, however, is that closed hybrids refuse to consider that problems might be caused by internal factors. They assume the difficulties arise from an improper interpretation of the host country environment. In contrast, open hybrid firms are willing to consider that they themselves might be the cause of some problems and, hence, are willing to look for internal adjustments.

Exportive and adaptive types are characterised by rather minor adjustments. That is, the initial templates fit reasonably such that only minor revisions are called for. The follow-up undertaken in this project reveals that this was not always true in the long term. In several instances, firms *chose* to perceive only minor problems when, in reality, the misalignment with local requirements was great. For example, a photochemical company based in the southern USA felt comfortable with its management system after two years of being in operation. 'Yes, there are problems', one US manager told us, 'but they'll be resolved over time.' A follow-up telephone interview nine months later revealed that the problems had only increased.

This raises another important point. Because learning is ongoing, firms may move from one type to another. This is most often the case with exportive and adaptive types. Over time some management systems that had seemed to work well experienced major difficulties. Sometimes this was due to an initial bad fit that had been glossed over. At other times it was the result of shifting conditions in the host country or a change in the affiliate's strategic role within the larger organisation. Usually, such shifts caught the affiliate off guard, making the subsequent adjustment traumatic.

Retention

The final stage of the learning cycle involves retaining lessons from what did or did not work. This is where the four types diverge from one another. What exportive firms seem to learn is that the parent template works in the new setting. In other words, learning comes in the form of a confirmation that initial assessments were correct. In concert with this learning is the perception that transference of the parent template primarily requires fine-tuning. The result is an emergent belief by the parent that its management template is 'universal'. Meanwhile, within the affiliate there is little inclination to question this belief, nor is there much attention directed at monitoring local conditions closely.

Closed hybrid firms learn, albeit often reluctantly, that the parent template does not fit the local environment well. Given the belief that management constitutes a core competency of the parent, other learning from the experience is predicated on maintaining a consistent self-image. That is, firms in this group 'learn' that the pressures of the host country environment require that the management system be buffered in various ways. Consequently, much of the learning centres on how to protect the system from local pressures. Given this orientation, it is not surprising that at the parent level little effort is made to absorb that which has been learned locally.

Adaptive firms learn about the local environment and what is required to succeed there. This knowledge is often embedded in the affiliate managers themselves, as characterised by a deep knowledge of how to accommodate local, state and government labour regulations. Because it is context-specific, affiliates find it hard to disseminate this knowledge beyond their own borders.

Finally, open hybrid firms acquire an understanding in three areas: namely, host country environment and what the affiliate management system needs to do to work well there; the affiliate itself – what its strengths and weaknesses are; and how the affiliate's experiences fit within the larger organisation, that is, what it could teach others and what it could learn from them. In a sense, such firms have a fundamentally different mind-set that is oriented to looking for connections between experiences in ways that downplay host country distinctiveness in favour of pursuing possible similarities with other areas of the organisation.

IMPLICATIONS FOR LEARNING

This section addresses more specifically various aspects of learning that grow out of the overseas affiliate's efforts at establishing a management system. First the learning implications are approached, in terms of differences among the four types, after which some of the larger implications for Japanese MNCs and other MNCs are considered.

The identification of four types of learning organisation leads us to consider the various effects and implications for learning. Several issues are addressed in the following section. Then, stepping back from the experiences of the firms in this study, the larger implications of learning in large, complex MNCs are reflected upon.

Implications of the Four Models

Type of Learning

Argyris and Schon (1978) make a distinction between *single-loop* and *double-loop* learning. Single-loop learning is characterised as 'an ability to detect and correct error in relation to a given set of operating norms' (Morgan, 1986: 88). By contrast, double-loop learning is described as an ability 'to take a "double-look" at the situation by questioning the relevance of operating norms' (Morgan, 1986: 88). Of the four learning types identified in the study, only the open hybrid exhibits comprehensive double-loop learning capabilities (see Table 13.2). Exportive firms and adaptive firms are convinced of the correctness of operating norms, and consequently their only concern is with making minor corrections to conform to norms. Closed hybrid firms, in the face of evidence that operating norms are not effective, choose instead to focus on ways to preserve norms rather than change them. This is one facet of the label 'closed'. They may experience double-loop learning in the affiliate, but it stops there.

Table 13.2 Implications of the four models for parent and affiliate learning

	Exportive	*Closed hybrid*	*Adaptive*	*Open hybrid*
Type of learning	Single loop	Single loop	Single loop	Double loop
Transferability of learning	Explicit	Tacit	Tacit	Tacit and explicit
Sharing of learning	Widespread; confirms original template	Limited; maintains self-image	Limited; focused on local knowledge	Widespread; multi-directional; connective

Transferability of Learning

A second aspect of learning is the extent to which it can be transmitted to others, namely its transferability. Nonaka and Takeuchi (1995) point out that knowledge comes in two varieties – explicit and tacit. Explicit knowledge is just that: easily explained or transmitted to others. Tacit knowledge is difficult to state or explain. It is embedded in understandings that cannot be easily codified. Much of the learning that adaptive and closed hybrid firms experience is tacit. It cannot easily be explained or transmitted outside the affiliate. Often it is embedded in the experiences of individual managers, who understood how things are done locally but see neither the need nor the way to explain it to the parent. 'Things are simply done differently here; headquarters doesn't understand,' was a phrase one manager used in characterising this learning in his firm.

Exportive firms acquire explicit, albeit shallow, knowledge. Many of the changes to policies they make are straightforward and transparent, as for example an overtime policy that needed to be modified to conform to host county regulations.

Open hybrid affiliates acquire both explicit and tacit knowledge. Because they experience double-loop learning, the tacit knowledge is both about how the affiliate can be effective locally, as well as how different policies fit together or coincide with the management philosophy. Explicit learning also focuses on two aspects of learning: first, on specific policies and the ways in which they work within the affiliate, and second, on how they would work in other settings. Quite often the latter type of explicit knowledge is developed through parent-designed workshop which bring together personnel managers from different affiliates within a region.

Sharing of Learning

The preceding discussion shows that knowledge may be more or less difficult to transfer. Whether or not it actually is transferred is another question. The final concern centres on the extent to which learning at the affiliate level is shared within the larger organisation. For exportive firms sharing is widespread, but superficial. Adaptive and closed hybrid affiliates engage in only limited sharing. In contrast, open hybrid firms share widely in a give-and-take fashion. They seek opportunities to pass on what they have learned to other units. In addition, they also actively seek input on what they are currently doing. Perhaps the most distinctive attribute of the open hybrid type is its openness to learning.

Larger Implications

The vast complexity of large MNCs, their institutional qualities, and the ambiguity of working across national and cultural boundaries raise a myriad of concerns. Although it is impossible to address all of them, several are particularly cogent to this work with Japanese MNCs and their overseas affiliates.

Learning when the Cycle is Incomplete

The discussion above is predicated on the assumption that learning cycles are complete. Hedberg (1981) suggests that complex, highly unstable environments (typical of the international arena) may create situations where the learning cycle is short-circuited or remains incomplete. This was certainly true of the Japanese firms studied in this project. Key managers were transferred, objectives changed, parent constraints prevented revisions to the existing system and so forth. In such instances, two types of outcomes were prevalent. In the first, the affiliate found itself repeating the mistakes of a previous administration as new managers acted on the basis of their own understandings, which were naïve and not contextually grounded. This often led to a deterioration of morale and the exit of persons possessing the appropriate knowledge to help the new manager correct errors. In the second, new adjustments were made before the efficacy of prior adjustments could be determined. Consequently, the affiliate seemed to be always in a state of flux, never stable long enough to confirm that difficulties had been properly diagnosed and remedied. This, in turn, developed into a downward spiral of morale and performance in which problems grew faster than responses could handle them.

Unlearning to Learn

Parent organisations, no matter how neutral or objective they attempt to be, introduce perspectives and ways of doing thing that are predicated on prior learning. In this sense, 'learning' in the Japanese overseas affiliate actually consisted of two different activities – learning and unlearning. This may be most easily understood if brought down to the level of the individual general manager. Japanese expatriates interviewed found it necessary to *unlearn* the Japanese parent's management system before they were able to *learn* local ways of doing things. This was also true for host country managers, who needed to unlearn local management approaches before they could comprehend the parent's system. Though this is certainly not a new observation, what was striking was the extent to which this consistently surfaced as a problematic issue, particularly in the case of Japanese parent managers who appeared to have a very difficult time envisioning non-Japanese approaches.

This suggests that humility and patience, as well as open-mindedness are essential qualities for affiliates and affiliate managers. Open-mindedness is needed to see the possibilities for doing things differently. Humility is required to let go of preferred or accepted ways of doing things, and patience is required because the process of unlearning and learning takes time. A similar assessment can be applied to parent companies.

The Strategic Dimension of Tactical Decisions in Learning

The discussion of organisational learning in Japanese affiliate management systems began by noting the variety of tactical decisions associated with setting up operations overseas. While there is no desire to blur the distinction between 'tactical' and 'strategic', these findings suggest that what many Japanese MNCs perceived as tactical decisions are in actuality strategic. Indeed, when it comes to the establishment of a new system within the overseas affiliate, prudence seems to point toward viewing most of the decisions as strategic. Foremost among those tactical decisions found in this study to have had a powerful strategic dimension, was that of selecting a general manager and other key personnel to staff the new operation. These are the individuals responsible for determining the template to be applied and then applying it. It is not unusual for them to imbue the template and its application with their own unique and personal flavour. In many instances it may well have been that case that success or failure of the template hinged more on the idiosyncratic character of the implementers or administrators of the system than the system itself. During the interviews the authors were impressed with the frequency with which a managing director, plant manager, or key personnel executive was referred to as the key to the affiliate's success or failure. Indeed, it was concluded that the single most important decision a Japanese firm may make in setting up its overseas affiliates is in the selection of the person responsible for managing it.

CONCLUSIONS

In this chapter, a typology of organisation learning models has been introduced and used to compare and contrast differences across Japanese MNCs in how they learn and the levels at which they learn. The typology and its application to JMNCs has a number of valuable implications for practitioners and international management researchers.

For practitioners, the typology and the examination of its effects on organisation learning offers useful guidance in the design of management systems for overseas affiliates. As with any improvement, whether it be in product or in process, the first step is understanding what the present product or process is actually like. For managers in MNCs, the typology offered in this chapter is unique in its identification of the component parts of the managerial systems that operate in foreign affiliates, from selection of a template, to the level at which it is applied, to what guides adjustments in the template. This disaggregation of a managerial system into its essential elements provides a framework that may be useful in understanding the degree to which other managerial systems contribute to organisational learning.

These organisational learning types have an important influence on the firm's ability to learn at a higher order level than its competitors. In addition to the type of learning that occurs, managers must examine whether learning is occurring at all, and if so, what mechanisms are being used to achieve the transfer of knowledge. As the resource-based view of the firm indicates (Barney, 1986; Grant, 1991), to the degree that firms can outperform competitors in these areas, they can create a 'learning organisation' in which they have the capability to integrate knowledge flexibly within the organisation, a capability that can be a source of enduring competitive advantage in a growing number of industries (Hamel and Prahalad, 1994; Henderson and Cockburn, 1994; Senge, 1990).

For management theorists, this chapter contributes important refinements and extensions of previous theory in the areas of organisational learning and international management (Cole, 1995; Dodgson, 1993). Drawing on the seminal work of Cyert and March (1963), Weick (1969) and Campbell (1965), the enactment–selection–retention model has been applied to an important problem facing MNCs: the design of the managerial systems of the firm. One of the critical tasks facing MNCs is how to design managerial systems such that the appropriate balance between integration and localisation is achieved

(Bartlett and Ghoshal, 1989; Taylor *et al.*, 1996). The four types of organisational learning presented in this chapter represent approaches to the integration–localisation problem that show *intermediate* points along the continuum. Moreover, the typology is dynamic, showing how systems can evolve over time, moving from one approach to another. The dynamic evolution of systems and their contribution to firm competitiveness is a perspective acquiring increasing importance (Collis, 1994).

Several other results of the study presented in this chapter should be noted by international management theorists. First, the finding that *perceived* cultural distance may be as important as *actual* cultural distance may have considerable import for researchers in the areas both of cross-cultural management and of international strategy. That is, while absolute differences based on such frameworks of cultural values as Hofstede (1980) have been utilised routinely by theorists, this chapter points to the possibility that it may be the perception of cultural distance of those in decision-making positions that actually affects the design of management systems and of international strategies. A second important result should be noted by those involved in international human resource management, particularly in the selection of expatriates. The key role that the general manager seems to play in selection of a template for design of the organisational system has received only minimal research attention (for example, Black *et al.*, 1994). The research reported here offers a framework by which to conceive of the different roles expatriates play in the development of an organisational learning type within an MNC. The role of expatriates in learning from overseas affiliates has important implications for international selection decisions, training, and performance appraisal.

In conclusion, this study of JMNCs illuminate both the process and the outcomes of organisational learning processes within the multinational network. While complex to study and difficult to manage, these processes are critical to the long-term survival of all MNCs.

References

Abo, T. (1994) *Hybrid Factory: The Japanese Production System in the United States*, New York: Oxford University Press.

Argyris, C. (1976) 'Leadership, Learning, and Changing the Status Quo', *Organizational Dynamics*, 4 (Winter), 29–43.

Argyris, C. and D. Schon (1978) *Organizational Learning: A Theory of Action Perspective*, Reading, Mass.: Addison-Wesley.

Barney, J. (1986) 'Types of Competition and the Theory of Strategy: Toward an Integrative Framework', *Academy of Management Review*, 11, 791–800.

Bartlett, C. and S. Ghoshal (1989) *Managing Across Borders*, Boston, Mass.: Harvard Business School Press.

Beechler, S. and A. Bird (1994) 'The Best of Both Worlds? An Exploratory Study of Human Resource Management Practices in US-Based Japanese Affiliates', in N. Campbell (ed.), *The Global Kaisha*, London: Blackwell.

Beechler, S., A. Bird and S. Raghuram (1993) 'Linking Business Strategy and Transnational Human Resource Management Practices', *Advances in International and Comparative Management*, 8, 199–215.

Bird, A. and S. Beechler (1995) 'Links Between Business Strategy and Human Resource Management Strategies in US-Based Japanese Subsidiaries: An Empirical Investigation', *Journal of International Business Studies*, 26, 23–45.

Black, S., M. Mendenhall and G. Oddou, (1992) *Global Assignments*, San Francisco: Jossey-Bass.

Campbell, D.T. (1959) 'Methodological Suggestions from a Comparative Psychology of Knowledge Processes', *Inquirry*, 2, 152–82.

Campbell, D.T. (1965) 'Variation and Selective Retention in Socio-cultural Evolution', in H.R. Barringer, G.I. Blanksten and R.W. Mack (eds), *Social Change in Developing Areas*, Cambridge, Mass.: Schenkman, 19–49.

Cole, R. (1995) 'Reflections on Organizational Learning in US and Japanese Industry', in J. Liker and J. Ettlie (eds), *Managing Technology Through Organizations: US and Japanese Approaches*, New York: Oxford University Press.

Collis, D. (1994) 'How Valuable are Organizational Capabilities?', *Strategic Management Journal*, 15, 143–152.

Cyert, R. and J. March (1963) *A Behavioral Theory of the Firm*, Englewood Cliffs, NJ: Prentice-Hall.

Dodgson, M. (1993) 'Organizational Learning: A Review of Some Literatures', *Organizational Studies*, 14, 375–96.

Grant, R. (1991) 'The Resource-Based Theory of Competitive Advantage: Implications for Strategy Formulation', *California Management Review*, Spring, 114–35.

Hamel, G. and C. Prahalad (1994) *Competing for the Future*, Boston, Mass.: Harvard Business School Press.

Hedberg, B. (1981) 'How Organizations Learn and Unlearn', in P.C. Nystrom and W.H. Starbuck (eds), *Handbook of Organizational Design.*, 1, New York: Oxford University Press, 3–27.

Henderson, R. and I. Cockburn (1994) 'Measuring Competence? Exploring Firm Effects in Pharmaceutical Research', *Strategic Management Journal*, 15, 63–84.

Hofstede, G. (1980) *Culture's Consequences*, Newbury Park, Calif.: Sage.
Kagono, T, I. Nonaka, H. Sakakibara and A. Okumura (1986) *Strategic versus Evolutionary Management*, Amsterdam: North-Holland.
Kidder, L.H. (1981) *Sellitz, Wrightsman and Cook's Research Methods in Social Relations*, New York: Holt, Rinehart & Winston.
March, J. and H. Simon (1958) *Organizations*, New York: Wiley.
Morgan, G. (1986) *Images of Organization*, Beverly Hills, Califf.: Sage.
Nonaka, I. and H. Takeuchi (1995) *The Knowledge-Creating Company*, New York: Oxford University Press.
Pfeffer, J. (1994) *Competitive Advantage Through People*, San Francisco: Jossey-Bass.
Schein, E. (1985) *Organizational Culture and Leadership*, San Francisco: Jossey-Bass.
Schuler, R.S. (1989) 'Strategic Human Resource Management and Industrial Relations', *Human Relations*, 42, 157–84.
Senge, P. (1990) 'The Leader's New Work: Building Learning Organizations', *Sloan Management Review*, 32, 7–23.
Stinchcombe, A.L. (1965) 'Social Structure and Organizations', in James G. March (ed.), *Handbook of Organizations*, Chicago: Rand McNally, 142–93.
Taylor, S., S. Beechler and N. Napier (1996) 'Toward an Integrative Theory of Strategic International Human Resource Management', *Academy of Management Review*, 21 (4), 959–85.
Weick, K. (1969) *The Social Psychology of Organizing*, Reading, Mass.: Addison-Wesley.

14 Conclusions and Policy Implications

Julian Birkinshaw and Neil Hood

INTRODUCTION

Chapter 1 of this volume established the context in which research into subsidiary management has emerged and set the scene for the twelve empirical studies. This final chapter stands back from the findings and attempts to evaluate them from the perspective of four different types of interest, namely those of MNEs as parents and corporate entities; of host governments; of managers within MNE subsidiaries; and of academics with a particular interest in this aspect of international business. Clearly, these interests do not necessarily coincide in matters of subsidiary development. Thus, for example, a parent MNE may recognise some of the creative tensions considered in the foregoing chapters when it comes to balancing subsidiary and corporate ambition in any one location within its network. On the other hand, a host government committed to investment attraction and development may be in favour of a 'beggar thy neighbour' policy which leads to the maximum value added within MNE subsidiaries within its territory. This book was not, however, designed to provide a comprehensive view of all of these issues. Moreover, it is recognised that, while the book represents a wide range of academic research on subsidiary development and involves over twenty authors working in fourteen countries, it can only selectively cover a number of illustrations of the different interests in the topic. Care must therefore be exercised when it comes to making generalisations on the basis of this evidence alone, and this will be avoided in the ensuing paragraphs. At the same time, the earlier chapters contain some interesting pointers which are likely to stimulate both policy interest and future academic research.

FINDINGS AND IMPLICATIONS

This section reviews some of these for each of the four constituencies identified above, distinguishing between them for the purposes of analysis and clarity, while recognising that some issues are relevant for several of the interested parties.

Multinational Corporate Parents

MNE subsidiary development takes place within the policy framework established, to a greater or lesser degree, by the parent or nodal company within the network. The evidence in these papers reminds MNEs that these frameworks cannot be static, and that there are many internal and external forces acting to change the roles of subsidiaries, while at the same time allowing many of them to develop their own dynamic in the interests of corporate competitiveness. Some MNE strategy managers might be tempted to suggest that the interests reflected here in the subsidiary development process is largely academic, and that it is a function of the ambitions of local managers or of host governments and their agencies. Yet it is evident that, in more mature corporate networks at least, the focus of innovation and creative market exploitation is increasingly diffuse, placing more emphasis on an enabling corporate centre that fosters the achievement of group goals by acknowledging the positive gains from subsidiary development.

A number of the chapters (including 3, 4, 7 and 10) develop taxonomies to classify subsidiaries, mostly based on the perspective from the subsidiary rather than the corporate level. There is further interesting work to be done in comparing these perspectives and testing the extent to which such taxonomies match when viewed from each of them. Taggart (Chapter 2) suggests that the coordination–configuration paradigm, which has largely been used as a corporate-level tool, can be shown to be equally relevant in categorising subsidiary strategy and allocating roles within networks. This chapter and others like it can invariably identify the desired end point that would satisfy local managers in any given path of subsidiary development. This has interesting implications for parent companies, because relatively few subsidiaries are likely to be allowed to attain these goals. The traditional corporate solution to this is of course to move the high-flying and aspirant country managers who harbour these ambitions away from the subsidiary and into the corporate HQ fast track. But this solution may be less valid if the proposition is accepted that many MNEs will require more highly developed subsidiaries as part of their developing competitive advantage, as some of the studies in this book suggest.

Continuing on this theme, the more macro study by Randøy and Li (Chapter 4) finds that distinctive subsidiary types can be discerned on an industry-by-industry basis in relation to the resource flows of capital, knowledge and products. The distinctive strategic industry groups were found to be related to the direction and intensity of subsidiary network integrations. In an era where there is intense interest in 'benchmarking' on an intra- and inter-sectoral basis, this work is potentially interesting. Perhaps MNEs do not always pay enough attention to the relative effectiveness of different mixes of subsidiary roles when comparing their own networks to those of their competitors. Such a line of thought could bring a new twist to the 'strategy v. structure' debate that has preoccupied management theorists for several decades.

It has long been evident from the management literature that corporate structures, and those of MNEs in particular, are subject to fashion shifts and discarded paradigms. With this in mind, Schütte's study (Chapter 5) of regional headquarters (RHQs) identified these as a type of special-purpose subsidiary that stands between headquarters and national subsidiaries. They are also shown to be prone to the same cycles of ascendancy, decendency and role change that is the hallmark of most subsidiaries. This study suggests that parent companies should limit their aspirations for RHQs in that, while they were found to be instrumental in integrating their regions by the provision of functional support activities, they were rarely able or willing to create synergies between different business or divisions. While the companies concerned perceived the RHQ role as an important ingredient of their regional success, and expected them to become more powerful in the future, there were evident limitations to their role. Among the challenging issues arising from this is that of striking an appropriate balance between using RHQs as an instrument of regional strategy where this is required, and allowing mature and fully fledged national subsidiaries to take the initiative consistent with building competitiveness in the region.

One important manifestation of such initiatives is reflected in the Irish study in Chapter 9, which shows that technology is becoming an important basis for subsidiary development. In this sample, technological capabilities are deployed by the subsidiary as a means of extending their business domain. The evidence presented suggested that most of this had involved backward integrating the subsidiary deeper into process technology development, and that this was especially attractive where the parent company had both strong technology and growth. This is an important finding for MNE parents. Not all parents are tolerant of this type of subsidiary action, and there is evidently a cumulative effect whereby the confidence engendered by some technological strength in the parent encourages initiative within the network. These results suggest that parents should foster subsidiary technological accumulation in a positive way, under a clearly specified brief, but with a sufficient degree of subsidiary autonomy. Put another way, parents have to ask themselves whether they have created the necessary environment to achieve the desired level of innovation of all kinds from their subsidiaries. It may well be that such innovation is a necessary condition for the evolution of the most productive subsidiaries in MNE networks in the future.

The material in Chapter 12, based on the case of Sony in the USA, provides some interesting insights into the role of the parent company in driving the subsidiary development process. The context is relevant here, in that the case is a reflection of a particular set of trade and market imperatives acting to encourage Japanese MNEs to add more value in key US and European markets at that period of time. For many such companies the twin drivers of defending market share based on home region exports and that of avoiding potential trade friction, encouraged the transfer of production and technology. This example acts as a reminder that subsidiary development is not only a matter of local management 'pull', but also one of corporate 'push' – the latter shown to include both functional migration and line of business entry. The Sony case illustrates that subsidiary evolution is a dynamic and adapted process, with actions, feedback, evaluation and further actions. Part of the parent company challenge is to develop and maintain a climate within its subsidiary network that is capable of the continual adaptation which this process model implies, as the operation adjusts to both internal and external stimuli. As Chapter 12 indicates, there is a valid question as to whether the iterative Sony model based on many feedback loops is the model upon which MNEs should base subsidiary evolution in an increasingly global business environment. There is much useful research to be done to explore the national and cultural differences that may influence the means adopted to achieve such development ends.

The final comment in this section with reference to Chapter 13 also concerns Japanese MNEs, in this case as part of a major study of the nature of management systems in Japanese overseas affiliates. The Beechler, Bird and Taylor project proffers a useful typology which identifies the component parts of the management systems operating in foreign affiliates, from selecting a template, considering the level of its application and the principles by which the template is adjusted. There is little doubt that this chapter touches upon some central questions for MNEs, not least in the context of creating an international 'learning organisation', which is now deemed so critical for ensuring knowledge generation and flows. At the same time the notion of 'templates' is a vexed one where MNEs are adopting complex matrix structures in many different environments, are fostering network-based structures and are less precious about the initial roots of their management philosophy. Yet it is evident, as this chapter shows, that MNEs need to interrogate and review their processes, regularly testing them for effectiveness and efficiency in organisational learning.

Host Governments

It is evident that not all host governments take the same degree of interest in the subsidiary development process in MNEs operating within their boundaries. Some would regard themselves as broadly neutral to the ebb and flow of business growth within any single corporation. Others, in perhaps a growing proportion of countries, would see a close link between economic development and the strategies which MNCs were pursuing. The governments of such countries would not necessarily take a proactive approach either to the attraction of MNE investment or to its development, but would confine their attention to reacting to plant rationalisation, restructuring or closure. There is ample evidence that individual host governments invariably play a limited role in such eventualities, especially when major external market, technological and competitive changes are driving these adjustments on a pan-national basis.

However, on the basis of the pursuit of economic development objectives, it is clear that over the past two or three decades an ever increasing number of countries have been vigorously promoting themselves, in whole or part, as appropriate locations for fdi. Moreover, where extensive numbers of MNE subsidiaries are present, as in most developed economies, there is a growing trend to attempt to foster expansion and value-adding projects within existing MNE subsidiaries, whether by ensuring that an appropriately supportive infrastructure is in place or by direct forms of subsidiary or tax breaks. The ensuing competitiveness between nations for a share of MNE growth and expansion has been well chronicled in the literature and is beyond the scope of this book. Nevertheless, a number of the chapters bring out some important findings for governments, predicated on the assumption that a prudent policy towards 'monitoring' MNE subsidiaries requires an understanding of their development dynamics.

One particular area of interest to host governments is the distribution of research and development activity within subsidiary networks, not least because it is linked with higher levels of autonomy, created embeddedness in the local environment and so on. Papanastassiou and Pearce (Chapter 3) suggest that, in responding to more intense global competition, MNEs are implementing their technology strategy in a much more decentralised and differentiated fashion. This in turn is creating, at least on the basis of this evidence, a new balance of centralisation and decentralisation of R&D activity in subsidiaries. This work again points to the sustaining of more creative subsidiaries, which need to be encouraged by their parent companies to individualise their knowledge scope, yet do so within a group framework. Were this to become a general trend, it would open up further opportunities for proactive host governments to encourage local R&D within MNE subsidiaries by educational and infrastructure investment and, in some instances, by the use of risk-sharing incentive schemes. Less desirably, perhaps, is the likelyhood of even more intensive competition for mobile R&D projects between countries in regions such as Europe.

On a related theme, and ever conscious of the locational options open to MNEs, host governments have a vested interest in identifying and fostering 'centres of excellence' among subsidiaries. They normally recognise that this is a subset of the total local stock of subsidiaries. All of the chapters in Part II of this volume contribute to our understanding of this concept. The Forsgren and Pedersen (Chapter 6) study recognises the difficulty of developing precise definitions of centres of excellence, but develops a conceptualisation based on their characteristics. One interesting conclusion, and rather contrary to some thinking, is that interdependence rather than autonomy was the crucial variable when assessing whether a subsidiary was a centre of excellence – provided that it had a well-established product mandate in the first place. Host governments should recognise the power of this finding, in that in order for any subsidiary to be an important part of an MNEs strategic plans, it has to have a level of corporate embeddedness with the rest of its network. In itself this finding acts as a constraint to the expectations that host governments should have as to how much activity can actually take place at a local level no matter how sophisticated is that environment.

Surlemont (Chapter 7) pursues the quest for a typology of centres within MNEs with considerable analytical rigour. Some of the principles explored in this chapter are very relevant for host governments, who pursue active policies of aftercare directed to the installed base of MNE subsidiaries in their region. One key element of this is identifying subsidiaries wherein the prospects of growth and expansion are best, and this often requires some typology by which these can be clarified and upon which resource allocation can be based. Some of the managerial implications of the Surlemont study will be commented upon later.

The final essay in Section 2 by Fratocchi and Holm (Chapter 8) points to the limited occurrence in Swedish MNEs of multi-functional centres of excellence with both production and marketing responsibilities. It also serves to remind host governments of the frequent sequence of marketing centres being established first, followed by manufacturing centres. On occasion, the investment attraction strategies of some countries fail to recognise such sequences, and pursue production units that frequently do not add on marketing responsibilities. This evidence suggests other factors that might exert a strong influence on the progression to multi functional centres, including the fact that the psychic distance between the subsidiary and its headquarters is an important predictor of whether marketing centres ever emerge.

In fostering development prospects within MNE subsidiaries, every host government is highly dependent upon the intrapreneurial skills of the local managers. There are some interesting lessons on this in both of the Irish studies (Chapters 9 and 10). The Egelhoff, Gorman and McCormick chapter illustrates a variety of technology-based initiatives by which the sample subsidiaries sought to extend their strategic domains based on lower local factor costs, suggesting that they were technology-based because of the lack of a significant local market. Clearly the route adopted might be different in other contexts, but the principles are similar. Of course, there is a limited contribution to be made by host governments when it comes to stimulating managerial initiative within MNE subsidiaries, but there is evidence of government agencies doing so by experimental programmes with subsidiary peer groups, encouraging inter-corporation management skilling, industry fora and so on. As this study shows, these may be a necessary, but not a sufficient stimulus, because many subsidiaries lack both the resources and autonomy to launch meaningful initiatives.

In Chapter 10 Delany presents a very interesting model, showing the various phases of subsidiary mandate development. Host government officials could find this intriguing and highly seductive, in that they would wish to be able to plot local MNE subsidiaries within this and thus inform their monitoring process. Life is never quite so simple as that, but the model is relevant. For example, it usefully distinguishes between domain consolidating and developing, while showing that domain defending and maintaining (corporate) credibility are ever present realities, independent of the stage of subsidiary development. Host governments would do well to factor such considerations into their support strategies. This requires, for example, a reasonable understanding of how (and with whom) local subsidiaries are benchmarked within the corporate network. It also lays continued stress on the performance of subsidiaries, by both internal and external measures, as an important determinant as to whether it will be in the frame for development projects.

The paper by Birkinshaw (Chapter 11) is the only one in this volume designed to examine subsidiary development from a host country point of view. Based on Swedish evidence, the study findings reflect the local context both in terms of geography and with regard to the long period over which inward foreign direct investment (FDI) was not encouraged. In many ways therefore Sweden is an unusual case, being a late entrant to investment attraction, but a long-term supporter of outward FDI by Swedish MNEs. At the macro level, there are lessons for host governments, both from the diverse mixture of subsidiaries present within the country and from the limited evidence that was found of subsidiary initiative except in the special case of large scale acquisitions. Birkinshaw draws out some important lessons for attracting investment to Sweden, given its relative disadvantages in terms of the fundamentals of market size and costs. Among these is the need to focus investment promotion on the leading-edge clusters of telecommunications and healthcare. Countries do not always play to their strengths in this regard, not least because they might view FDI as a diversification strategy in terms of their current industrial structure. Another point is well made, and has general applicability, namely the role that subsidiary managers can play in supporting investment promotion. There is ample evidence in more remote or otherwise disadvantaged regions, such as Ireland and Scotland, that there is considerable power in the example shown by existing subsidiaries and their managers when it comes to advising new entrants.

MNE Subsidiary Managers

There are lessons for subsidiary managers throughout this book, but they are limited in number for one important reason.

The authors of this chapter have spent a great deal of time working in, and with, MNE subsidiaries in many different countries. From this it is evident that the experience of many subsidiary managers is not well captured in words such as 'development', 'initiative' and 'subsidiary strategy'. Their roles are relatively routine and highly constrained, with little prospect of domain extension or the enlargement of their scope. Clearly, managers with such experiences could not readily relate to the more positive and opportunistic note in which most of the chapters are written. That said, maybe the lesson for such managers is to be mobile and follow the opportunities!

With these caveats in mind, there are some specific points that have emerged and that subsidiary managers should note. For example, the very title of Chapter 3 draws attention to individualism as a characteristic of subsidiaries that has to be balanced with interdependence. This study suggests that there is a premium to be placed in certain corporate contexts upon innovation of all types as part of the evolution of subsidiaries. This raises the question as to whether this can, to some extent, be negotiated by subsidiary managers who are alive to the opportunities afforded to them. At the very least, an MNE subsidiary manager should be aware that there is plenty of evidence both that subsidiary development is not merely part of a deterministic process, but that it is also a function of entrepreneurship at local level.

Surlemont (Chapter 7) raises some interesting principles, albeit deriving from a particular type of centre in a single country, namely Belgium. The first concerns the development of relationships with other subsidiaries as a way to extend more cross-border influence; the other argues for identifying and pursuing a range of specialist services for other group companies. The point is made that focus, specialisation and expertise seem to be preferable in order to gain internal credibility and global influence as a centre of excellence. It has to be recognised that many subsidiary managers may be constrained in the extent to which they can alter there three variables, and they may not be able to aspire to manage the strategic centres of excellence which Surlemont identifies.

Some final comments derive from Chapter 12 concerning the Sony US case. The authors make the important observation that evolution is not inevitable or automatic, nor is it steady or symmetrical across lines of business. Equally critical is the view that concerted efforts are required at all stages and that the necessary skills differ sharply depending on the level of functional migration. Faced with these comments, some senior subsidiary managers may recognise the lack of a fully functional team that often characterises subsidiaries at the earlier stages of their development. And yet the process requires access to, if not ownership of, a diverse and quality skill base. Such situations, for example, can find subsidiary managers recruiting staff with technology skills in order to undertake unofficial development work as part of mounting a bid for a product development franchise. It is not surprising that the Sony case highlights that a successful process of functional migration is a complex managerial task calling for skills ranging from the technical to the political.

Academics

As the editors acknowledge in Chapter 1 and each set of authors recognise in their chapters, there are several research agendas to emerge from a volume such as this. There are hypothesis to be confirmed or disputed, models to be tested on a wider range of data, and much deeper work to be done on issues such as corporate and subsidiary perspectives on development. Each of the chapters attempts to place its contribution in the context of the debate so far, but it is recognised that this specific part of the MNE development debate is at an early stage and is worthy of much more research.

The directions which that research takes will as always be dependent upon individual or team preferences. For these authors and at this time, however, there are some issues worthy of highlighting. The centres of excellence research is worth taking further both in conceptual and empirical terms. Both corporations and governments have a close interest in this, and it has important public policy consequences. Equally, there is much more to be done in testing some of the taxonomies developed in the chapters, including those of Delany (Chapter 10) and Beechler *et al.* (Chapter 12). In the latter context the authors call for more research on the differences between perceived and actual cultural distance and on the role a subsidiary general manager plays in the selection of a template for the design of organisational systems. In a similar vein, Schütte (Chapter 11) calls for more longitudinal studies of regional headquarters in smaller numbers of MNEs, particularly in order to clarify various findings on the life expectancy of this type of organisational unit within MNEs, and to consider how it fits in with the globalisation of the firms.

In broader terms, the phenomenon of subsidiary development presents some interesting theoretical angles that could usefully be explored. For example, the patterns of subsidiary growth and decline can be seen as analogous to the growth and decline of independent firms, though obviously with additional constraints imposed by the limited autonomy of subsidiaries and their interdependencies with other parts of the MNE. As such, subsidiary 'evolution' represents a special case that can probably inform the more general work on the 'evolutionary theory of the firm' as presented by Penrose (1959), Nelson and Winter (1982), Kogut and Zander (1993) and others. In the same vein, subsidiary development processes also have the potential to shed light on some mainstream organisation theories (such as institutional theory, resource dependency theory, population ecology), again on the basis that the "special case" can inform the general theory.

Perhaps the best short- to-medium-term contribution this volume can make for academics is to bring together, perhaps for the first time, a range of papers that demonstrates some of the current research being undertaken on subsidiary development around the world. As noted, the coverage, though wide, is inevitably partial and is designed to stimulate interest and further research in this important multidisciplinary corner of the field of international business.

CONCLUSIONS

This chapter has sought to draw attention to some, but by no means all, of the main conclusions of this volume and extract some of the implications of the volume for four different types of audience. It is not, of course, a substitute for reading each contribution in greater detail, and individual readers will draw their own conclusions, interpreting and enriching the findings in the light of their own experience.

References

Kogut, B. and U. Zander (1993) 'Knowledge of the Firm and the Evolutionary Theory of the Multinational Corporation', *Journal of International Business Studies*, 24 (4), 625–45.

Nelson, R. and S. Winter (1982) *An Evolutionary Theory of Economic Change*, Cambridge, Mass.: Harvard University Press.

Penrose, E.T. (1959) *The Theory of the Growth of the Firm*, Oxford: Basil Blackwell.

Index